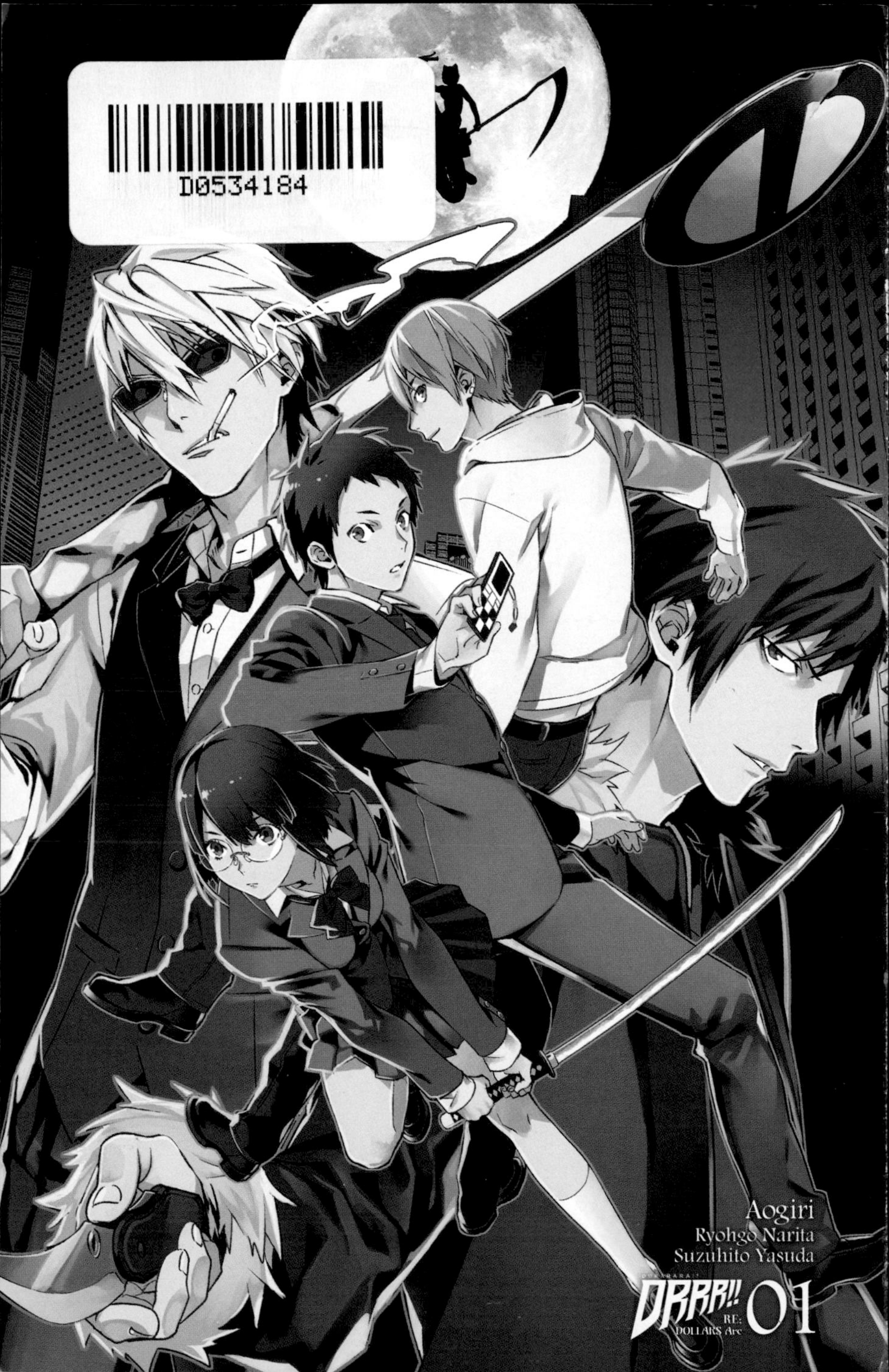
Aogiri
Ryohgo Narita
Suzuhito Yasuda
DRRR!! RE: DOLLARS Arc 01

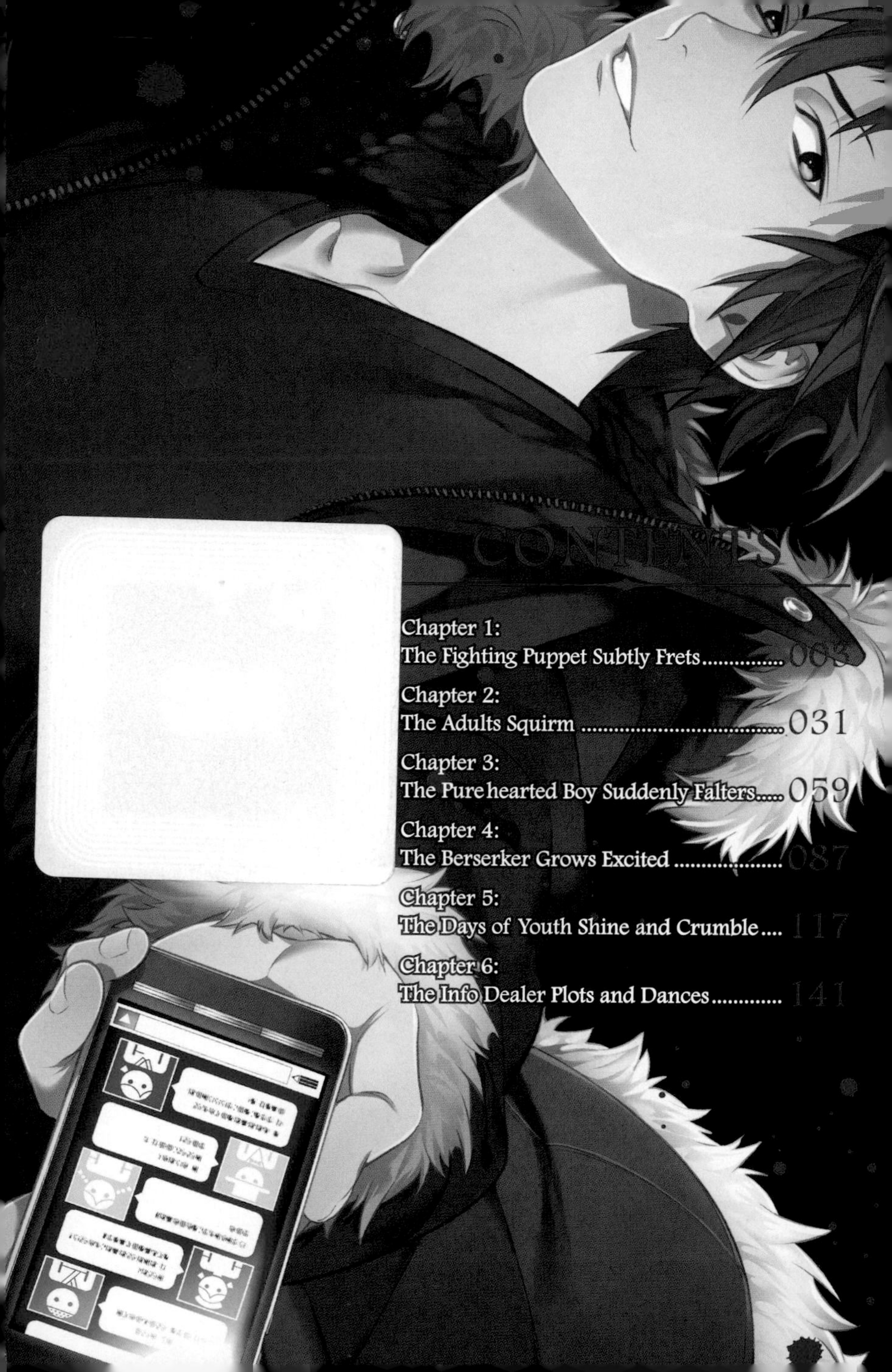

CONTENTS

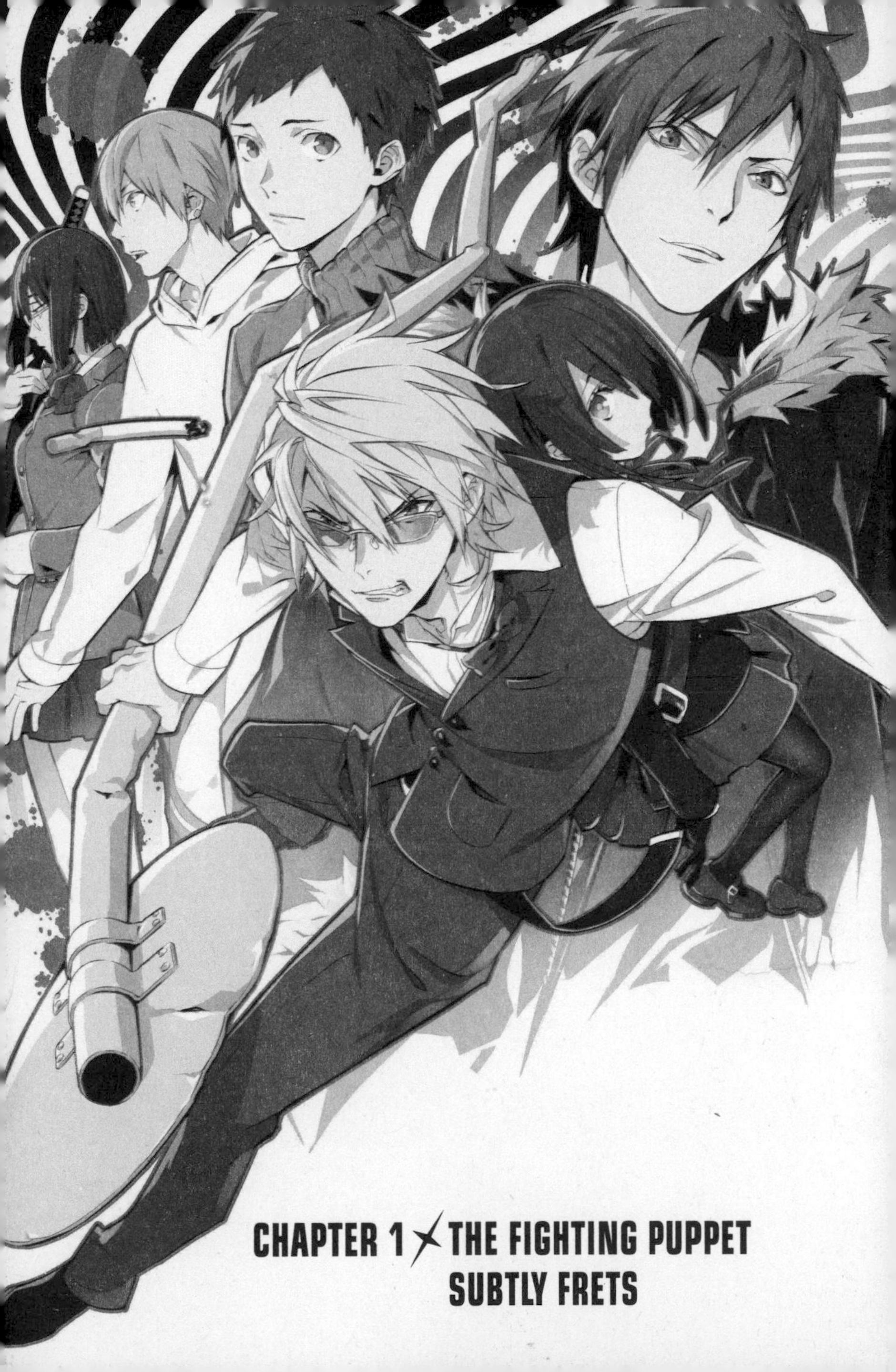

CHAPTER 1 ✗ THE FIGHTING PUPPET SUBTLY FRETS

DURARARA!!

DRRR!!

Re:Dollars Arc

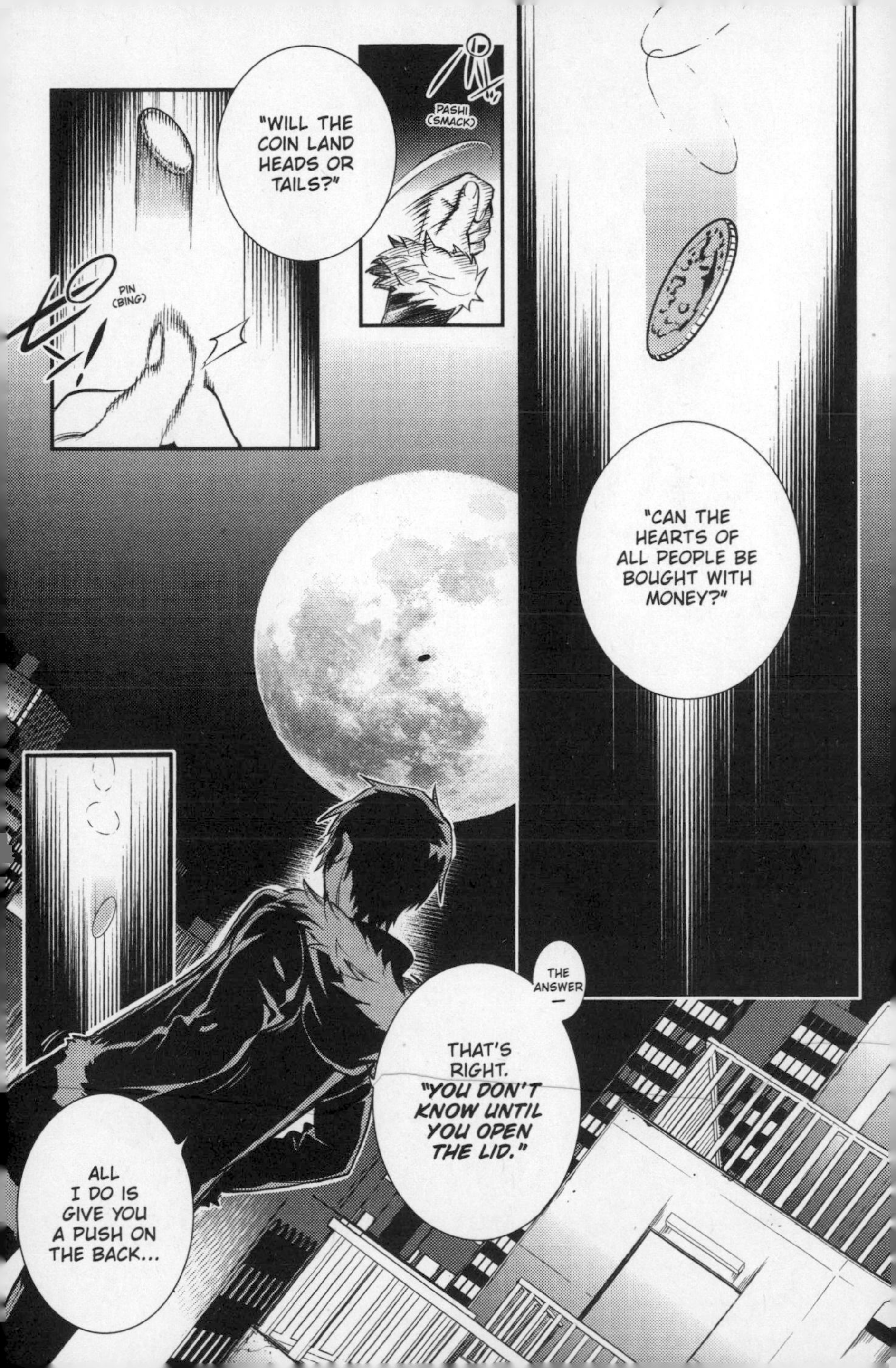
"CAN THE HEARTS OF ALL PEOPLE BE BOUGHT WITH MONEY?"
PASHI (SMACK)
"WILL THE COIN LAND HEADS OR TAILS?"
PIN (BING)
THE ANSWER—
THAT'S RIGHT. *"YOU DON'T KNOW UNTIL YOU OPEN THE LID."*
ALL I DO IS GIVE YOU A PUSH ON THE BACK...

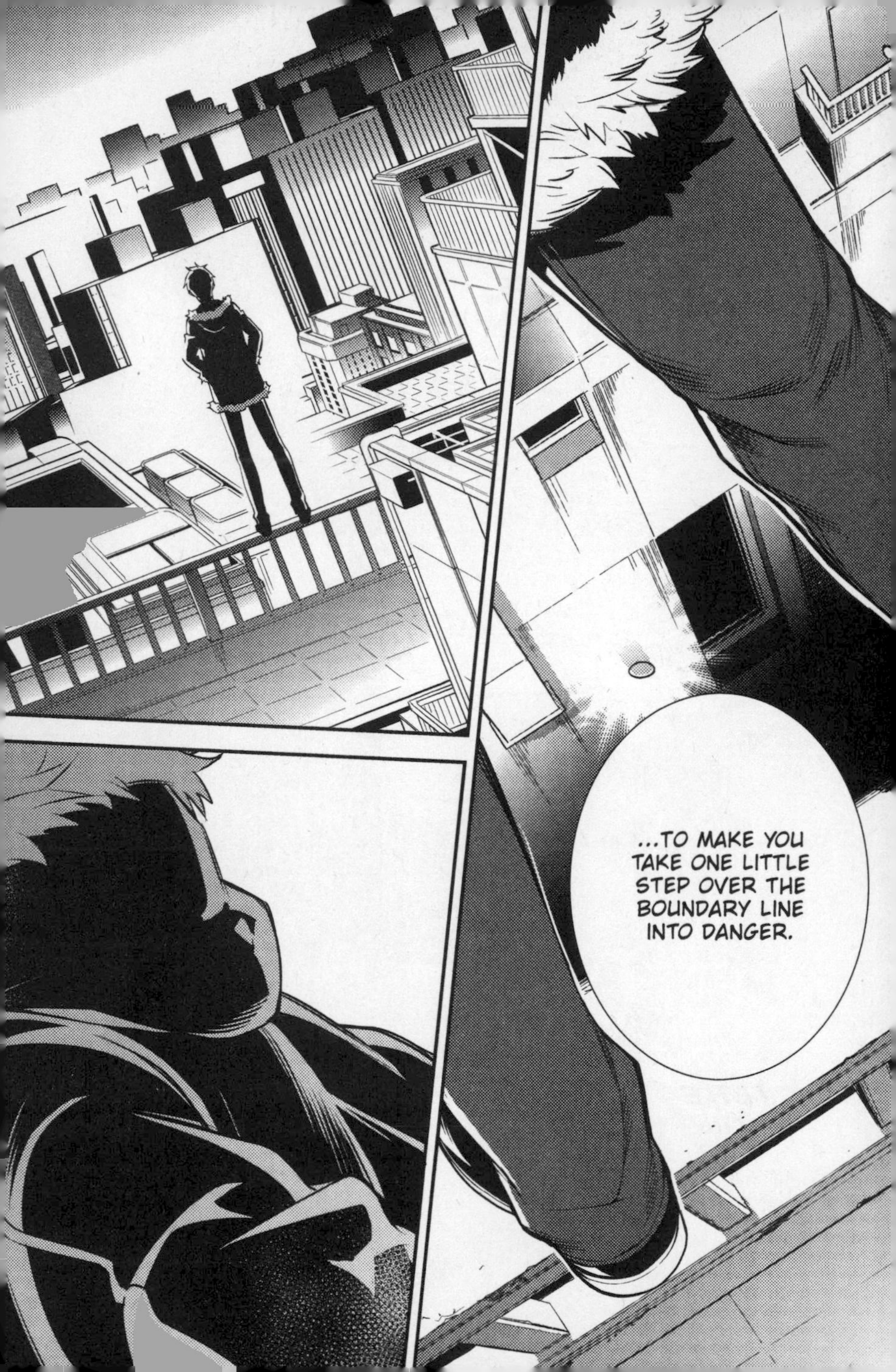
...TO MAKE YOU TAKE ONE LITTLE STEP OVER THE BOUNDARY LINE INTO DANGER.

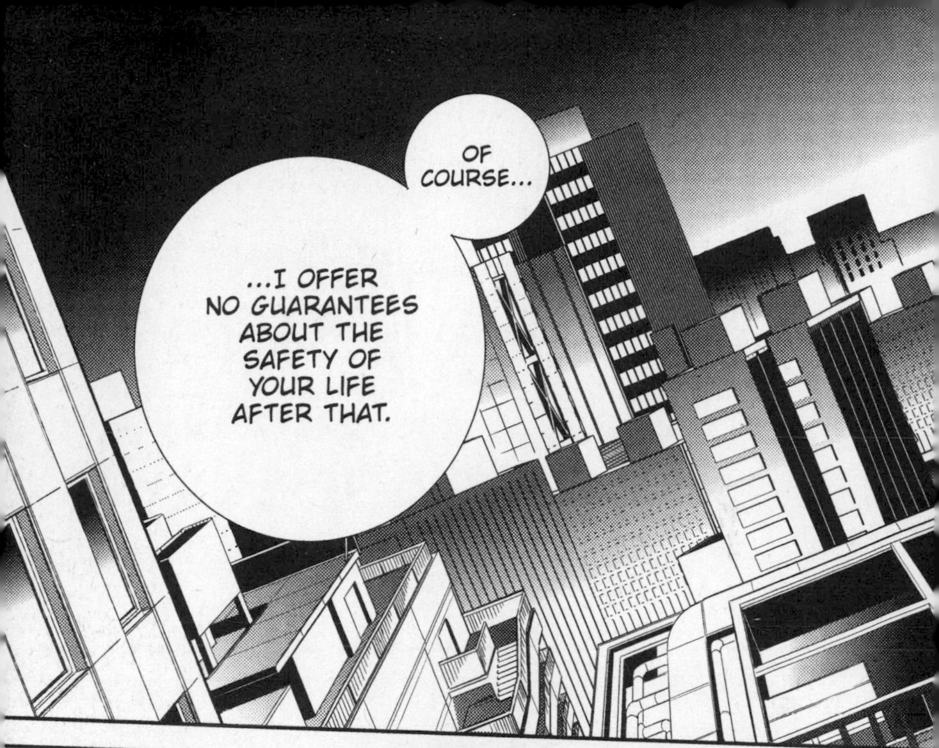
OF COURSE...
...I OFFER NO GUARANTEES ABOUT THE SAFETY OF YOUR LIFE AFTER THAT.
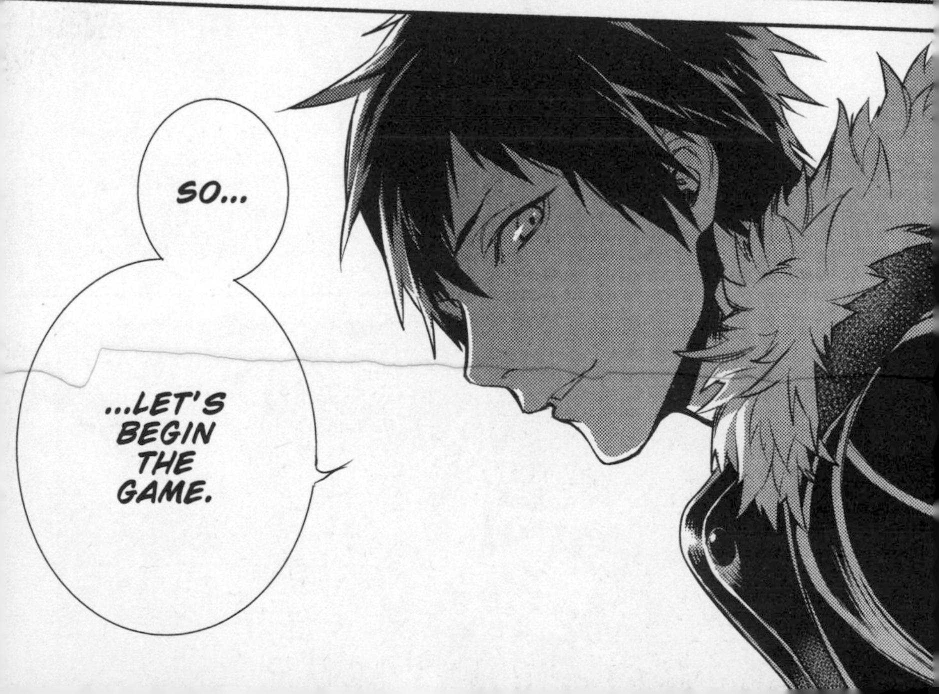
SO...
...LET'S BEGIN THE GAME.

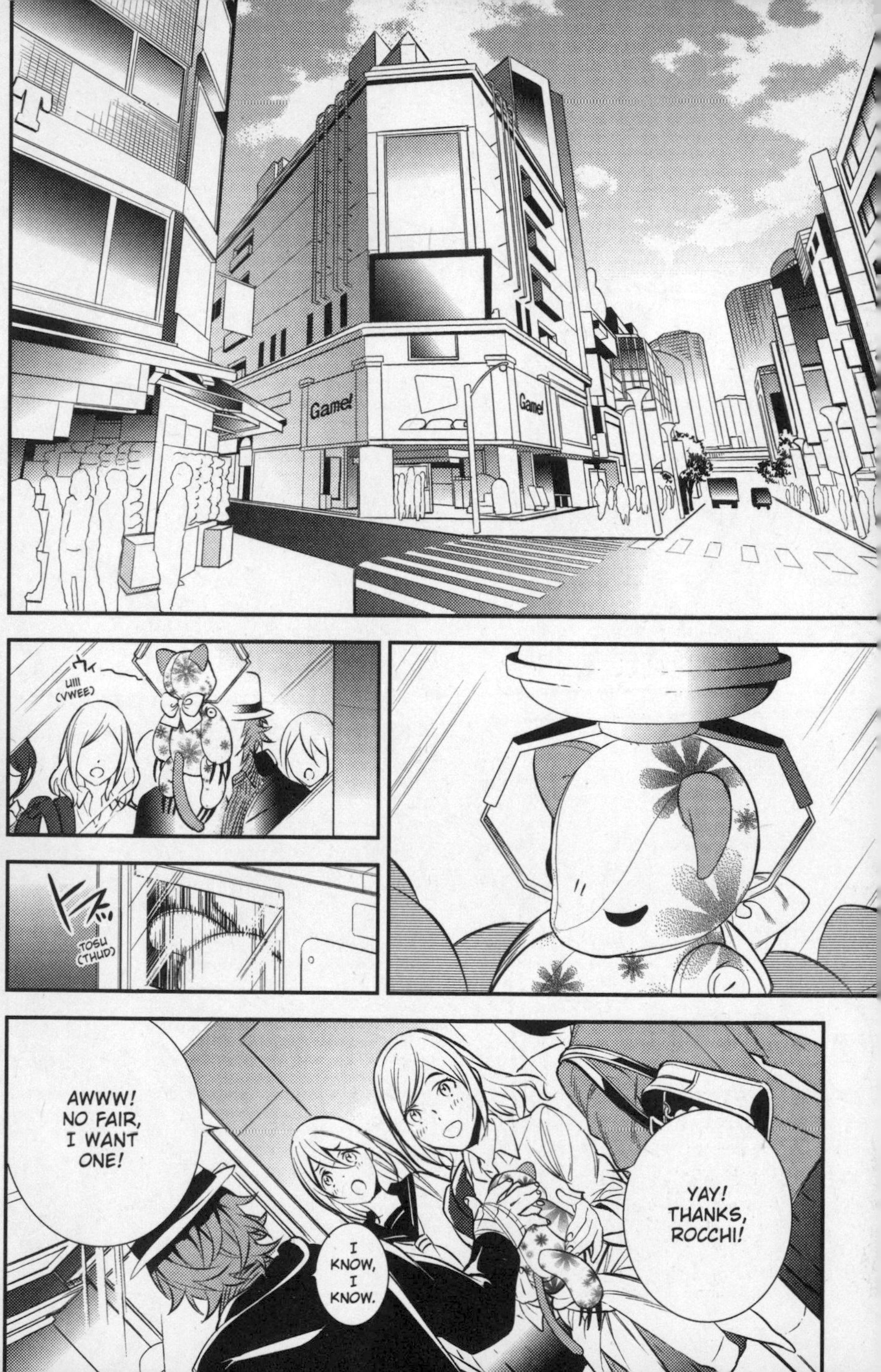
UIII (VWEE)
TOSU (THUD)
YAY! THANKS, ROCCHI!
I KNOW, I KNOW.
AWWW! NO FAIR, I WANT ONE!

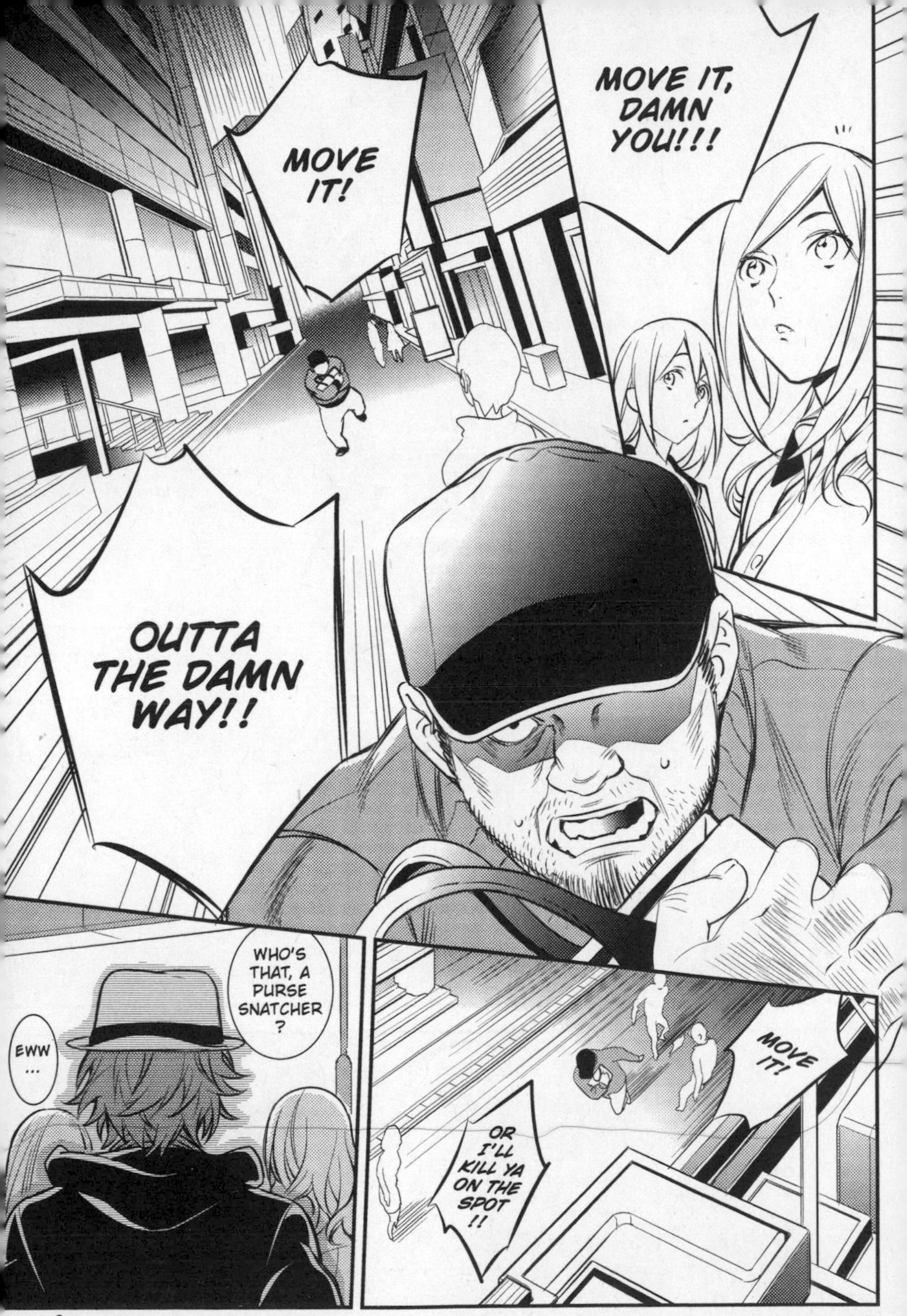

MOVE IT, DAMN YOU!!!
MOVE IT!
OUTTA THE DAMN WAY!!
MOVE IT!
OR I'LL KILL YA ON THE SPOT!!
WHO'S THAT, A PURSE SNATCHER?
EWW...

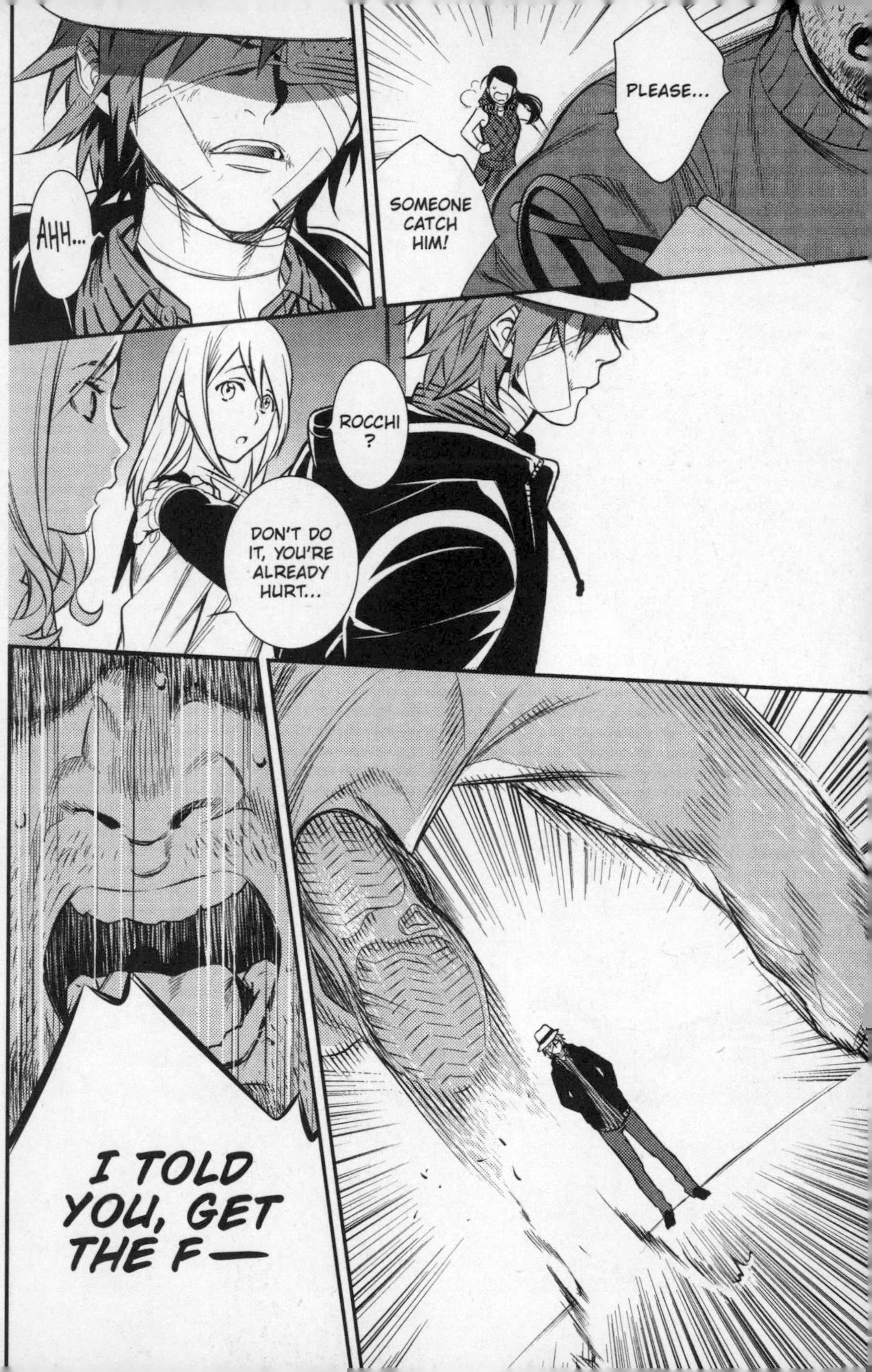
PLEASE...
SOMEONE CATCH HIM!
AHH...
ROCCHI?
DON'T DO IT, YOU'RE ALREADY HURT...
I TOLD YOU, GET THE F—

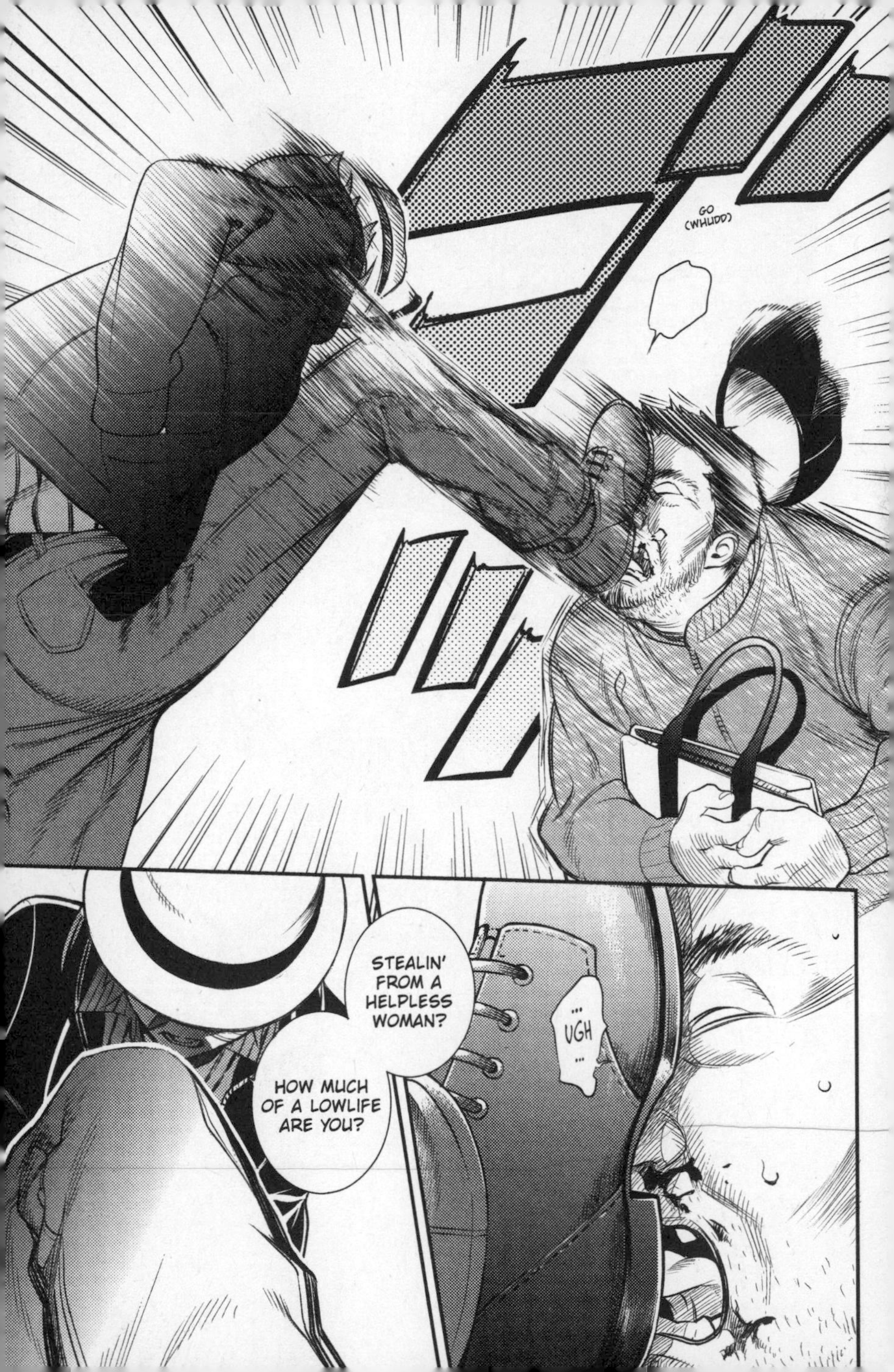
GO (WHUDD)
... UGH ...
STEALIN' FROM A HELPLESS WOMAN?
HOW MUCH OF A LOWLIFE ARE YOU?

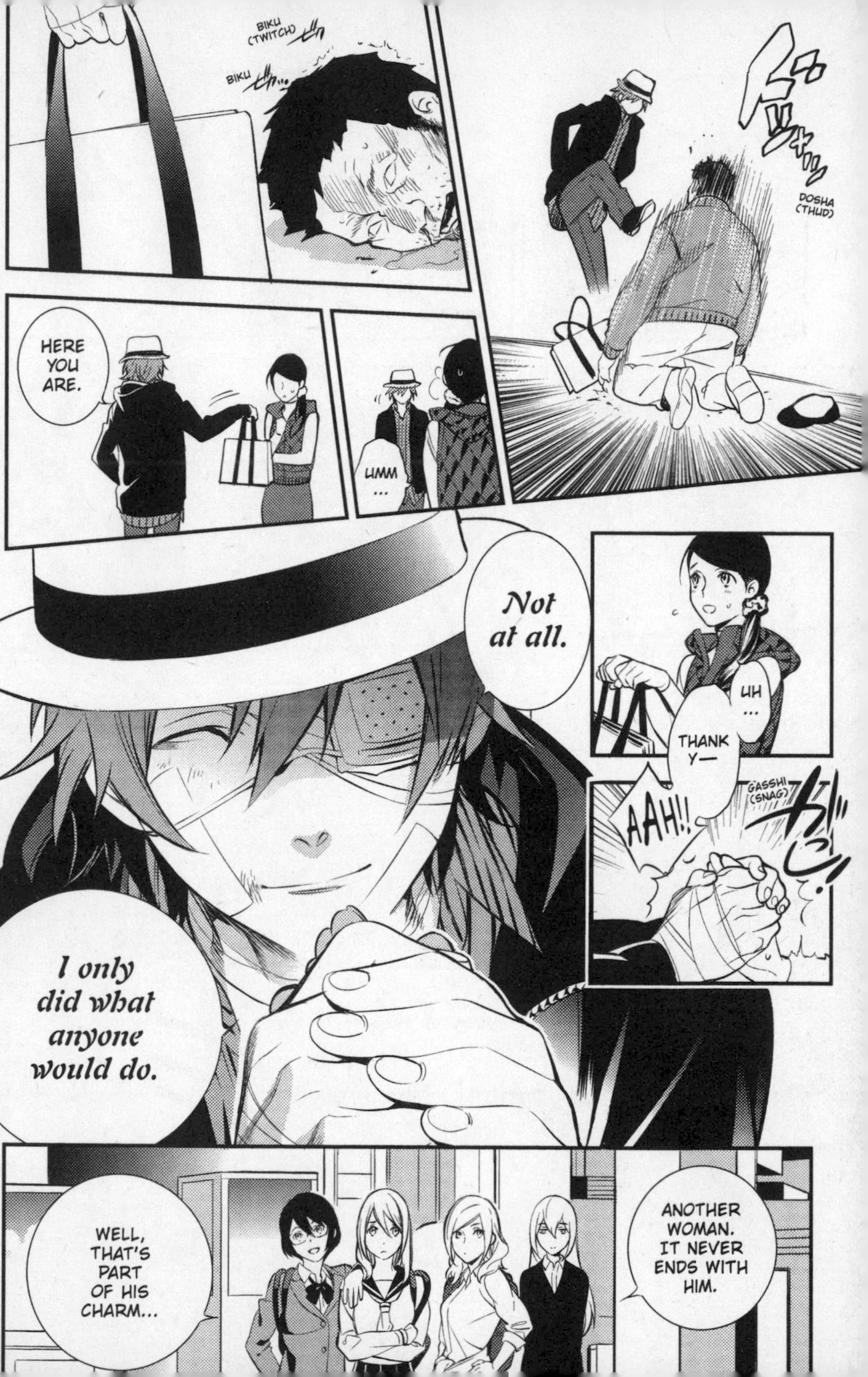
DOSHA (THUD)
BIKU (TWITCH)
BIKU
UMM ...
HERE YOU ARE.
UH ...
THANK Y—
GASSHI (SNAG)
AAH!!
Not at all.
I only did what anyone would do.
ANOTHER WOMAN. IT NEVER ENDS WITH HIM.
WELL, THAT'S PART OF HIS CHARM...

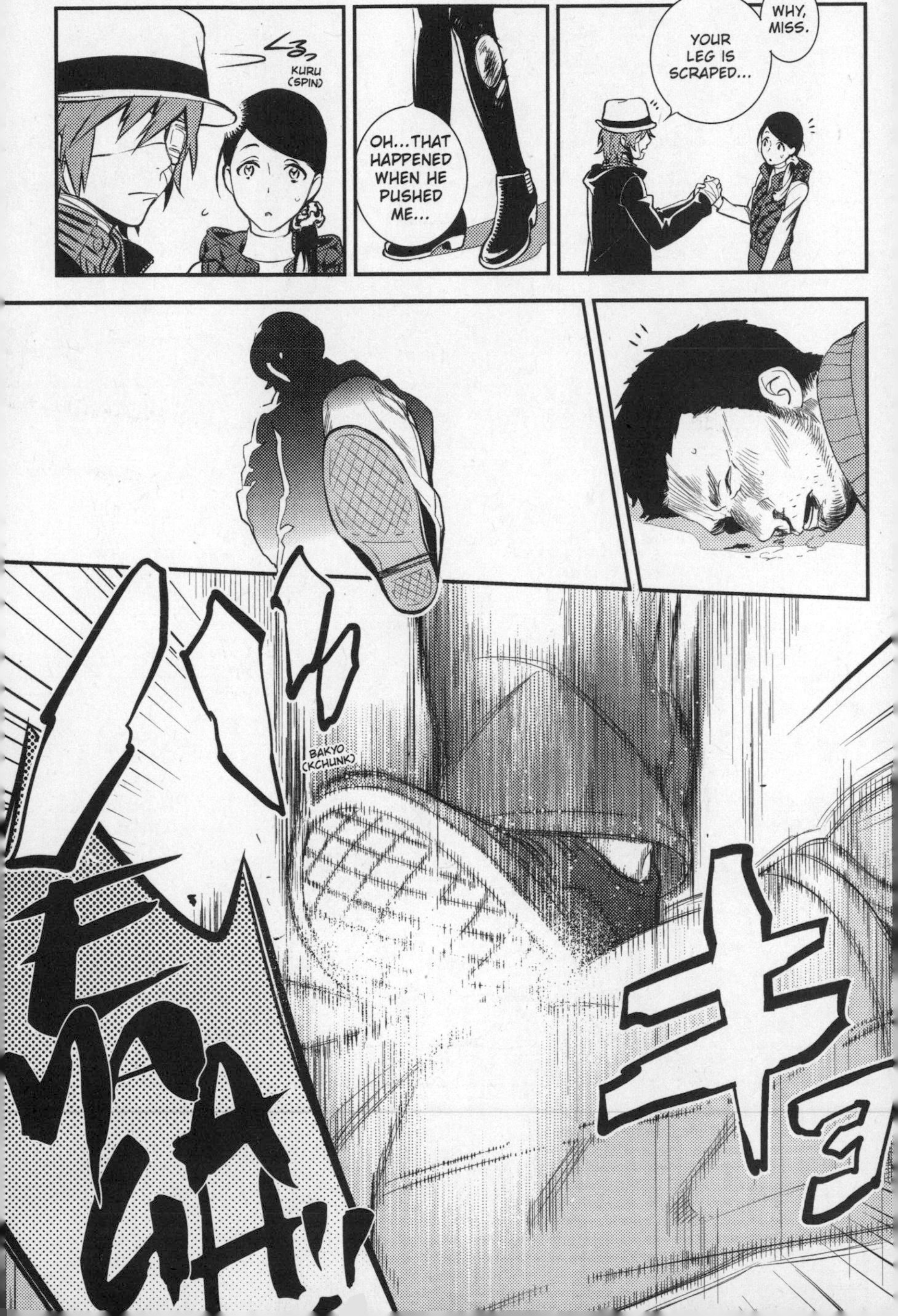
WHY, MISS.
YOUR LEG IS SCRAPED...
OH...THAT HAPPENED WHEN HE PUSHED ME...
KURU (SPIN)
BAKYO (KCHUNK)

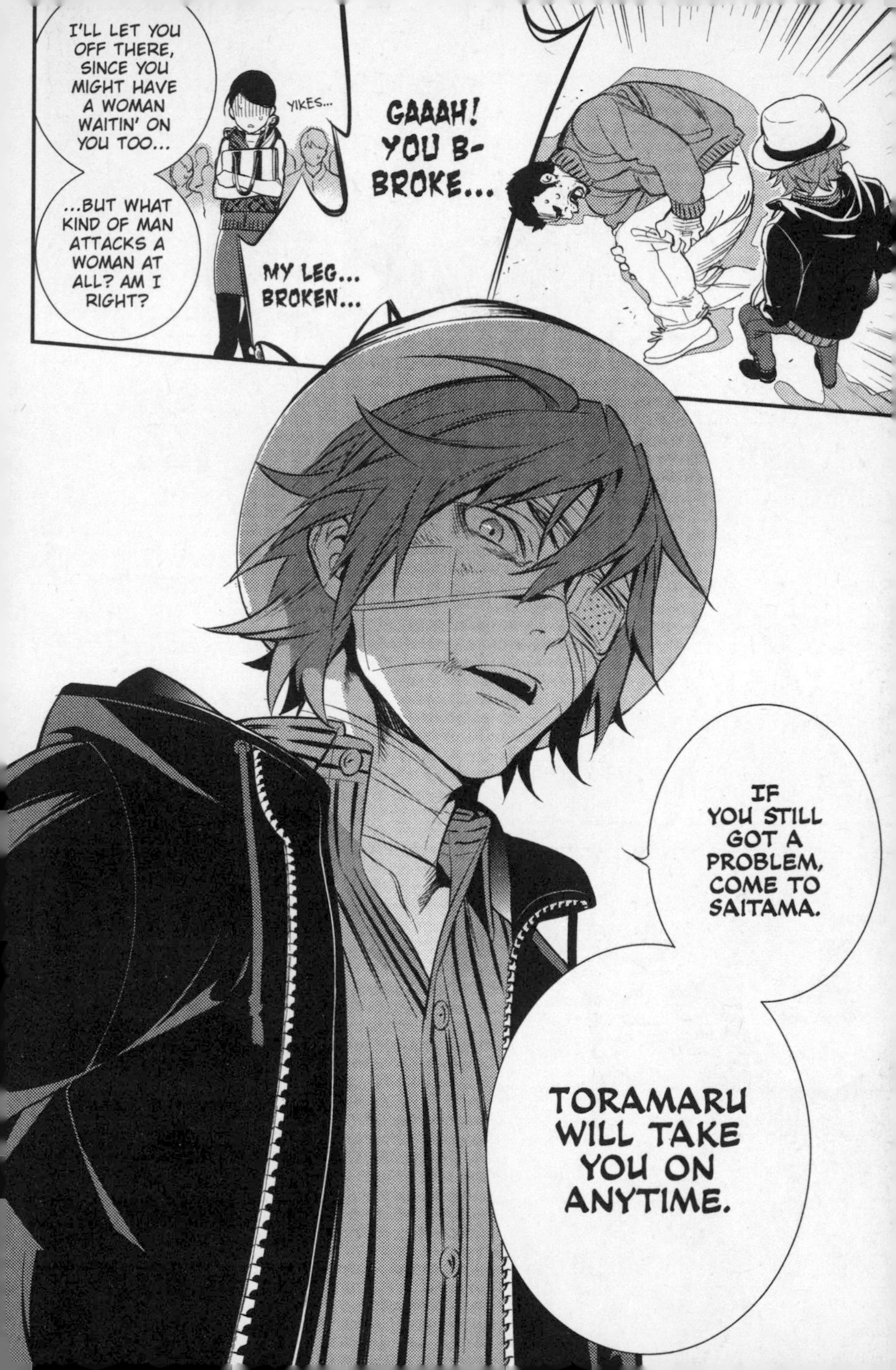
GAAAH! YOU B-BROKE...
MY LEG... BROKEN...
I'LL LET YOU OFF THERE, SINCE YOU MIGHT HAVE A WOMAN WAITIN' ON YOU TOO...
YIKES...
...BUT WHAT KIND OF MAN ATTACKS A WOMAN AT ALL? AM I RIGHT?
IF YOU STILL GOT A PROBLEM, COME TO SAITAMA.
TORAMARU WILL TAKE YOU ON ANYTIME.

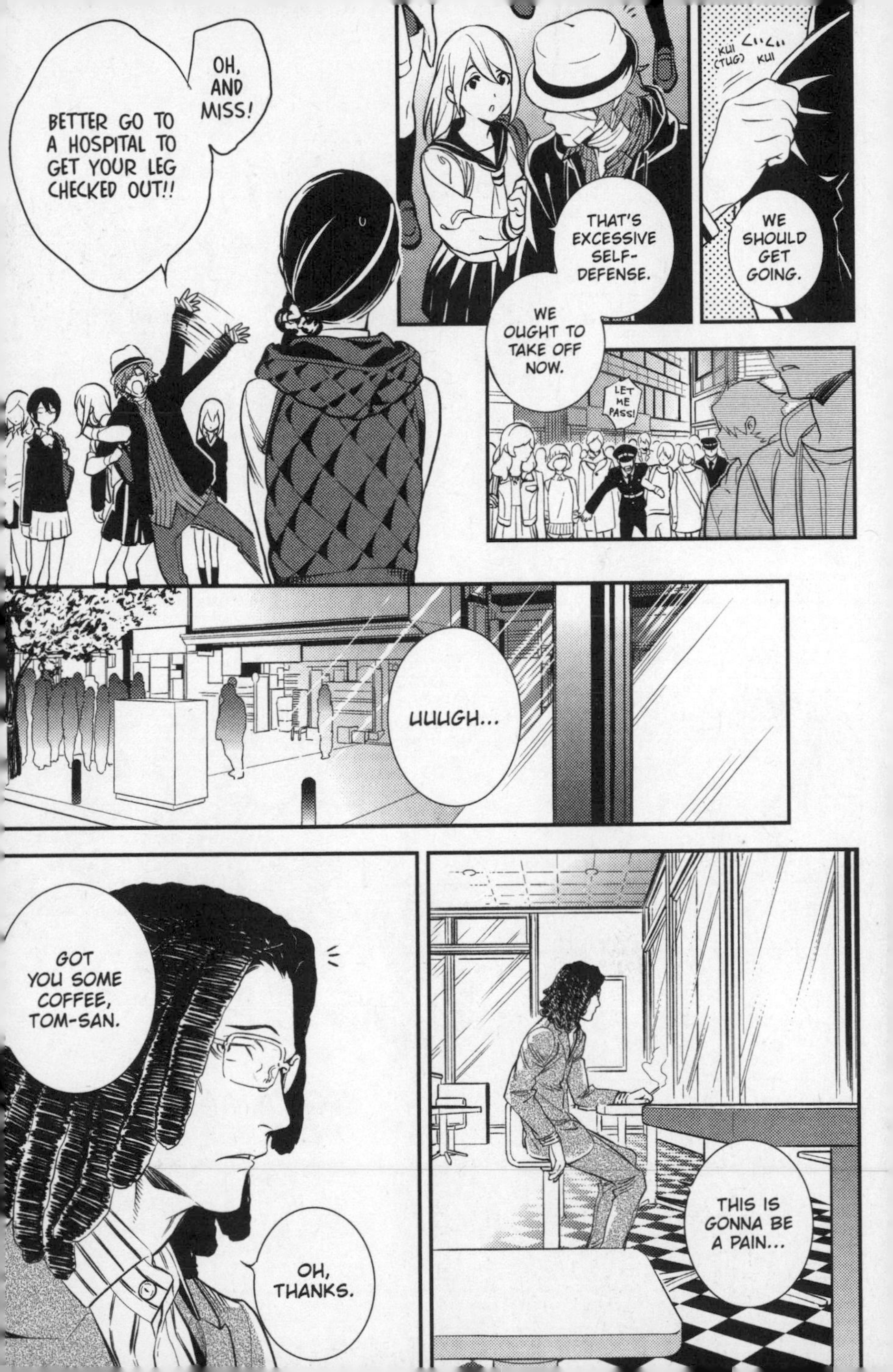

KUI くいくい (TUG) KUI
WE SHOULD GET GOING.
THAT'S EXCESSIVE SELF-DEFENSE.
WE OUGHT TO TAKE OFF NOW.
LET ME PASS!
OH, AND MISS!
BETTER GO TO A HOSPITAL TO GET YOUR LEG CHECKED OUT!!
UUUGH...
THIS IS GONNA BE A PAIN...
GOT YOU SOME COFFEE, TOM-SAN.
OH, THANKS.

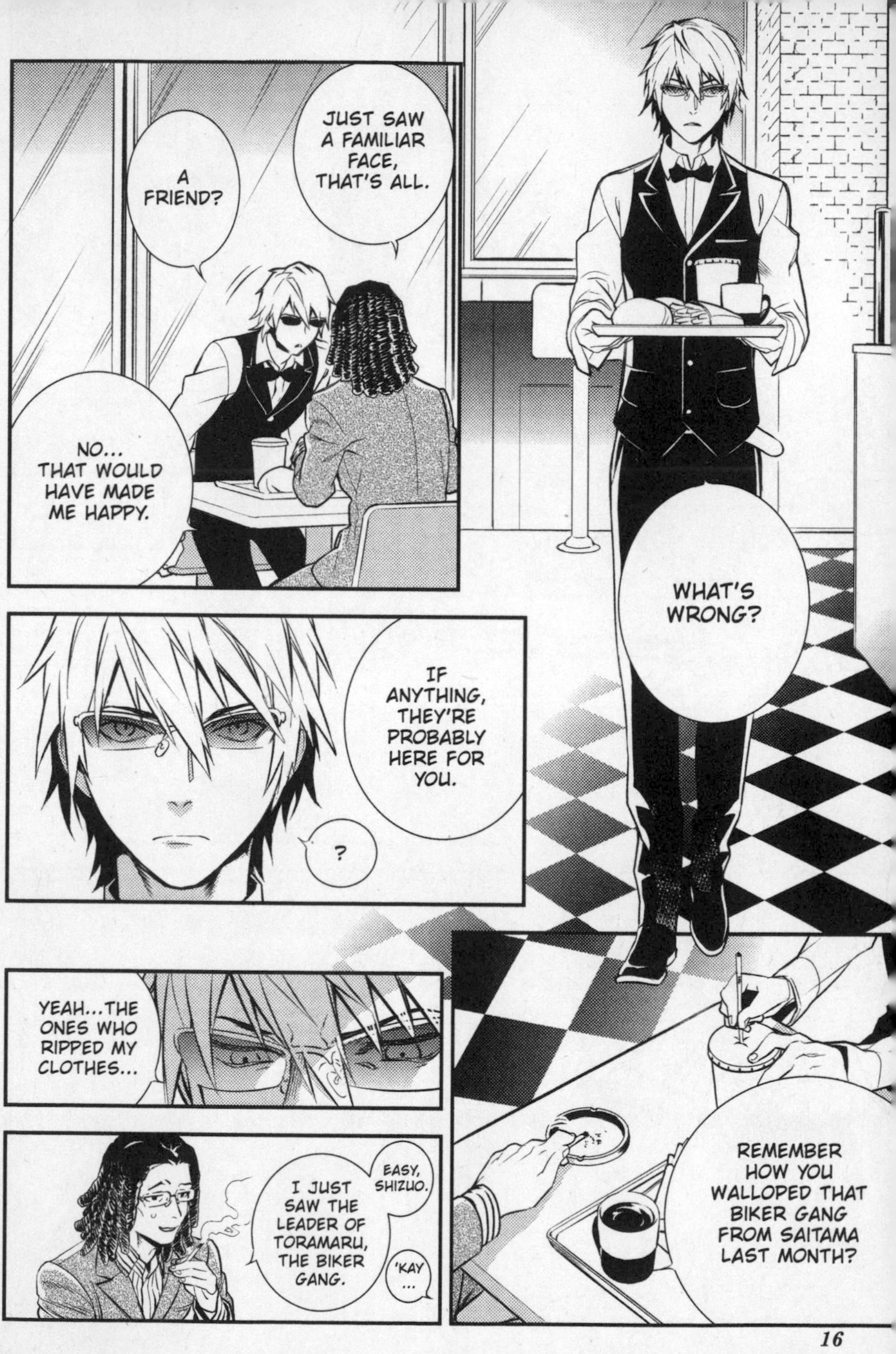
WHAT'S WRONG?
JUST SAW A FAMILIAR FACE, THAT'S ALL.
A FRIEND?
NO... THAT WOULD HAVE MADE ME HAPPY.
IF ANYTHING, THEY'RE PROBABLY HERE FOR YOU.
?
REMEMBER HOW YOU WALLOPED THAT BIKER GANG FROM SAITAMA LAST MONTH?
YEAH...THE ONES WHO RIPPED MY CLOTHES...
EASY, SHIZUO.
'KAY ...
I JUST SAW THE LEADER OF TORAMARU, THE BIKER GANG.

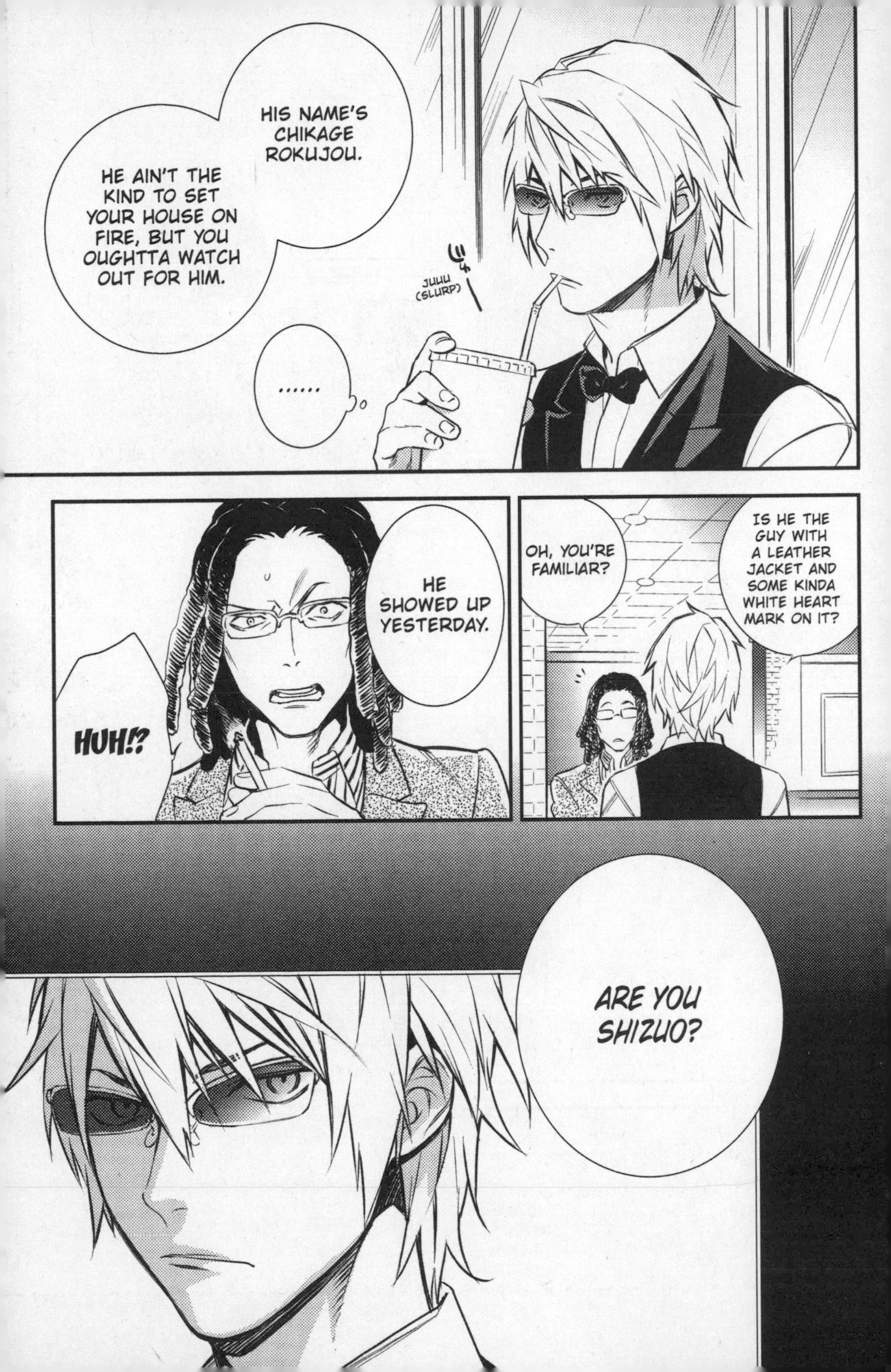
HIS NAME'S CHIKAGE ROKUJOU.
HE AIN'T THE KIND TO SET YOUR HOUSE ON FIRE, BUT YOU OUGHTTA WATCH OUT FOR HIM.
JUUU (SLURP)
......
IS HE THE GUY WITH A LEATHER JACKET AND SOME KINDA WHITE HEART MARK ON IT?
OH, YOU'RE FAMILIAR?
HE SHOWED UP YESTERDAY.
HUH!?
ARE YOU SHIZUO?

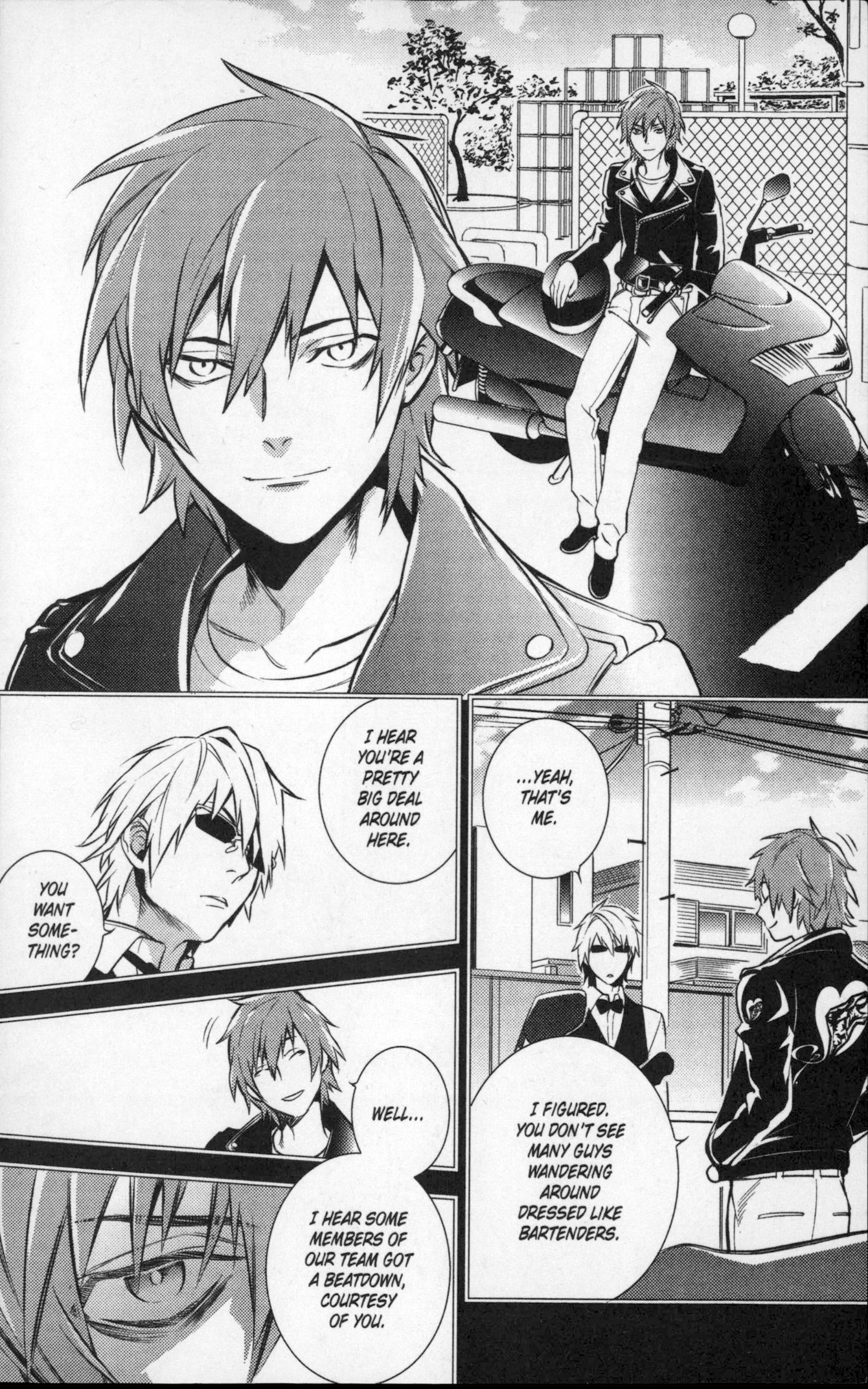
...YEAH, THAT'S ME.
I FIGURED. YOU DON'T SEE MANY GUYS WANDERING AROUND DRESSED LIKE BARTENDERS.
I HEAR YOU'RE A PRETTY BIG DEAL AROUND HERE.
YOU WANT SOME-THING?
WELL...
I HEAR SOME MEMBERS OF OUR TEAM GOT A BEATDOWN, COURTESY OF YOU.

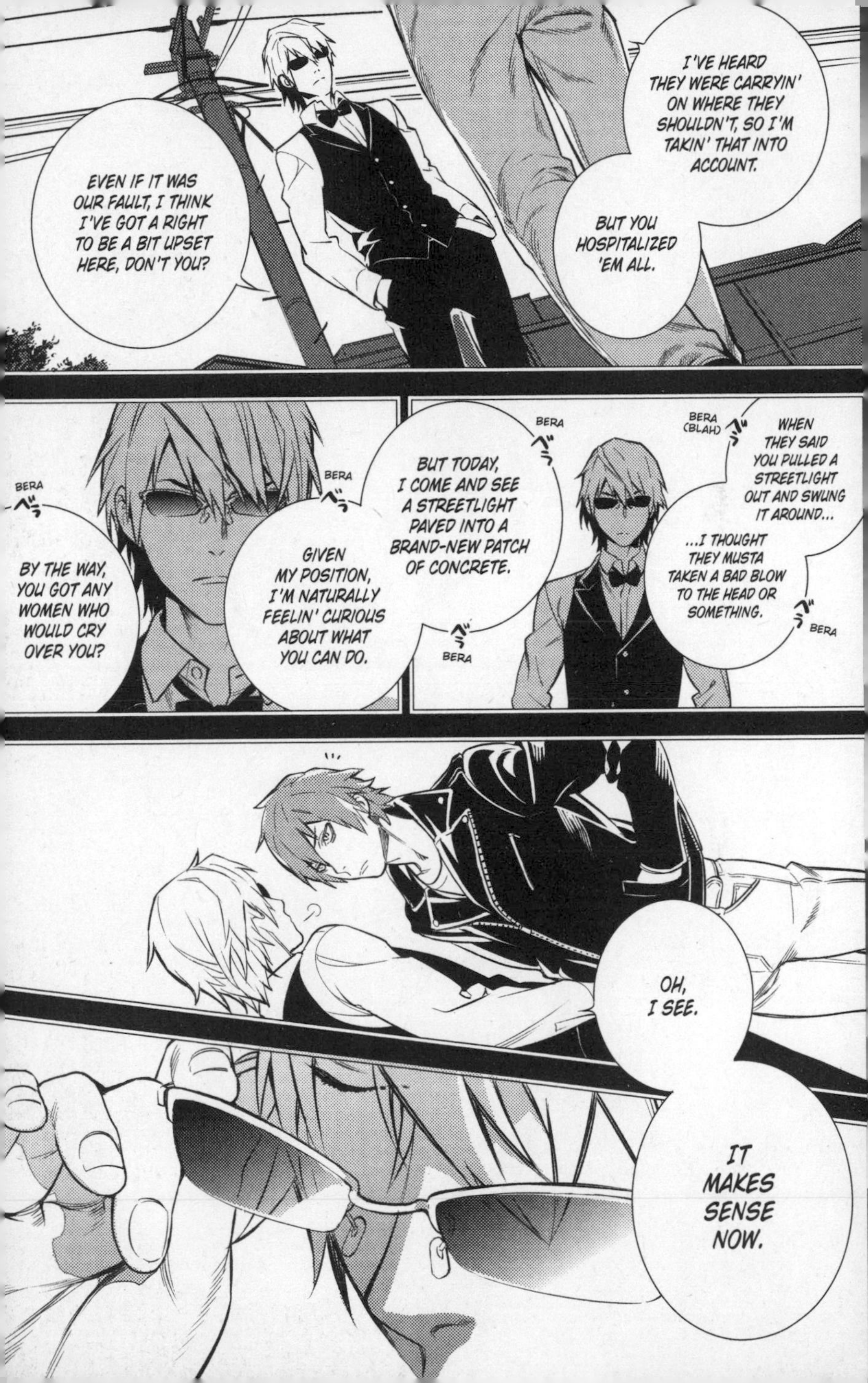
I'VE HEARD THEY WERE CARRYIN' ON WHERE THEY SHOULDN'T, SO I'M TAKIN' THAT INTO ACCOUNT.
BUT YOU HOSPITALIZED 'EM ALL.
EVEN IF IT WAS OUR FAULT, I THINK I'VE GOT A RIGHT TO BE A BIT UPSET HERE, DON'T YOU?
BERA (BLAH)
WHEN THEY SAID YOU PULLED A STREETLIGHT OUT AND SWUNG IT AROUND...
...I THOUGHT THEY MUSTA TAKEN A BAD BLOW TO THE HEAD OR SOMETHING.
BERA
BERA
BUT TODAY, I COME AND SEE A STREETLIGHT PAVED INTO A BRAND-NEW PATCH OF CONCRETE.
BERA
BERA
GIVEN MY POSITION, I'M NATURALLY FEELIN' CURIOUS ABOUT WHAT YOU CAN DO.
BERA
BY THE WAY, YOU GOT ANY WOMEN WHO WOULD CRY OVER YOU?
OH, I SEE.
IT MAKES SENSE NOW.

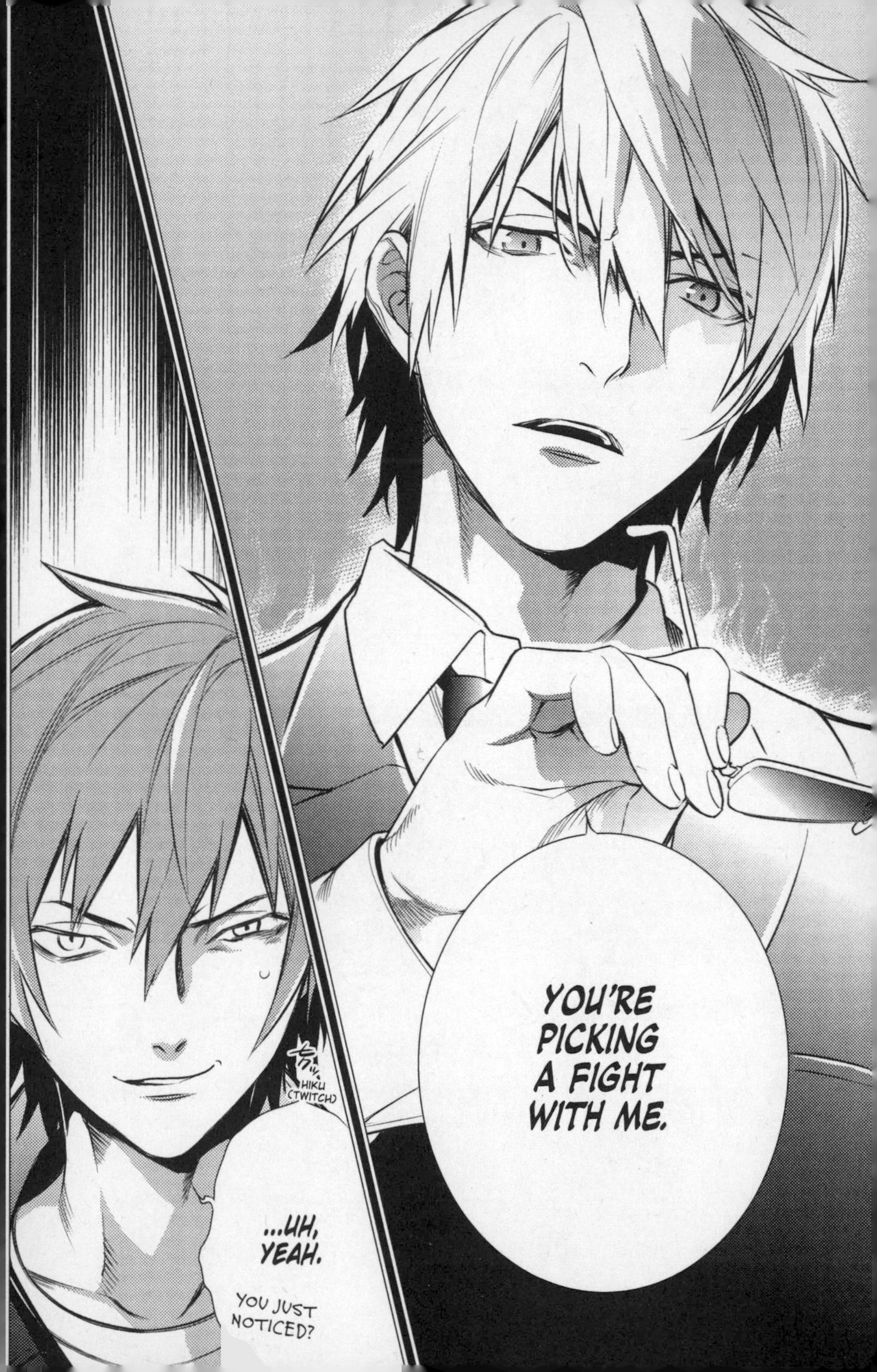
YOU'RE PICKING A FIGHT WITH ME.
HIKU (TWITCH)
...UH, YEAH.
YOU JUST NOTICED?

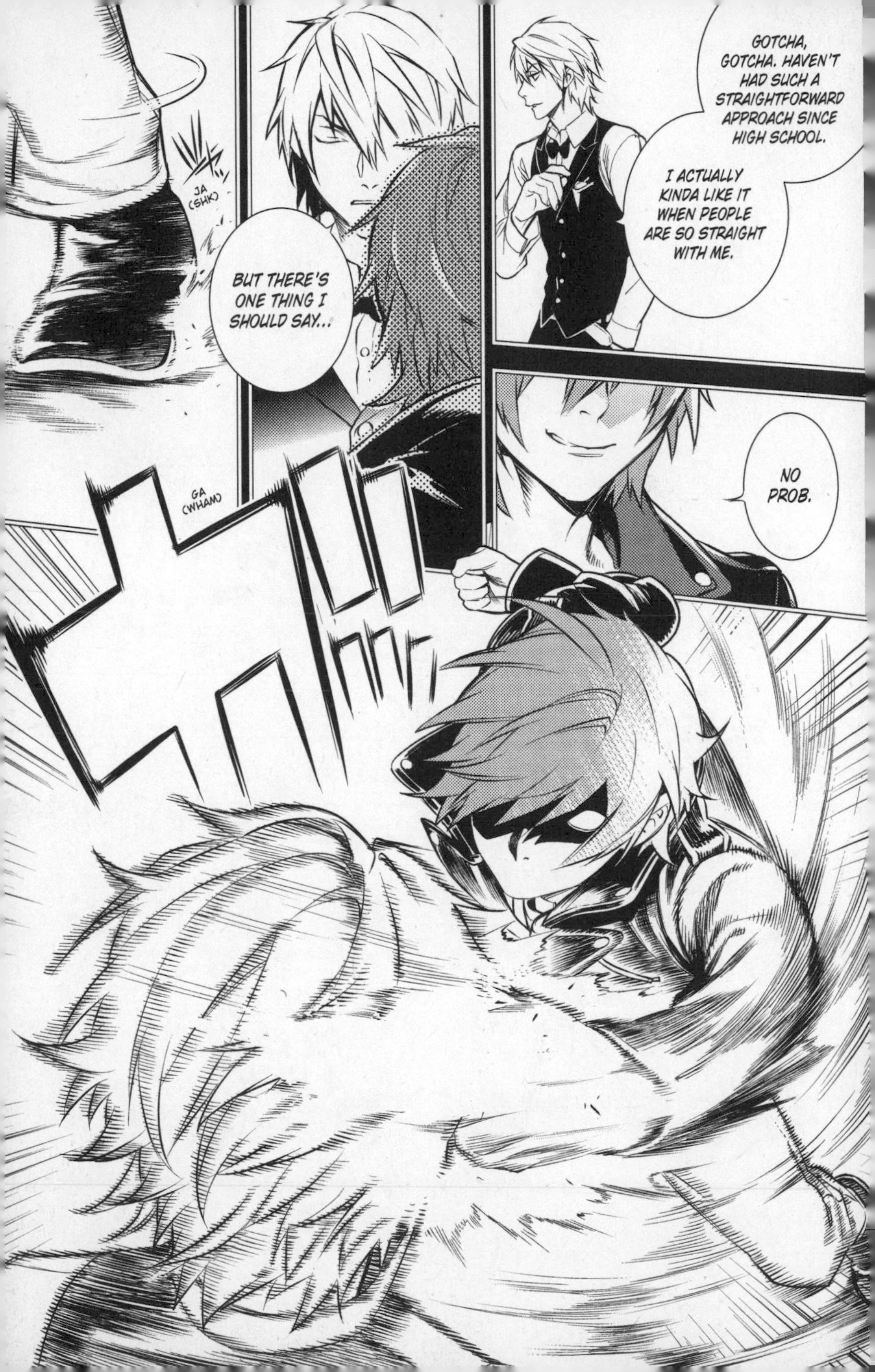
GOTCHA, GOTCHA. HAVEN'T HAD SUCH A STRAIGHTFORWARD APPROACH SINCE HIGH SCHOOL.
I ACTUALLY KINDA LIKE IT WHEN PEOPLE ARE SO STRAIGHT WITH ME.
NO PROB.
BUT THERE'S ONE THING I SHOULD SAY...
JA (SHK)
GA (WHAM)

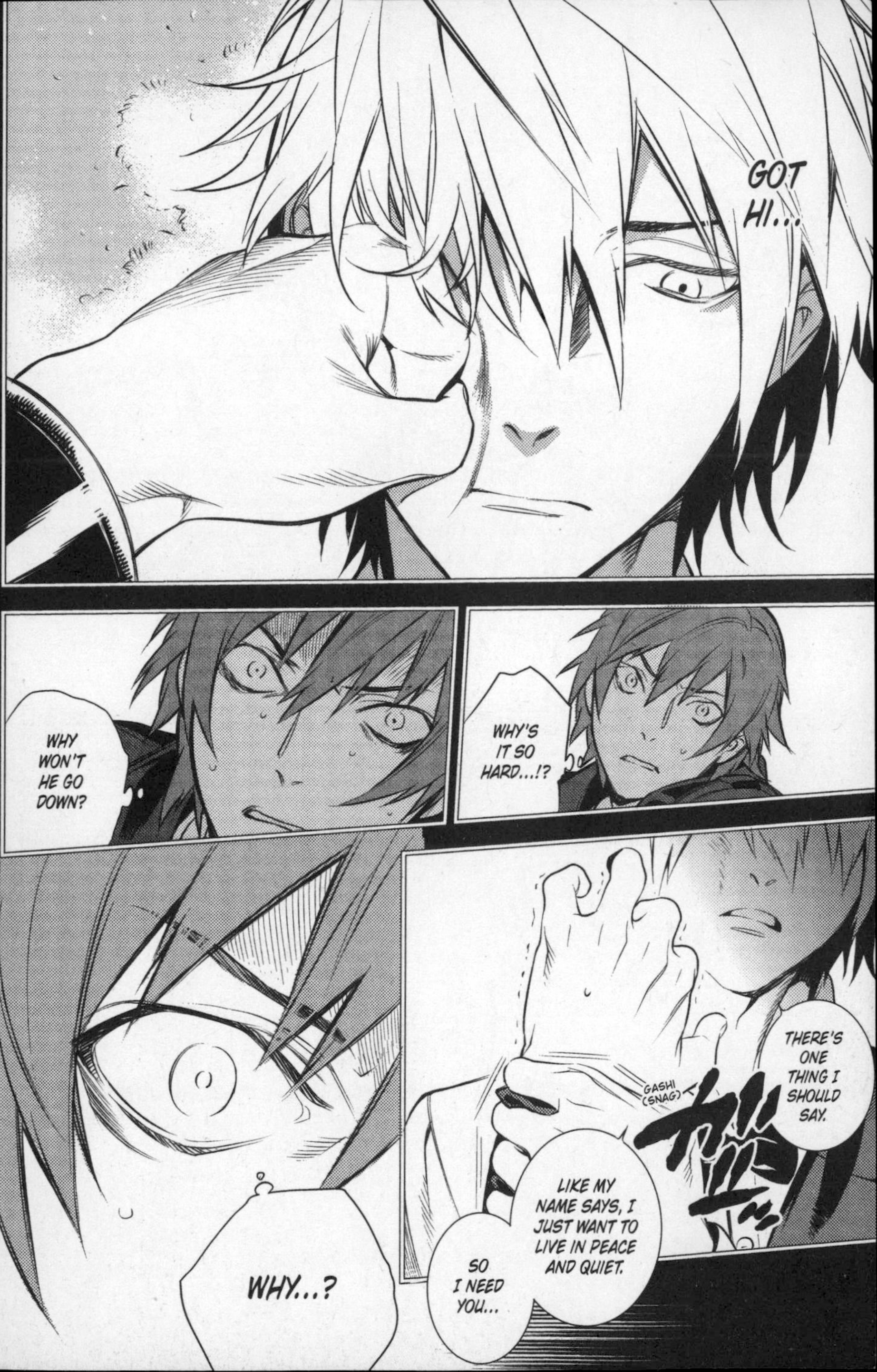
GOT HI...
WHY'S IT SO HARD...!?
WHY WON'T HE GO DOWN?
THERE'S ONE THING I SHOULD SAY.
GASHI (SNAG)
LIKE MY NAME SAYS, I JUST WANT TO LIVE IN PEACE AND QUIET.
SO I NEED YOU...
WHY...?

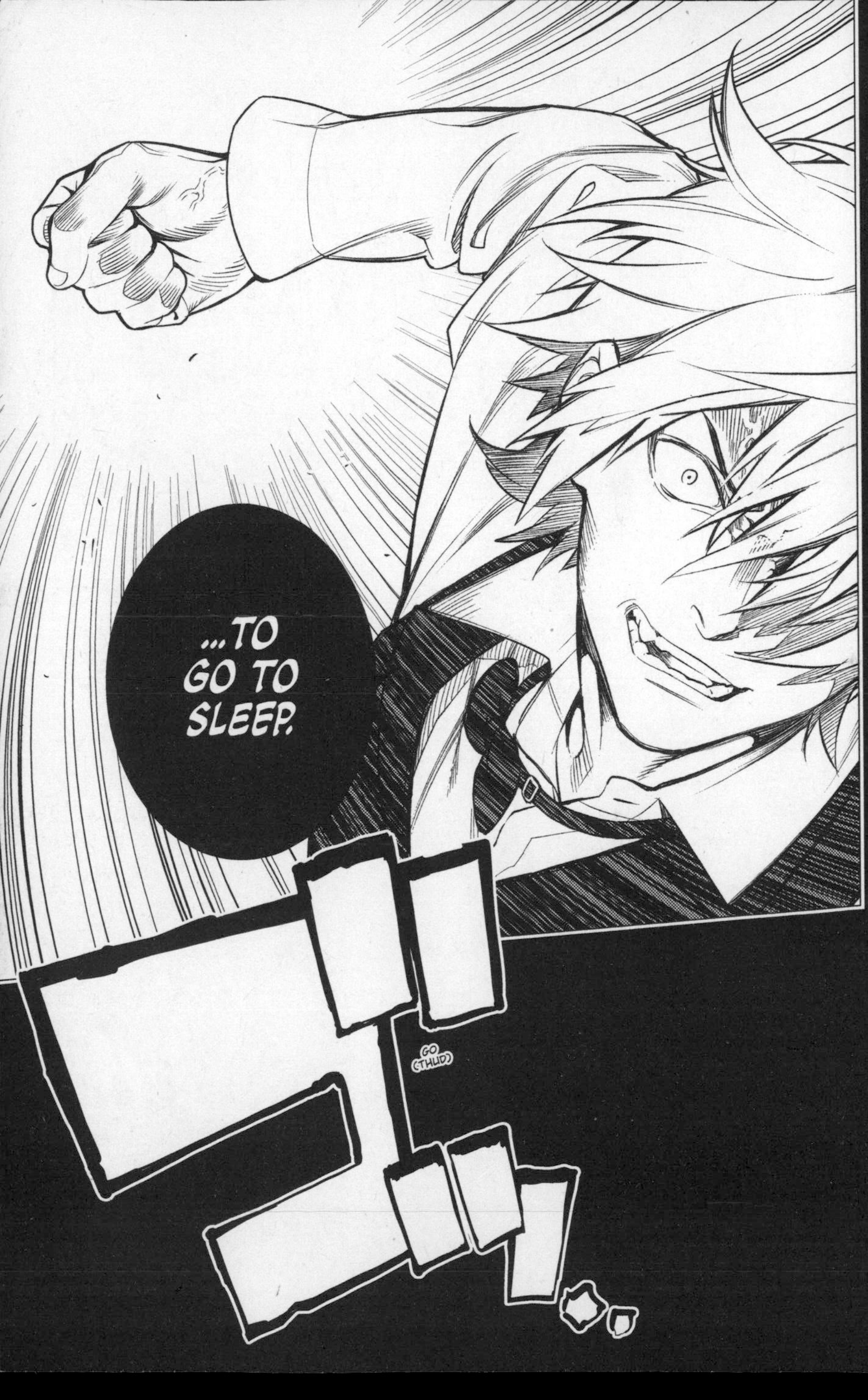
...TO GO TO SLEEP.
GO (THUD)

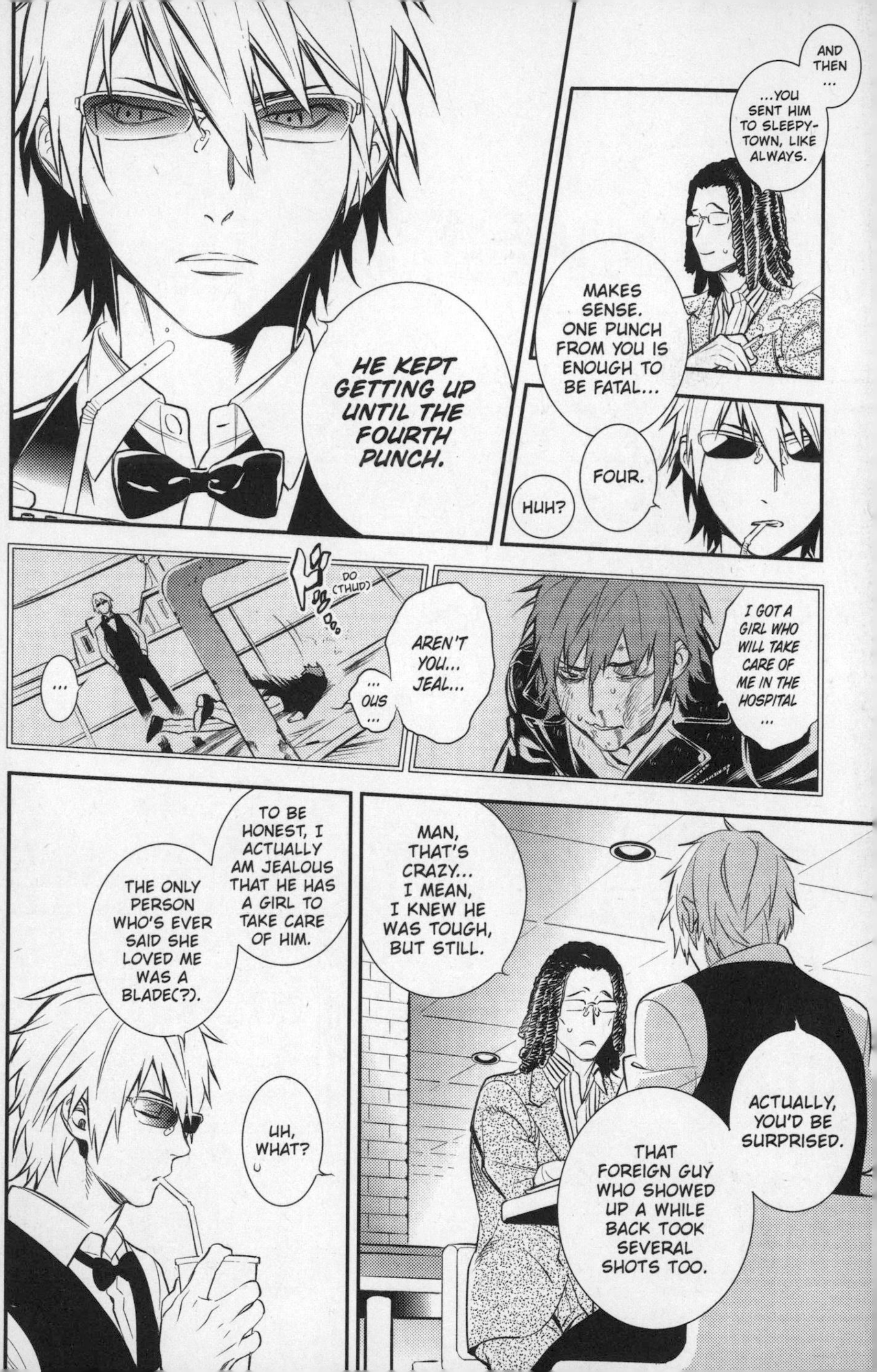

AND THEN ...
...YOU SENT HIM TO SLEEPY-TOWN, LIKE ALWAYS.
MAKES SENSE. ONE PUNCH FROM YOU IS ENOUGH TO BE FATAL...
FOUR.
HUH?
HE KEPT GETTING UP UNTIL THE FOURTH PUNCH.
I GOT A GIRL WHO WILL TAKE CARE OF ME IN THE HOSPITAL ...
AREN'T YOU... JEAL...
DO (THUD)
... OUS ...
...
MAN, THAT'S CRAZY... I MEAN, I KNEW HE WAS TOUGH, BUT STILL.
ACTUALLY, YOU'D BE SURPRISED.
THAT FOREIGN GUY WHO SHOWED UP A WHILE BACK TOOK SEVERAL SHOTS TOO.
TO BE HONEST, I ACTUALLY AM JEALOUS THAT HE HAS A GIRL TO TAKE CARE OF HIM.
THE ONLY PERSON WHO'S EVER SAID SHE LOVED ME WAS A BLADE(?).
UH, WHAT?

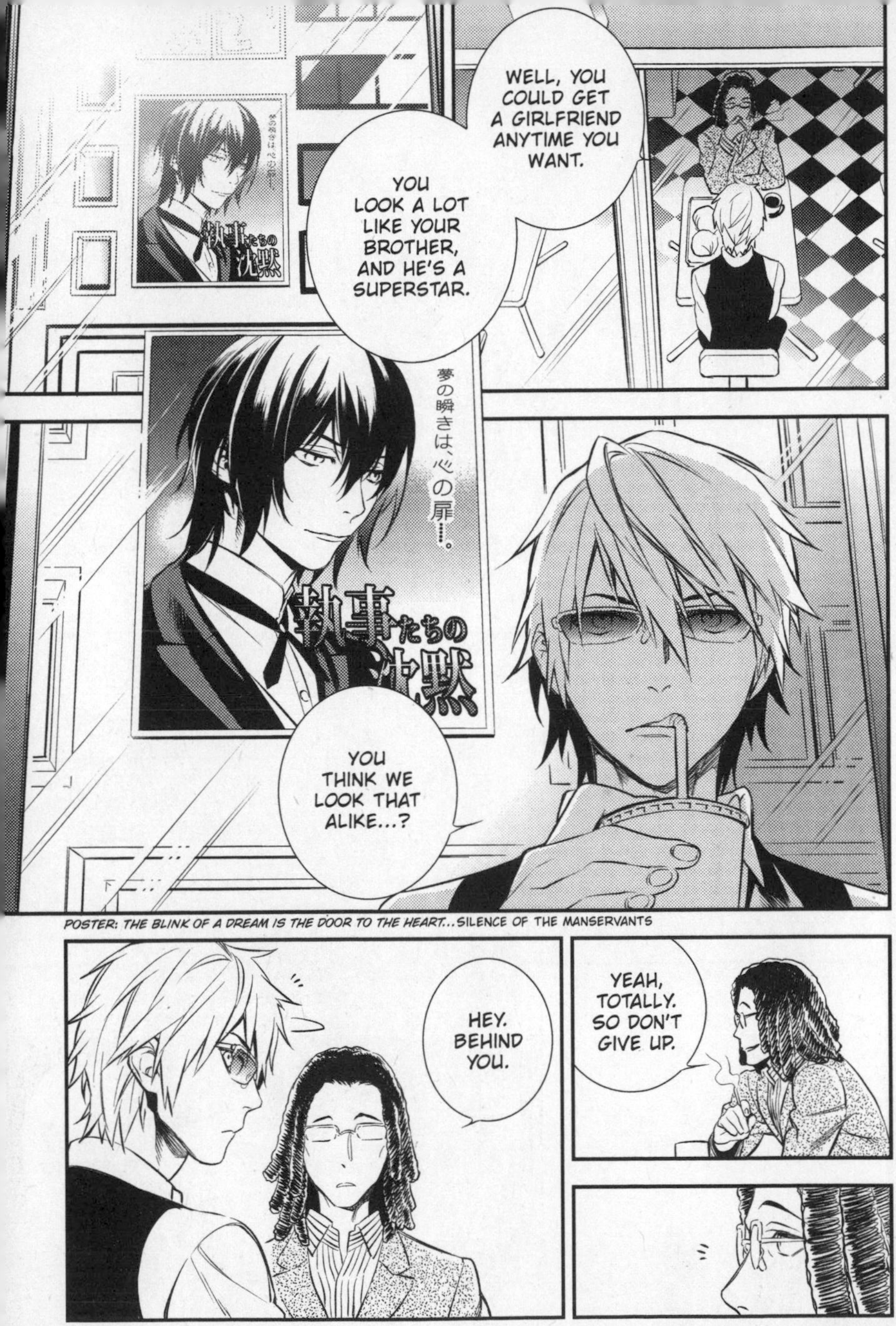
WELL, YOU COULD GET A GIRLFRIEND ANYTIME YOU WANT.
YOU LOOK A LOT LIKE YOUR BROTHER, AND HE'S A SUPERSTAR.
夢の瞬きは、心の扉……。
執事たちの沈黙
YOU THINK WE LOOK THAT ALIKE...?
POSTER: THE BLINK OF A DREAM IS THE DOOR TO THE HEART...SILENCE OF THE MANSERVANTS
YEAH, TOTALLY. SO DON'T GIVE UP.
HEY. BEHIND YOU.

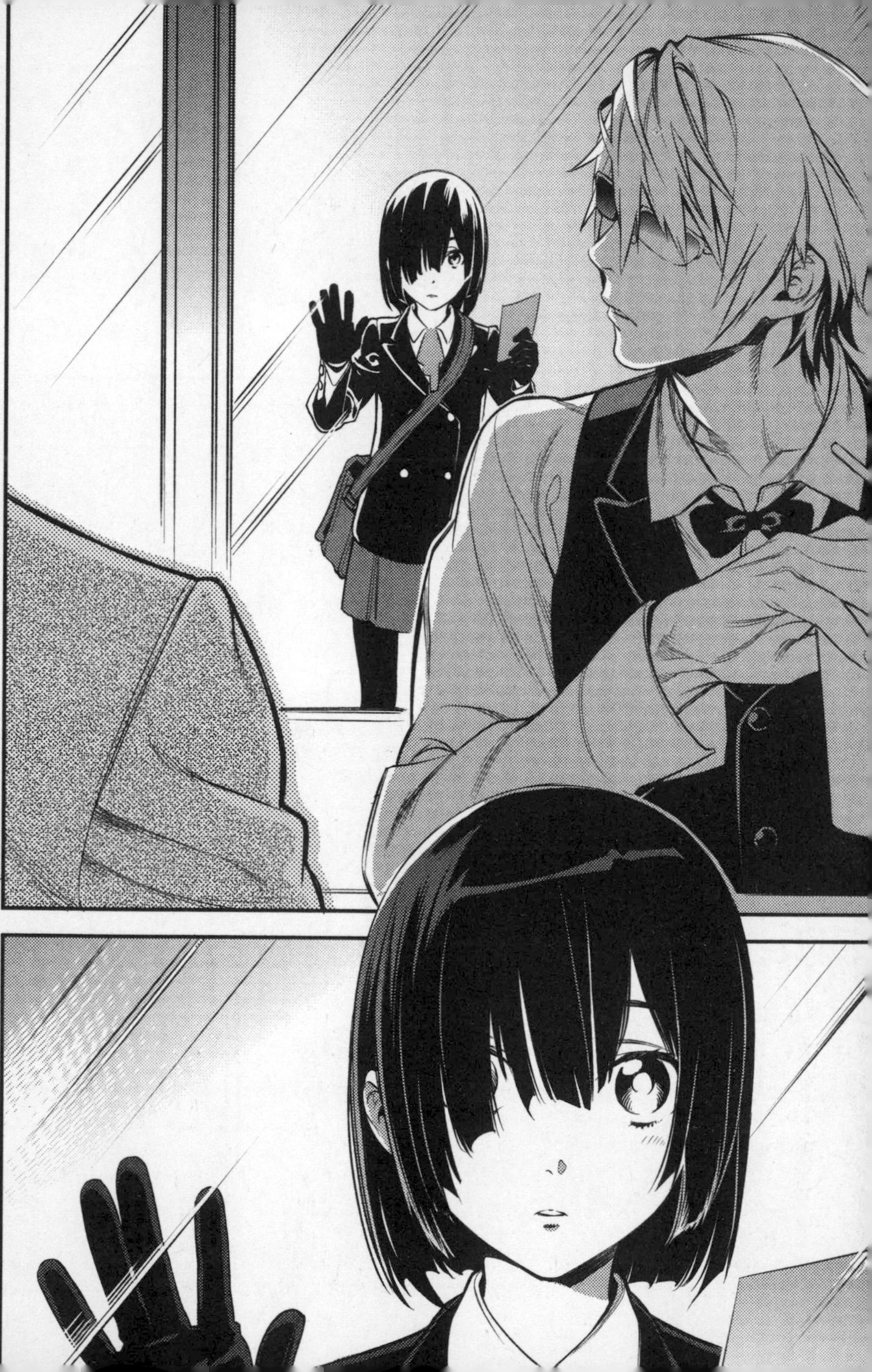

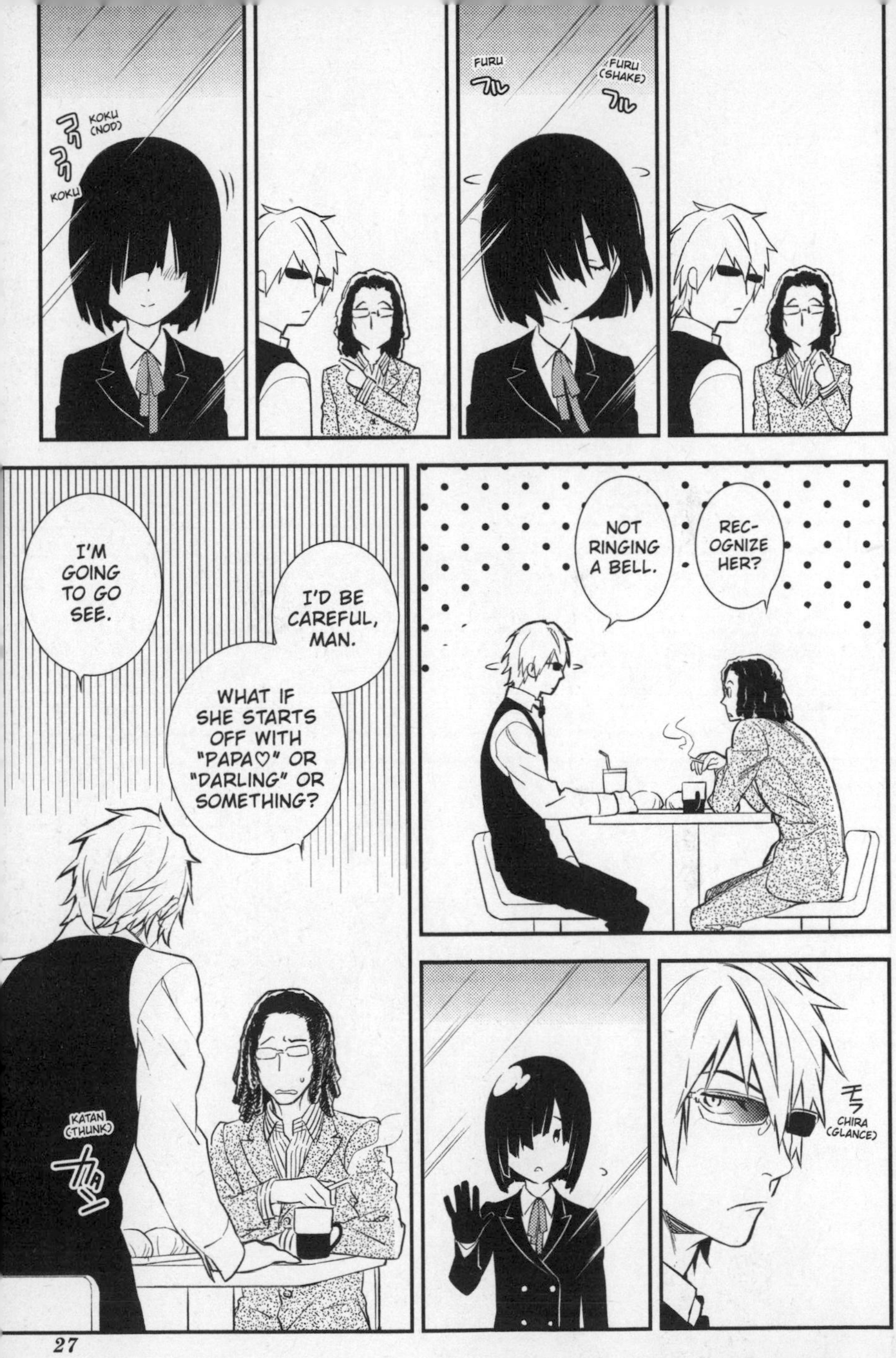
FURU (SHAKE)
FURU
KOKU (NOD)
KOKU
REC-OGNIZE HER?
NOT RINGING A BELL.
CHIRA (GLANCE)
I'D BE CAREFUL, MAN.
WHAT IF SHE STARTS OFF WITH "PAPA♡" OR "DARLING" OR SOMETHING?
I'M GOING TO GO SEE.
KATAN (THUNK)

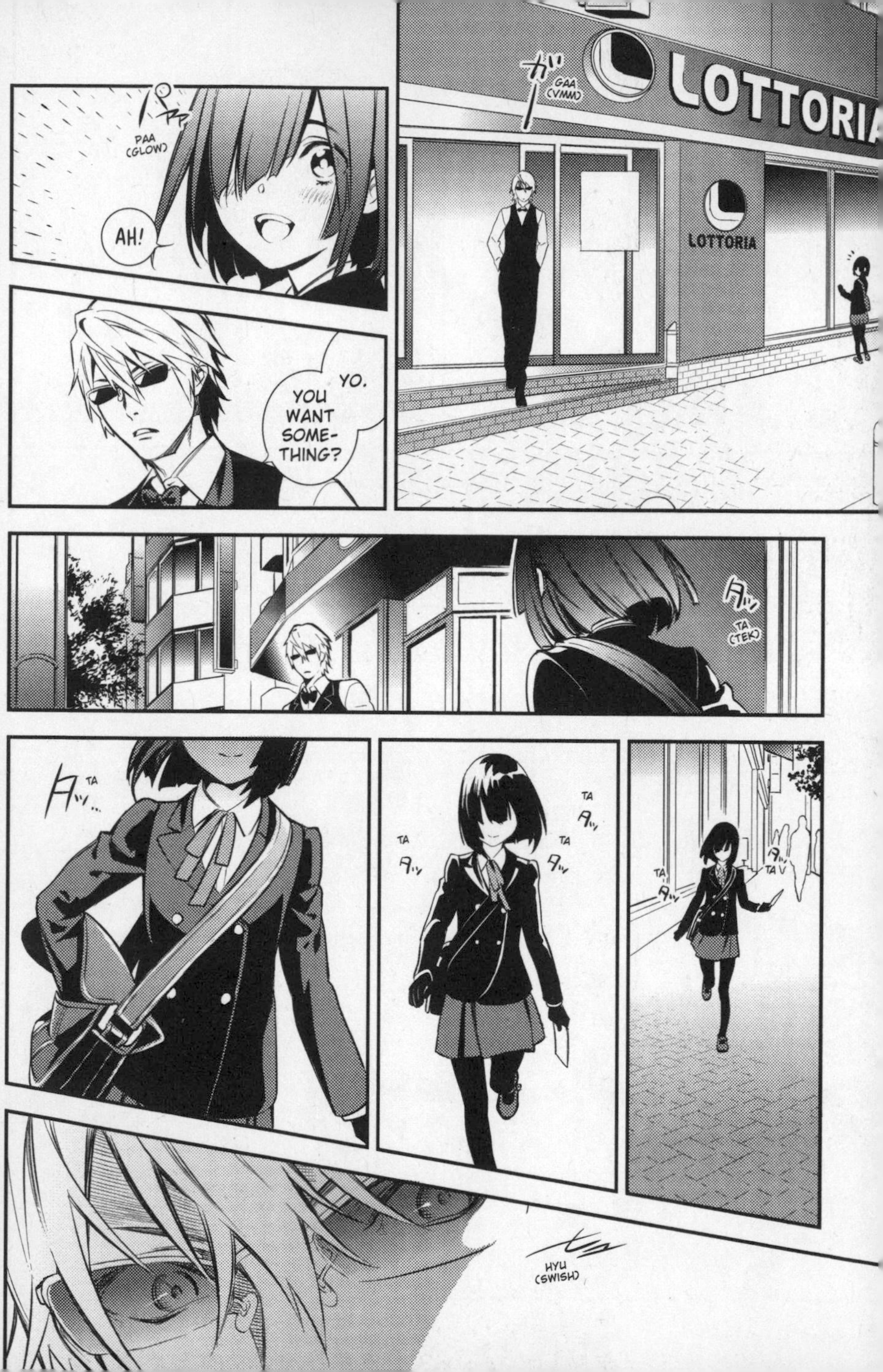
GAA (VMM)
LOTTORIA
LOTTORIA
PAA (GLOW)
AH!
YO. YOU WANT SOMETHING?
TA (TEK)
TA
TA V
TA
TA
TA
TA...
HYU (SWISH)

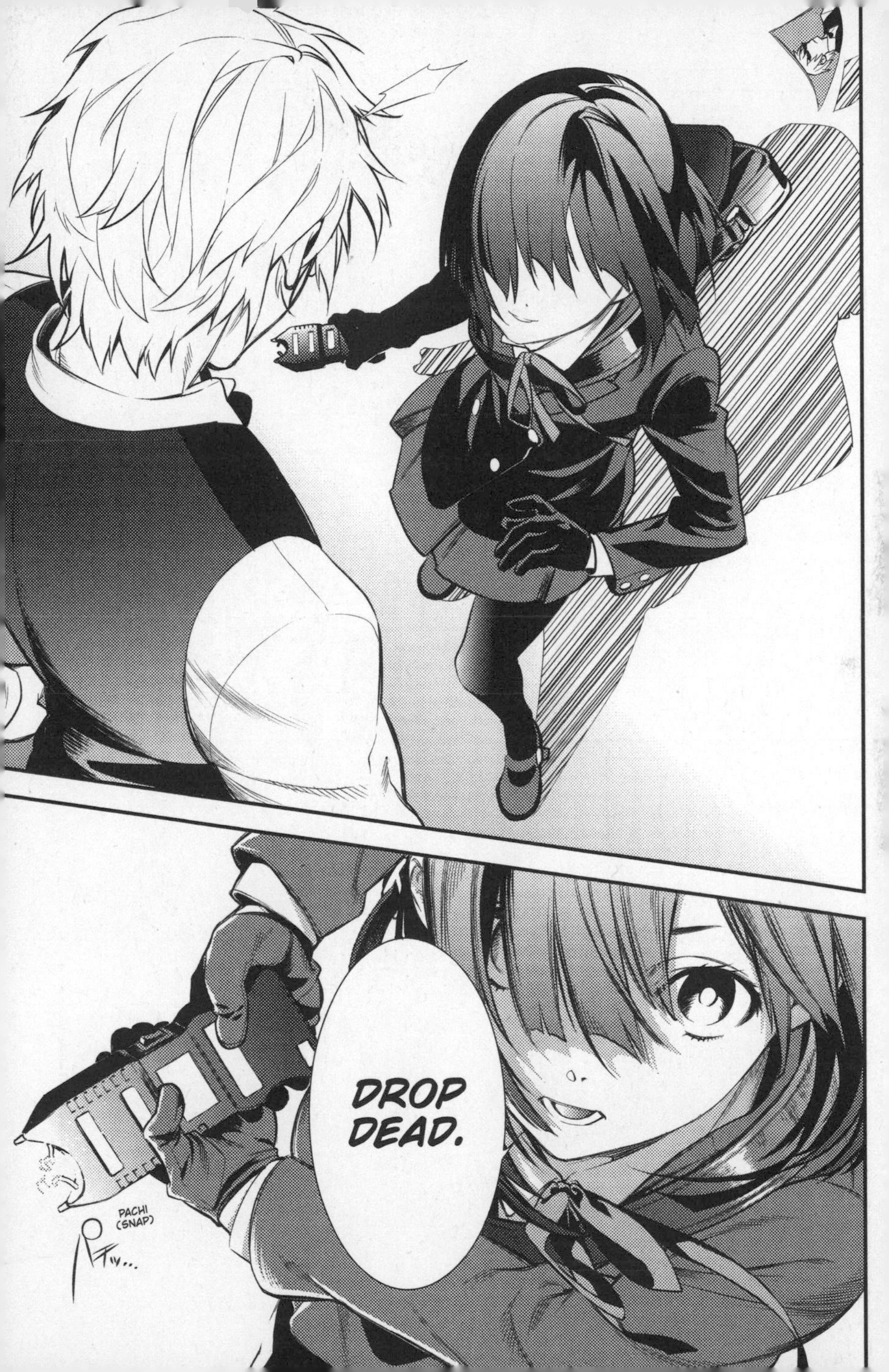
DROP DEAD.
PACHI (SNAP)

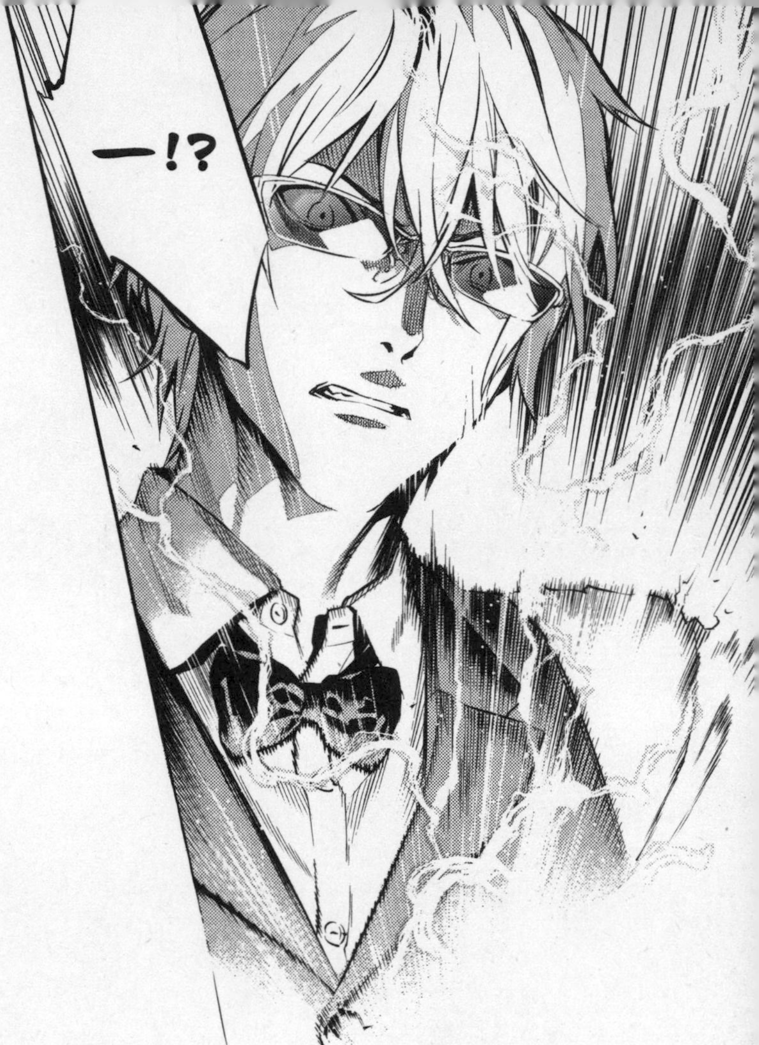
—!?

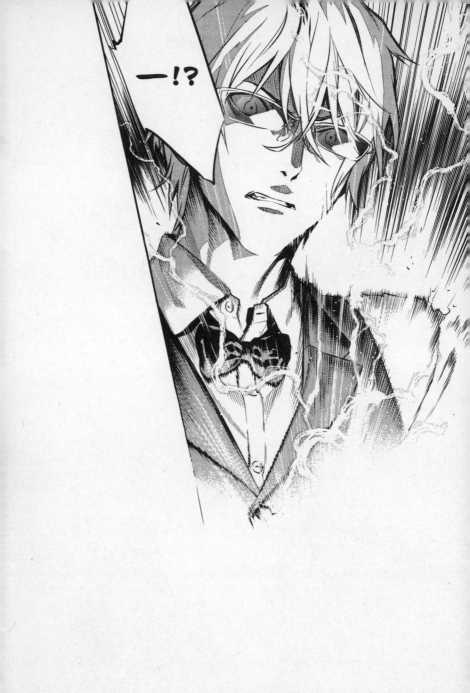

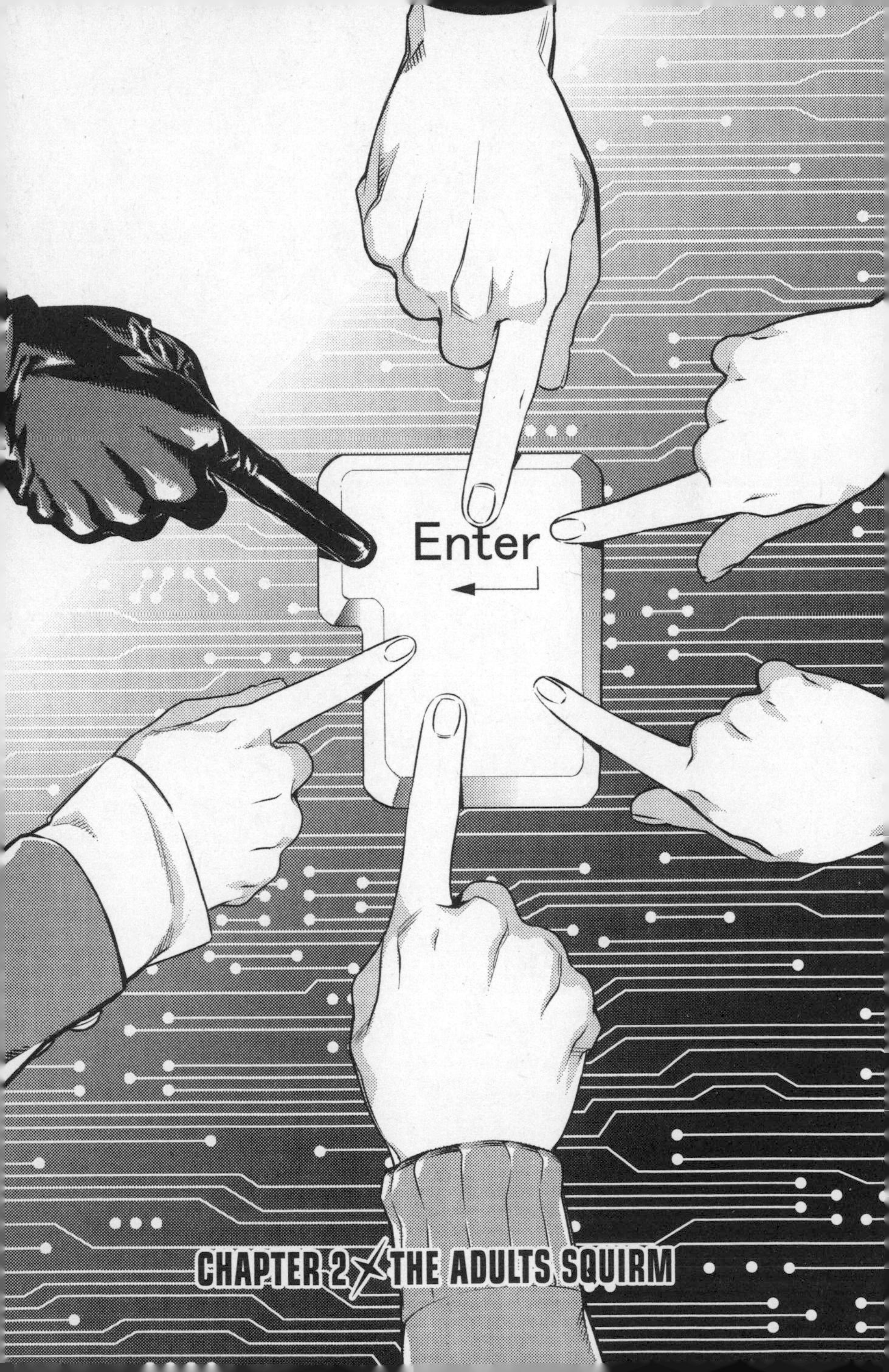
Enter
CHAPTER 2 THE ADULTS SQUIRM

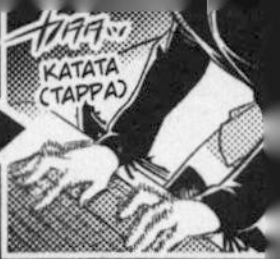
KATATA
(TAPPA)

Kuru: By the way, "Setton" is a very curious username. Where does it come from? Did you borrow it from the movie producer Maxwell Setton?

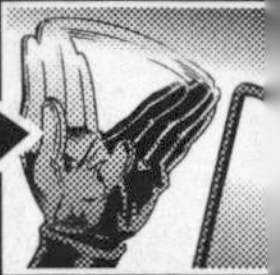

Setton: No, my username is just a play on my actual name.

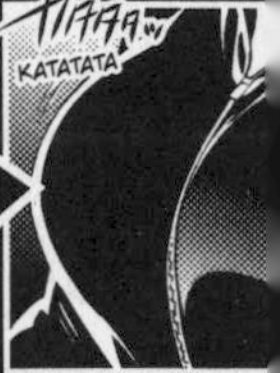
KATATATA

Kuru: My goodness, I did not realize it was that simple. Oh dear, I just called you simple. Please accept my deepest apologies and recognize that it was a harmless mistake. But do you realize you have given us an angle to decipher your identity? You could be Sanpei Seto...Anna Setouchi...and who else?

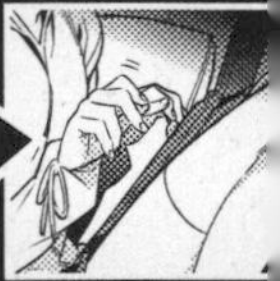

Mai: —(This message contains an inappropriate word and cannot be displayed)—

Mai: Huh?

—TAROUTANAKA HAS ENTERED THE CHAT—

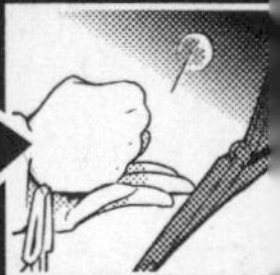

Mai: —(This message contains an inappropriate word and cannot be displayed)—

Mai: Oh, you can't type that word

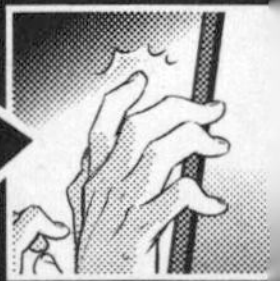

TarouTanaka: Good eveni—whoa...I've never seen anyone set off that feature before.

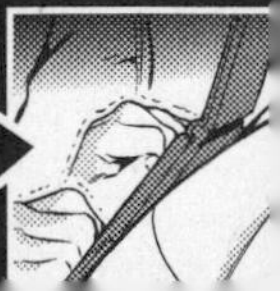

Mai: Ouch.

got pinched.

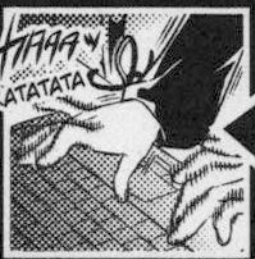
KATATATA

Kuru: Please forgive me. We are using separate computers next to each other, and I noticed that Mai was entering a terribly rude word and took it upon myself to punish her in real life for soiling the mood. Please be reassured that I am in control.

—BACURA HAS ENTERED THE CHAT—
—SAIKA HAS ENTERED THE CHAT—

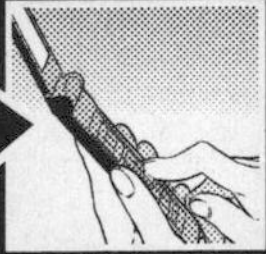

Saika: good evening

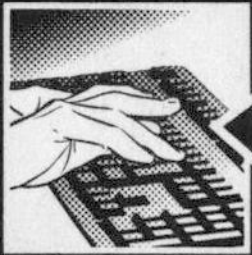

Bacura: 'Suuup.

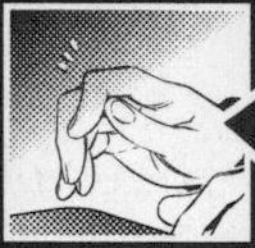

Kuru: Oh, it's the playboy who plays the recorder.

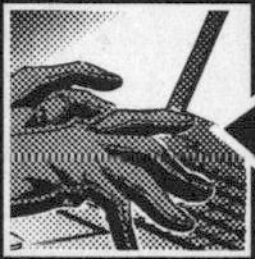

Setton: Good evening, Saika-san. That timing was practically synchronized.

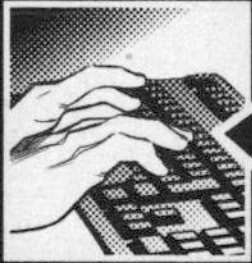

Bacura: Are you still on about the recorder thing!?

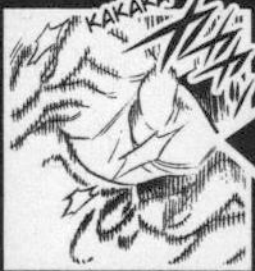
KAKAKA

Kuru: My very first encounter with this chat room brought me face-to-face with that embarrassingly trite poem, so it seems to have been etched into my mind. If anything, I ought to demand an apology and restitution.

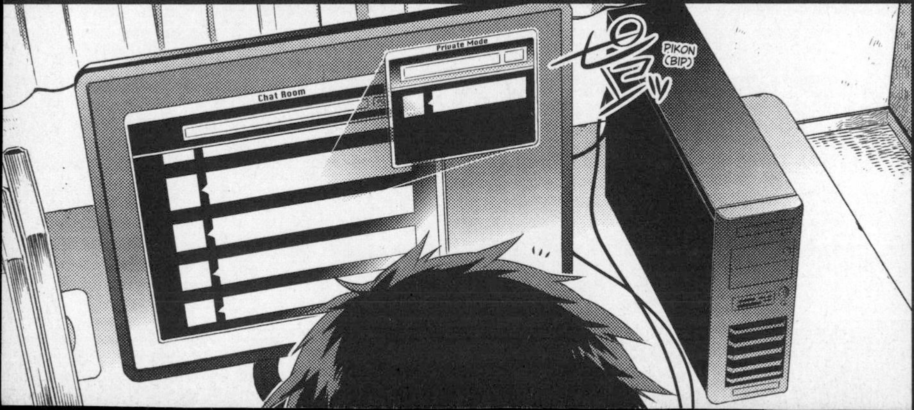
PIKON (BIP)
Private Mode
Chat Room

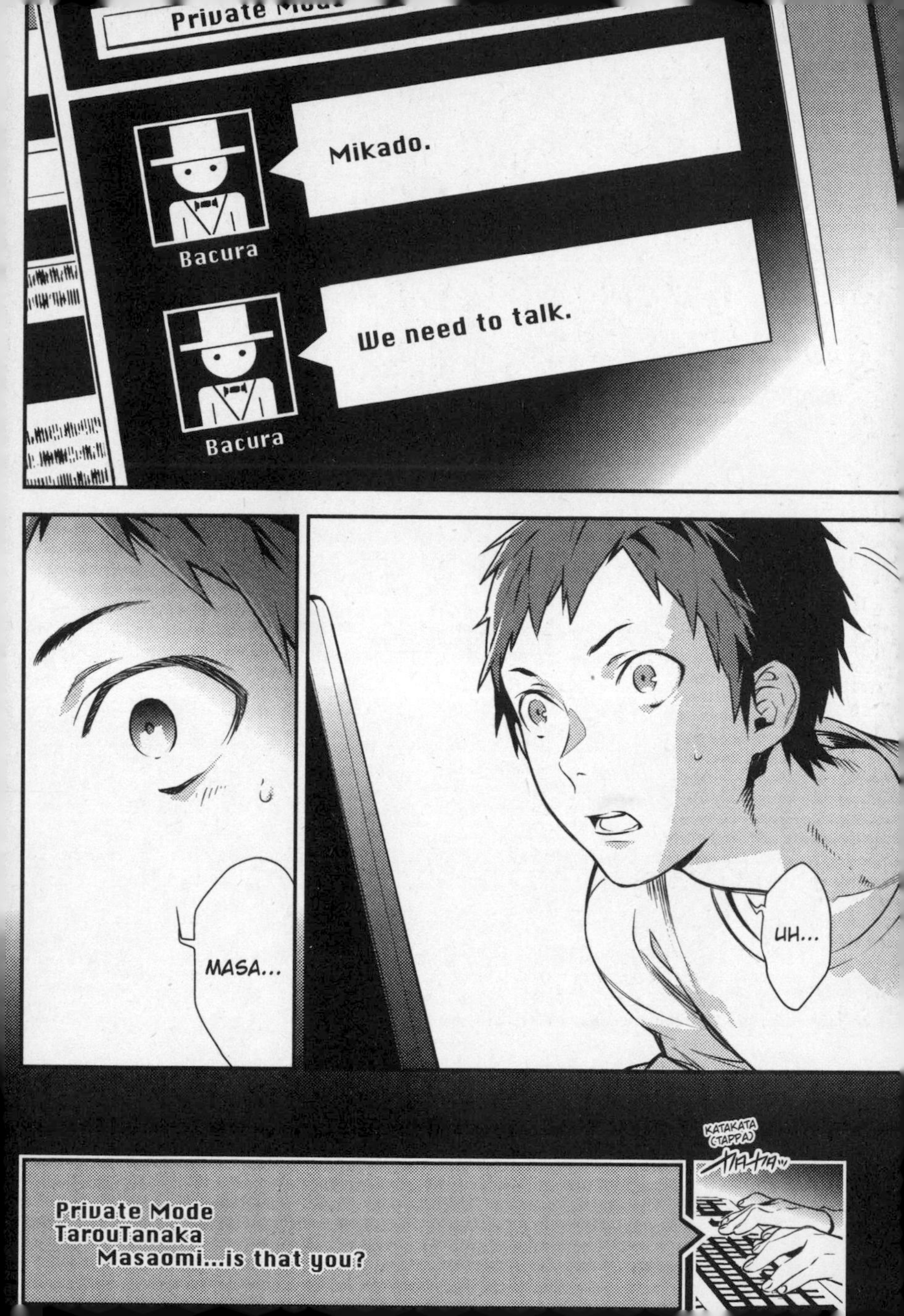

Private Mod
Mikado.
Bacura
We need to talk.
Bacura
UH...
MASA...
KATAKATA (TAPPA)
Private Mode
TarouTanaka
Masaomi...is that you?

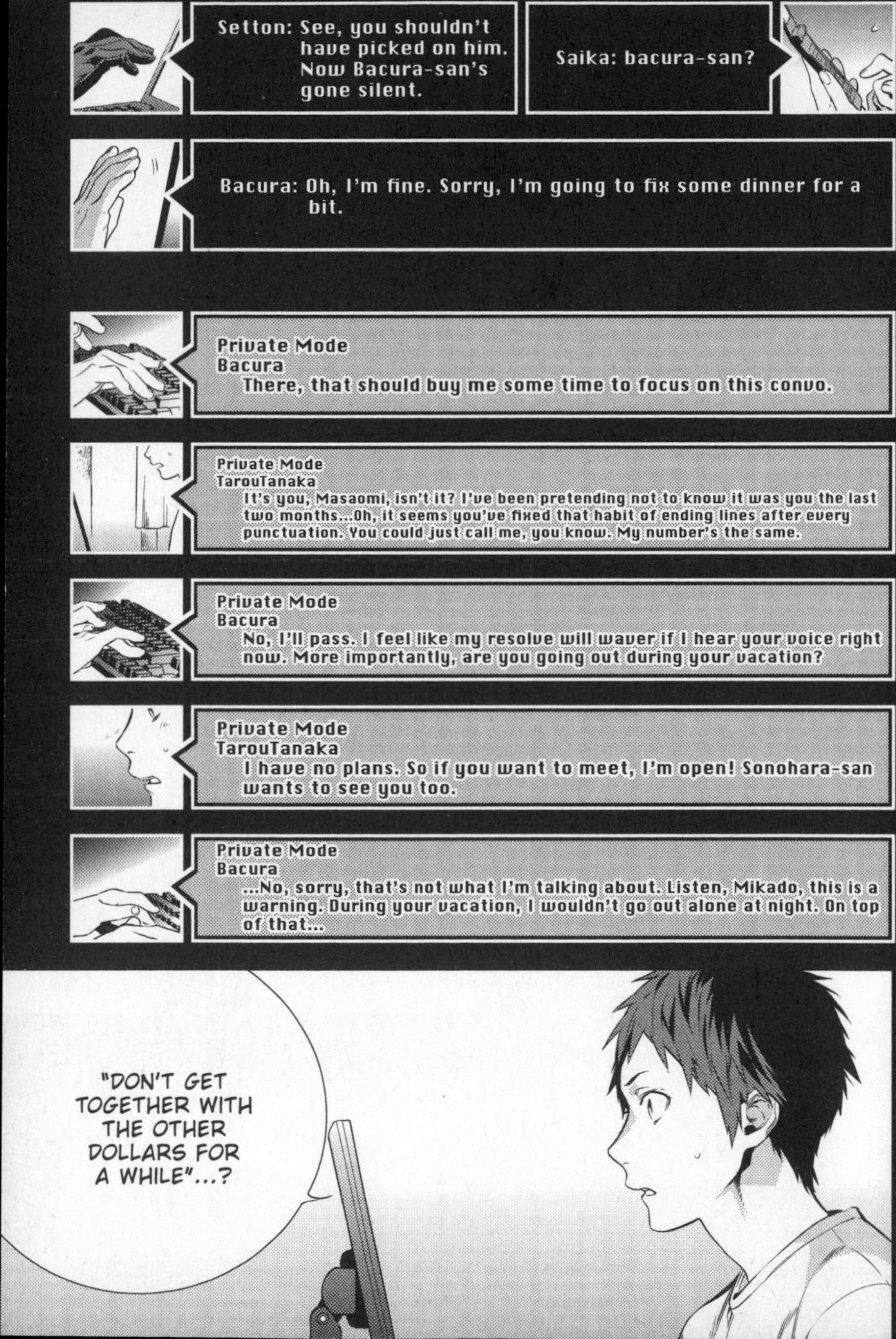
Saika: bacura-san?
Setton: See, you shouldn't have picked on him. Now Bacura-san's gone silent.
Bacura: Oh, I'm fine. Sorry, I'm going to fix some dinner for a bit.
Private Mode
Bacura
There, that should buy me some time to focus on this convo.
Private Mode
TarouTanaka
It's you, Masaomi, isn't it? I've been pretending not to know it was you the last two months...Oh, it seems you've fixed that habit of ending lines after every punctuation. You could just call me, you know. My number's the same.
Private Mode
Bacura
No, I'll pass. I feel like my resolve will waver if I hear your voice right now. More importantly, are you going out during your vacation?
Private Mode
TarouTanaka
I have no plans. So if you want to meet, I'm open! Sonohara-san wants to see you too.
Private Mode
Bacura
...No, sorry, that's not what I'm talking about. Listen, Mikado, this is a warning. During your vacation, I wouldn't go out alone at night. On top of that...
"DON'T GET TOGETHER WITH THE OTHER DOLLARS FOR A WHILE"...?

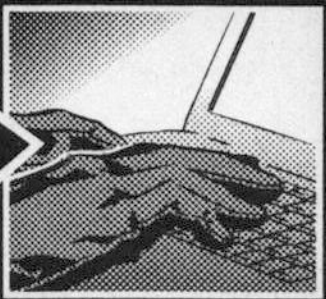

Setton: Tarou-san hasn't responded for a while. He must be AFK. I've noticed Kanra-san isn't here today either.

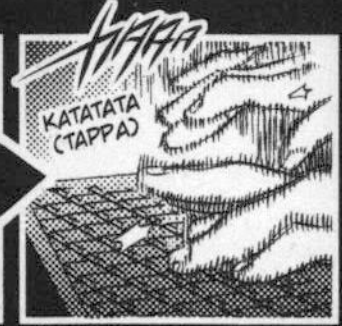
KATATATA (TAPPA)

Kuru: He is a very busy and wicked person, after all. If he were always spending his free time in here, it would mean more peace for the rest of the world.

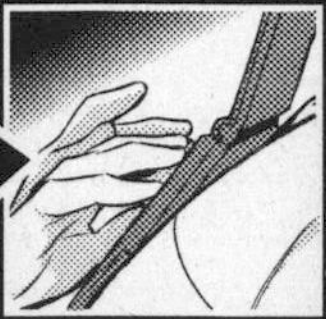

Mai: He's an evil bastard.

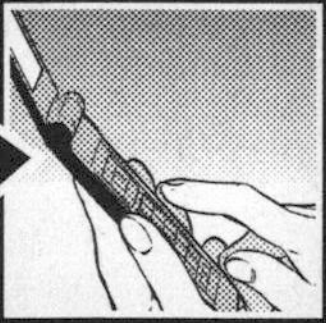

Saika: kanra-san doesnt seem bad to me
i have not met in person though

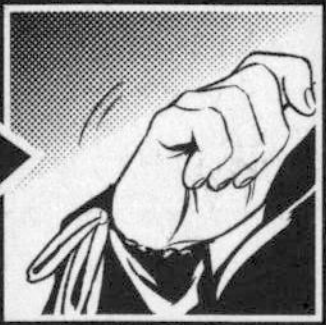

Kuru: Alas, it seems that even here, we have another unfortunate soul taken in by Kanra-san's honeyed lies...

⋮

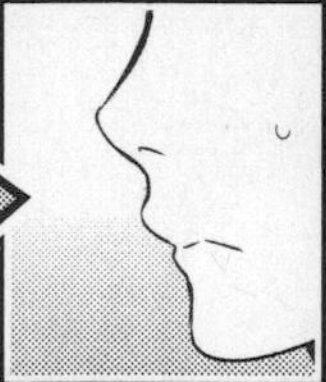

Private Mode
TarouTanaka
What do you mean?

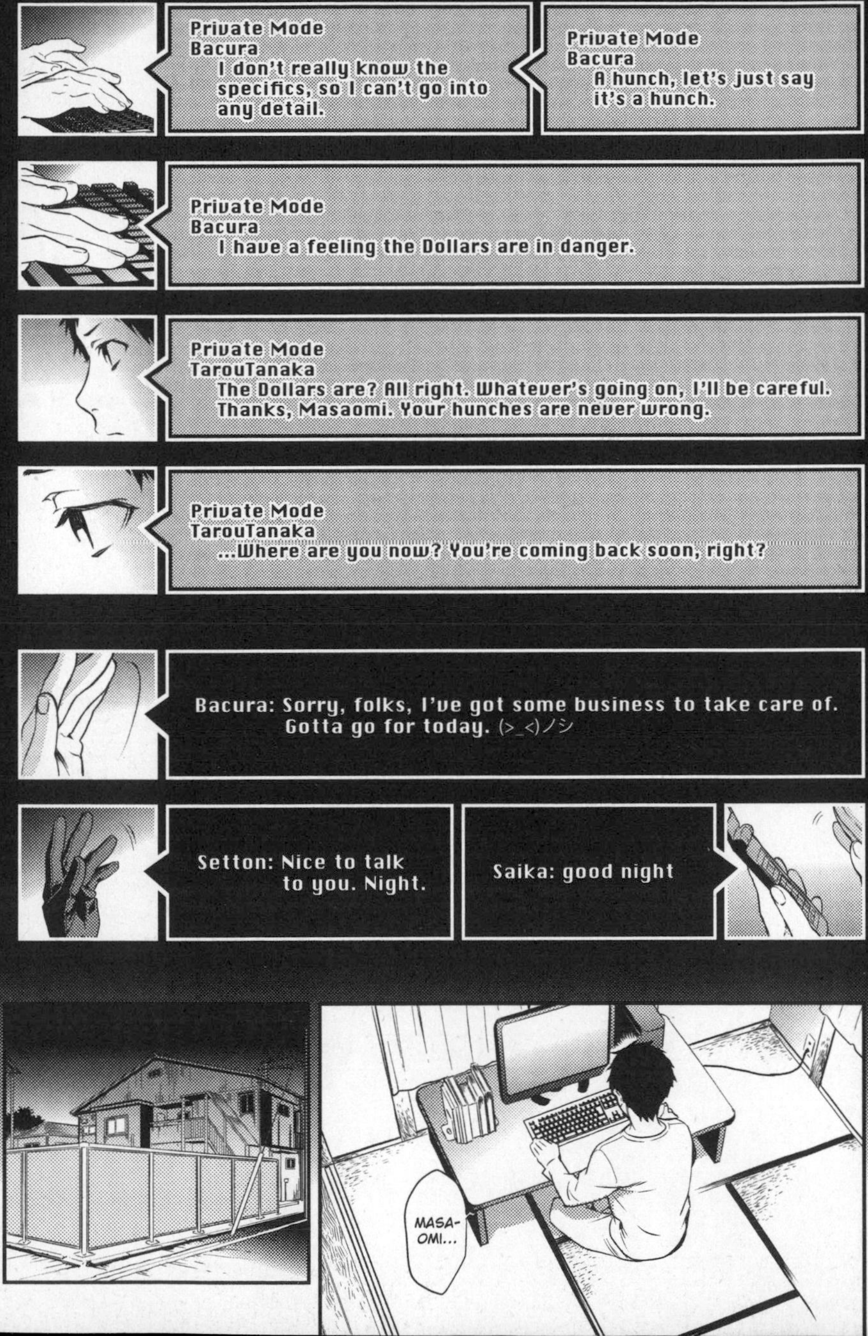

Private Mode
Bacura
A hunch, let's just say it's a hunch.
Private Mode
Bacura
I don't really know the specifics, so I can't go into any detail.
Private Mode
Bacura
I have a feeling the Dollars are in danger.
Private Mode
TarouTanaka
The Dollars are? All right. Whatever's going on, I'll be careful. Thanks, Masaomi. Your hunches are never wrong.
Private Mode
TarouTanaka
...Where are you now? You're coming back soon, right?
Bacura: Sorry, folks, I've got some business to take care of. Gotta go for today. (>_<)ノシ
Saika: good night
Setton: Nice to talk to you. Night.
MASA-OMI...

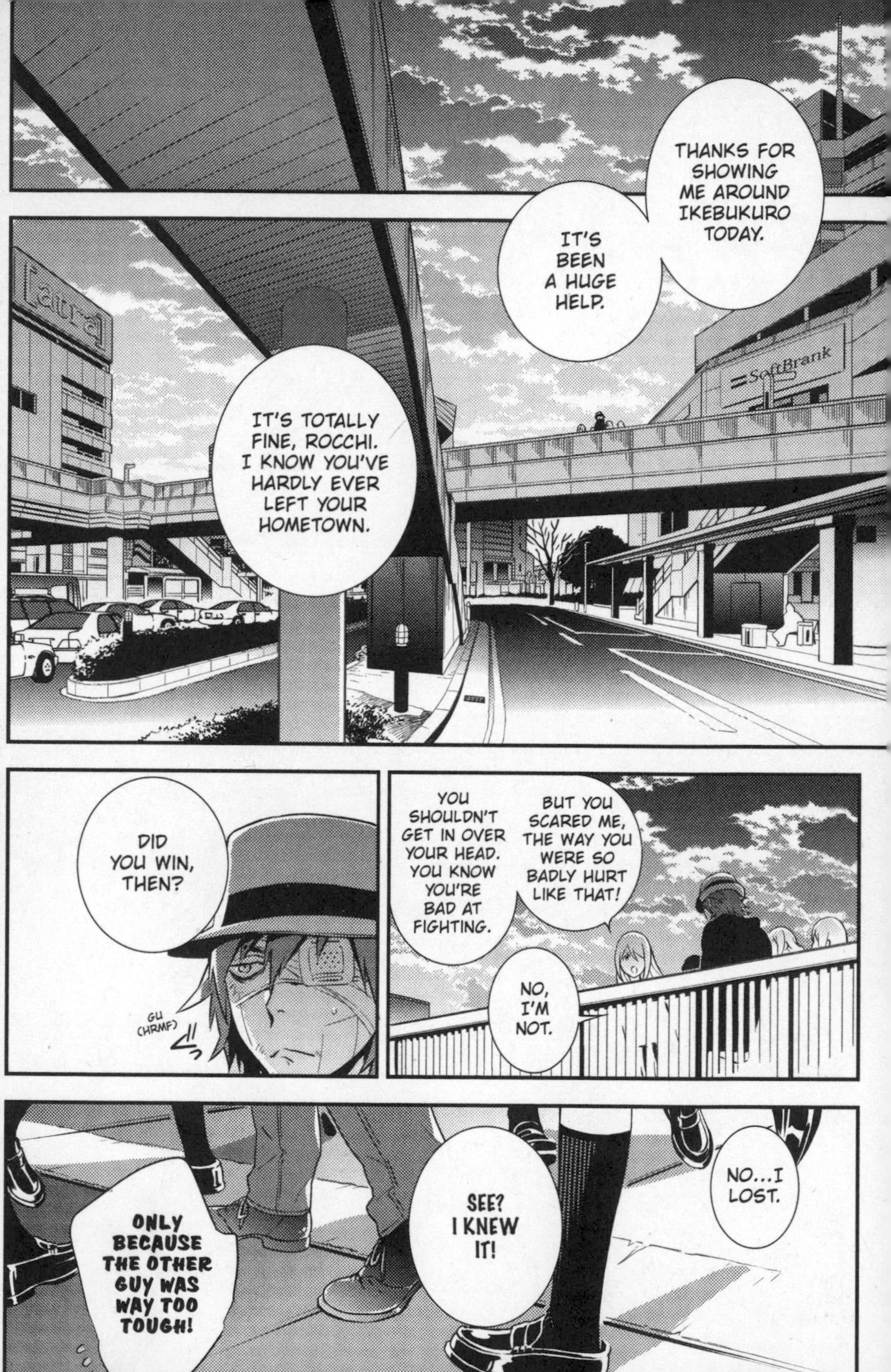
THANKS FOR SHOWING ME AROUND IKEBUKURO TODAY.
IT'S BEEN A HUGE HELP.
SoftBrank
IT'S TOTALLY FINE, ROCCHI. I KNOW YOU'VE HARDLY EVER LEFT YOUR HOMETOWN.
BUT YOU SCARED ME, THE WAY YOU WERE SO BADLY HURT LIKE THAT!
YOU SHOULDN'T GET IN OVER YOUR HEAD. YOU KNOW YOU'RE BAD AT FIGHTING.
NO, I'M NOT.
DID YOU WIN, THEN?
GU (HRMF)
NO...I LOST.
SEE? I KNEW IT!
ONLY BECAUSE THE OTHER GUY WAS WAY TOO TOUGH!

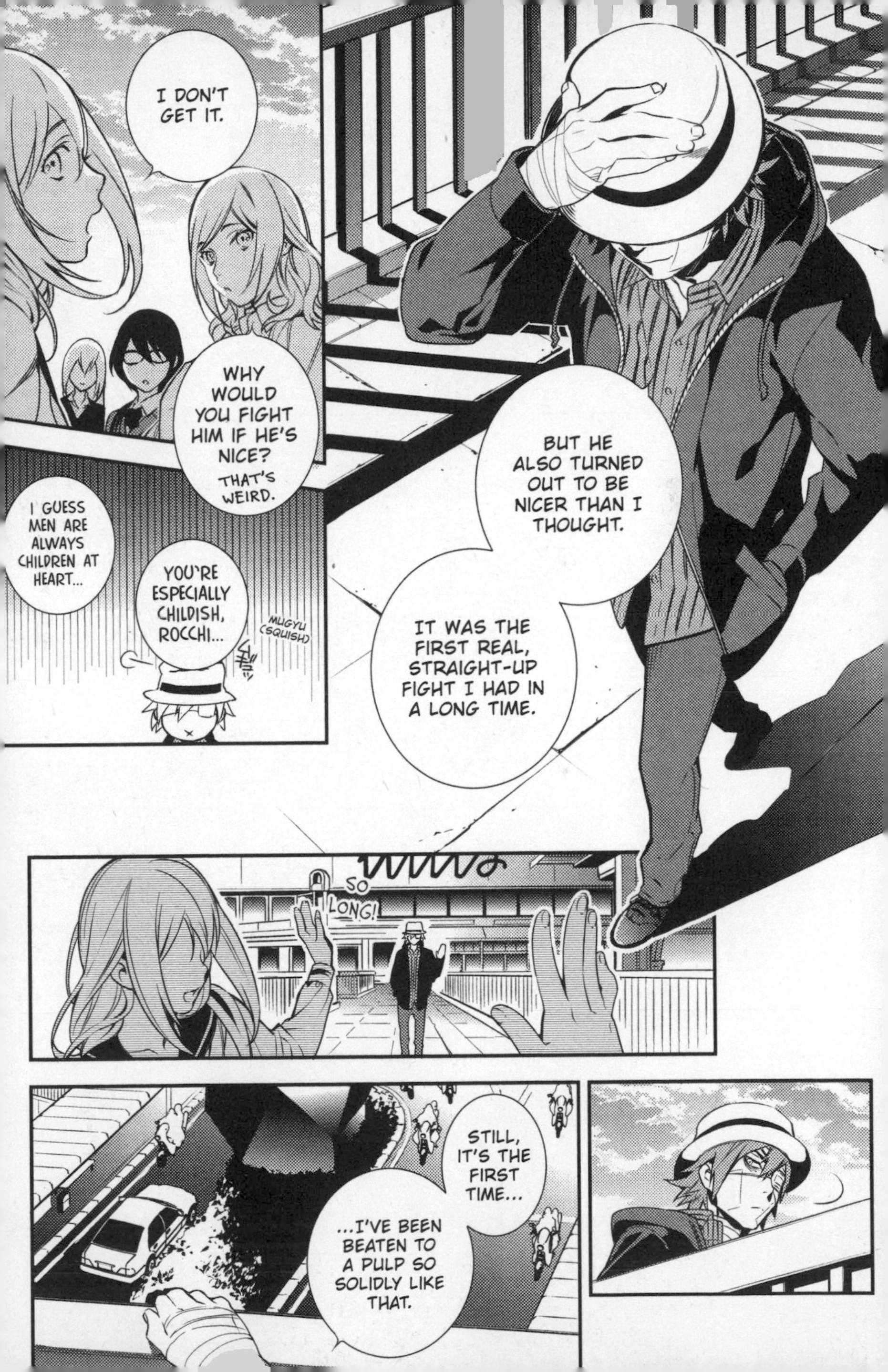
BUT HE ALSO TURNED OUT TO BE NICER THAN I THOUGHT.
IT WAS THE FIRST REAL, STRAIGHT-UP FIGHT I HAD IN A LONG TIME.
I DON'T GET IT.
WHY WOULD YOU FIGHT HIM IF HE'S NICE?
THAT'S WEIRD.
I GUESS MEN ARE ALWAYS CHILDREN AT HEART...
YOU'RE ESPECIALLY CHILDISH, ROCCHI...
MUGYU (SQUISH)
SO LONG!
STILL, IT'S THE FIRST TIME...
...I'VE BEEN BEATEN TO A PULP SO SOLIDLY LIKE THAT.

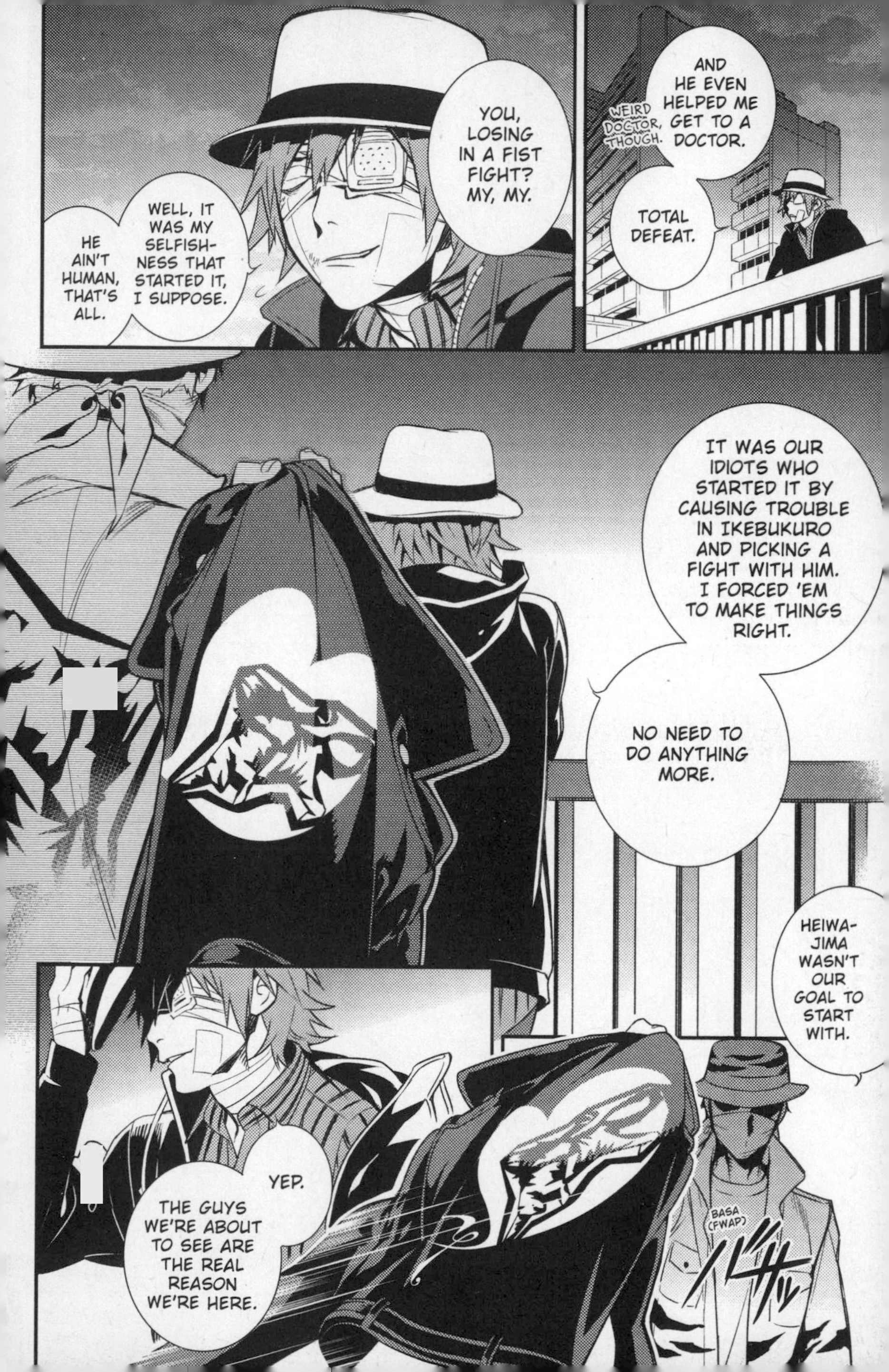
AND HE EVEN HELPED ME GET TO A DOCTOR.
WEIRD DOCTOR, THOUGH.
TOTAL DEFEAT.
YOU, LOSING IN A FIST FIGHT? MY, MY.
WELL, IT WAS MY SELFISH-NESS THAT STARTED IT, I SUPPOSE.
HE AIN'T HUMAN, THAT'S ALL.
IT WAS OUR IDIOTS WHO STARTED IT BY CAUSING TROUBLE IN IKEBUKURO AND PICKING A FIGHT WITH HIM. I FORCED 'EM TO MAKE THINGS RIGHT.
NO NEED TO DO ANYTHING MORE.
HEIWA-JIMA WASN'T OUR GOAL TO START WITH.
BASA (FWAP)
YEP.
THE GUYS WE'RE ABOUT TO SEE ARE THE REAL REASON WE'RE HERE.

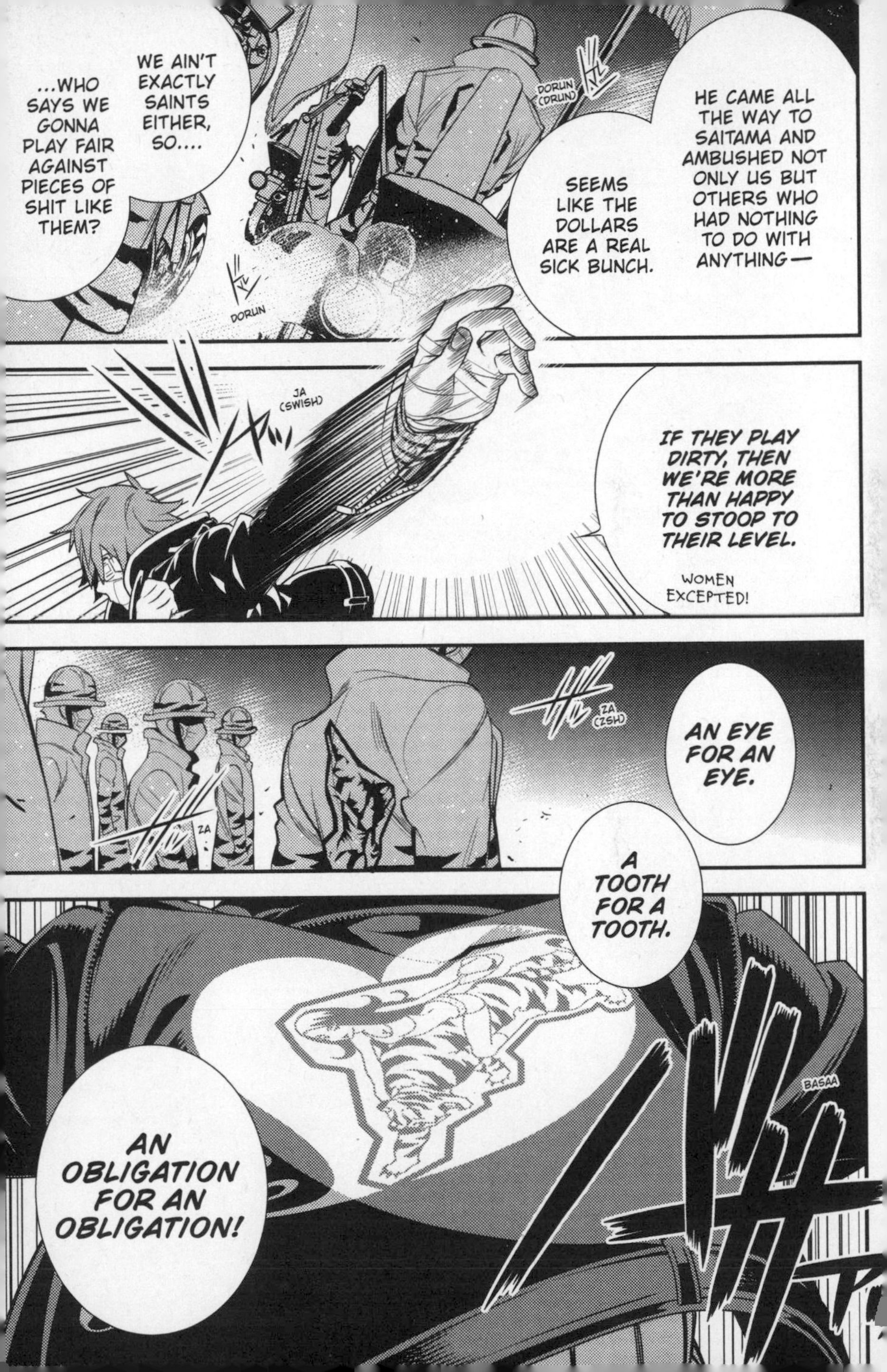
HE CAME ALL THE WAY TO SAITAMA AND AMBUSHED NOT ONLY US BUT OTHERS WHO HAD NOTHING TO DO WITH ANYTHING—
SEEMS LIKE THE DOLLARS ARE A REAL SICK BUNCH.
DORUN (DRUN)
WE AIN'T EXACTLY SAINTS EITHER, SO....
...WHO SAYS WE GONNA PLAY FAIR AGAINST PIECES OF SHIT LIKE THEM?
DORUN
IF THEY PLAY DIRTY, THEN WE'RE MORE THAN HAPPY TO STOOP TO THEIR LEVEL.
WOMEN EXCEPTED!
JA (SWISH)
AN EYE FOR AN EYE.
ZA (ZSH)
ZA
A TOOTH FOR A TOOTH.
BASAA
AN OBLIGATION FOR AN OBLIGATION!

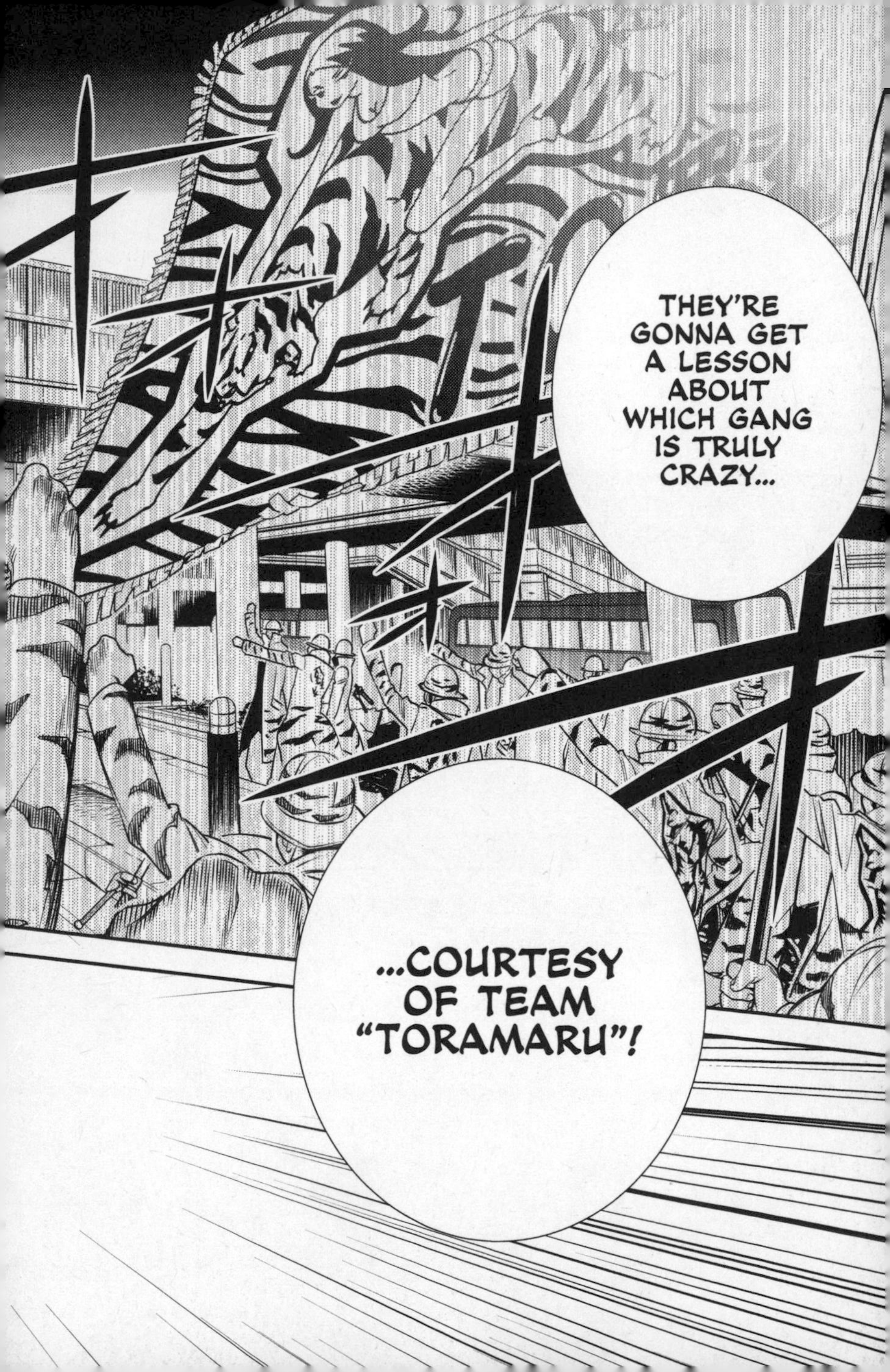
THEY'RE GONNA GET A LESSON ABOUT WHICH GANG IS TRULY CRAZY...
...COURTESY OF TEAM "TORAMARU"!

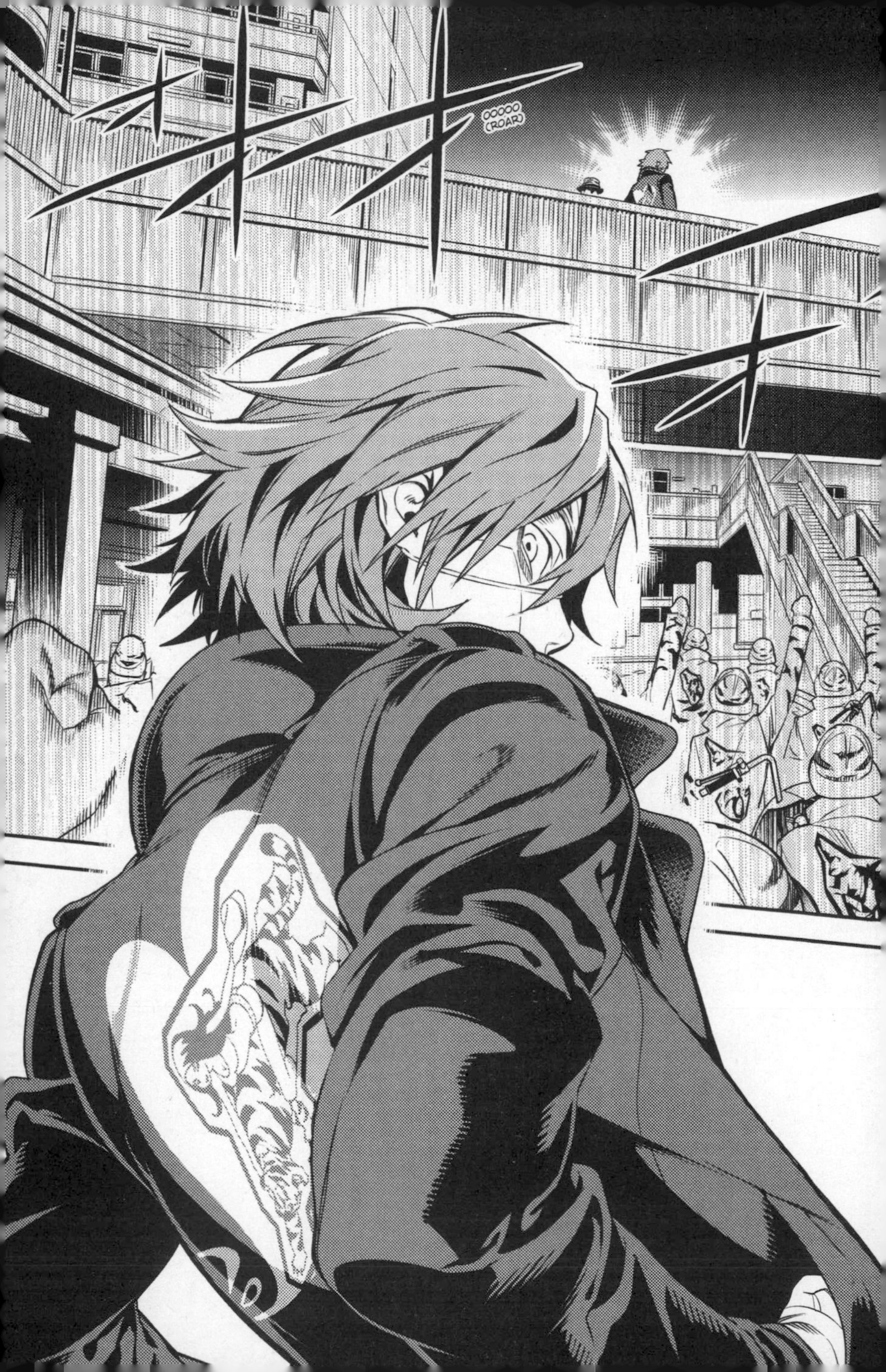
OOOOO
(ROAR)

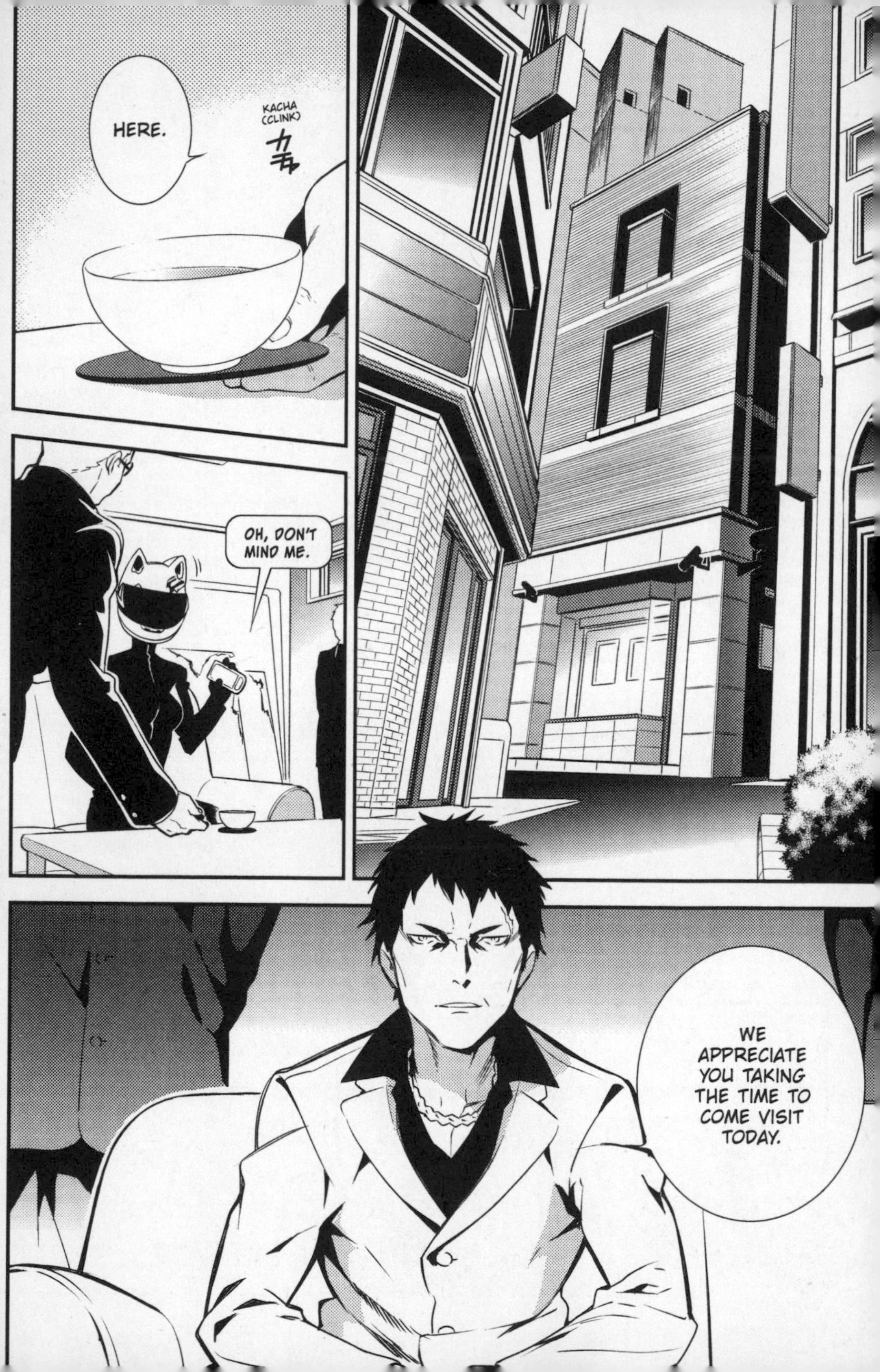
HERE.
KACHA (CLINK)
カチャ
OH, DON'T MIND ME.
WE APPRECIATE YOU TAKING THE TIME TO COME VISIT TODAY.

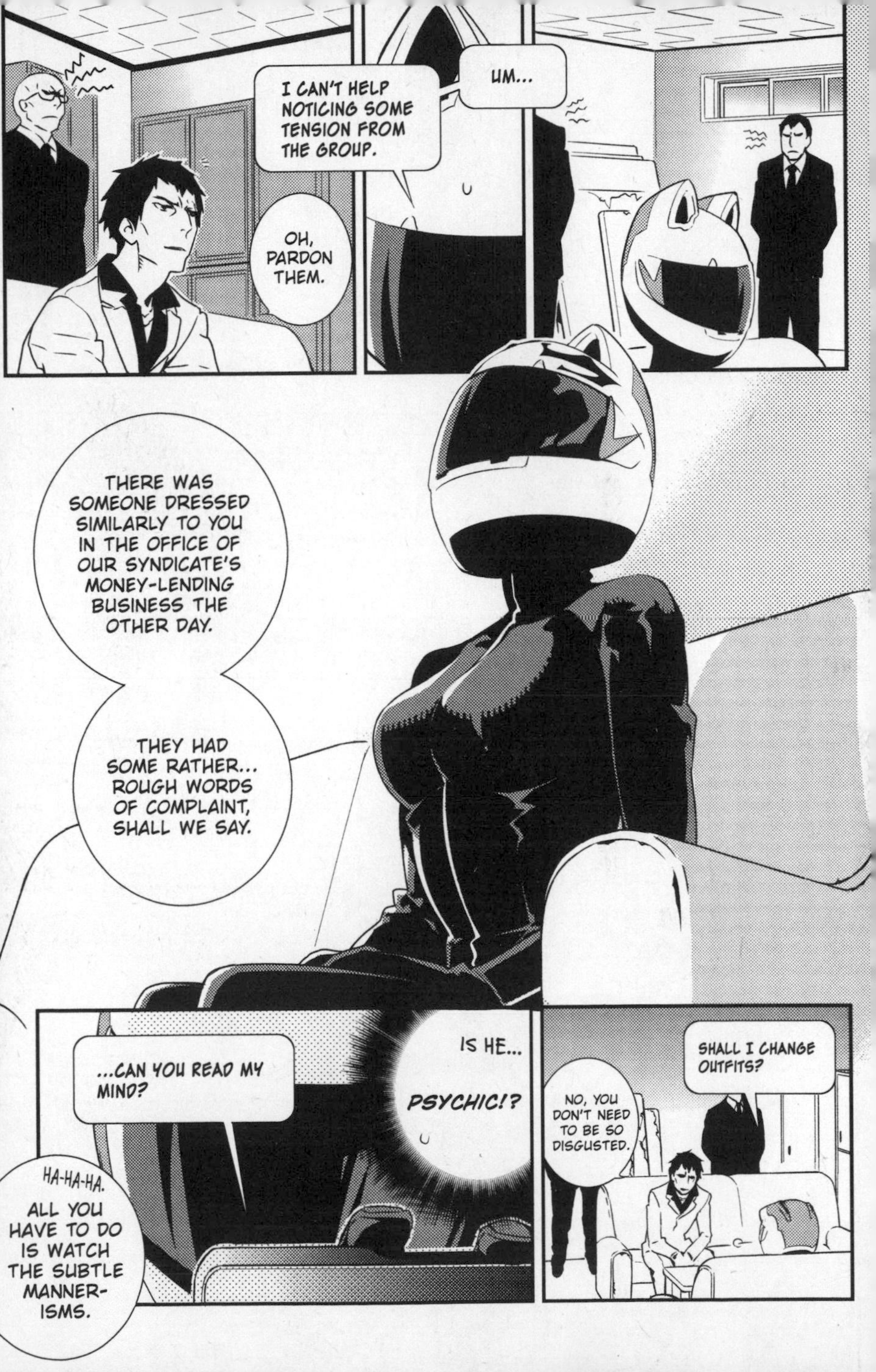
UM...
I CAN'T HELP NOTICING SOME TENSION FROM THE GROUP.
OH, PARDON THEM.
THERE WAS SOMEONE DRESSED SIMILARLY TO YOU IN THE OFFICE OF OUR SYNDICATE'S MONEY-LENDING BUSINESS THE OTHER DAY.
THEY HAD SOME RATHER... ROUGH WORDS OF COMPLAINT, SHALL WE SAY.
SHALL I CHANGE OUTFITS?
NO, YOU DON'T NEED TO BE SO DISGUSTED.
IS HE...
PSYCHIC!?
...CAN YOU READ MY MIND?
HA-HA-HA.
ALL YOU HAVE TO DO IS WATCH THE SUBTLE MANNER-ISMS.

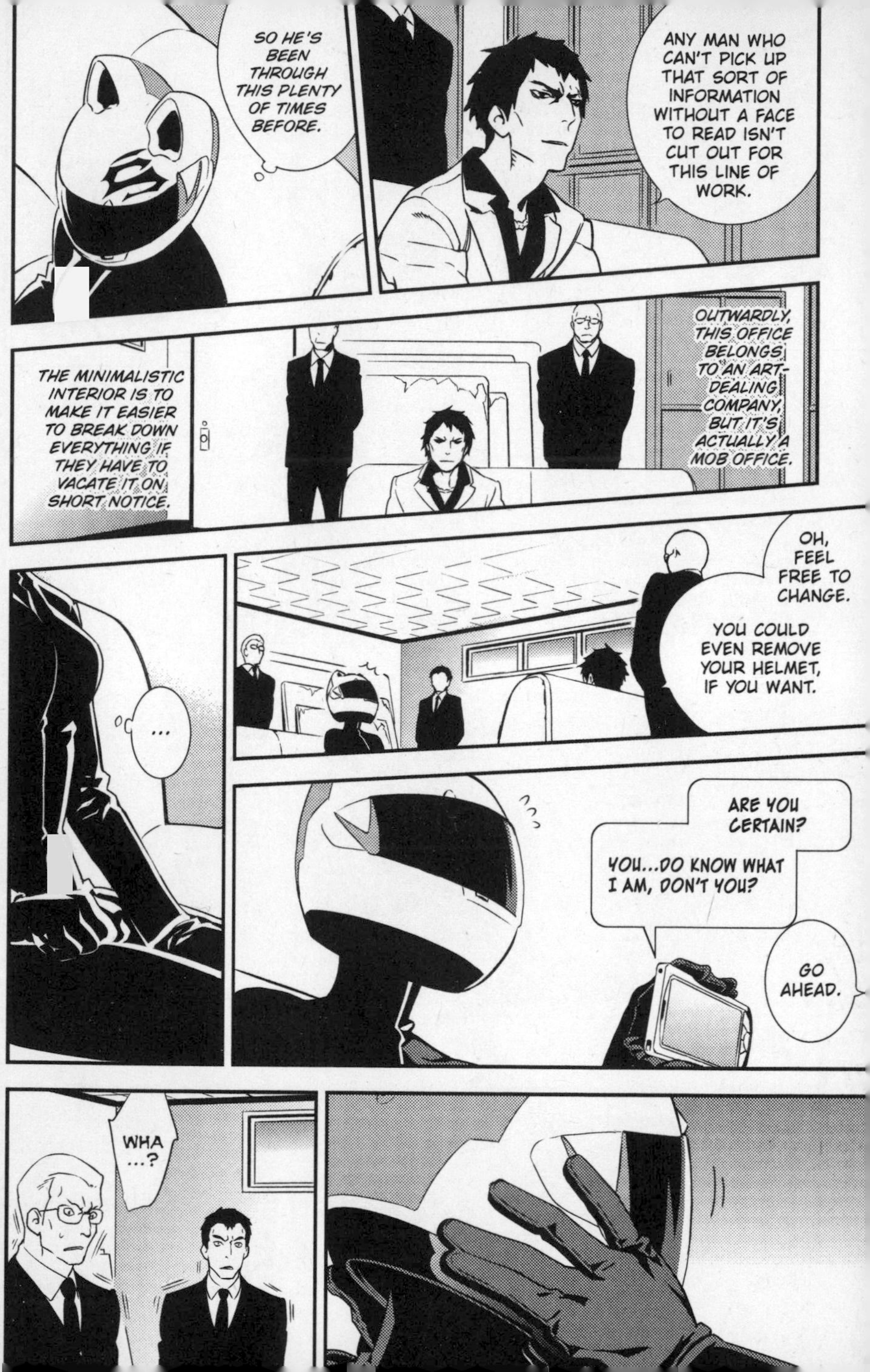
ANY MAN WHO CAN'T PICK UP THAT SORT OF INFORMATION WITHOUT A FACE TO READ ISN'T CUT OUT FOR THIS LINE OF WORK.
SO HE'S BEEN THROUGH THIS PLENTY OF TIMES BEFORE.
OUTWARDLY, THIS OFFICE BELONGS TO AN ART-DEALING COMPANY, BUT IT'S ACTUALLY A MOB OFFICE.
THE MINIMALISTIC INTERIOR IS TO MAKE IT EASIER TO BREAK DOWN EVERYTHING IF THEY HAVE TO VACATE IT ON SHORT NOTICE.
OH, FEEL FREE TO CHANGE.
YOU COULD EVEN REMOVE YOUR HELMET, IF YOU WANT.
ARE YOU CERTAIN?
YOU...DO KNOW WHAT I AM, DON'T YOU?
GO AHEAD.
...
WHA ...?

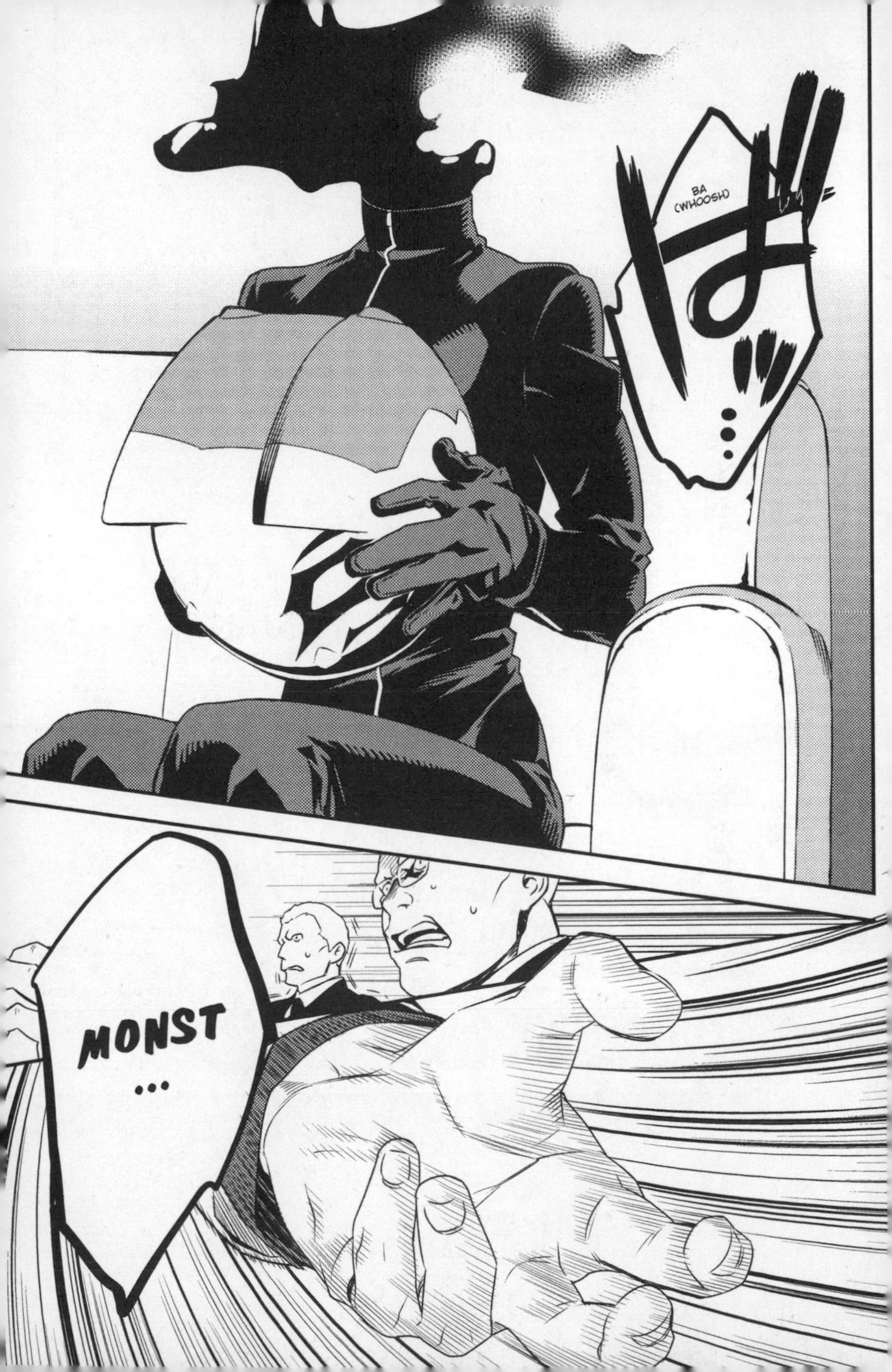
BA
(WHOOSH)
MONST
...

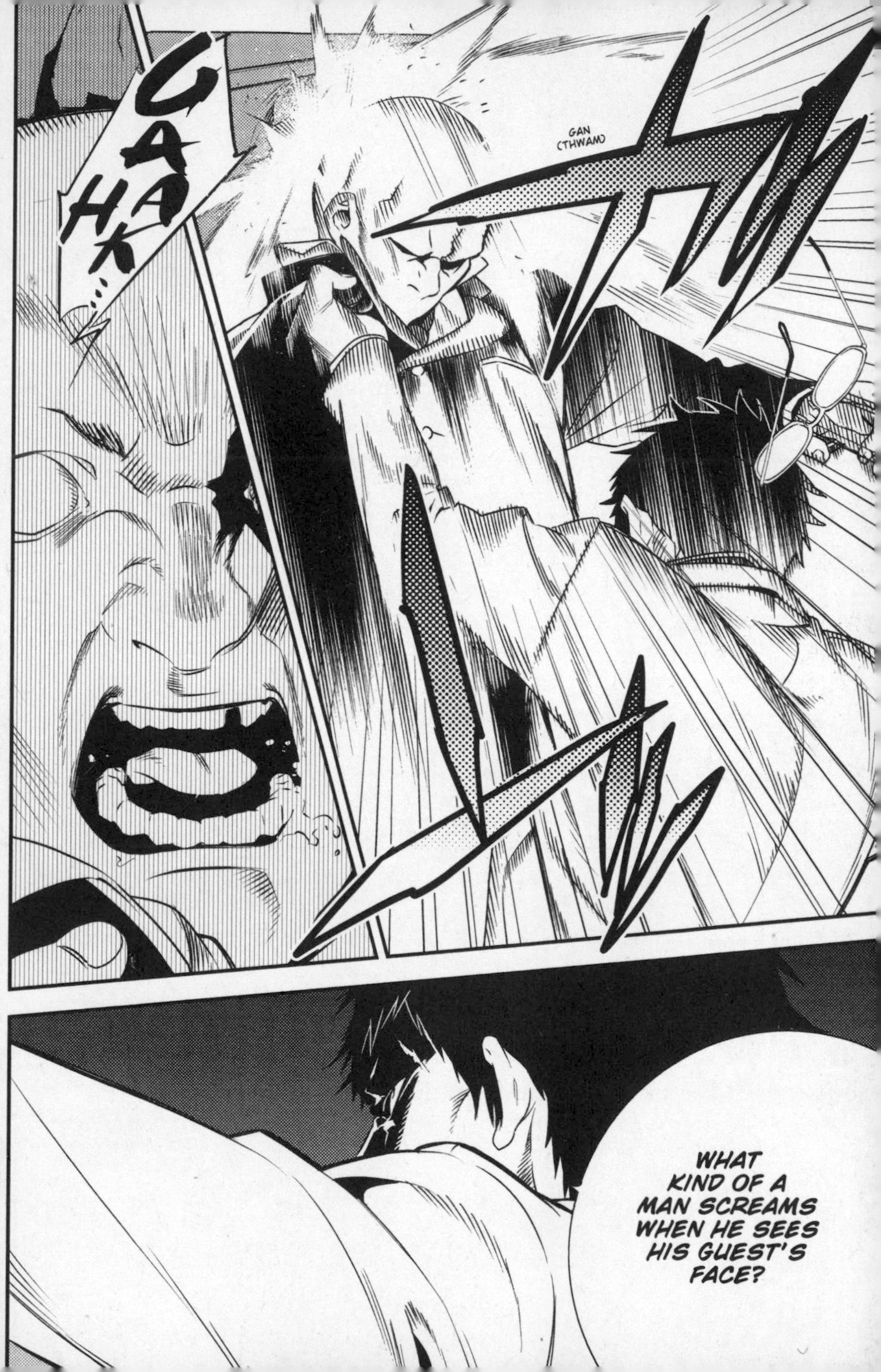
GAN (THWAM)
GAHK...
WHAT KIND OF A MAN SCREAMS WHEN HE SEES HIS GUEST'S FACE?

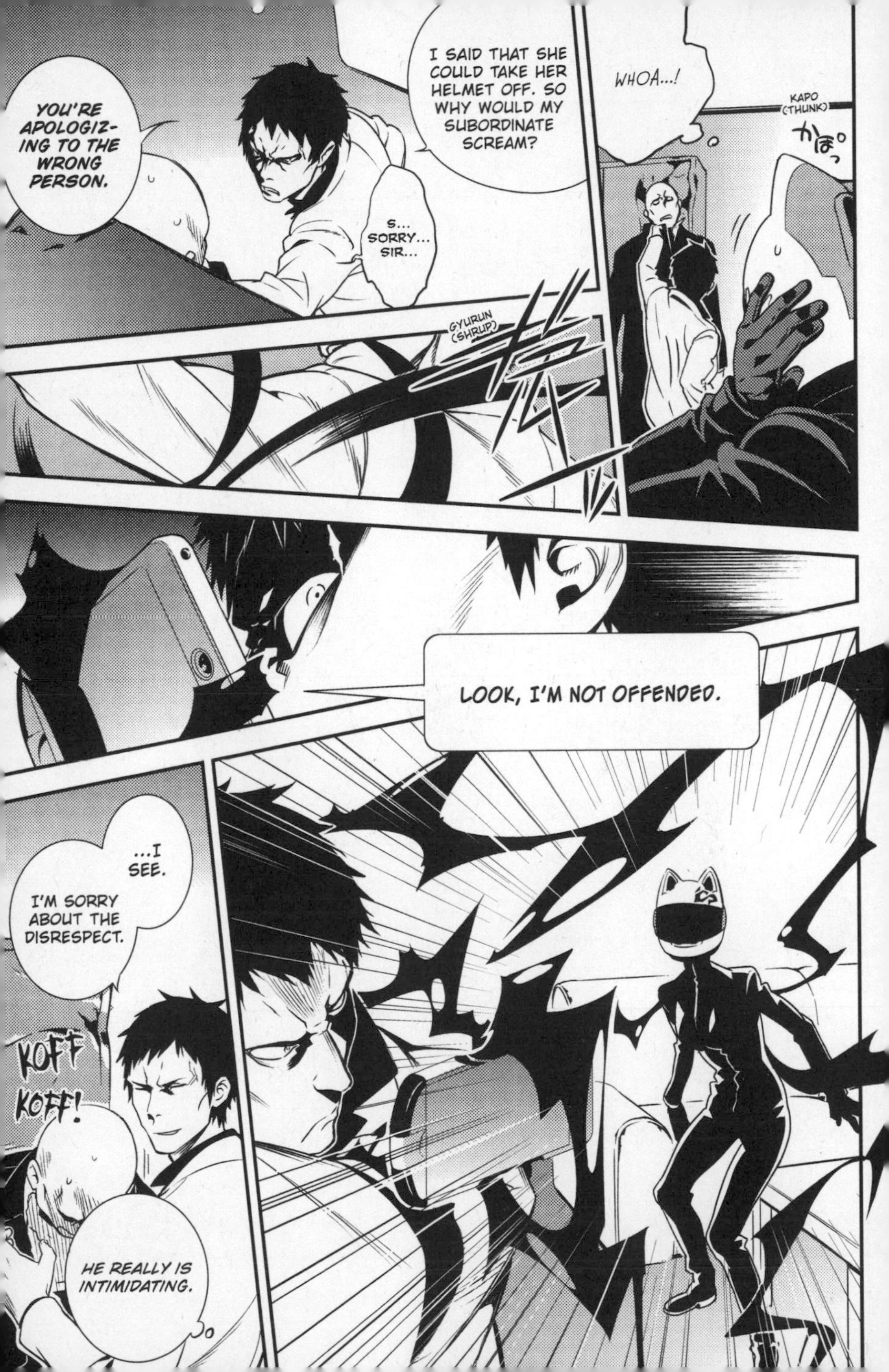

WHOA...!
KAPO (THUNK)
かぽっ
I SAID THAT SHE COULD TAKE HER HELMET OFF. SO WHY WOULD MY SUBORDINATE SCREAM?
YOU'RE APOLOGIZING TO THE WRONG PERSON.
S... SORRY... SIR...
GYURUN (SHRUP)
LOOK, I'M NOT OFFENDED.
...I SEE.
I'M SORRY ABOUT THE DISRESPECT.
KOFF KOFF!
HE REALLY IS INTIMIDATING.

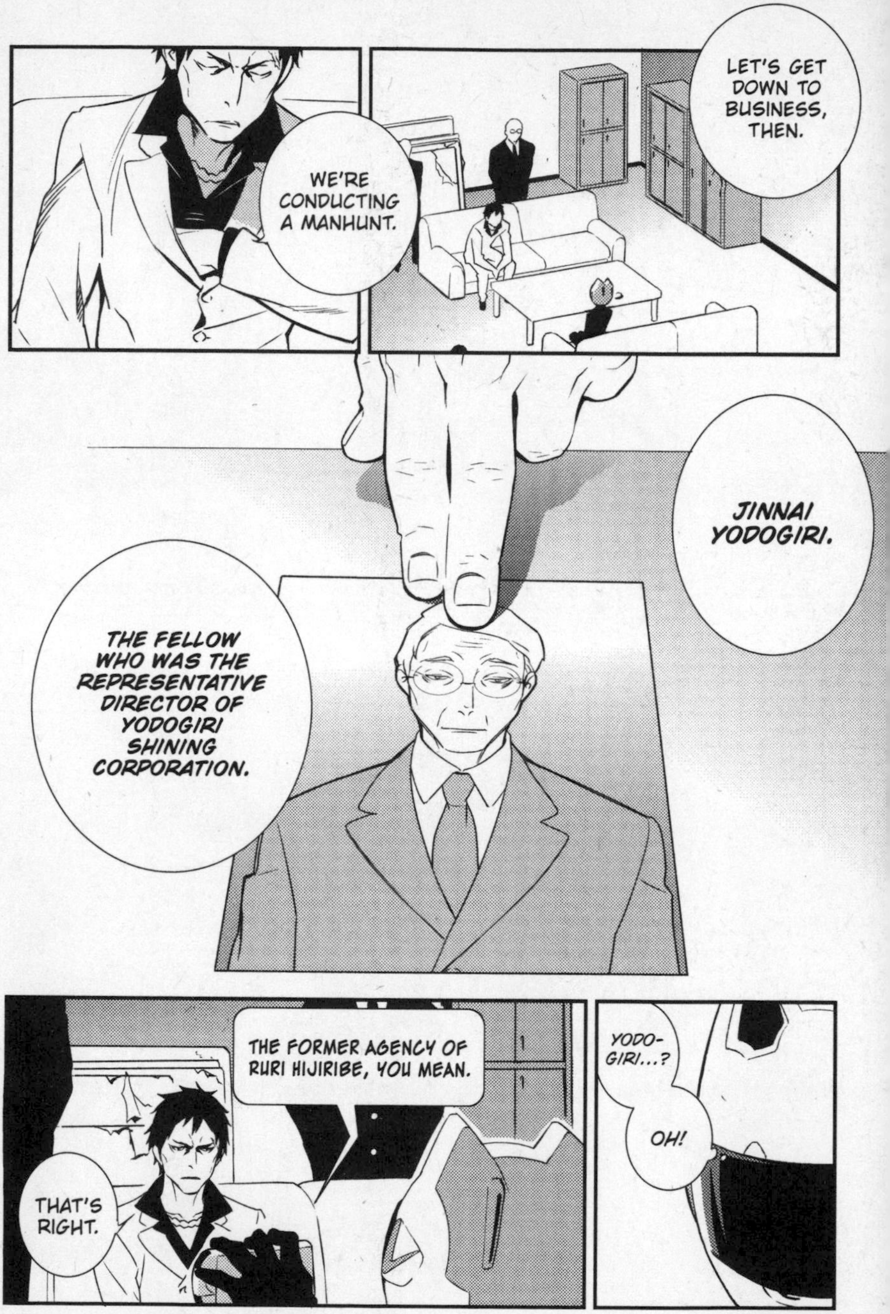
LET'S GET DOWN TO BUSINESS, THEN.
WE'RE CONDUCTING A MANHUNT.
JINNAI YODOGIRI.
THE FELLOW WHO WAS THE REPRESENTATIVE DIRECTOR OF YODOGIRI SHINING CORPORATION.
YODO-GIRI...?
OH!
THE FORMER AGENCY OF RURI HIJIRIBE, YOU MEAN.
THAT'S RIGHT.

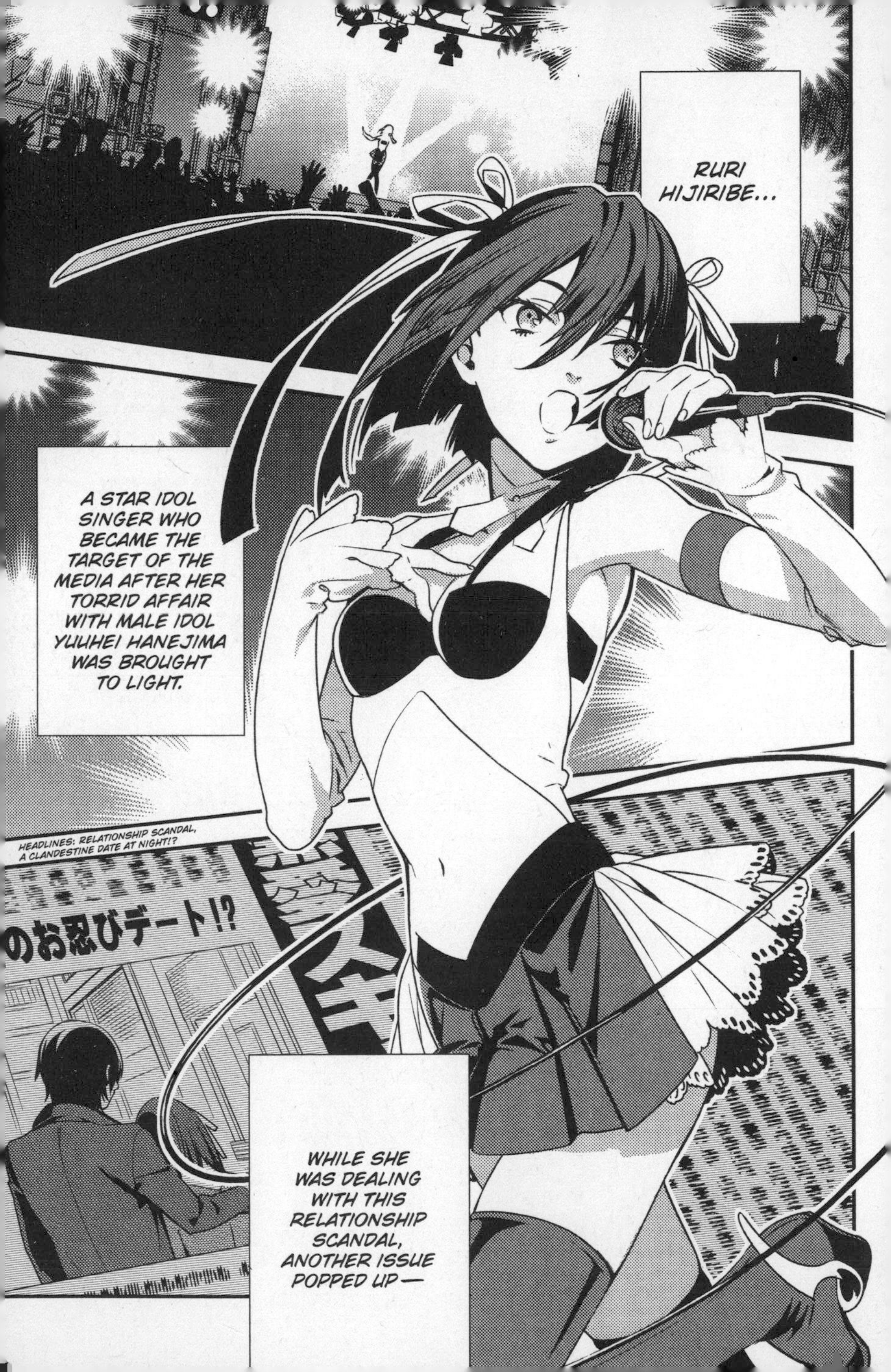
RURI HIJIRIBE...
A STAR IDOL SINGER WHO BECAME THE TARGET OF THE MEDIA AFTER HER TORRID AFFAIR WITH MALE IDOL YUUHEI HANEJIMA WAS BROUGHT TO LIGHT.
HEADLINES: RELATIONSHIP SCANDAL, A CLANDESTINE DATE AT NIGHT!?
のお忍びデート!?
WHILE SHE WAS DEALING WITH THIS RELATIONSHIP SCANDAL, ANOTHER ISSUE POPPED UP—

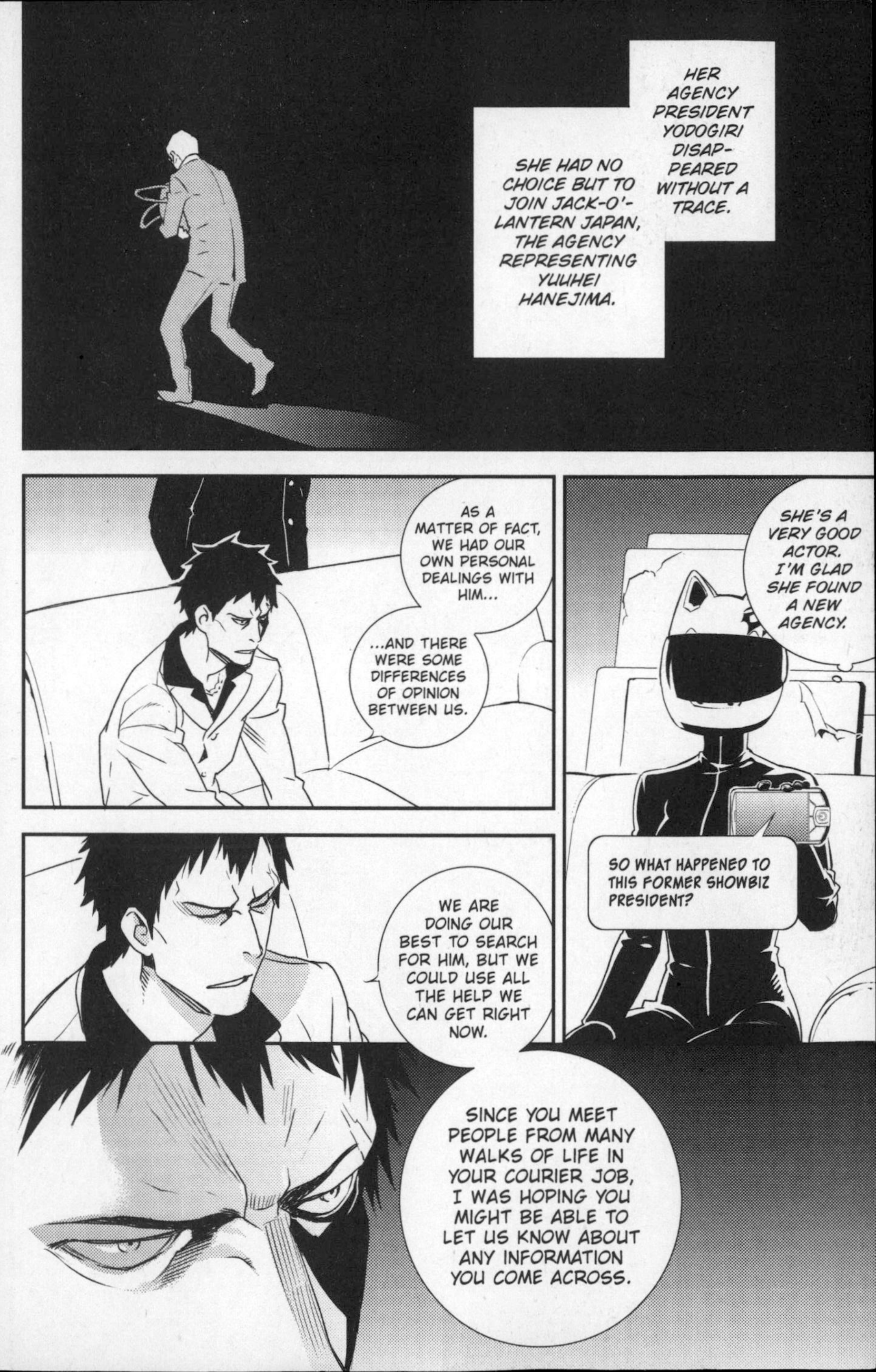
HER AGENCY PRESIDENT YODOGIRI DISAP-PEARED WITHOUT A TRACE.
SHE HAD NO CHOICE BUT TO JOIN JACK-O'-LANTERN JAPAN, THE AGENCY REPRESENTING YUUHEI HANEJIMA.
SHE'S A VERY GOOD ACTOR. I'M GLAD SHE FOUND A NEW AGENCY.
SO WHAT HAPPENED TO THIS FORMER SHOWBIZ PRESIDENT?
AS A MATTER OF FACT, WE HAD OUR OWN PERSONAL DEALINGS WITH HIM...
...AND THERE WERE SOME DIFFERENCES OF OPINION BETWEEN US.
WE ARE DOING OUR BEST TO SEARCH FOR HIM, BUT WE COULD USE ALL THE HELP WE CAN GET RIGHT NOW.
SINCE YOU MEET PEOPLE FROM MANY WALKS OF LIFE IN YOUR COURIER JOB, I WAS HOPING YOU MIGHT BE ABLE TO LET US KNOW ABOUT ANY INFORMATION YOU COME ACROSS.

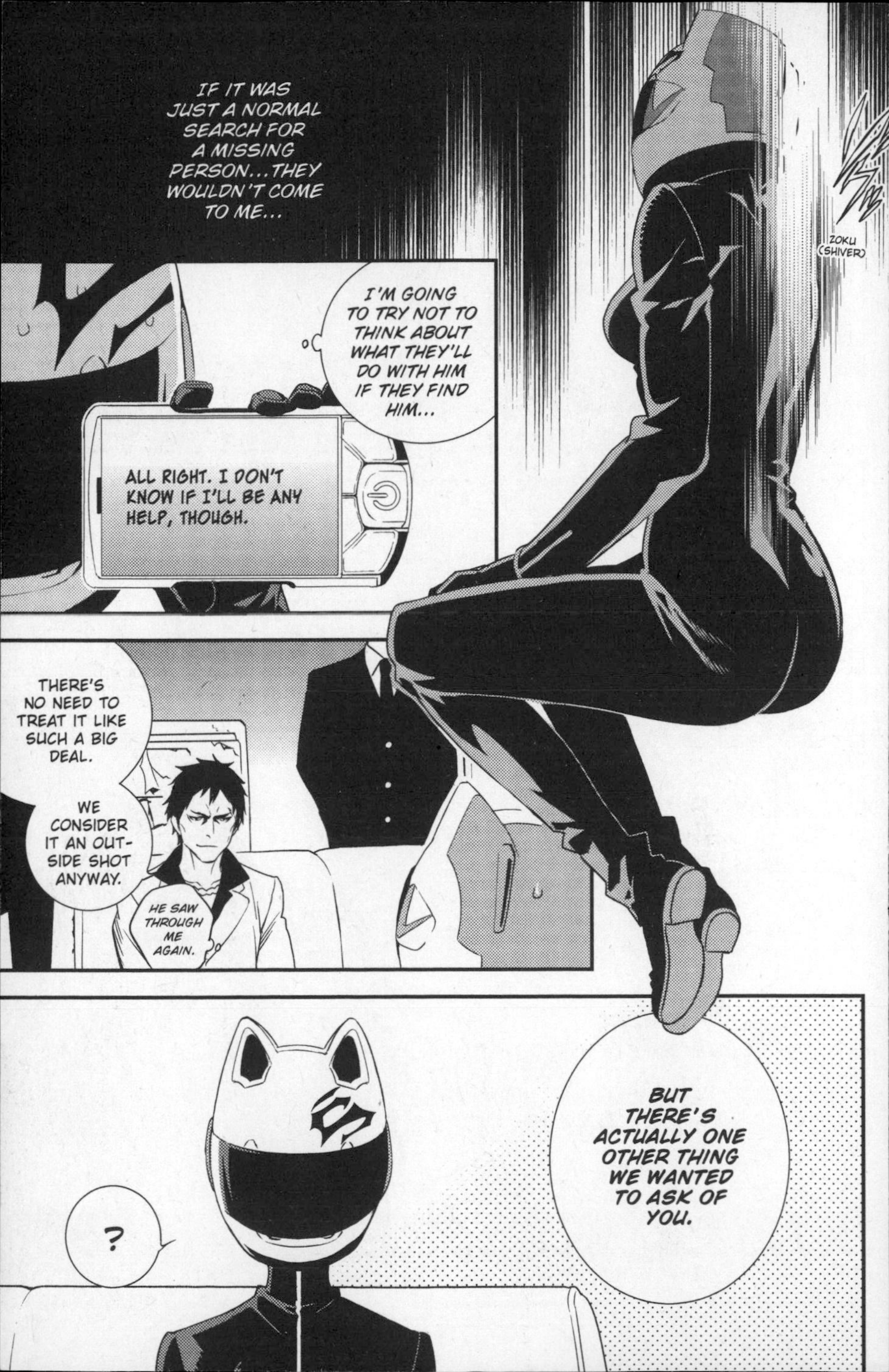
IF IT WAS JUST A NORMAL SEARCH FOR A MISSING PERSON...THEY WOULDN'T COME TO ME...
ZOKU (SHIVER)
I'M GOING TO TRY NOT TO THINK ABOUT WHAT THEY'LL DO WITH HIM IF THEY FIND HIM...
ALL RIGHT. I DON'T KNOW IF I'LL BE ANY HELP, THOUGH.
THERE'S NO NEED TO TREAT IT LIKE SUCH A BIG DEAL.
WE CONSIDER IT AN OUT-SIDE SHOT ANYWAY.
HE SAW THROUGH ME AGAIN.
BUT THERE'S ACTUALLY ONE OTHER THING WE WANTED TO ASK OF YOU.
?

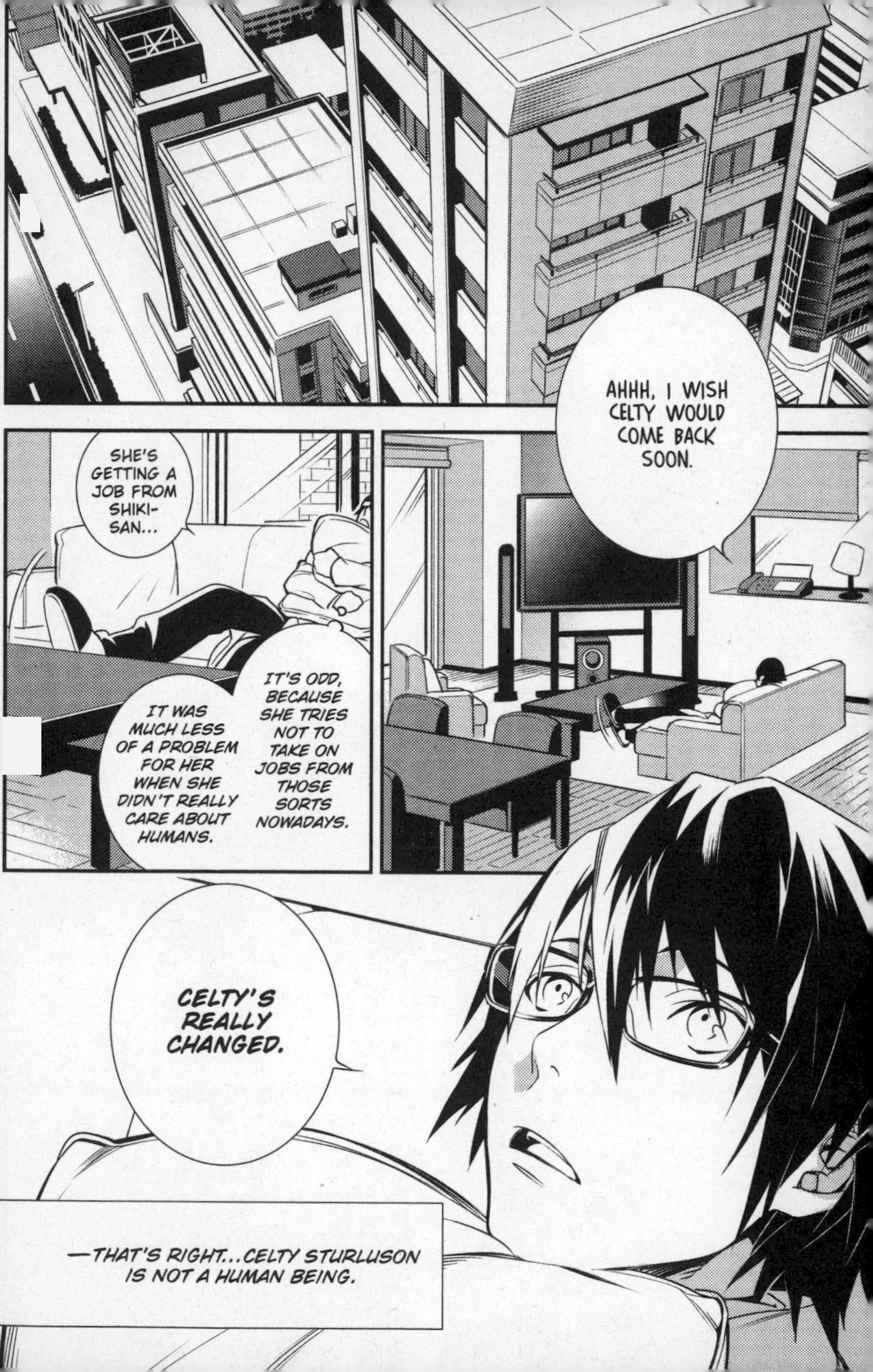

AHHH, I WISH CELTY WOULD COME BACK SOON.
SHE'S GETTING A JOB FROM SHIKI-SAN...
IT'S ODD, BECAUSE SHE TRIES NOT TO TAKE ON JOBS FROM THOSE SORTS NOWADAYS.
IT WAS MUCH LESS OF A PROBLEM FOR HER WHEN SHE DIDN'T REALLY CARE ABOUT HUMANS.
CELTY'S REALLY CHANGED.
—THAT'S RIGHT...CELTY STURLUSON IS NOT A HUMAN BEING.

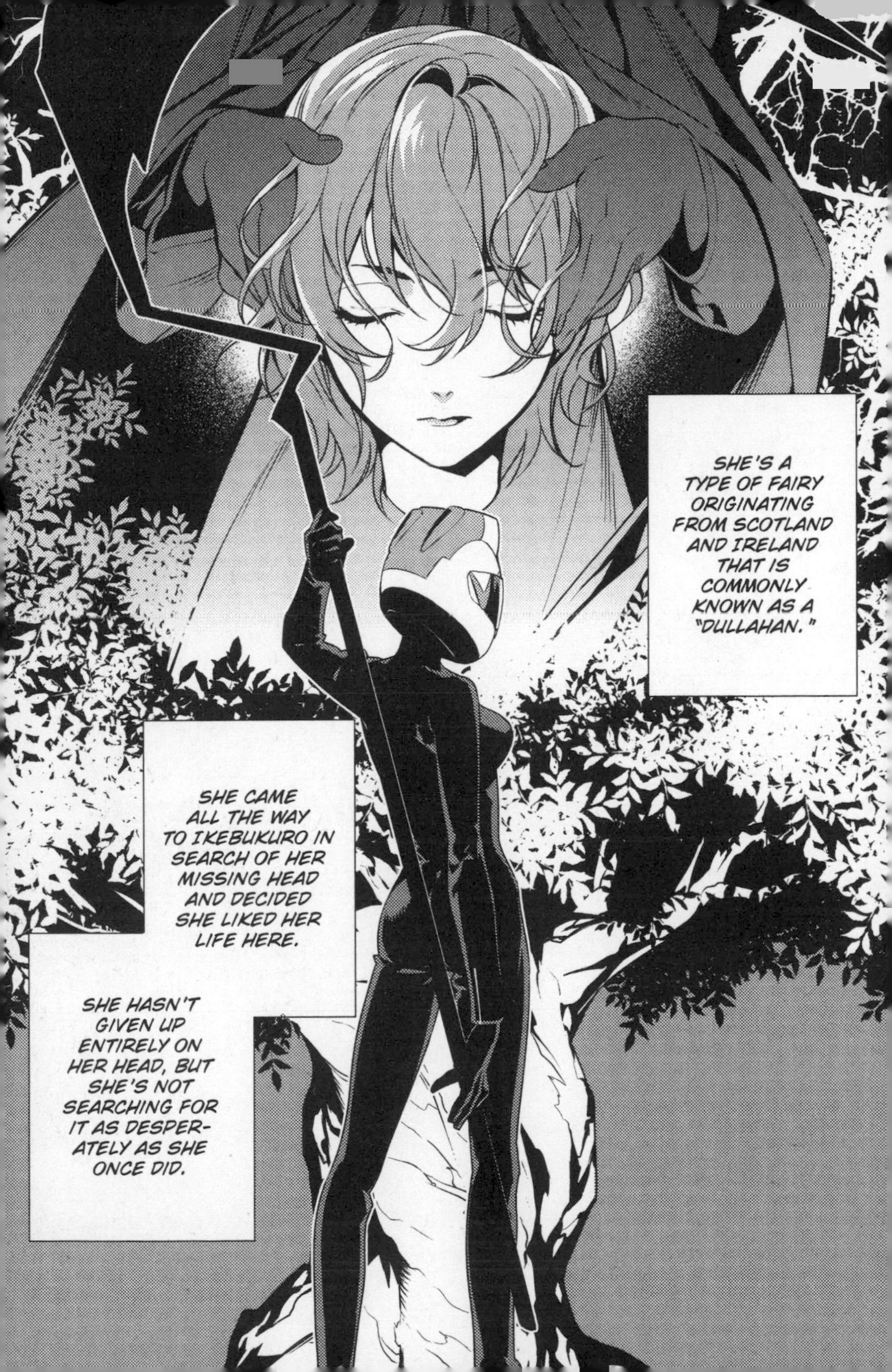
SHE'S A TYPE OF FAIRY ORIGINATING FROM SCOTLAND AND IRELAND THAT IS COMMONLY KNOWN AS A "DULLAHAN."
SHE CAME ALL THE WAY TO IKEBUKURO IN SEARCH OF HER MISSING HEAD AND DECIDED SHE LIKED HER LIFE HERE.
SHE HASN'T GIVEN UP ENTIRELY ON HER HEAD, BUT SHE'S NOT SEARCHING FOR IT AS DESPER-ATELY AS SHE ONCE DID.

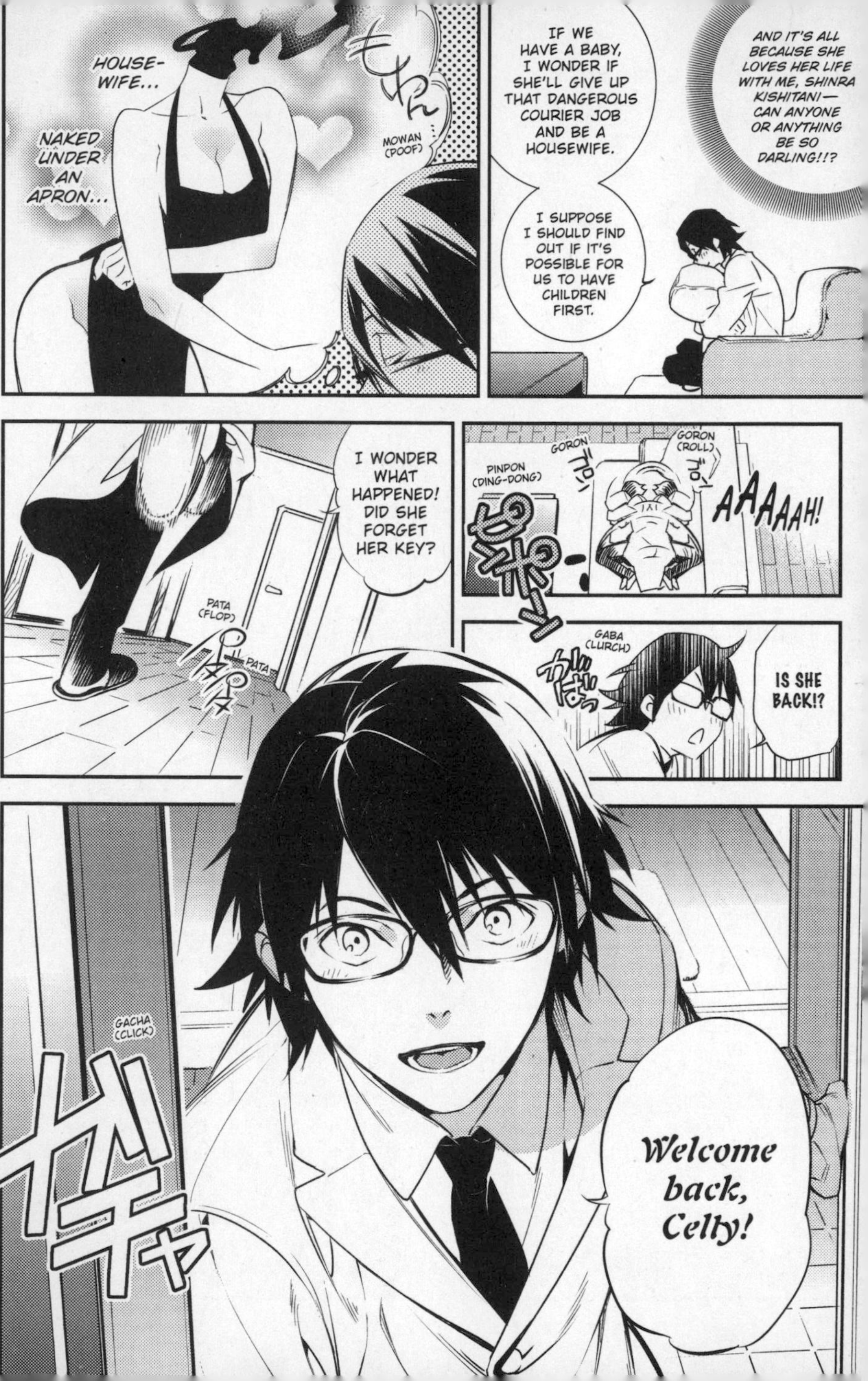

AND IT'S ALL BECAUSE SHE LOVES HER LIFE WITH ME, SHINRA KISHITANI—CAN ANYONE OR ANYTHING BE SO DARLING!!?
IF WE HAVE A BABY, I WONDER IF SHE'LL GIVE UP THAT DANGEROUS COURIER JOB AND BE A HOUSEWIFE.
I SUPPOSE I SHOULD FIND OUT IF IT'S POSSIBLE FOR US TO HAVE CHILDREN FIRST.
もわん…
MOWAN (POOF)
HOUSE-WIFE…
NAKED UNDER AN APRON…
GORON (ROLL)
ゴロン
AAAAAH!
GORON
ゴロン
PINPON (DING-DONG)
ピンポーン
IS SHE BACK!?
GABA (LURCH)
がばっ
I WONDER WHAT HAPPENED! DID SHE FORGET HER KEY?
PATA (FLOP)
PATA
Welcome back, Celly!
GACHA (CLICK)
ガチャ

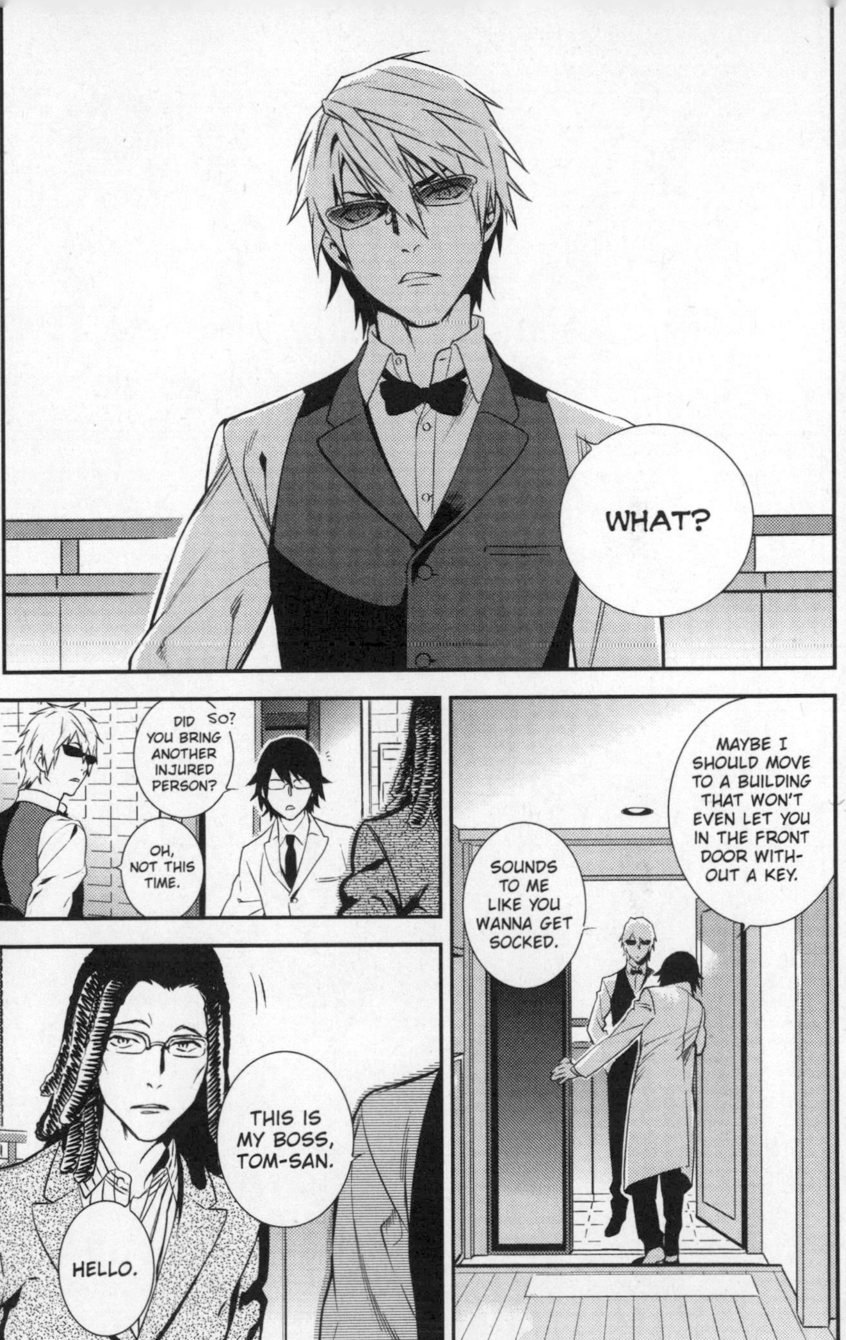
WHAT?
MAYBE I SHOULD MOVE TO A BUILDING THAT WON'T EVEN LET YOU IN THE FRONT DOOR WITH-OUT A KEY.
SOUNDS TO ME LIKE YOU WANNA GET SOCKED.
SO? DID YOU BRING ANOTHER INJURED PERSON?
OH, NOT THIS TIME.
THIS IS MY BOSS, TOM-SAN.
HELLO.

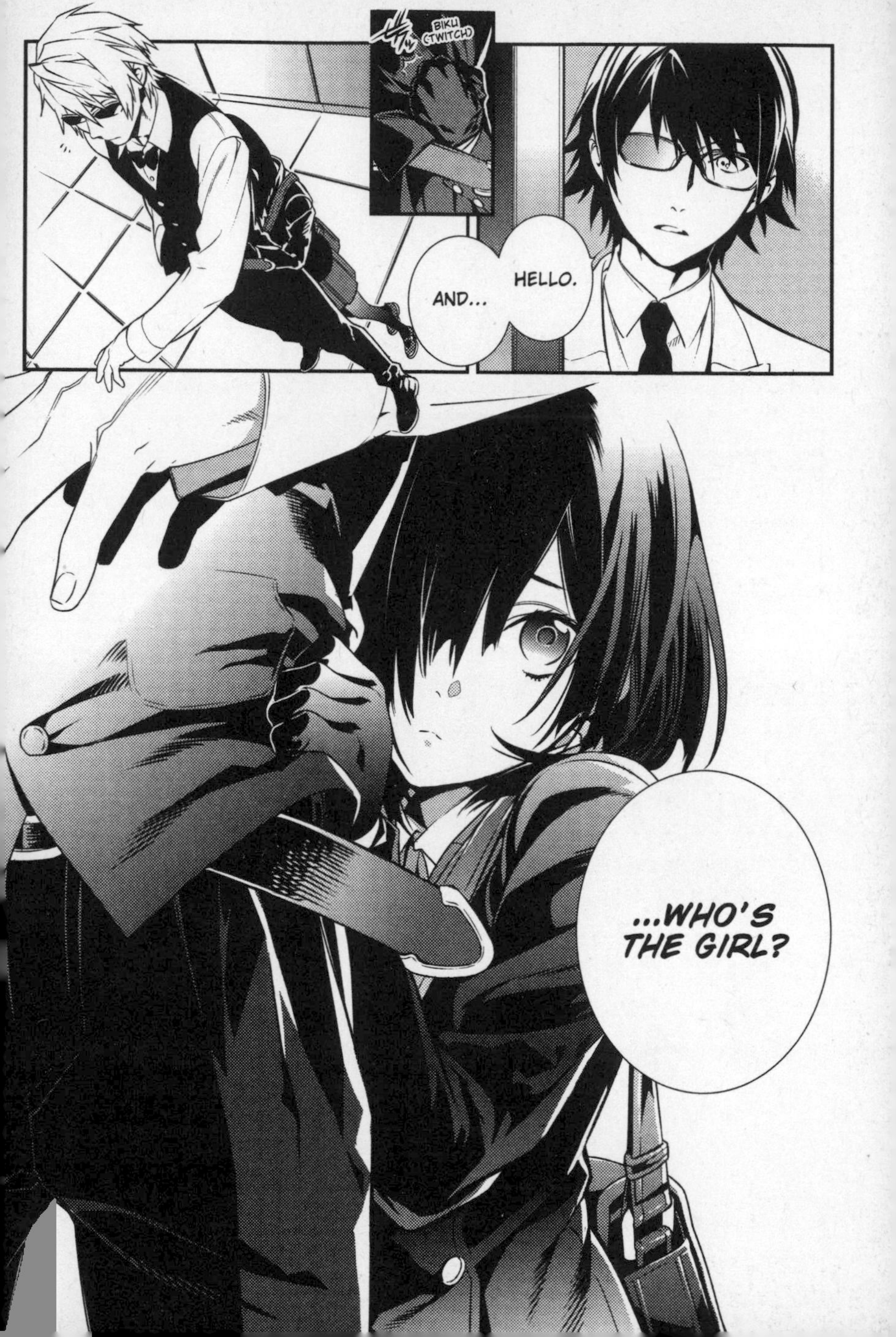
HELLO.
AND...
BIKU (TWITCH)
...WHO'S THE GIRL?

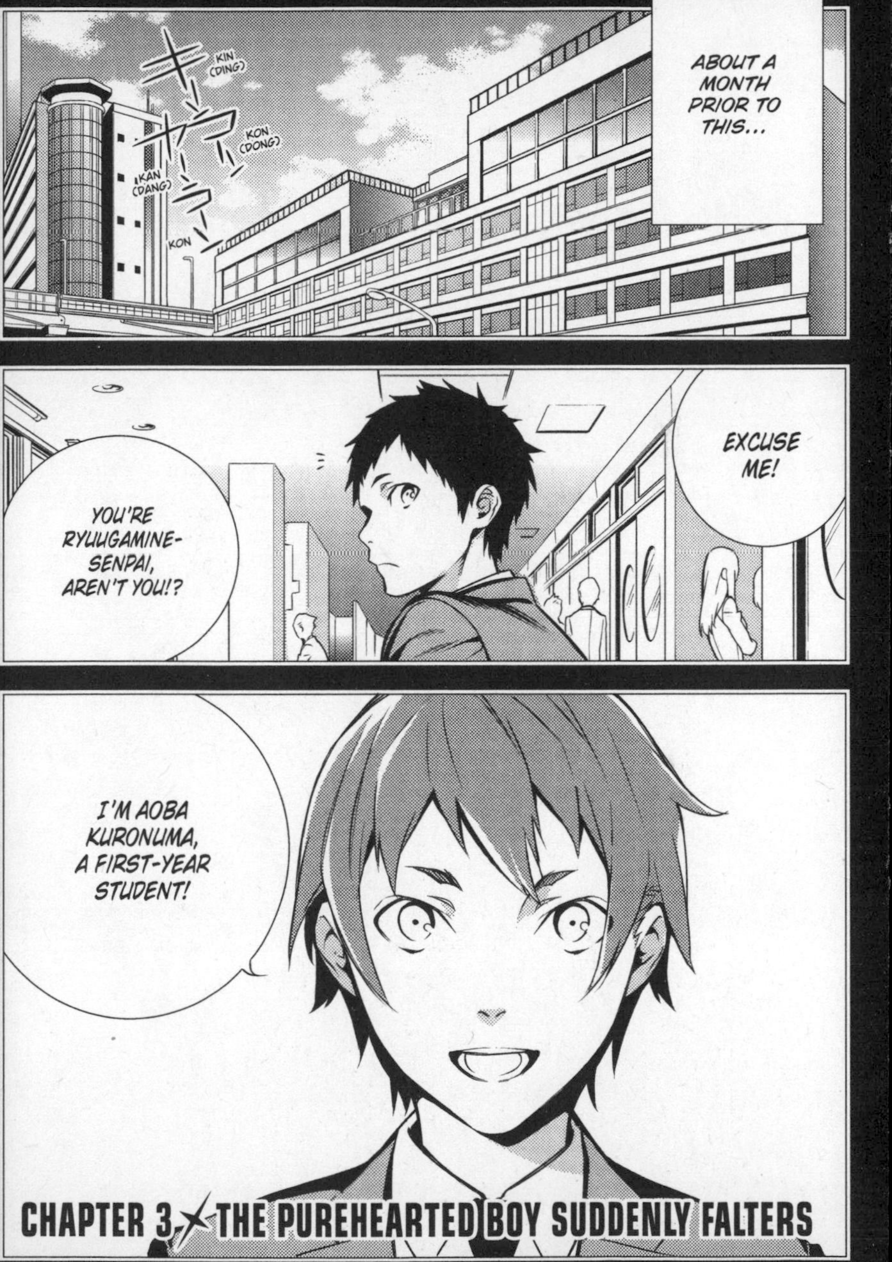
ABOUT A MONTH PRIOR TO THIS...
KIN (DING)
KON (DONG)
KAN (DANG)
KON
EXCUSE ME!
YOU'RE RYUUGAMINE-SENPAI, AREN'T YOU!?
I'M AOBA KURONUMA, A FIRST-YEAR STUDENT!
CHAPTER 3 THE PUREHEARTED BOY SUDDENLY FALTERS

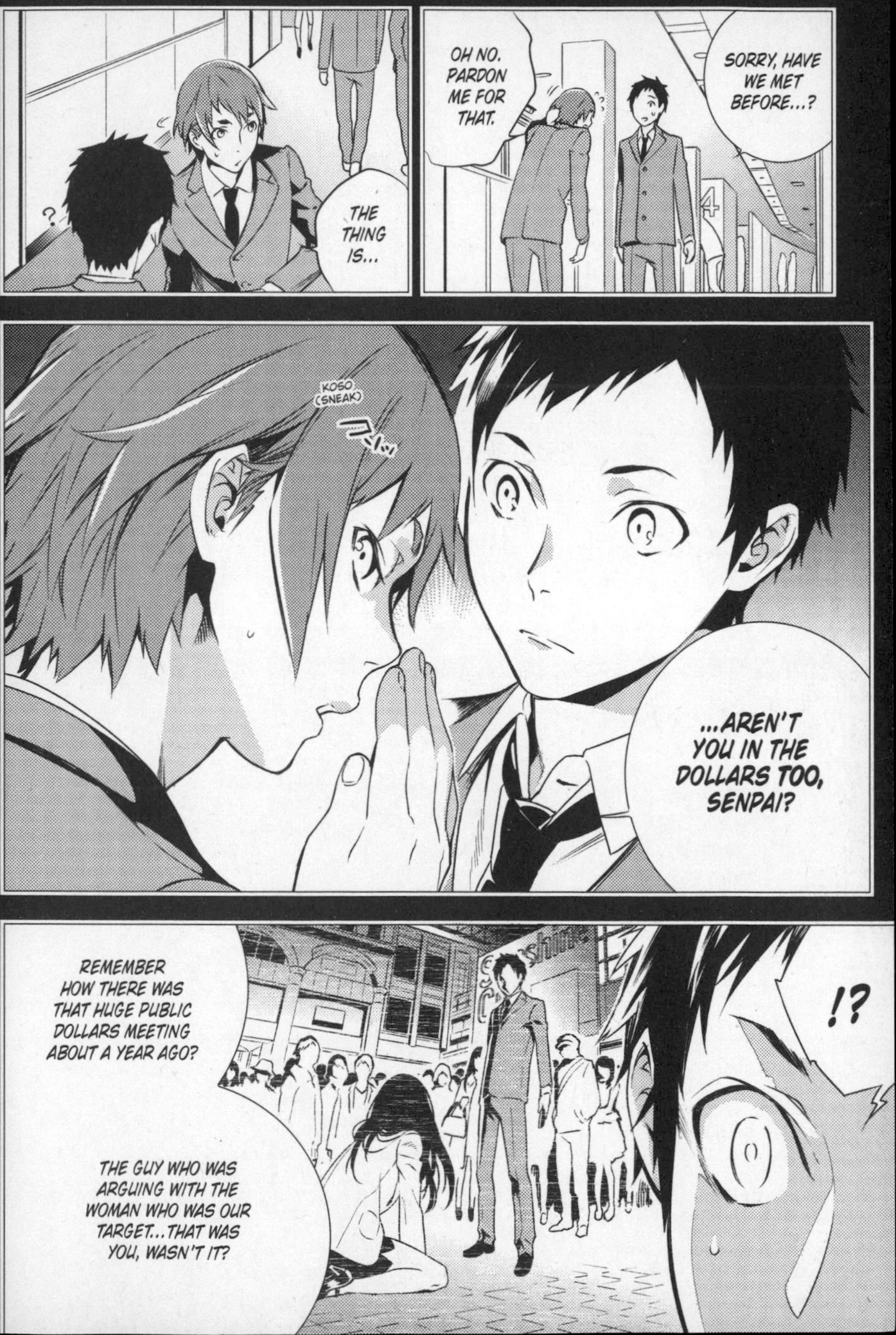
SORRY, HAVE WE MET BEFORE...?
OH NO. PARDON ME FOR THAT.
THE THING IS...
KOSO (SNEAK)
...AREN'T YOU IN THE DOLLARS TOO, SENPAI?
!?
REMEMBER HOW THERE WAS THAT HUGE PUBLIC DOLLARS MEETING ABOUT A YEAR AGO?
THE GUY WHO WAS ARGUING WITH THE WOMAN WHO WAS OUR TARGET...THAT WAS YOU, WASN'T IT?

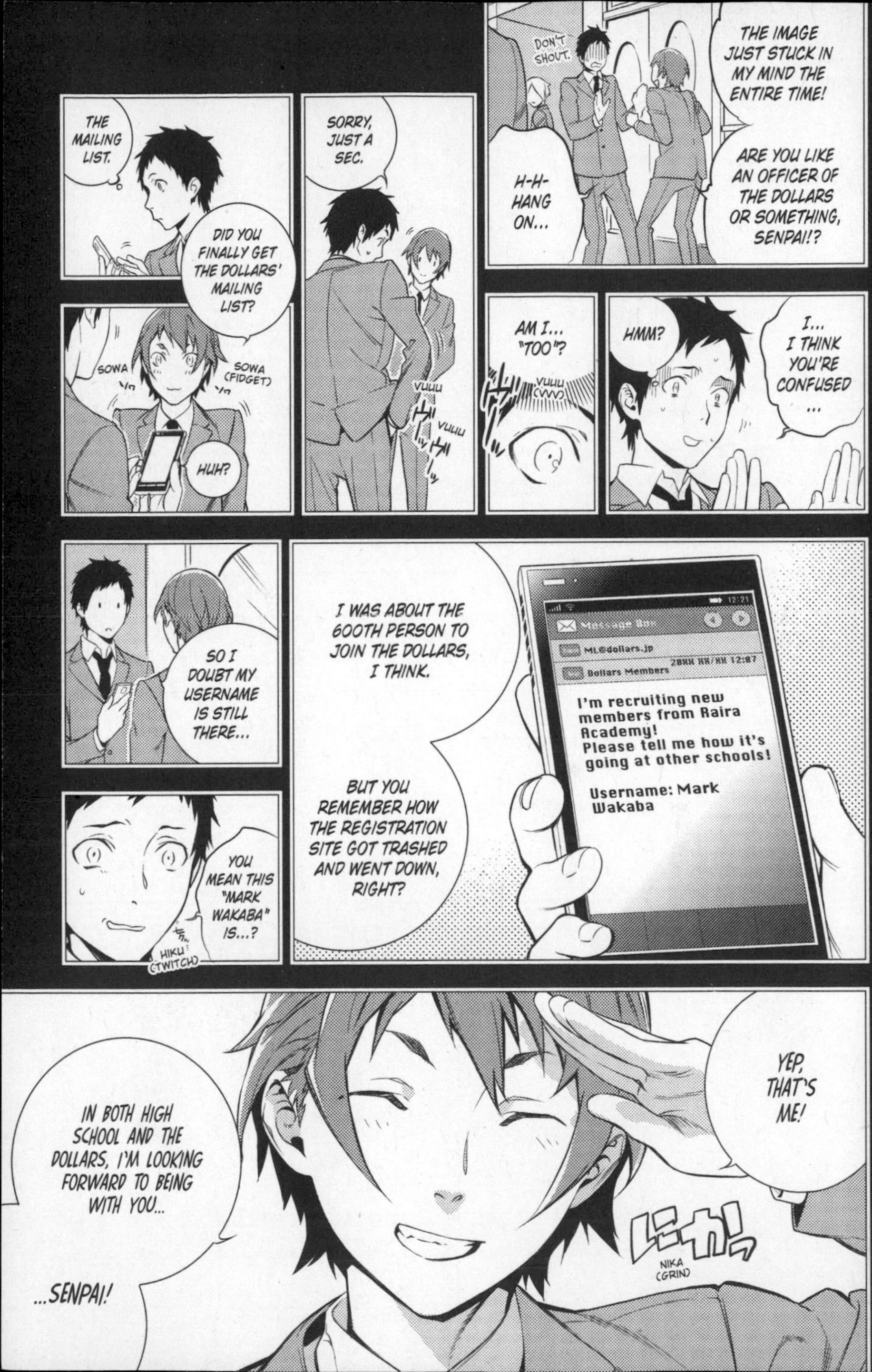
THE IMAGE JUST STUCK IN MY MIND THE ENTIRE TIME!
ARE YOU LIKE AN OFFICER OF THE DOLLARS OR SOMETHING, SENPAI!?
DON'T SHOUT.
H-H-HANG ON...
I... I THINK YOU'RE CONFUSED...
HMM?
AM I... "TOO"?
VUUU (VVV)
SORRY, JUST A SEC.
VUUU
VUUU
DID YOU FINALLY GET THE DOLLARS' MAILING LIST?
THE MAILING LIST.
SOWA (FIDGET)
SOWA
HUH?
I WAS ABOUT THE 600TH PERSON TO JOIN THE DOLLARS, I THINK.
BUT YOU REMEMBER HOW THE REGISTRATION SITE GOT TRASHED AND WENT DOWN, RIGHT?
Message Box
ML@dollars.jp
Dollars Members
I'm recruiting new members from Raira Academy! Please tell me how it's going at other schools!
Username: Mark Wakaba
SO I DOUBT MY USERNAME IS STILL THERE...
YOU MEAN THIS "MARK WAKABA" IS...?
HIKU (TWITCH)
YEP, THAT'S ME!
NIKA (GRIN)
IN BOTH HIGH SCHOOL AND THE DOLLARS, I'M LOOKING FORWARD TO BEING WITH YOU...
...SENPAI!

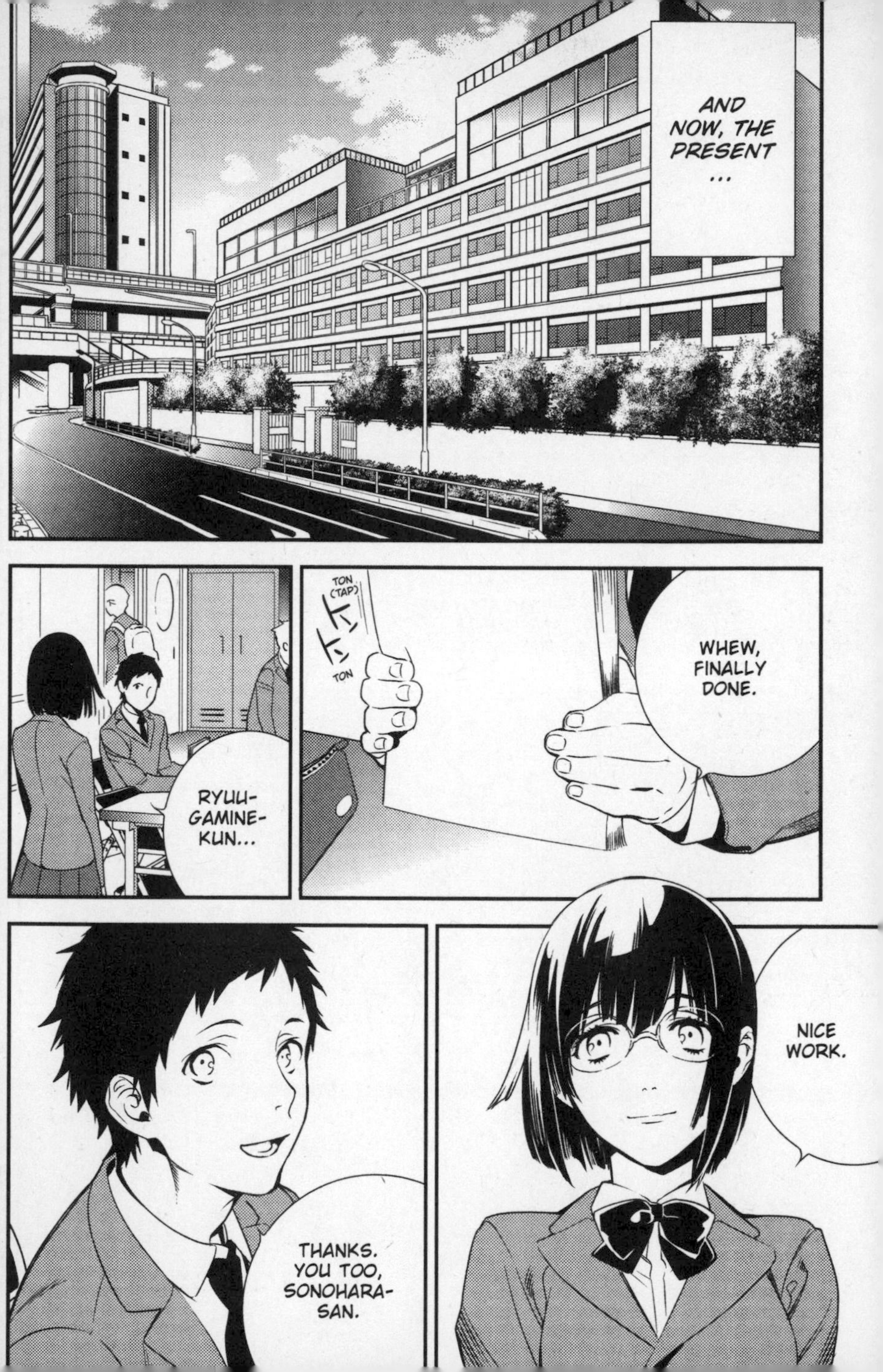
AND NOW, THE PRESENT ...
TON (TAP)
TON
WHEW, FINALLY DONE.
RYUU-GAMINE-KUN...
NICE WORK.
THANKS. YOU TOO, SONOHARA-SAN.

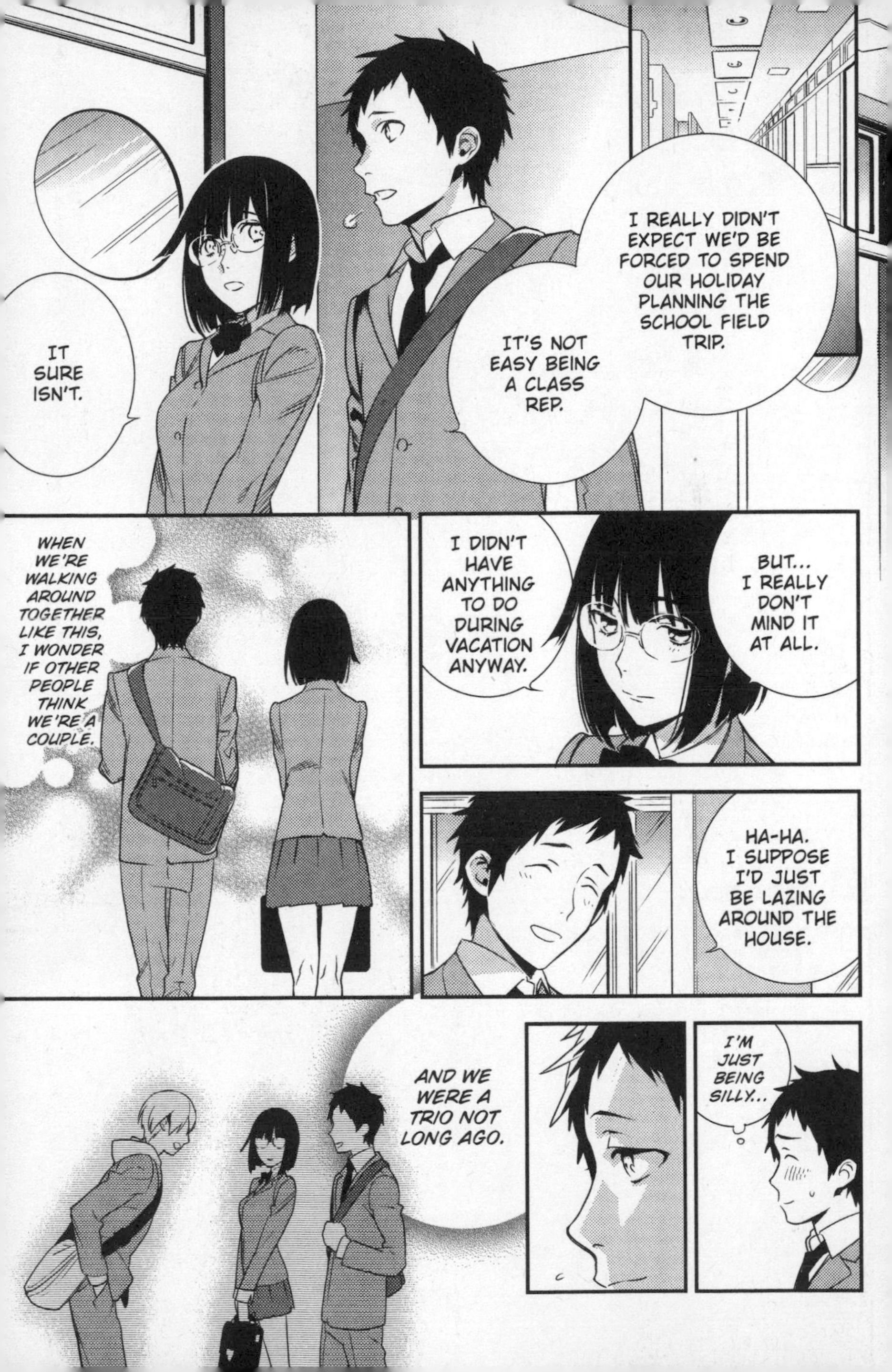
I REALLY DIDN'T EXPECT WE'D BE FORCED TO SPEND OUR HOLIDAY PLANNING THE SCHOOL FIELD TRIP.
IT'S NOT EASY BEING A CLASS REP.
IT SURE ISN'T.
BUT... I REALLY DON'T MIND IT AT ALL.
I DIDN'T HAVE ANYTHING TO DO DURING VACATION ANYWAY.
HA-HA. I SUPPOSE I'D JUST BE LAZING AROUND THE HOUSE.
WHEN WE'RE WALKING AROUND TOGETHER LIKE THIS, I WONDER IF OTHER PEOPLE THINK WE'RE A COUPLE.
I'M JUST BEING SILLY...
AND WE WERE A TRIO NOT LONG AGO.

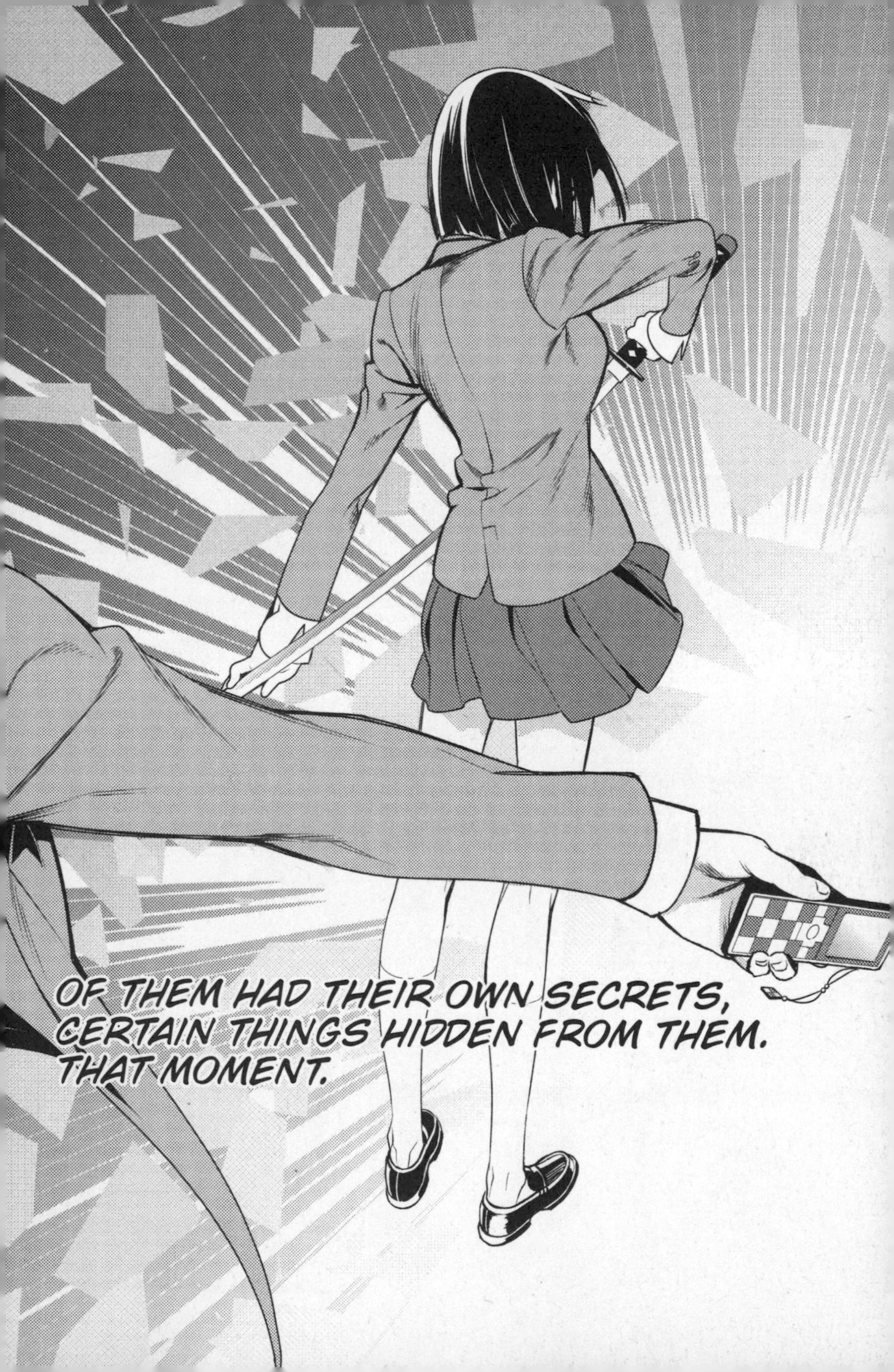
OF THEM HAD THEIR OWN SECRETS,
CERTAIN THINGS HIDDEN FROM THEM.
THAT MOMENT.

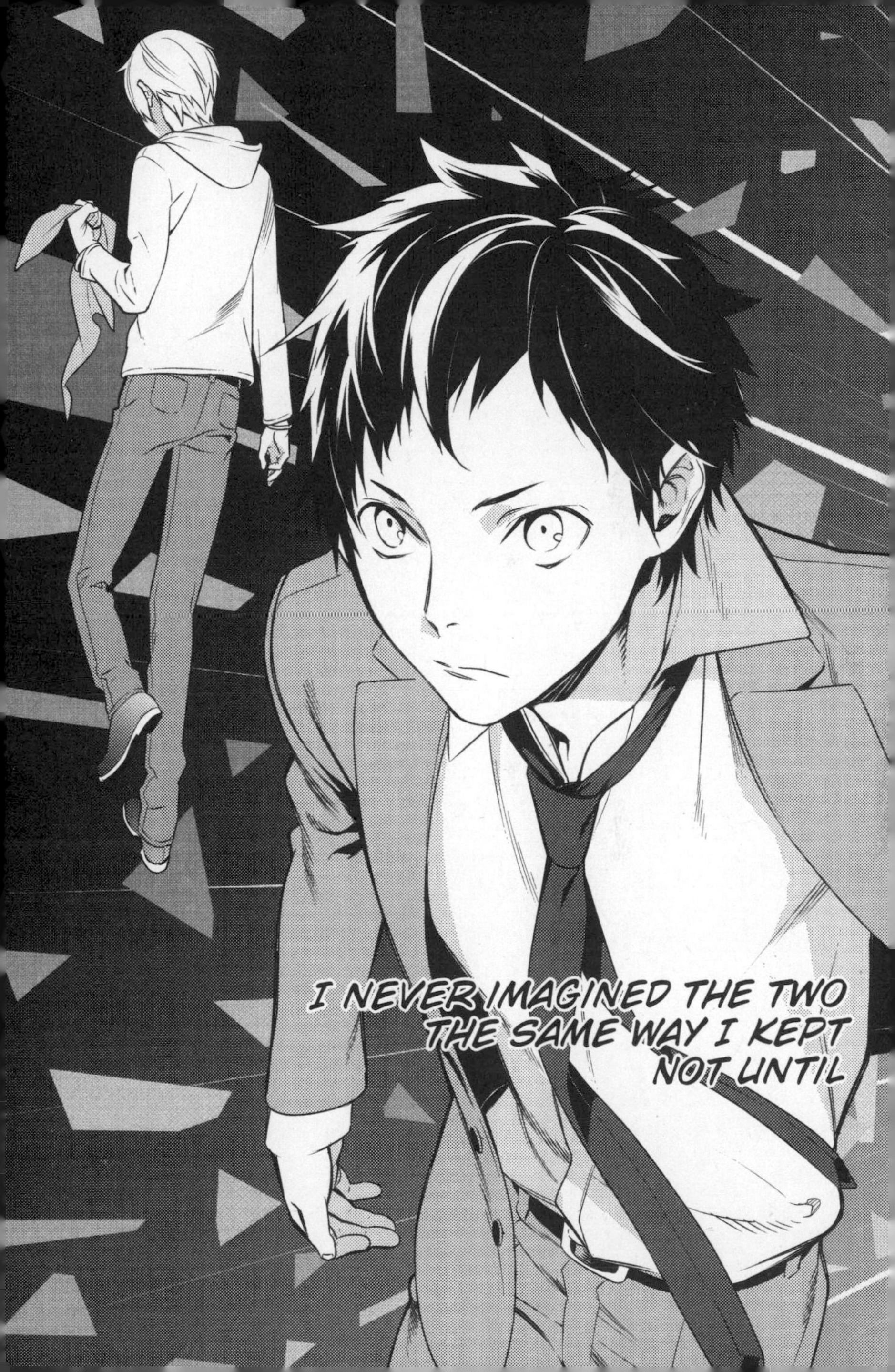
I NEVER IMAGINED THE TWO
THE SAME WAY I KEPT
NOT UNTIL

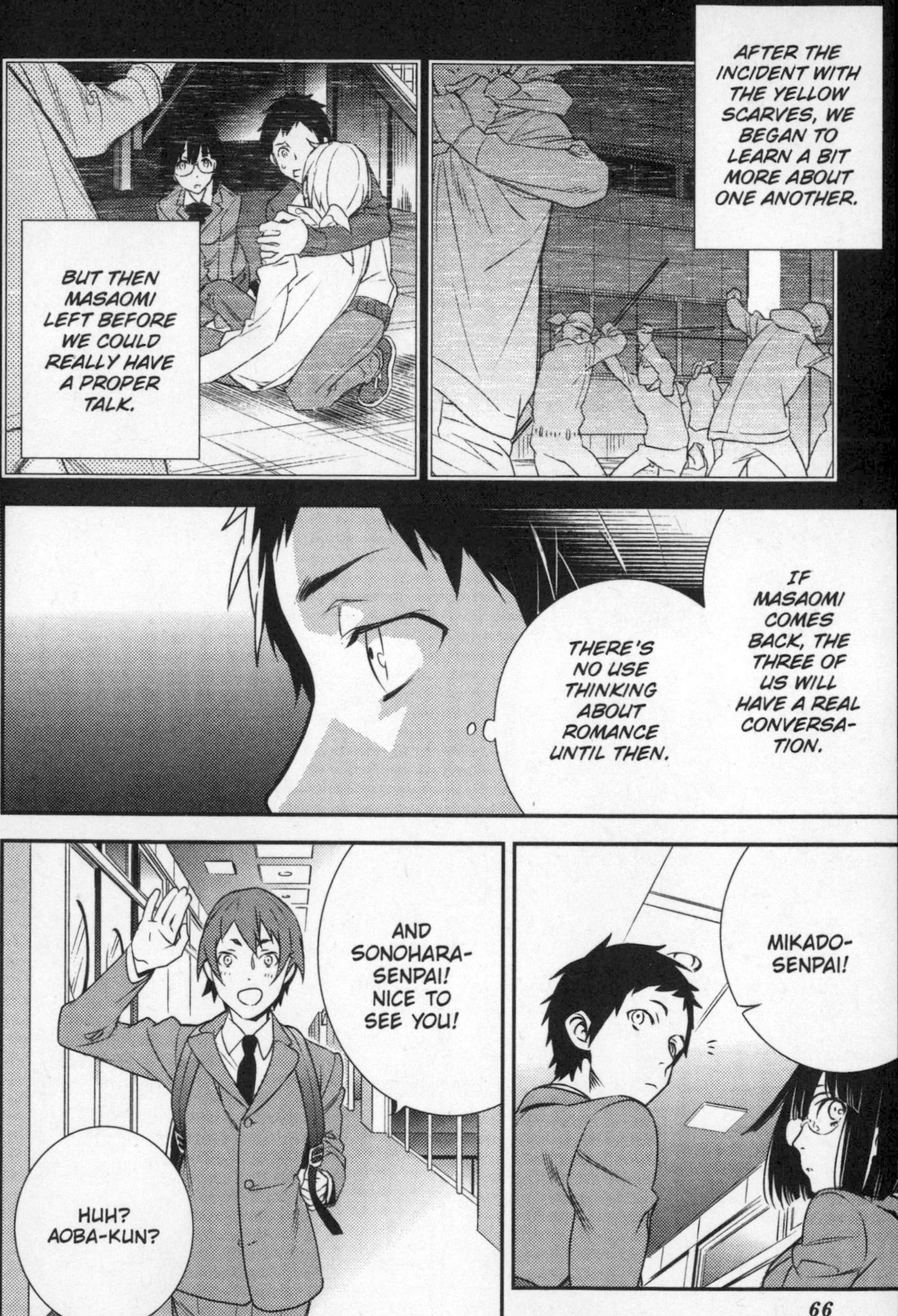
AFTER THE INCIDENT WITH THE YELLOW SCARVES, WE BEGAN TO LEARN A BIT MORE ABOUT ONE ANOTHER.
BUT THEN MASAOMI LEFT BEFORE WE COULD REALLY HAVE A PROPER TALK.
IF MASAOMI COMES BACK, THE THREE OF US WILL HAVE A REAL CONVERSA-TION.
THERE'S NO USE THINKING ABOUT ROMANCE UNTIL THEN.
MIKADO-SENPAI!
AND SONOHARA-SENPAI! NICE TO SEE YOU!
HUH? AOBA-KUN?

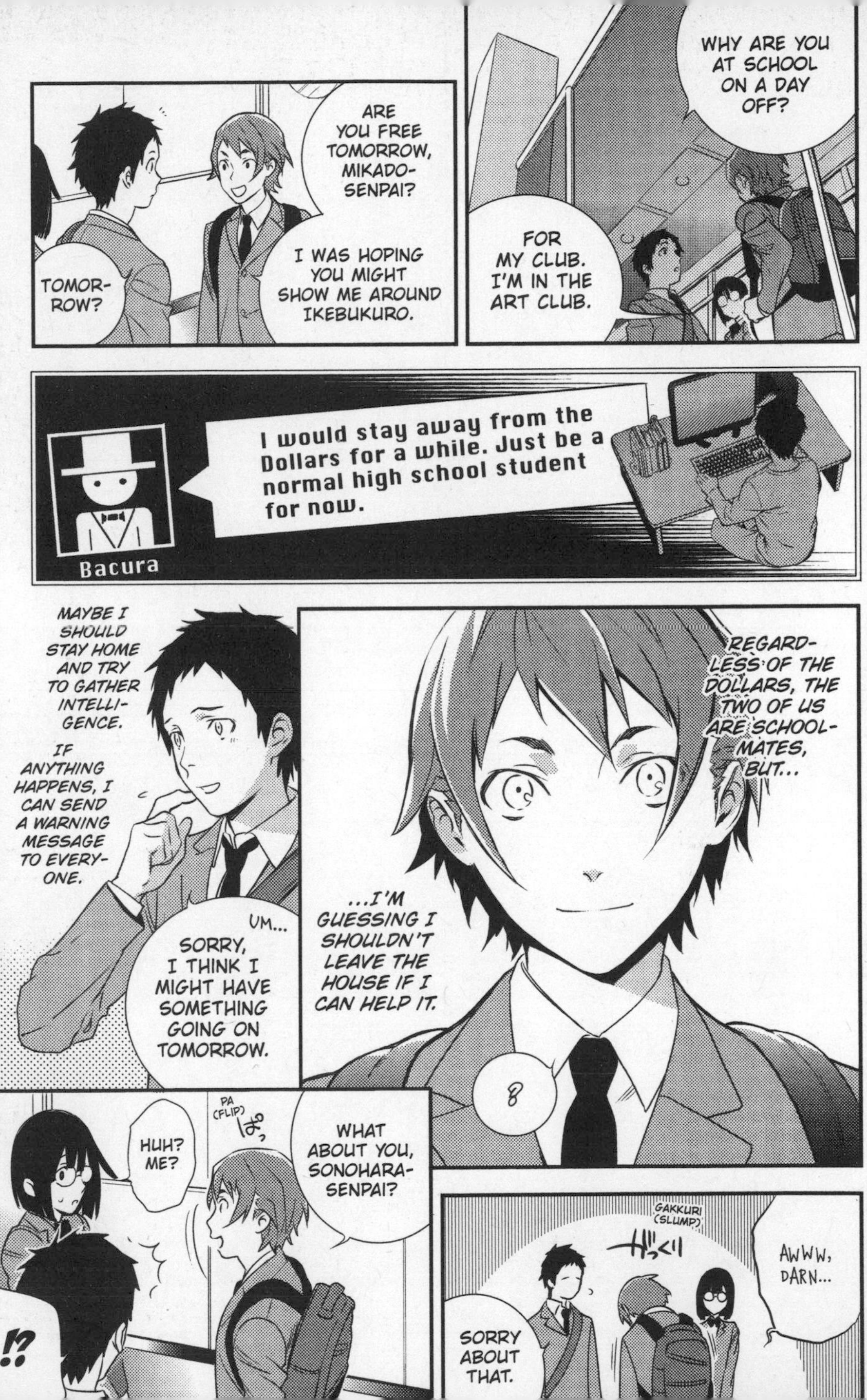
WHY ARE YOU AT SCHOOL ON A DAY OFF?
FOR MY CLUB. I'M IN THE ART CLUB.
ARE YOU FREE TOMORROW, MIKADO-SENPAI?
I WAS HOPING YOU MIGHT SHOW ME AROUND IKEBUKURO.
TOMOR-ROW?
I would stay away from the Dollars for a while. Just be a normal high school student for now.
Bacura
REGARD-LESS OF THE DOLLARS, THE TWO OF US ARE SCHOOL-MATES, BUT...
...I'M GUESSING I SHOULDN'T LEAVE THE HOUSE IF I CAN HELP IT.
?
MAYBE I SHOULD STAY HOME AND TRY TO GATHER INTELLI-GENCE.
IF ANYTHING HAPPENS, I CAN SEND A WARNING MESSAGE TO EVERY-ONE.
UM...
SORRY, I THINK I MIGHT HAVE SOMETHING GOING ON TOMORROW.
WHAT ABOUT YOU, SONOHARA-SENPAI?
PA (FLIP)
ぱっ
HUH? ME?
!?
AWWW, DARN...
GAKKURI (SLUMP)
がっくり
SORRY ABOUT THAT.

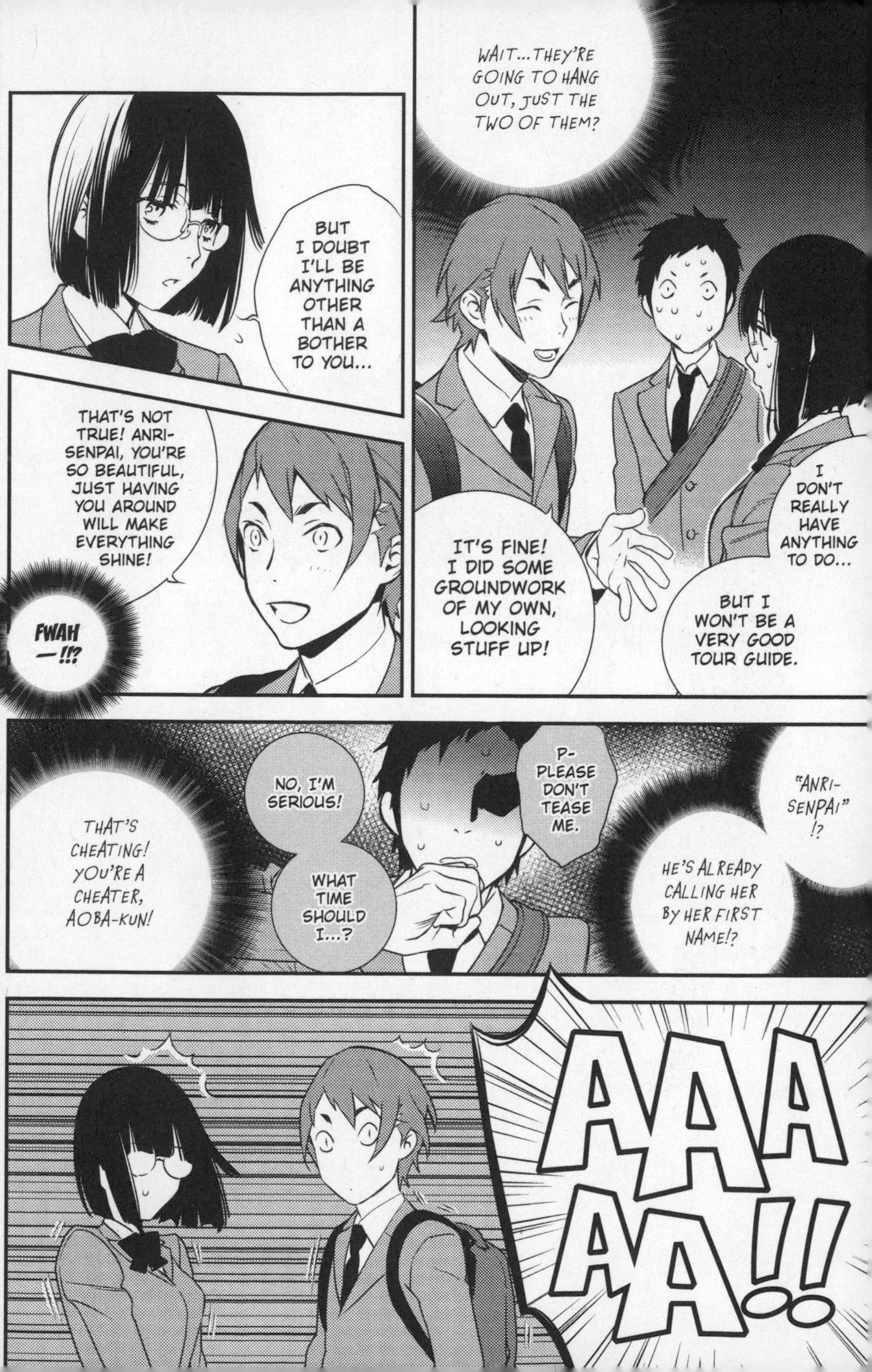
WAIT...THEY'RE GOING TO HANG OUT, JUST THE TWO OF THEM?
I DON'T REALLY HAVE ANYTHING TO DO...
BUT I WON'T BE A VERY GOOD TOUR GUIDE.
IT'S FINE! I DID SOME GROUNDWORK OF MY OWN, LOOKING STUFF UP!
BUT I DOUBT I'LL BE ANYTHING OTHER THAN A BOTHER TO YOU...
THAT'S NOT TRUE! ANRI-SENPAI, YOU'RE SO BEAUTIFUL, JUST HAVING YOU AROUND WILL MAKE EVERYTHING SHINE!
FWAH —!!?
"ANRI-SENPAI" !?
HE'S ALREADY CALLING HER BY HER FIRST NAME!?
P-PLEASE DON'T TEASE ME.
NO, I'M SERIOUS!
WHAT TIME SHOULD I...?
THAT'S CHEATING! YOU'RE A CHEATER, AOBA-KUN!
AAAAA!!

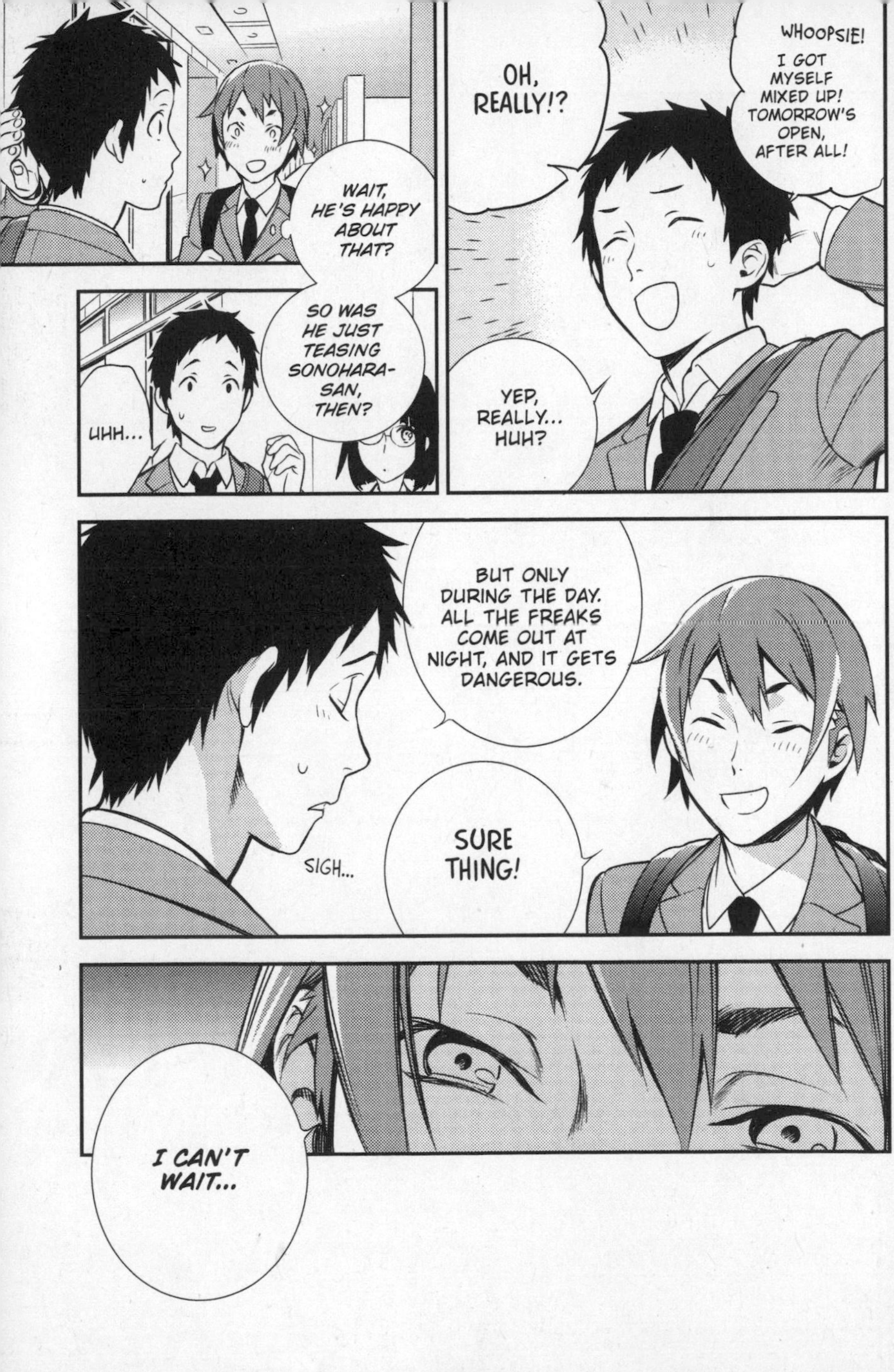
WHOOPSIE! I GOT MYSELF MIXED UP! TOMORROW'S OPEN, AFTER ALL!
OH, REALLY!?
YEP, REALLY... HUH?
WAIT, HE'S HAPPY ABOUT THAT?
SO WAS HE JUST TEASING SONOHARA-SAN, THEN?
UHH...
BUT ONLY DURING THE DAY. ALL THE FREAKS COME OUT AT NIGHT, AND IT GETS DANGEROUS.
SURE THING!
SIGH...
I CAN'T WAIT...

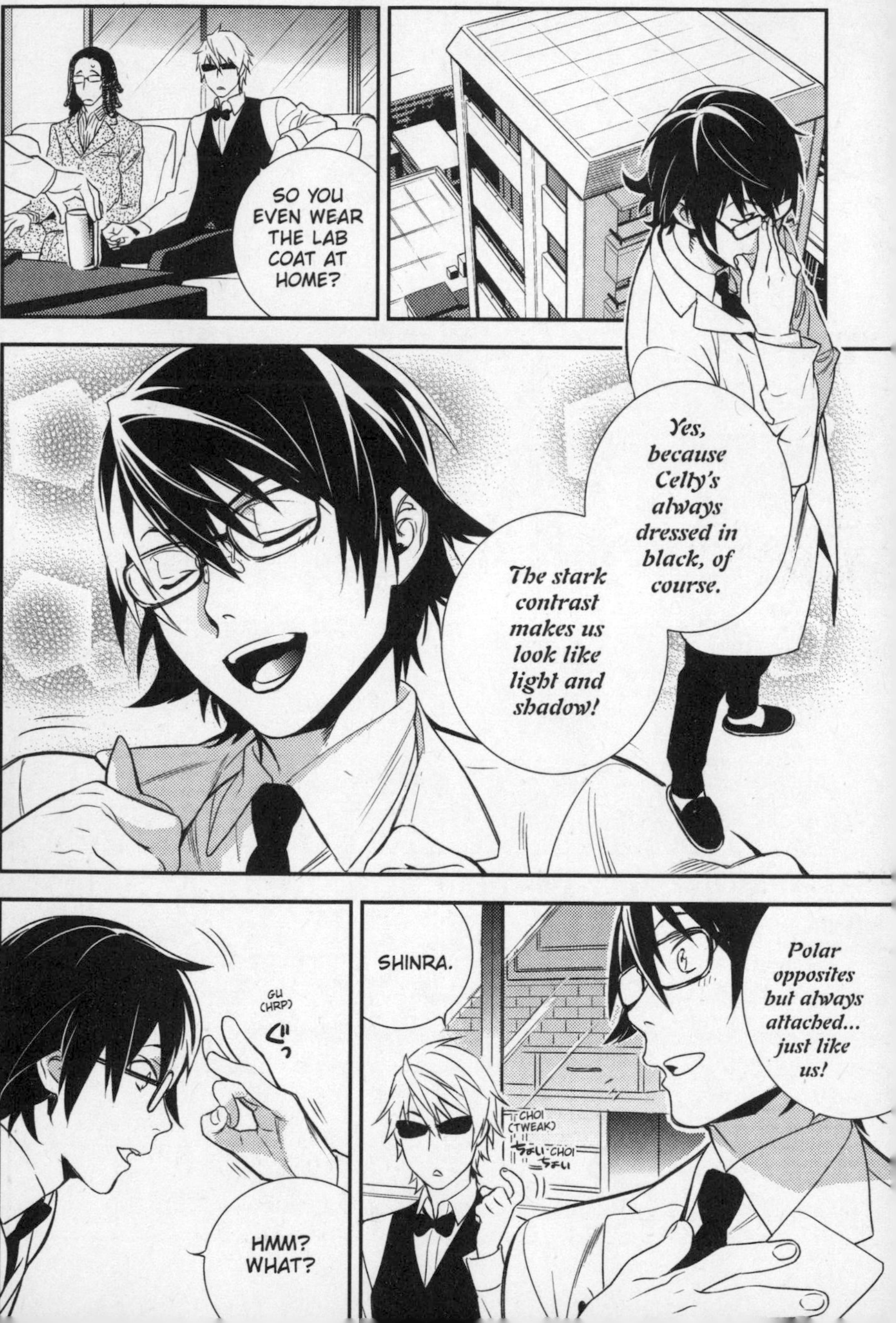
SO YOU EVEN WEAR THE LAB COAT AT HOME?
Yes, because Celly's always dressed in black, of course.
The stark contrast makes us look like light and shadow!
Polar opposites but always attached... just like us!
SHINRA.
CHOI (TWEAK) ちょい
CHOI ちょい
GU (HRP) ぐっ
HMM? WHAT?

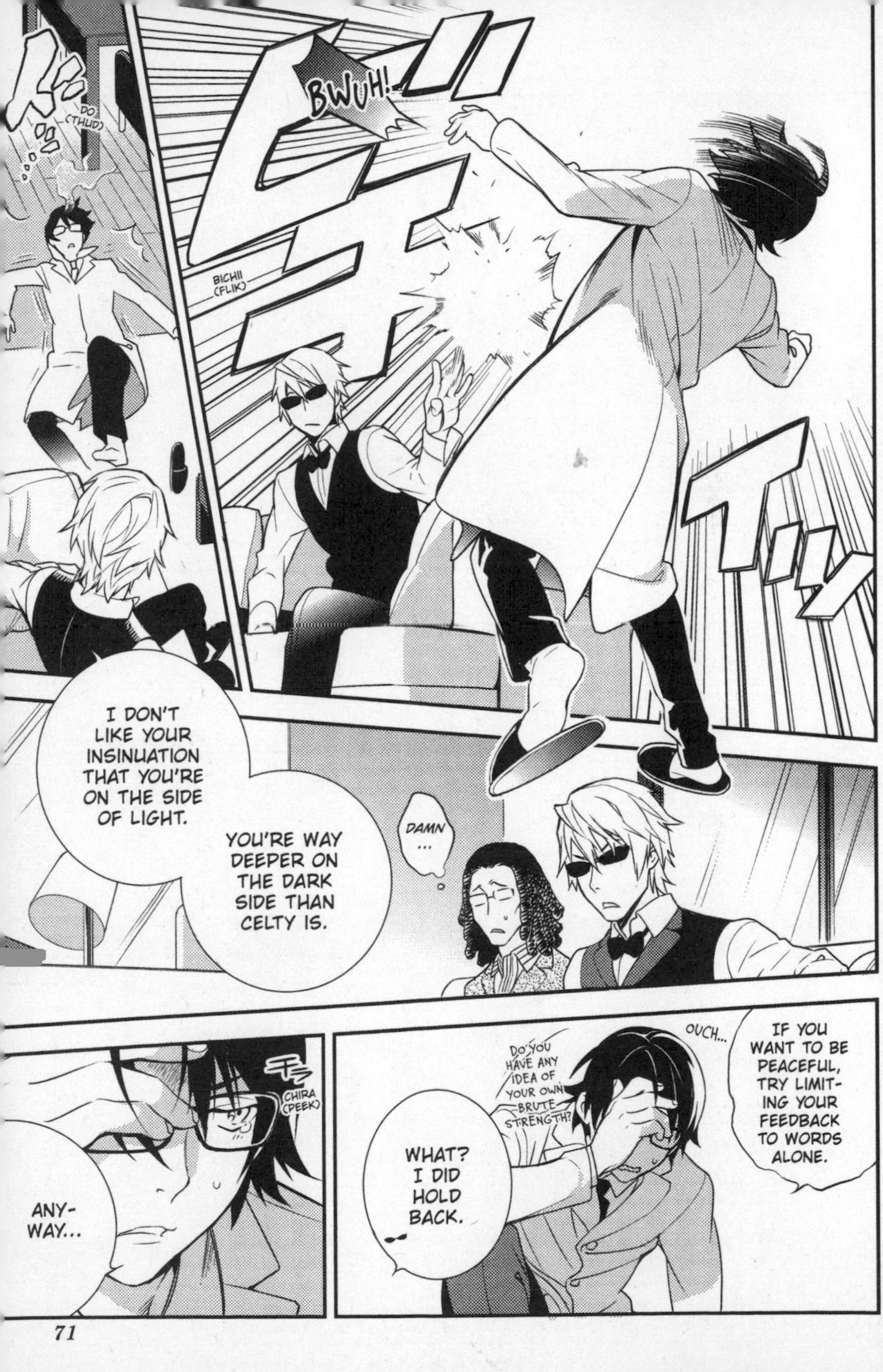
BWUH!
DO (THUD)
BICHII (FLIK)
I DON'T LIKE YOUR INSINUATION THAT YOU'RE ON THE SIDE OF LIGHT.
YOU'RE WAY DEEPER ON THE DARK SIDE THAN CELTY IS.
DAMN...
IF YOU WANT TO BE PEACEFUL, TRY LIMIT-ING YOUR FEEDBACK TO WORDS ALONE.
OUCH...
DO YOU HAVE ANY IDEA OF YOUR OWN BRUTE STRENGTH?
WHAT? I DID HOLD BACK.
CHIRA (PEEK)
ANY-WAY...

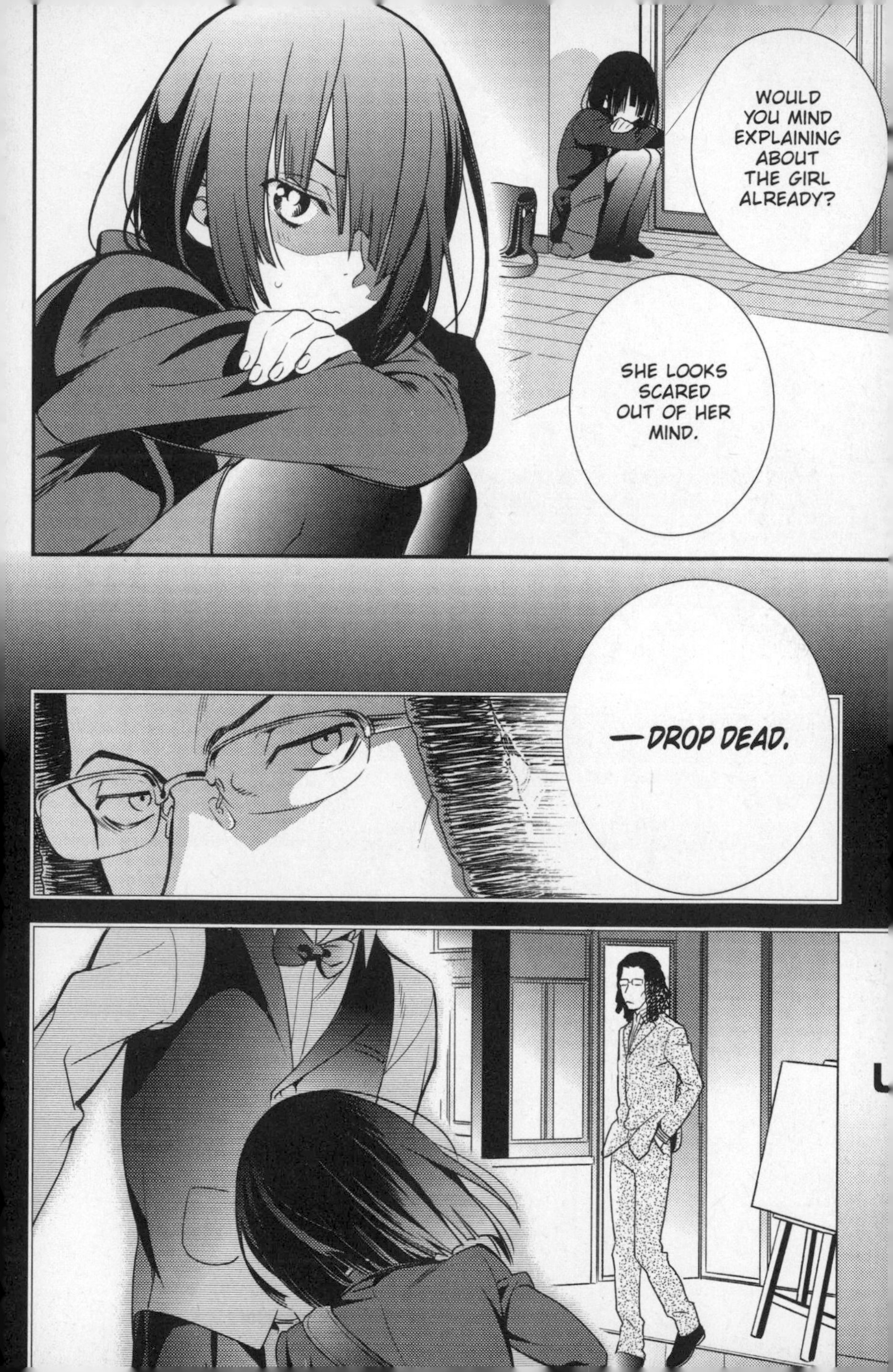
WOULD YOU MIND EXPLAINING ABOUT THE GIRL ALREADY?
SHE LOOKS SCARED OUT OF HER MIND.
—DROP DEAD.

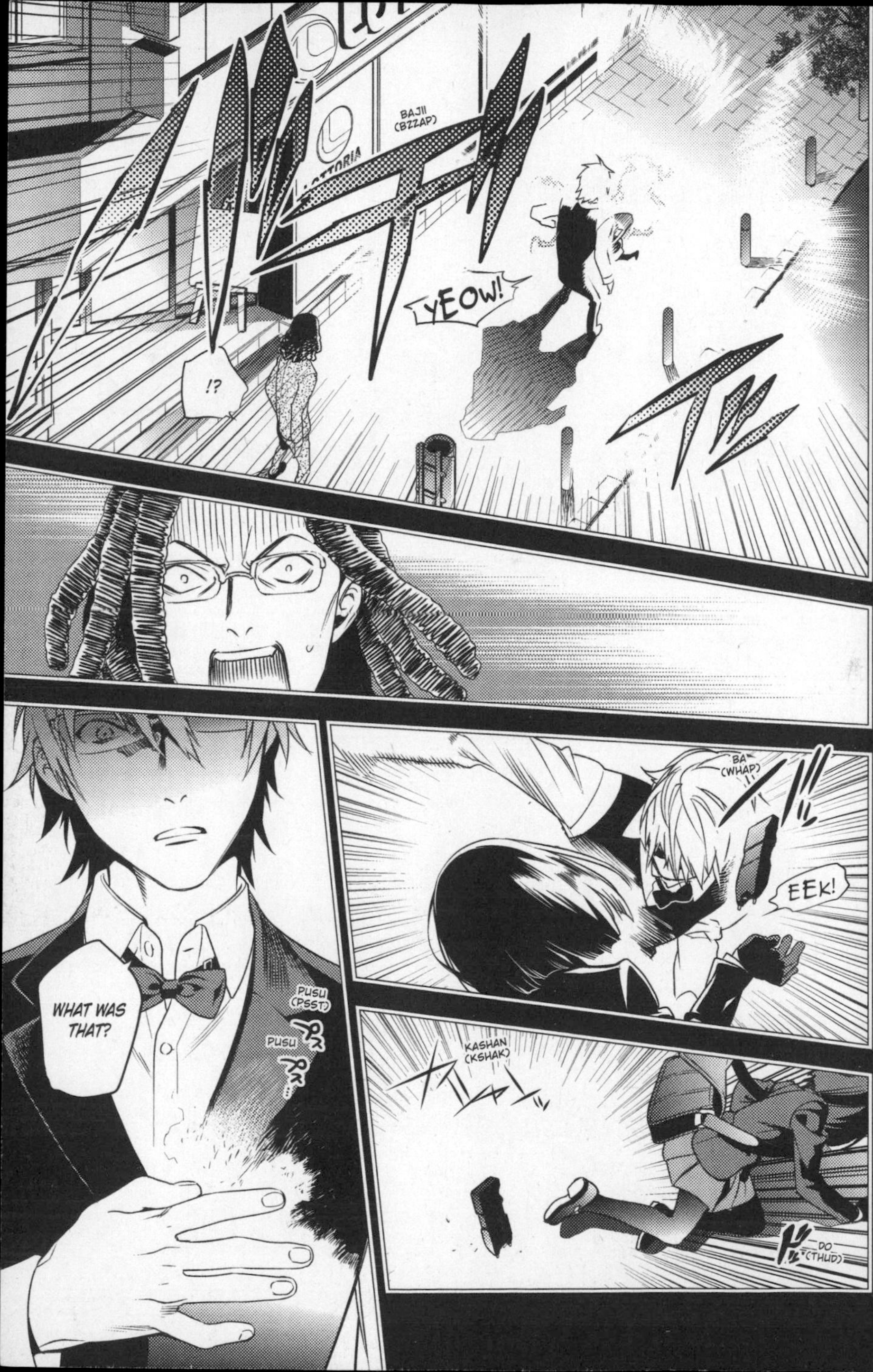
BAJII (BZZAP)
YEOW!
!?
BA (WHAP)
EEK!
KASHAN (KSHAK)
DO (THUD)
WHAT WAS THAT?
PUSU (PSST)
PUSU

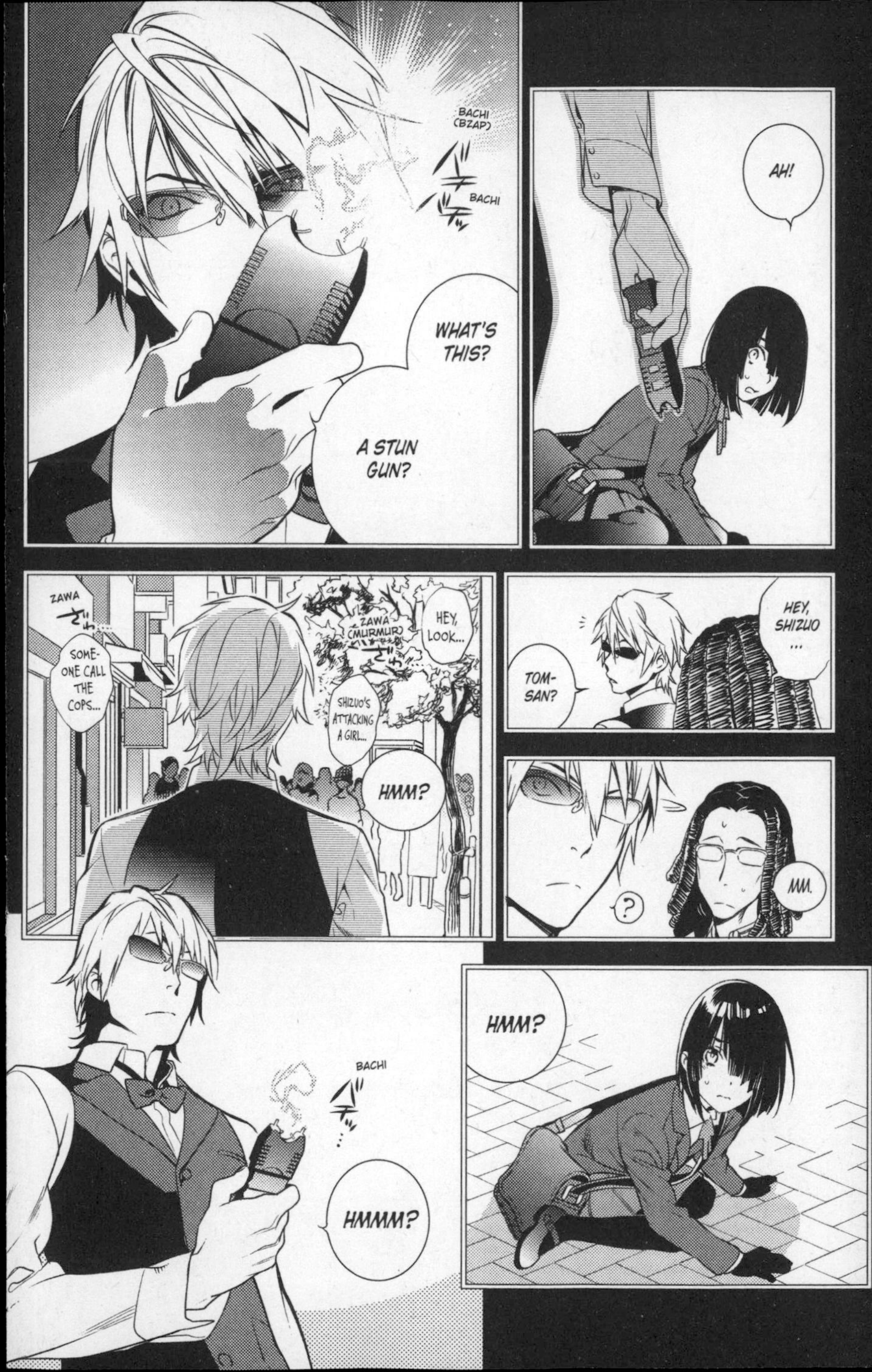
AH!
BACHI (BZAP)
BACHI
WHAT'S THIS?
A STUN GUN?
HEY, SHIZUO ...
TOM-SAN?
?
MM.
ZAWA (MURMUR)
HEY, LOOK...
SHIZUO'S ATTACKING A GIRL...
ZAWA
SOME-ONE CALL THE COPS...
HMM?
HMM?
BACHI
HMMM?

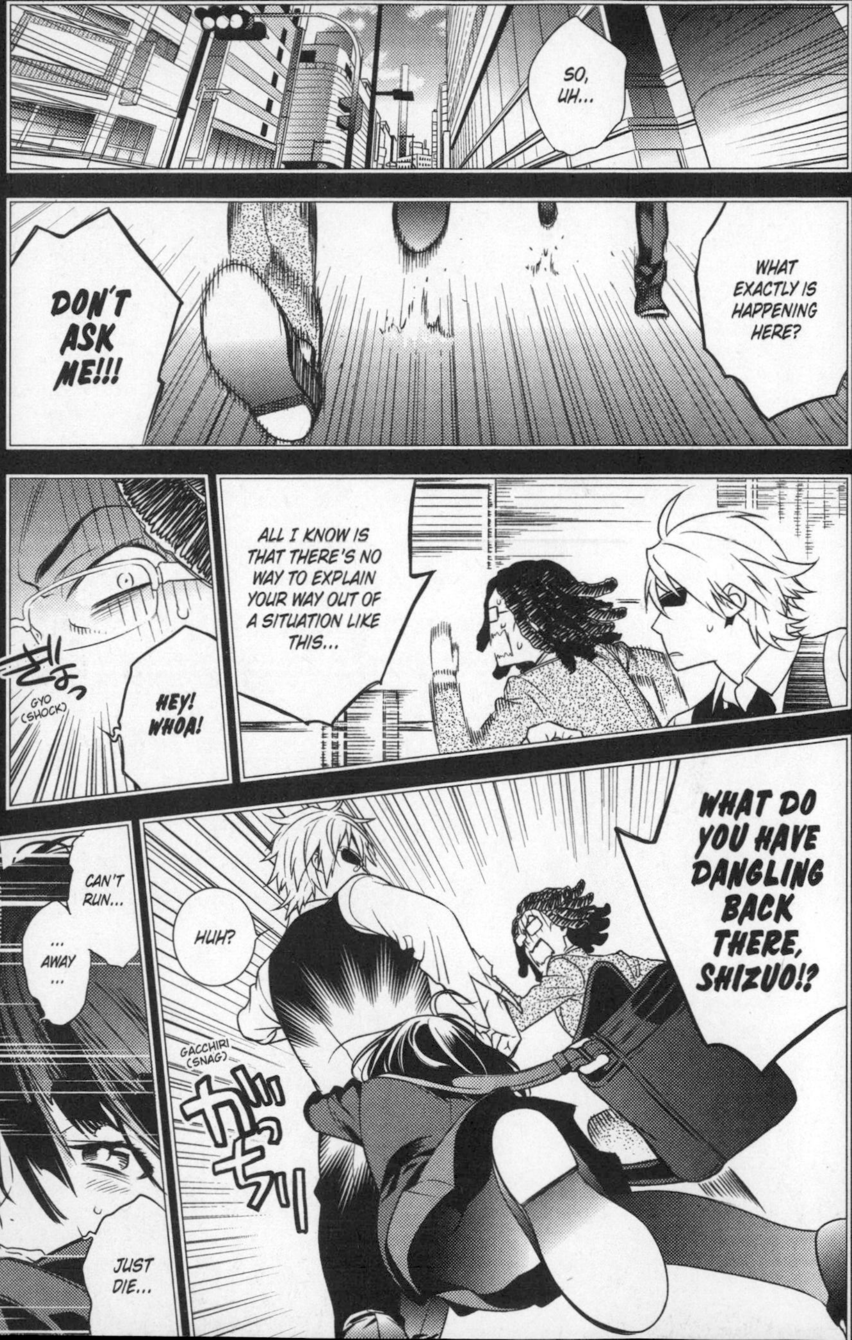

SO, UH...
WHAT EXACTLY IS HAPPENING HERE?
DON'T ASK ME!!!
ALL I KNOW IS THAT THERE'S NO WAY TO EXPLAIN YOUR WAY OUT OF A SITUATION LIKE THIS...
HEY! WHOA!
GYO (SHOCK)
WHAT DO YOU HAVE DANGLING BACK THERE, SHIZUO!?
HUH?
GACCHIRI (SNAG)
CAN'T RUN...
... AWAY ...
DIE.
JUST DIE...

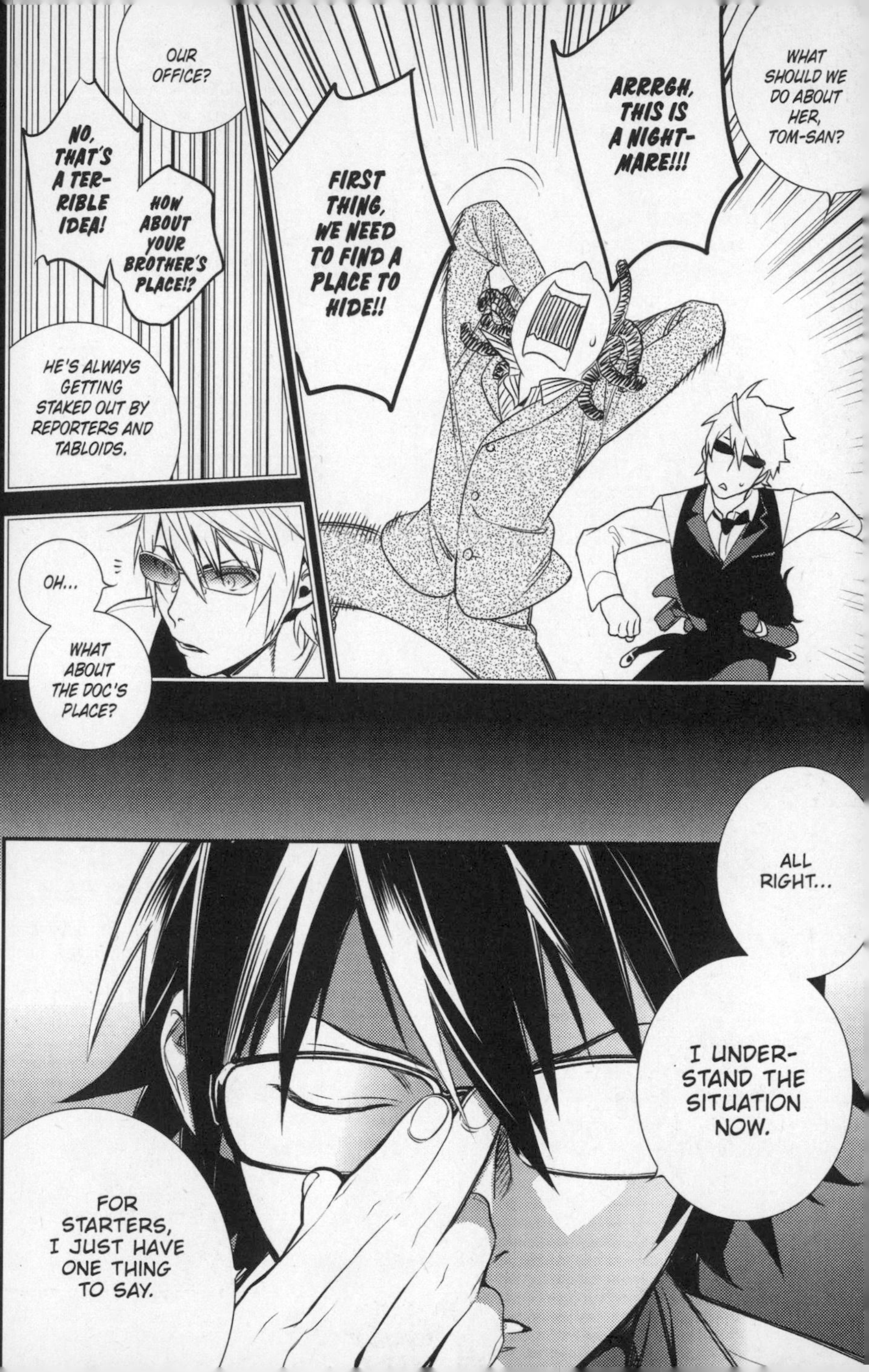
WHAT SHOULD WE DO ABOUT HER, TOM-SAN?
ARRRGH, THIS IS A NIGHT-MARE!!!
FIRST THING, WE NEED TO FIND A PLACE TO HIDE!!
OUR OFFICE?
NO, THAT'S A TER-RIBLE IDEA!
HOW ABOUT YOUR BROTHER'S PLACE!?
HE'S ALWAYS GETTING STAKED OUT BY REPORTERS AND TABLOIDS.
OH...
WHAT ABOUT THE DOC'S PLACE?
ALL RIGHT...
I UNDER-STAND THE SITUATION NOW.
FOR STARTERS, I JUST HAVE ONE THING TO SAY.

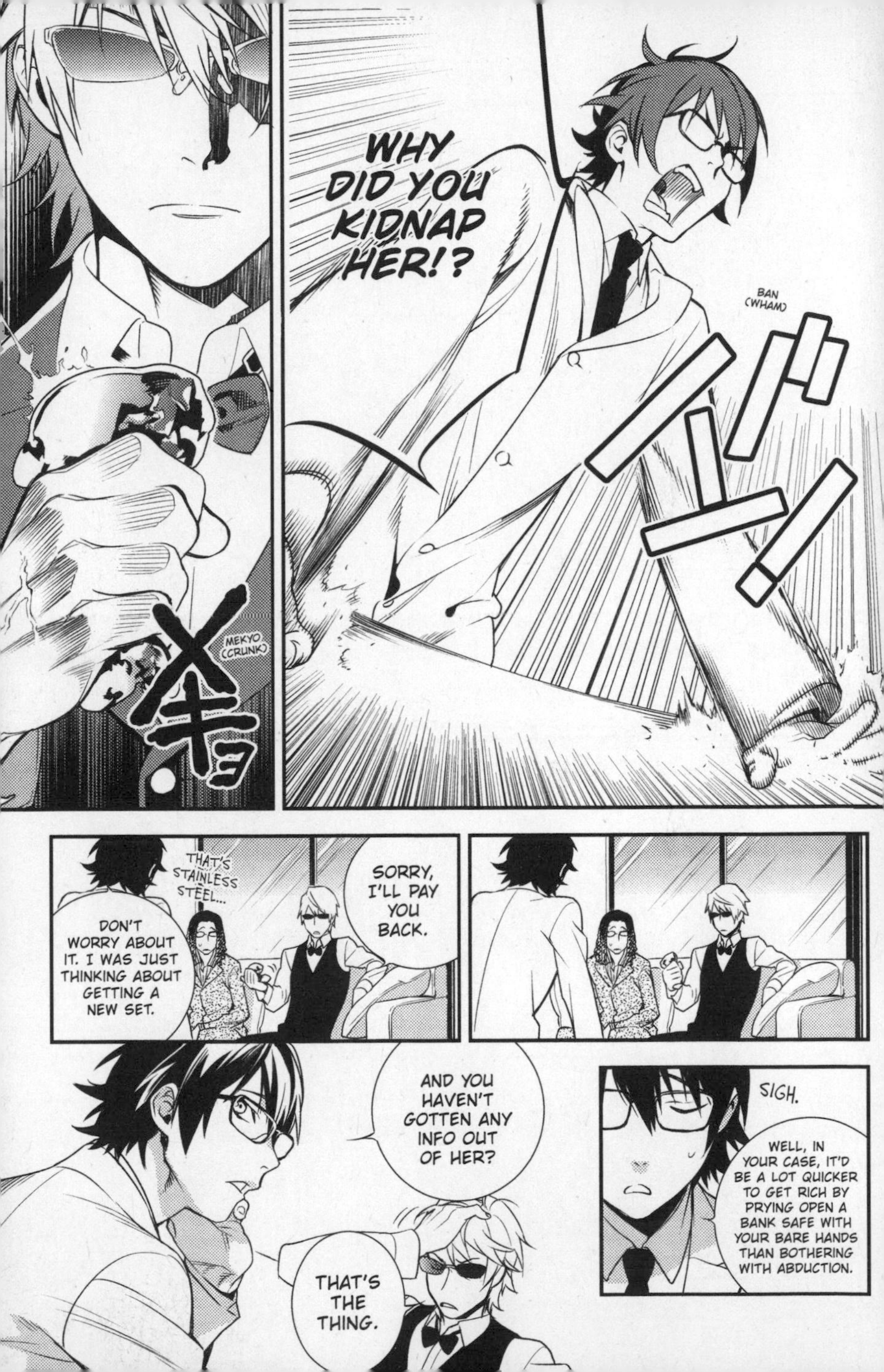
WHY DID YOU KIDNAP HER!?
BAN (WHAM)
MEKYO (CRUNK)
メキョ
SORRY, I'LL PAY YOU BACK.
THAT'S STAINLESS STEEL...
DON'T WORRY ABOUT IT. I WAS JUST THINKING ABOUT GETTING A NEW SET.
SIGH.
WELL, IN YOUR CASE, IT'D BE A LOT QUICKER TO GET RICH BY PRYING OPEN A BANK SAFE WITH YOUR BARE HANDS THAN BOTHERING WITH ABDUCTION.
AND YOU HAVEN'T GOTTEN ANY INFO OUT OF HER?
THAT'S THE THING.

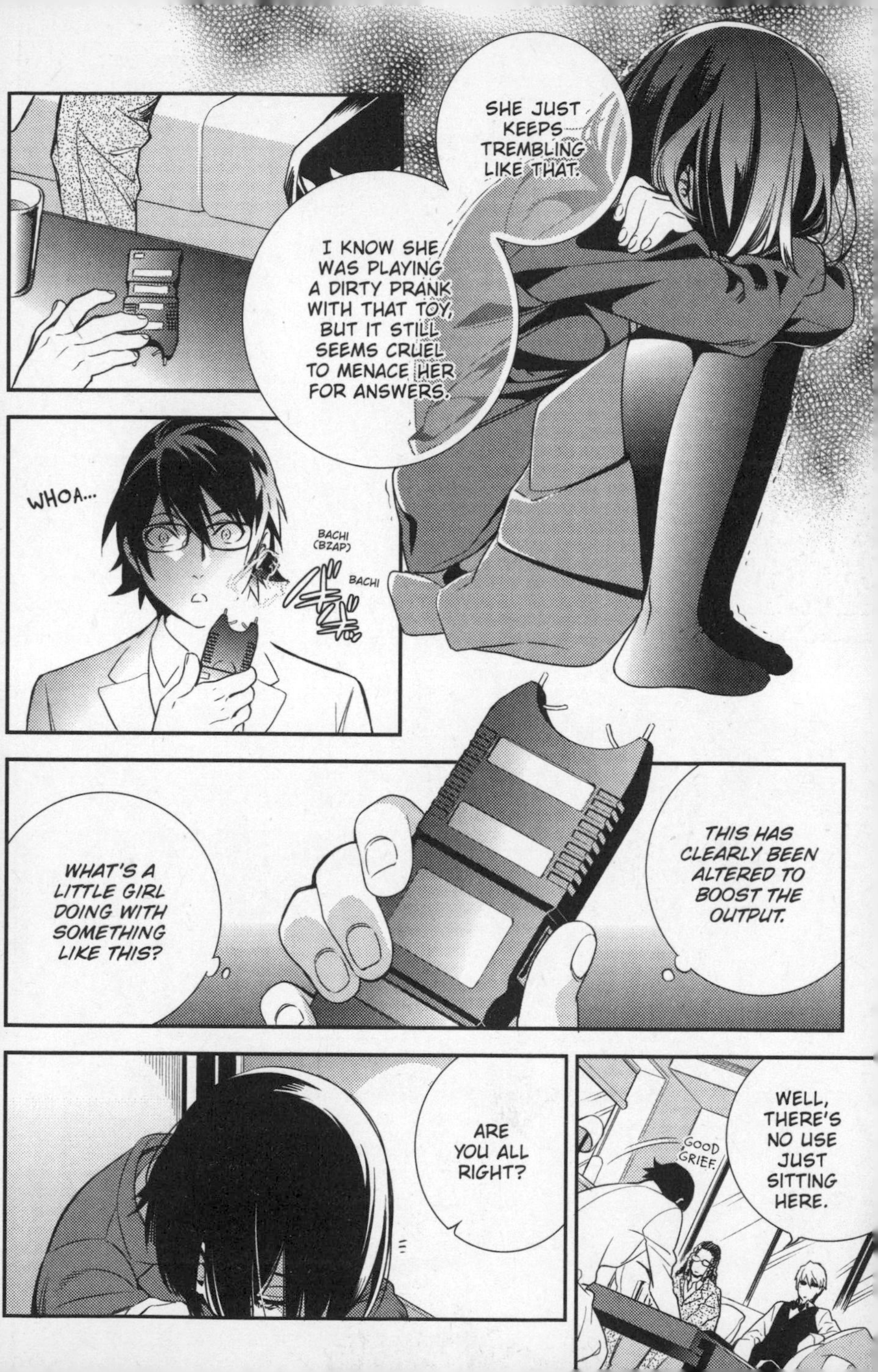

SHE JUST KEEPS TREMBLING LIKE THAT.
I KNOW SHE WAS PLAYING A DIRTY PRANK WITH THAT TOY, BUT IT STILL SEEMS CRUEL TO MENACE HER FOR ANSWERS.
BACHI (BZAP)
BACHI
WHOA...
THIS HAS CLEARLY BEEN ALTERED TO BOOST THE OUTPUT.
WHAT'S A LITTLE GIRL DOING WITH SOMETHING LIKE THIS?
WELL, THERE'S NO USE JUST SITTING HERE.
GOOD GRIEF.
ARE YOU ALL RIGHT?

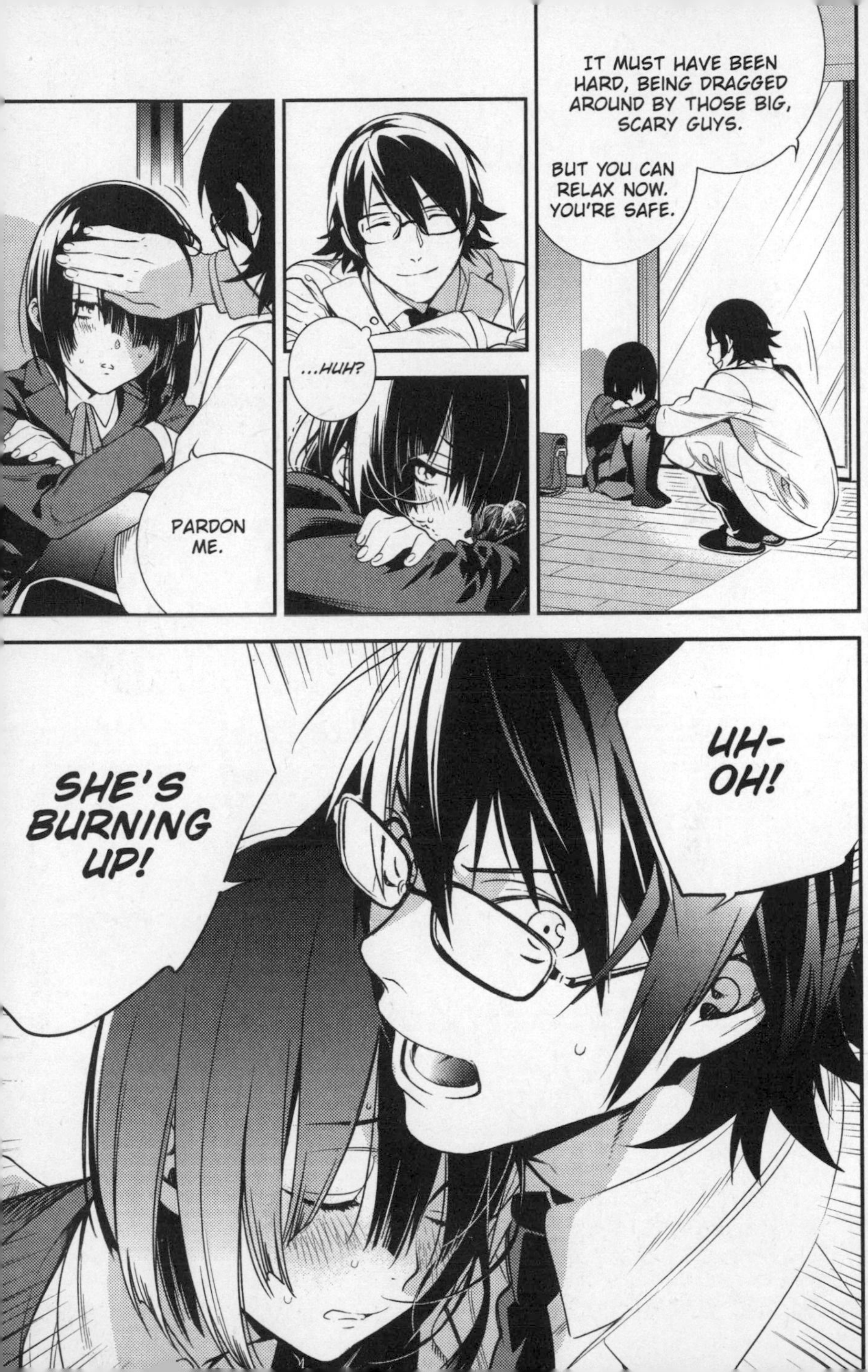
IT MUST HAVE BEEN HARD, BEING DRAGGED AROUND BY THOSE BIG, SCARY GUYS.
BUT YOU CAN RELAX NOW. YOU'RE SAFE.
...HUH?
PARDON ME.
UH-OH!
SHE'S BURNING UP!

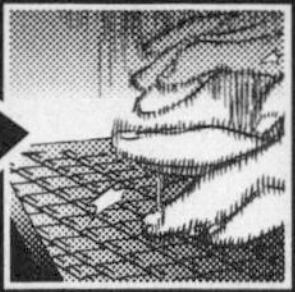

Kuru: I recently witnessed something interesting in town. There were several dozen men congregated around a pedestrian bridge, shouting about something. I believe they belonged to a motorcycle gang...

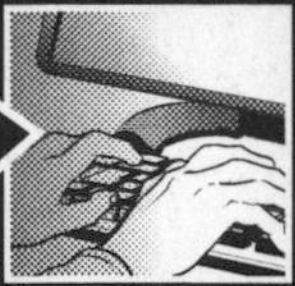

TarouTanaka: Ohh. Sounds scary...

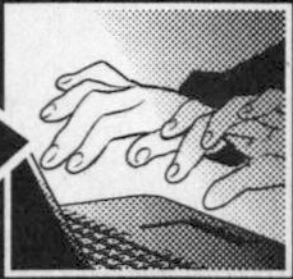

Kuru: Speaking of scary, is everyone here aware of the "Dollars"? They're a very mysterious gang! Despite being a classic color-based street gang, they choose no color at all or rep the color of "camouflage" to blend in with the city! It's an insane organization!

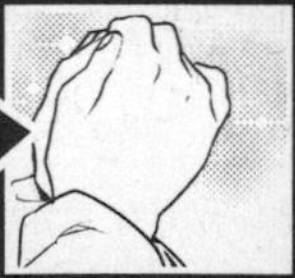

Mai: Really cool.

Saika: thats a bit scary

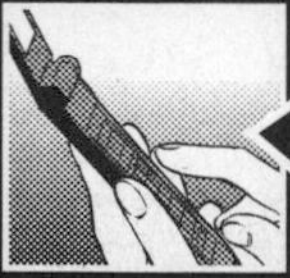

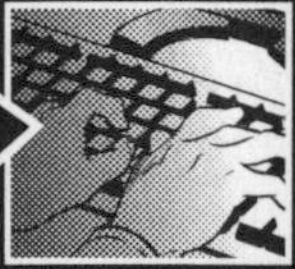

TarouTanaka: Calling them "insane" seems a bit much.

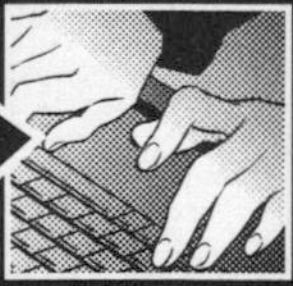

Kuru: But there's no way to know what they're after! At least with a normal color gang, you can identify them on sight and possibly understand certain things about them, but not with the Dollars. There's no way to know who might be a member. Perhaps even ordinary students, housewives, or friendly classmates might secretly be Dollars. They're like a security camera that's always recording the city, only the camera is the eyes of the crowd. You never know when they might detect and seize upon your most tender weakness.

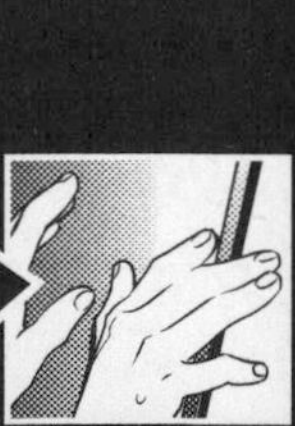

TarouTanaka: You're thinking way too hard about this. Are you sure it's not just like any old club?

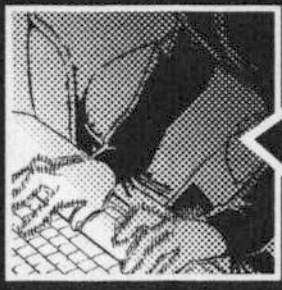

Kuru: That's just it. It's a gang that anyone can claim to be part of, at any time, for any reason. If you were a Dollars member, Tanaka-san, could you claim that no one else in the group has any ulterior motives, just because you don't?

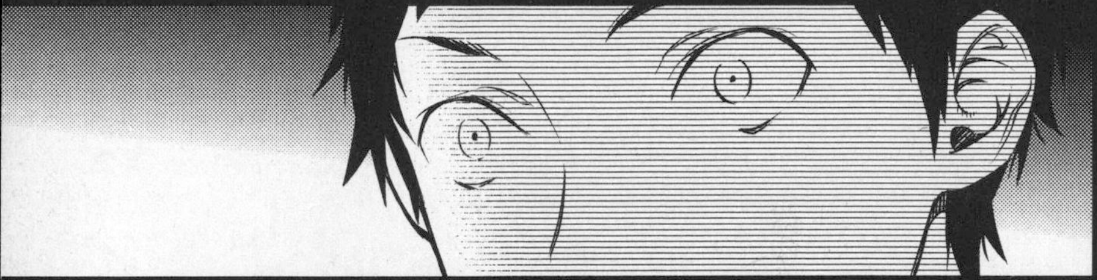

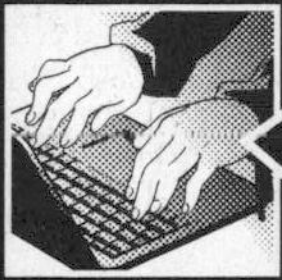

Kuru: There are many people in the Dollars, and I hear that no one knows who the others are...but if that was the case, don't you think someone could claim membership and use that to get away with something truly terrible?

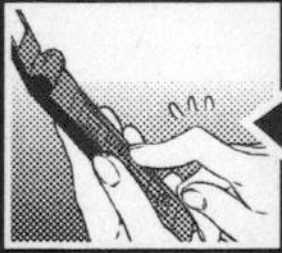

Saika: um

Saika: please dont fight

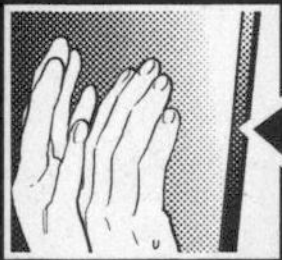

TarouTanaka: Uh, first, we're not fighting, lol.

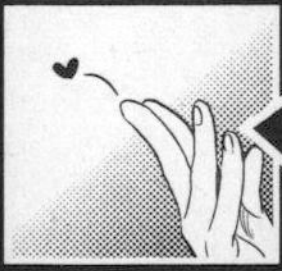

Kuru: Of course not. I do not have a single shred of personal hatred or anger toward TarouTanaka-san. The fact that we are members of the same chat room makes me like him enough to give him a kiss, in fact. Smooch!

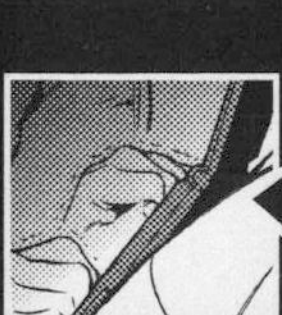

Mai: Gross.

Mai: Ouch.

Mai: I got pinched again.

Saika: im sorry

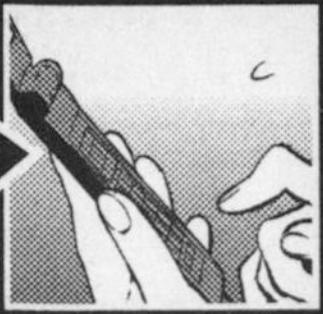

TarouTanaka: No, there's nothing to apologize for. Anyway, I haven't heard any bad rumors about the Dollars raising trouble in Ikebukuro, so it's probably not worth worrying about, okay?

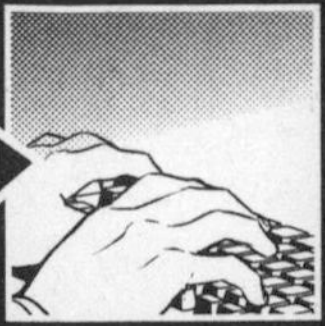

Kuru: But that's not the case. In fact, I understand that members of the Dollars have been picking fights with people from other prefectures.

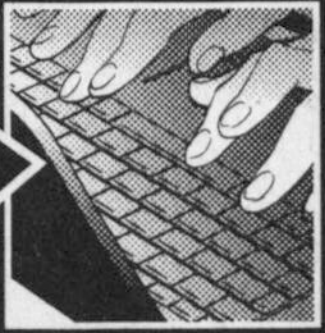

TarouTanaka: Huh?

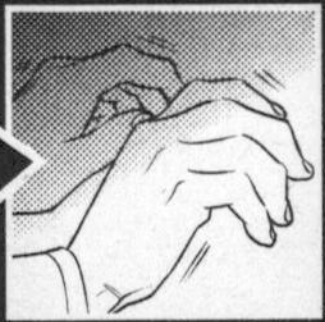

Kuru: In fact, it was less "picking" fights than "forcing" them. They just beat and beat and beat and beat and beat their victims, whether they wanted to fight or not. It must have been quite a sight.

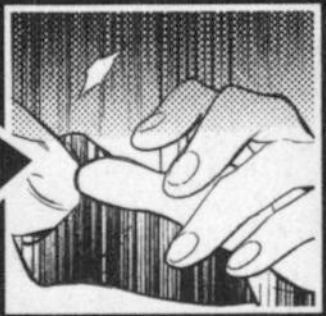

Mai: That the Dollars beat up some people from Saitama.

Mai: I heard that too.

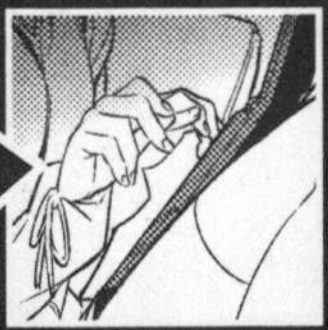

TarouTanaka: Is this true? Do you have a source for that info?

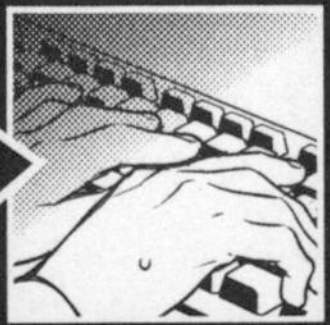

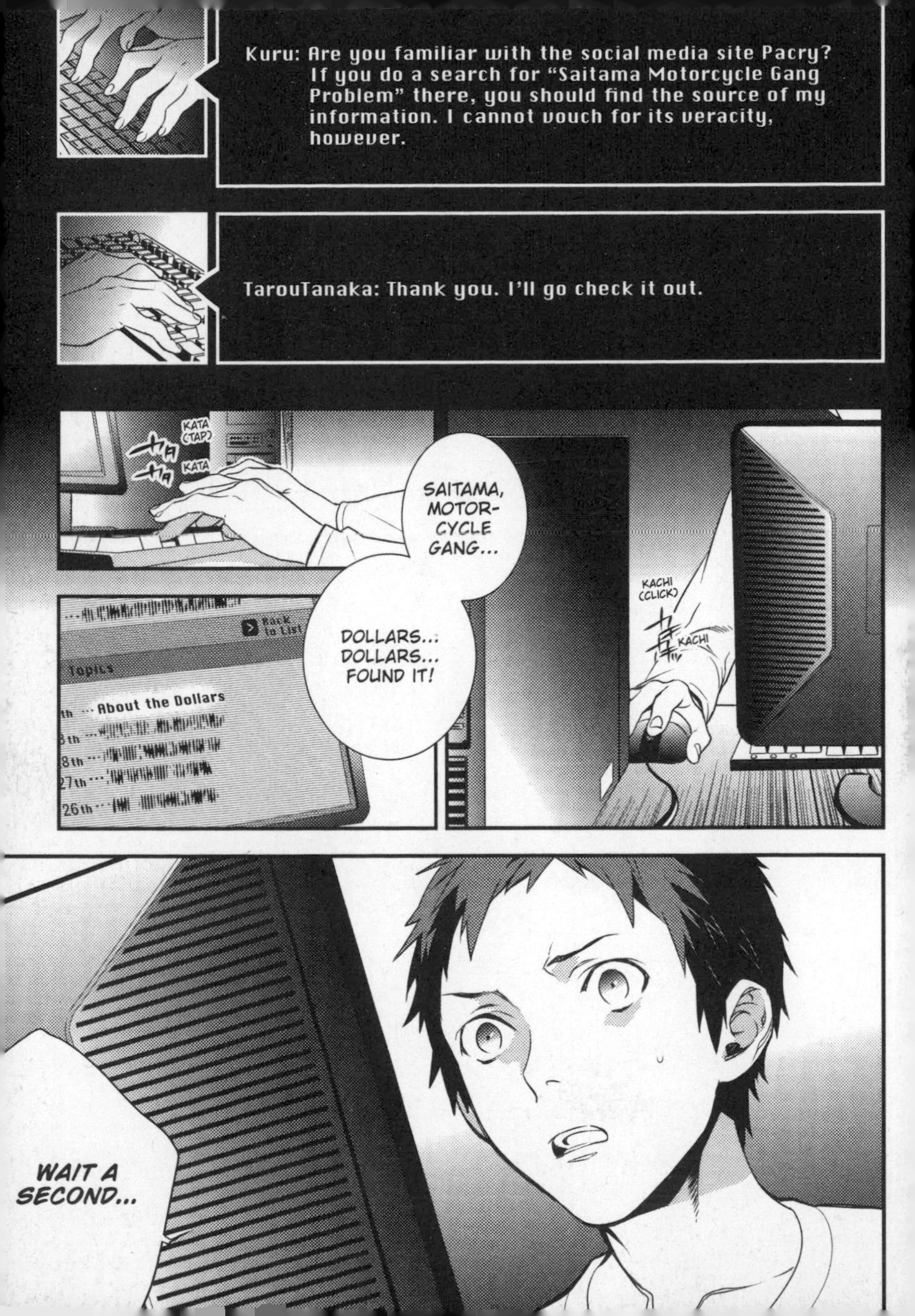
Kuru: Are you familiar with the social media site Pacry? If you do a search for "Saitama Motorcycle Gang Problem" there, you should find the source of my information. I cannot vouch for its veracity, however.
TarouTanaka: Thank you. I'll go check it out.
KACHI (CLICK)
KACHI
KATA (TAP)
KATA
SAITAMA, MOTORCYCLE GANG...
DOLLARS... DOLLARS... FOUND IT!
Back to List
Topics
About the Dollars
WAIT A SECOND...

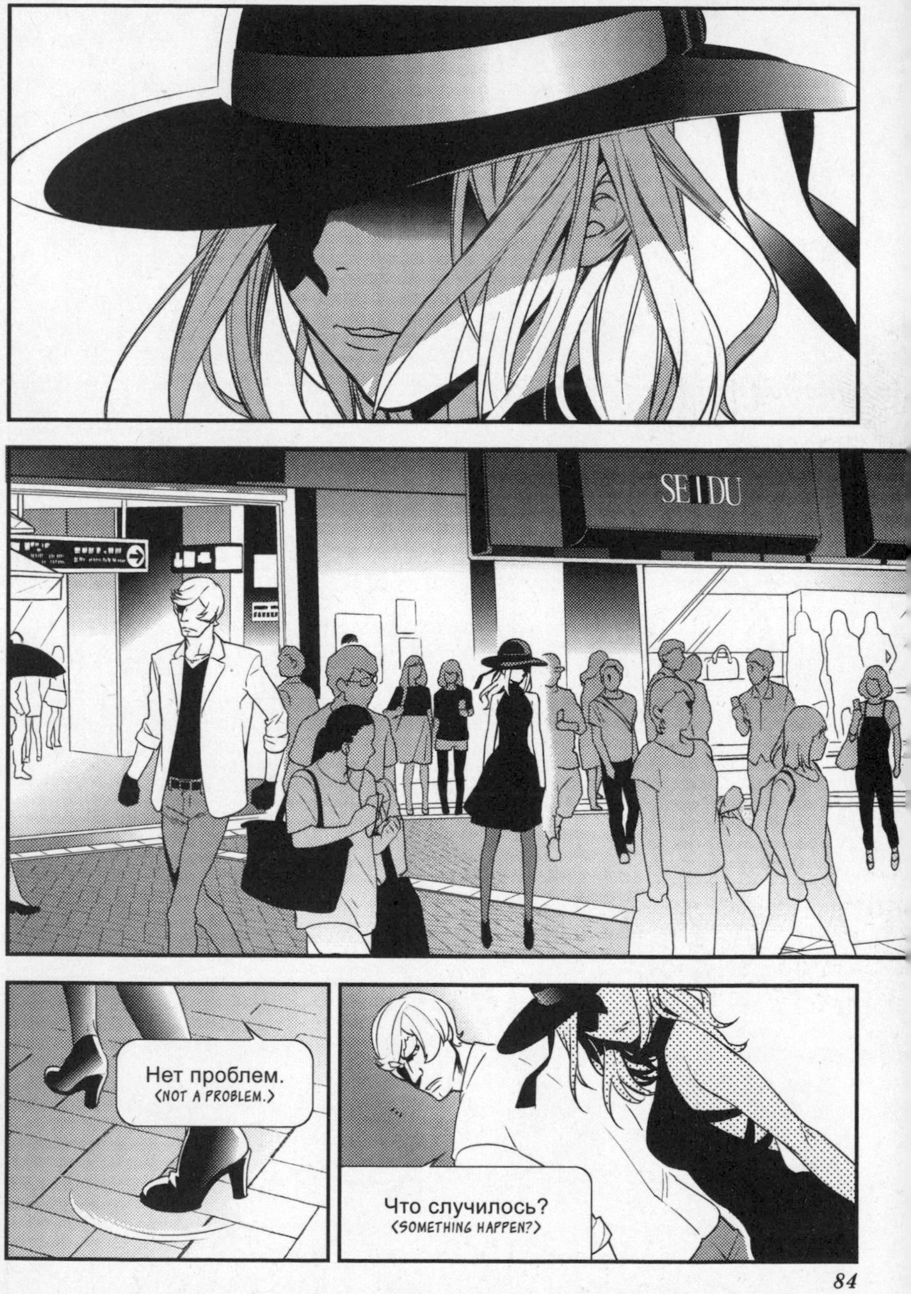
Что случилось?
⟨SOMETHING HAPPEN?⟩
Нет проблем.
⟨NOT A PROBLEM.⟩

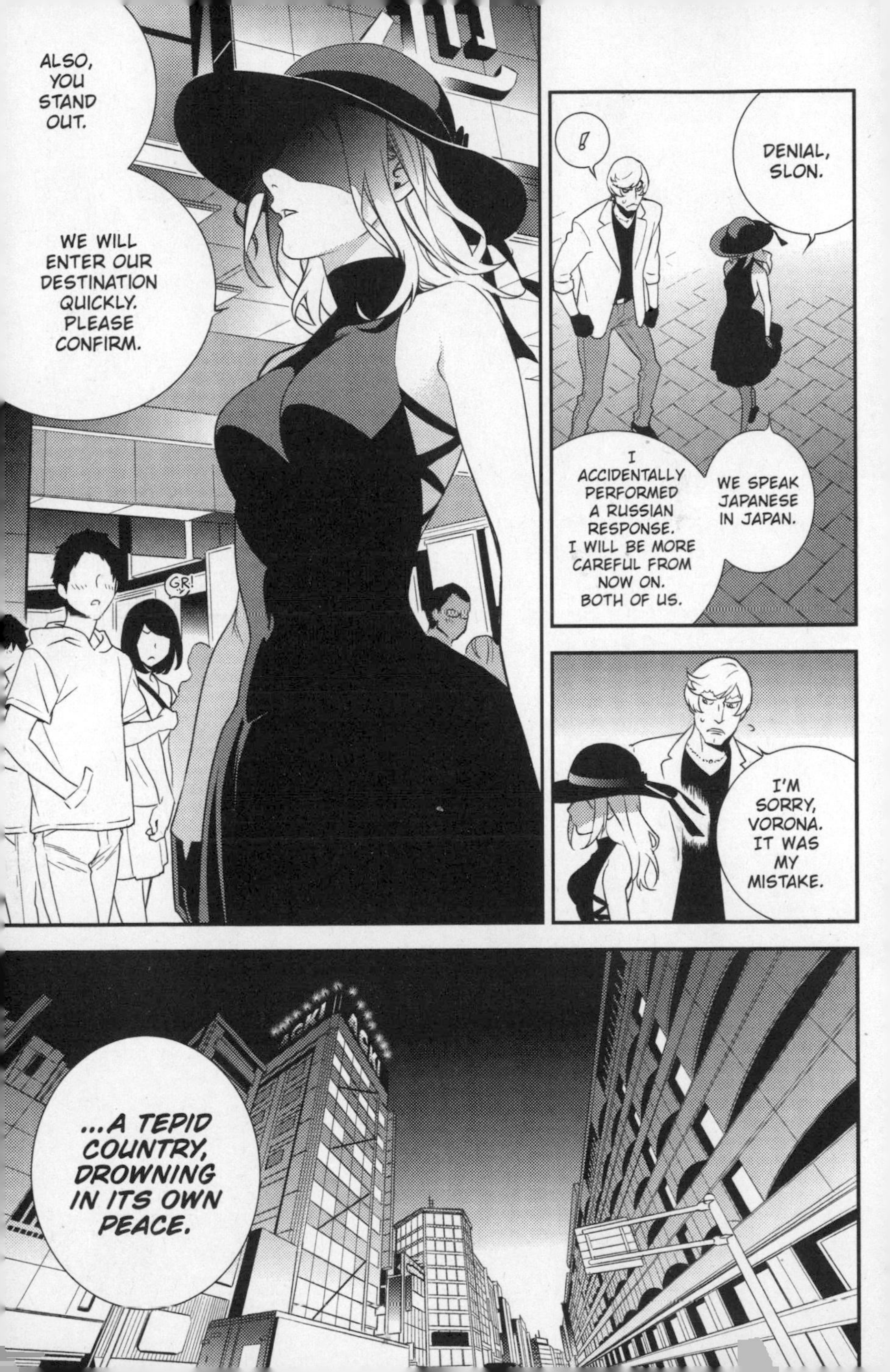
DENIAL, SLON.
!
WE SPEAK JAPANESE IN JAPAN.
I ACCIDENTALLY PERFORMED A RUSSIAN RESPONSE. I WILL BE MORE CAREFUL FROM NOW ON. BOTH OF US.
I'M SORRY, VORONA. IT WAS MY MISTAKE.
ALSO, YOU STAND OUT.
WE WILL ENTER OUR DESTINATION QUICKLY. PLEASE CONFIRM.
GR!
...A TEPID COUNTRY, DROWNING IN ITS OWN PEACE.

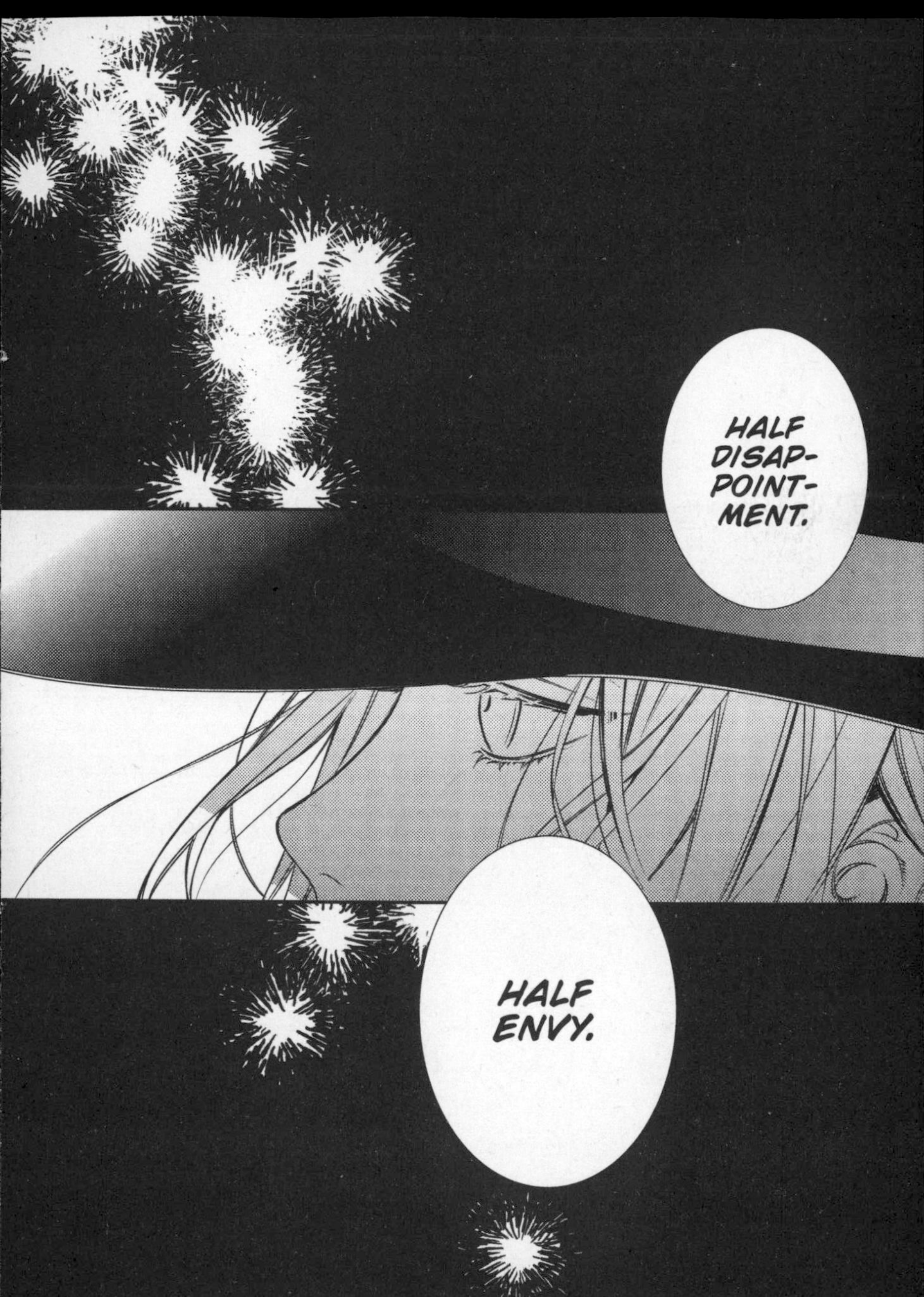
HALF DISAP-POINT-MENT.
HALF ENVY.

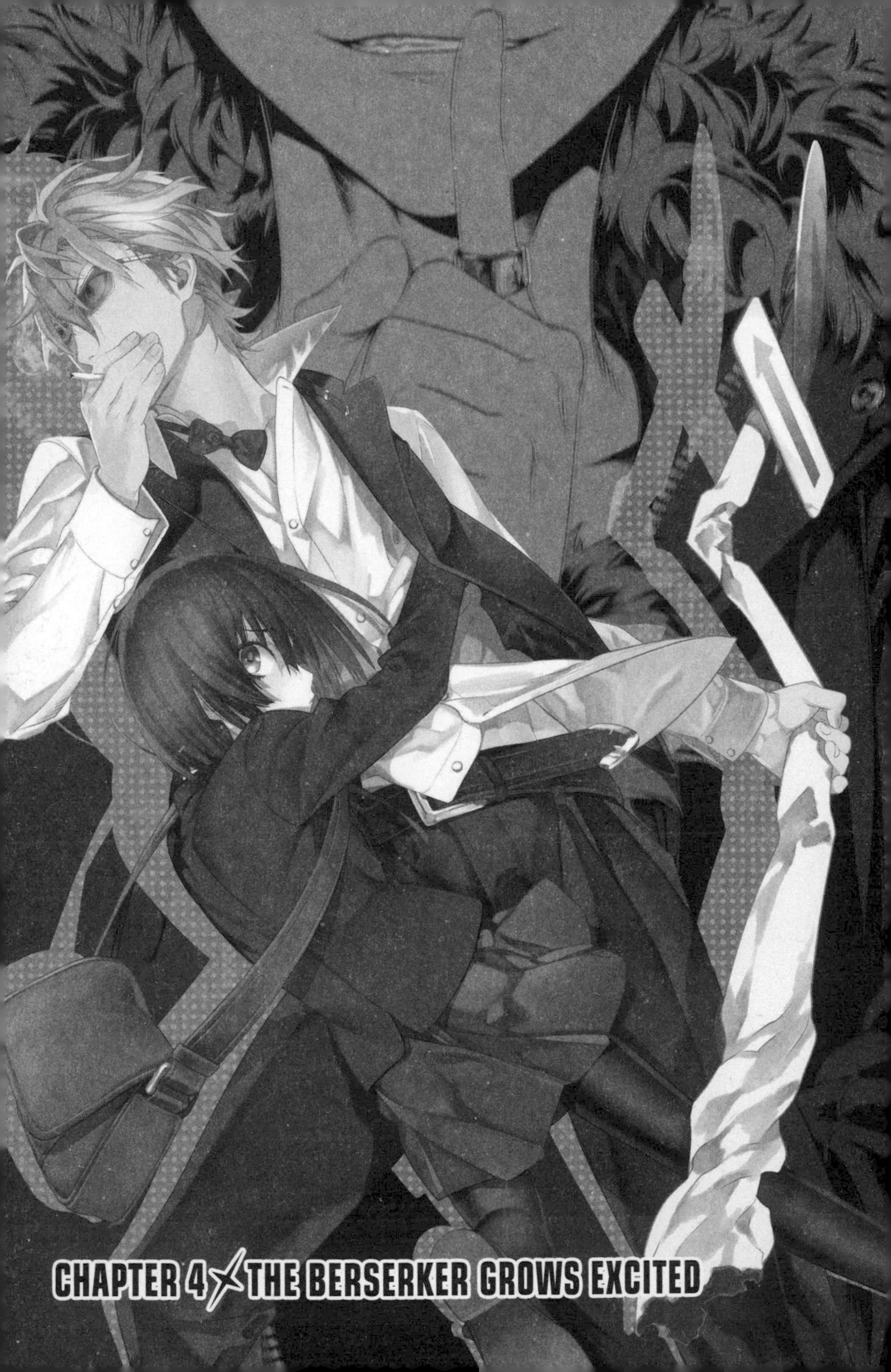

CHAPTER 4 THE BERSERKER GROWS EXCITED

DURARARA!!

DRRR!!

Re;Dollars Arc

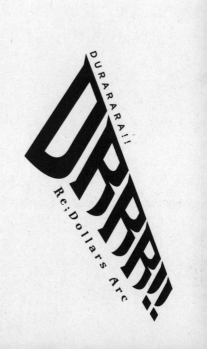

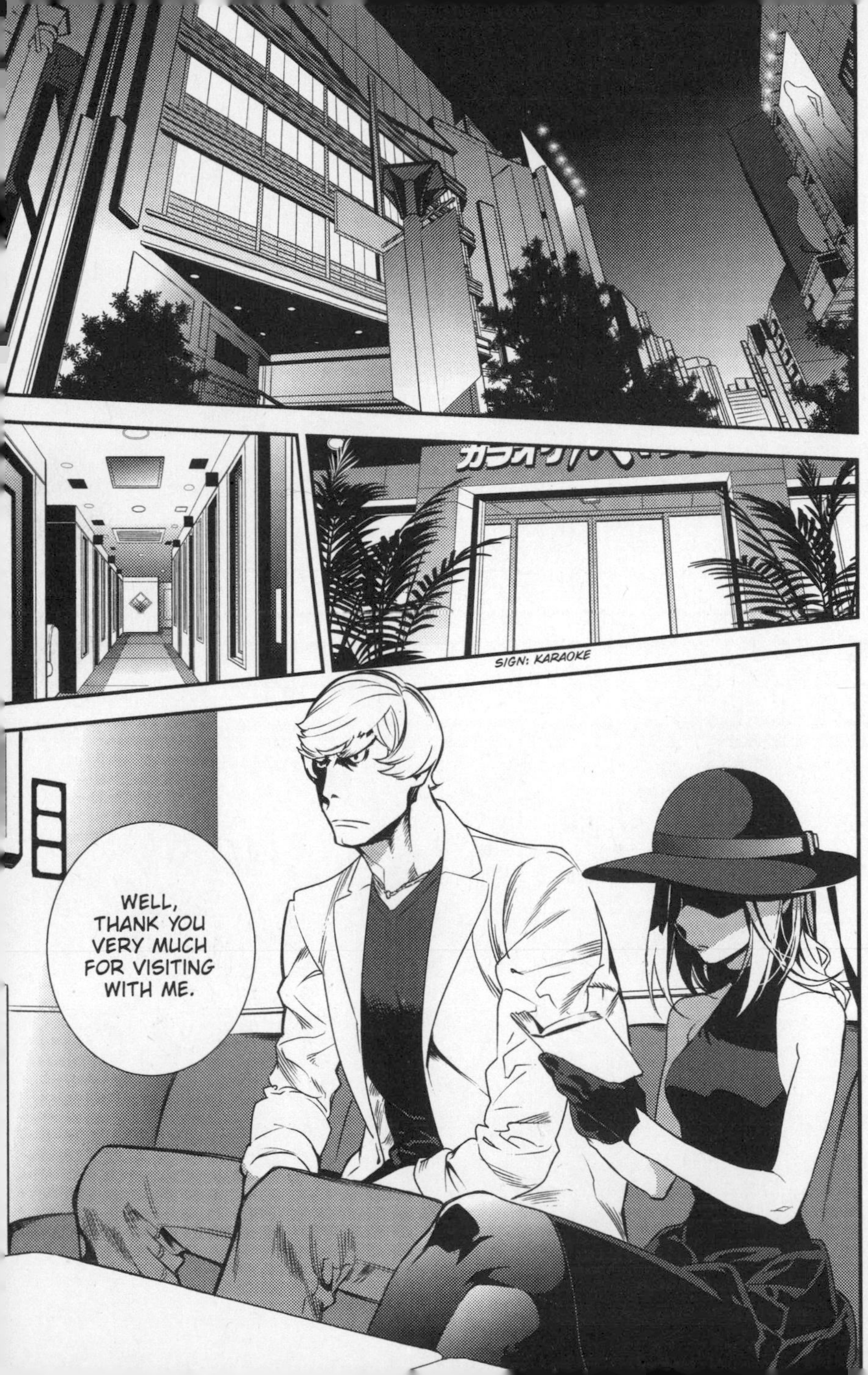
SIGN: KARAOKE
WELL, THANK YOU VERY MUCH FOR VISITING WITH ME.

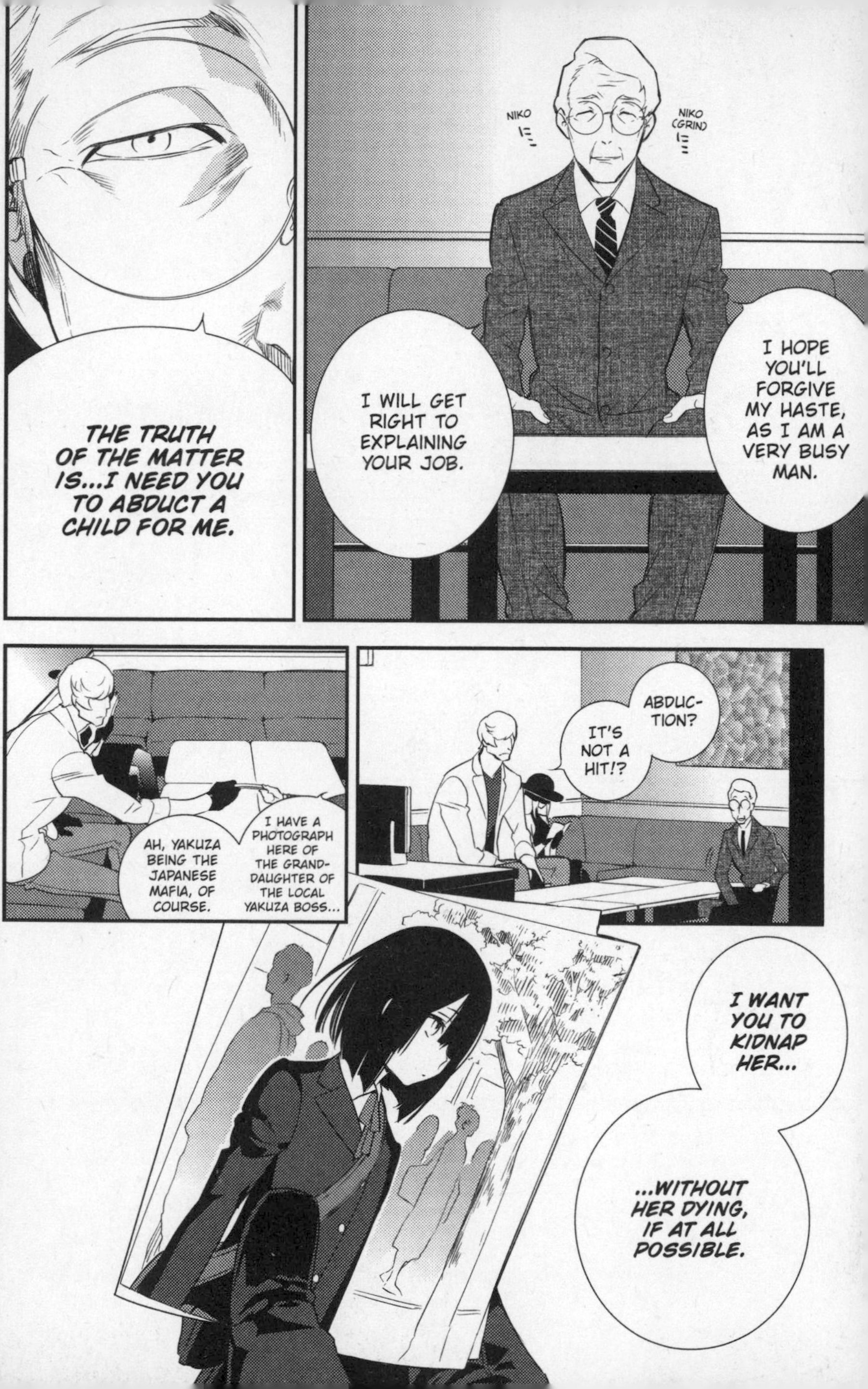
NIKO (GRIN)
NIKO
I HOPE YOU'LL FORGIVE MY HASTE, AS I AM A VERY BUSY MAN.
I WILL GET RIGHT TO EXPLAINING YOUR JOB.
THE TRUTH OF THE MATTER IS...I NEED YOU TO ABDUCT A CHILD FOR ME.
ABDUC-TION?
IT'S NOT A HIT!?
I HAVE A PHOTOGRAPH HERE OF THE GRAND-DAUGHTER OF THE LOCAL YAKUZA BOSS...
AH, YAKUZA BEING THE JAPANESE MAFIA, OF COURSE.
I WANT YOU TO KIDNAP HER...
...WITHOUT HER DYING, IF AT ALL POSSIBLE.

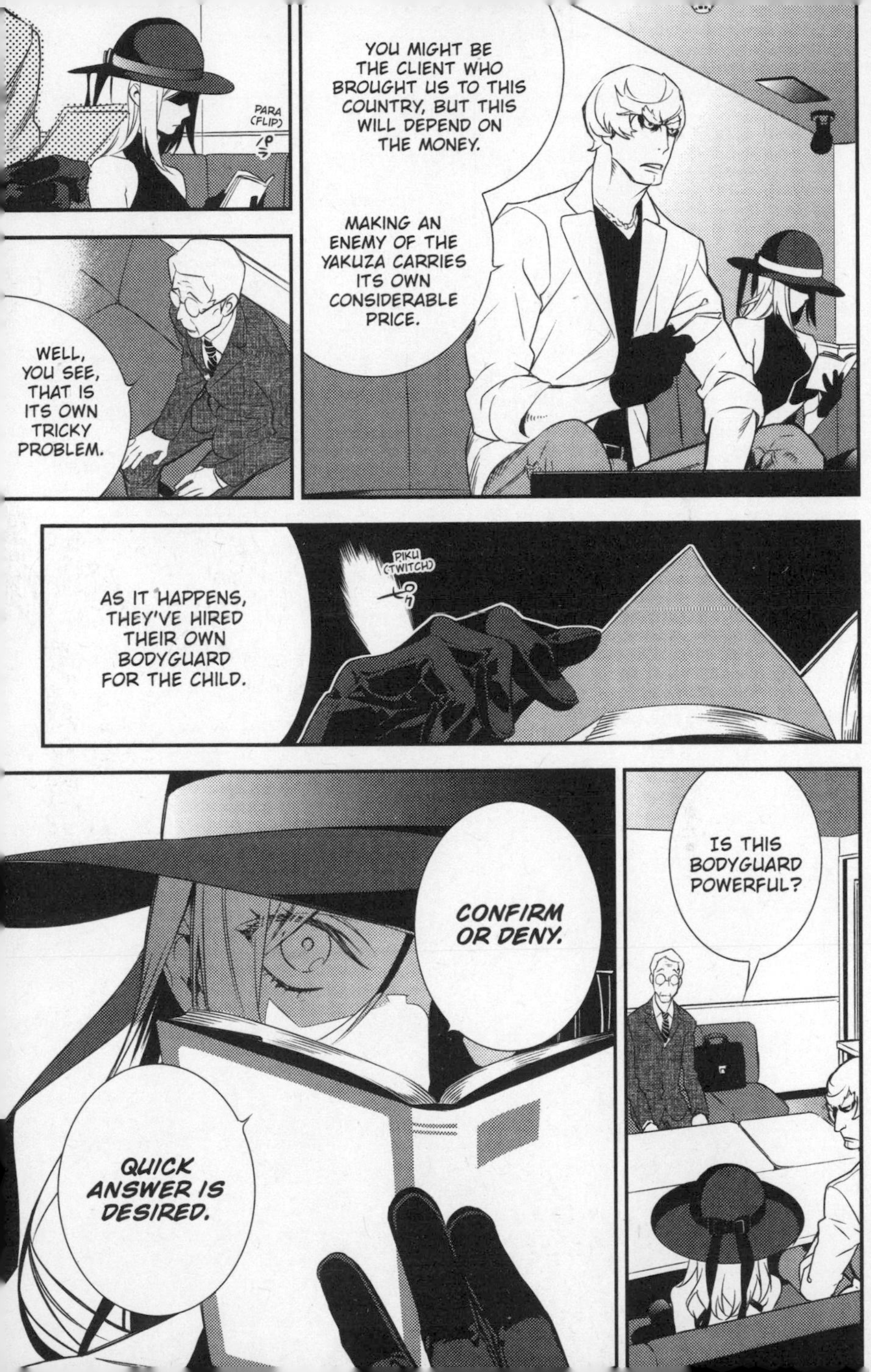

YOU MIGHT BE THE CLIENT WHO BROUGHT US TO THIS COUNTRY, BUT THIS WILL DEPEND ON THE MONEY.
MAKING AN ENEMY OF THE YAKUZA CARRIES ITS OWN CONSIDERABLE PRICE.
PARA (FLIP)
WELL, YOU SEE, THAT IS ITS OWN TRICKY PROBLEM.
PIKU (TWITCH)
AS IT HAPPENS, THEY'VE HIRED THEIR OWN BODYGUARD FOR THE CHILD.
IS THIS BODYGUARD POWERFUL?
CONFIRM OR DENY.
QUICK ANSWER IS DESIRED.

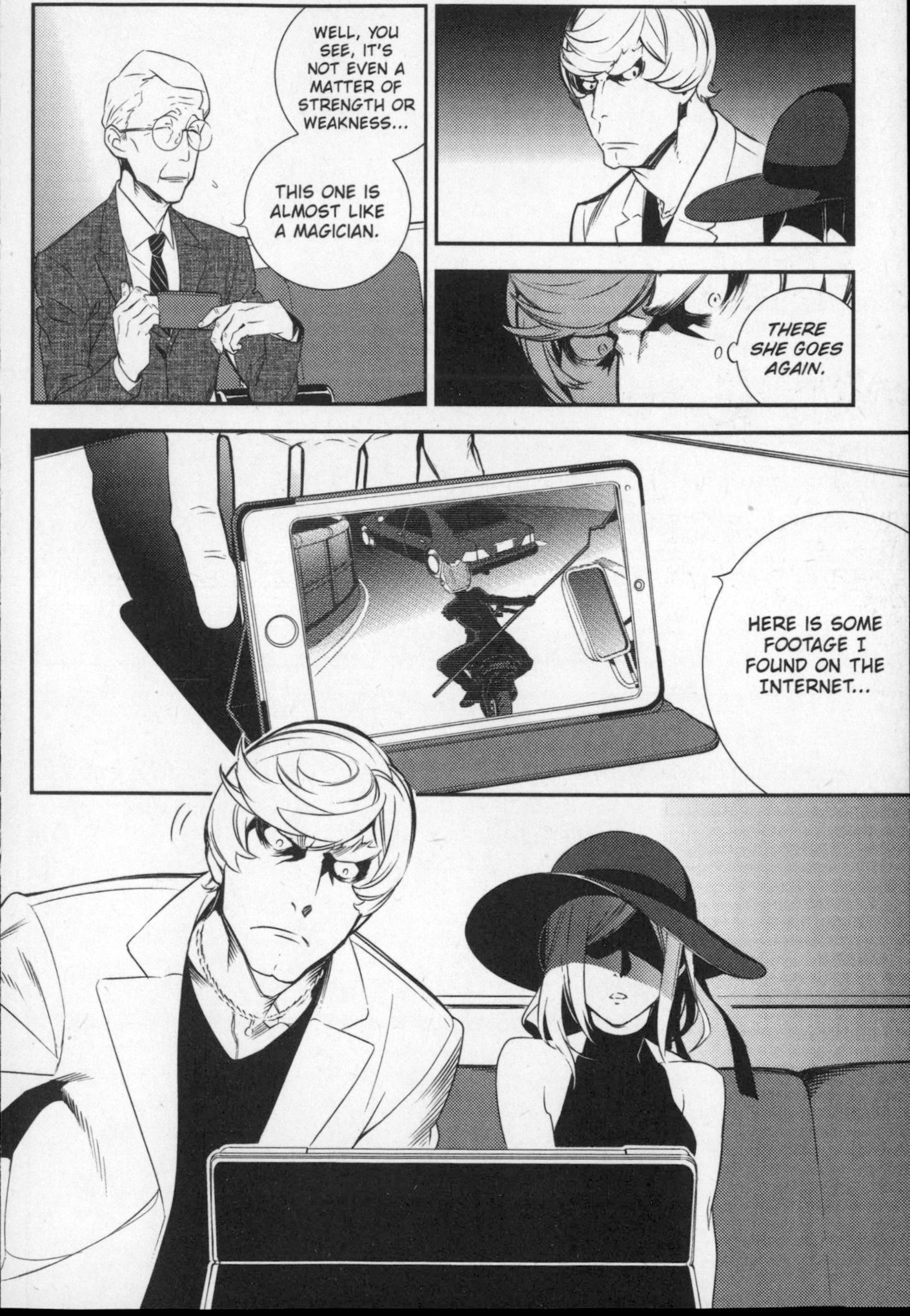
THERE SHE GOES AGAIN.
WELL, YOU SEE, IT'S NOT EVEN A MATTER OF STRENGTH OR WEAKNESS...
THIS ONE IS ALMOST LIKE A MAGICIAN.
HERE IS SOME FOOTAGE I FOUND ON THE INTERNET...

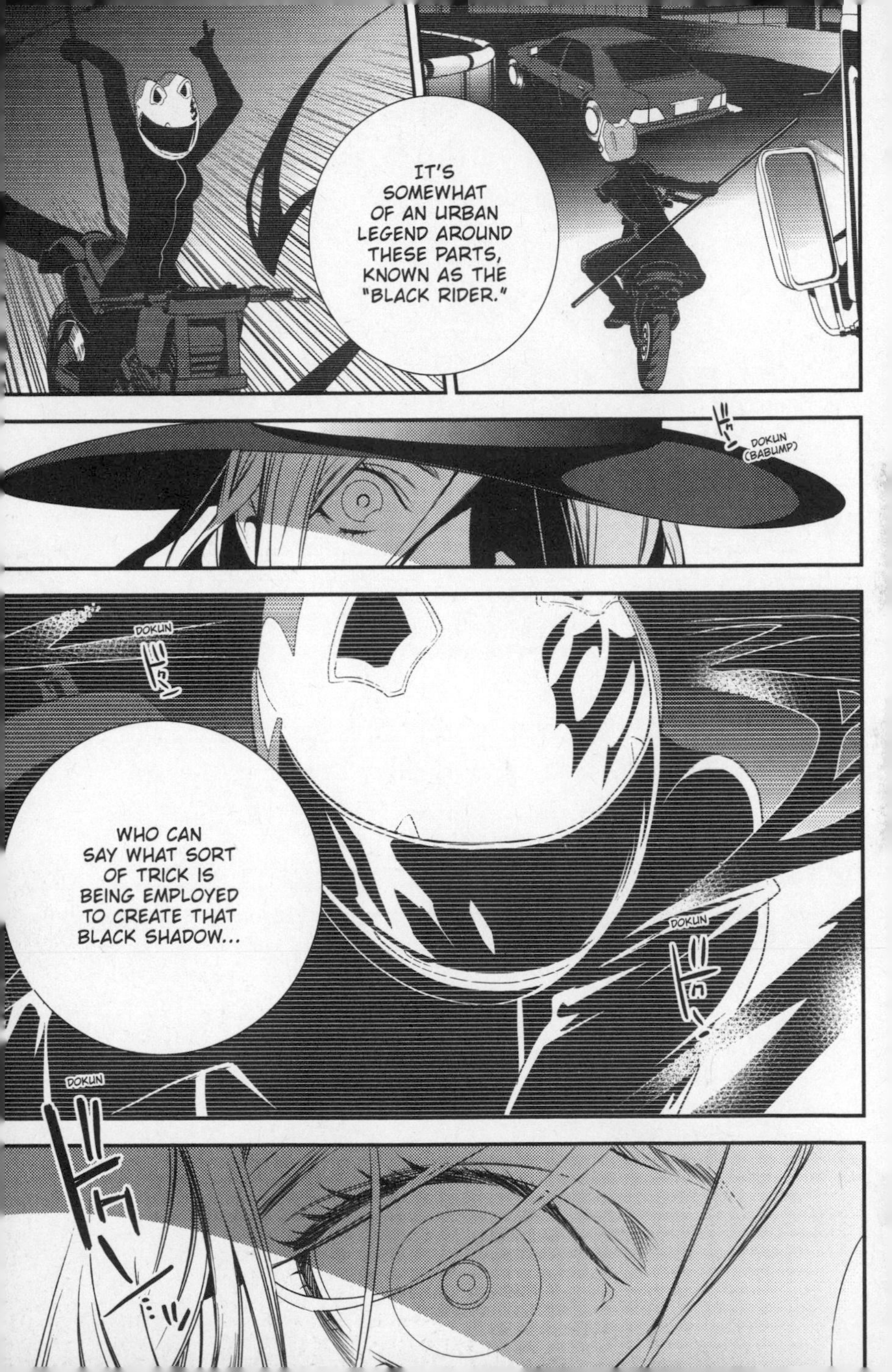
IT'S SOMEWHAT OF AN URBAN LEGEND AROUND THESE PARTS, KNOWN AS THE "BLACK RIDER."
DOKUN (BABUMP)
DOKUN
WHO CAN SAY WHAT SORT OF TRICK IS BEING EMPLOYED TO CREATE THAT BLACK SHADOW...
DOKUN
DOKUN

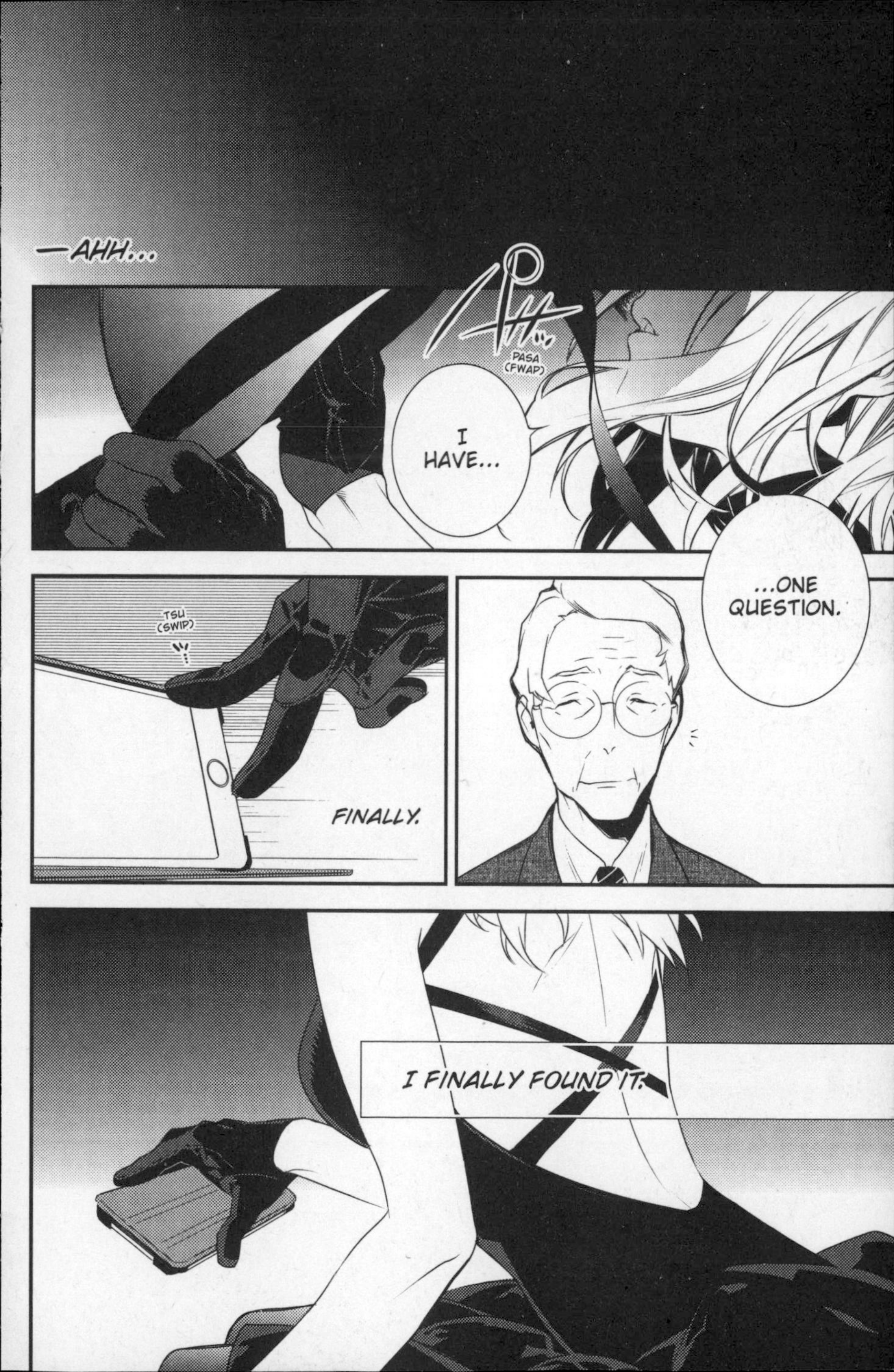
—AHH...
PASA (FWAP)
I HAVE...
...ONE QUESTION.
TSU (SWIP)
FINALLY.
I FINALLY FOUND IT.

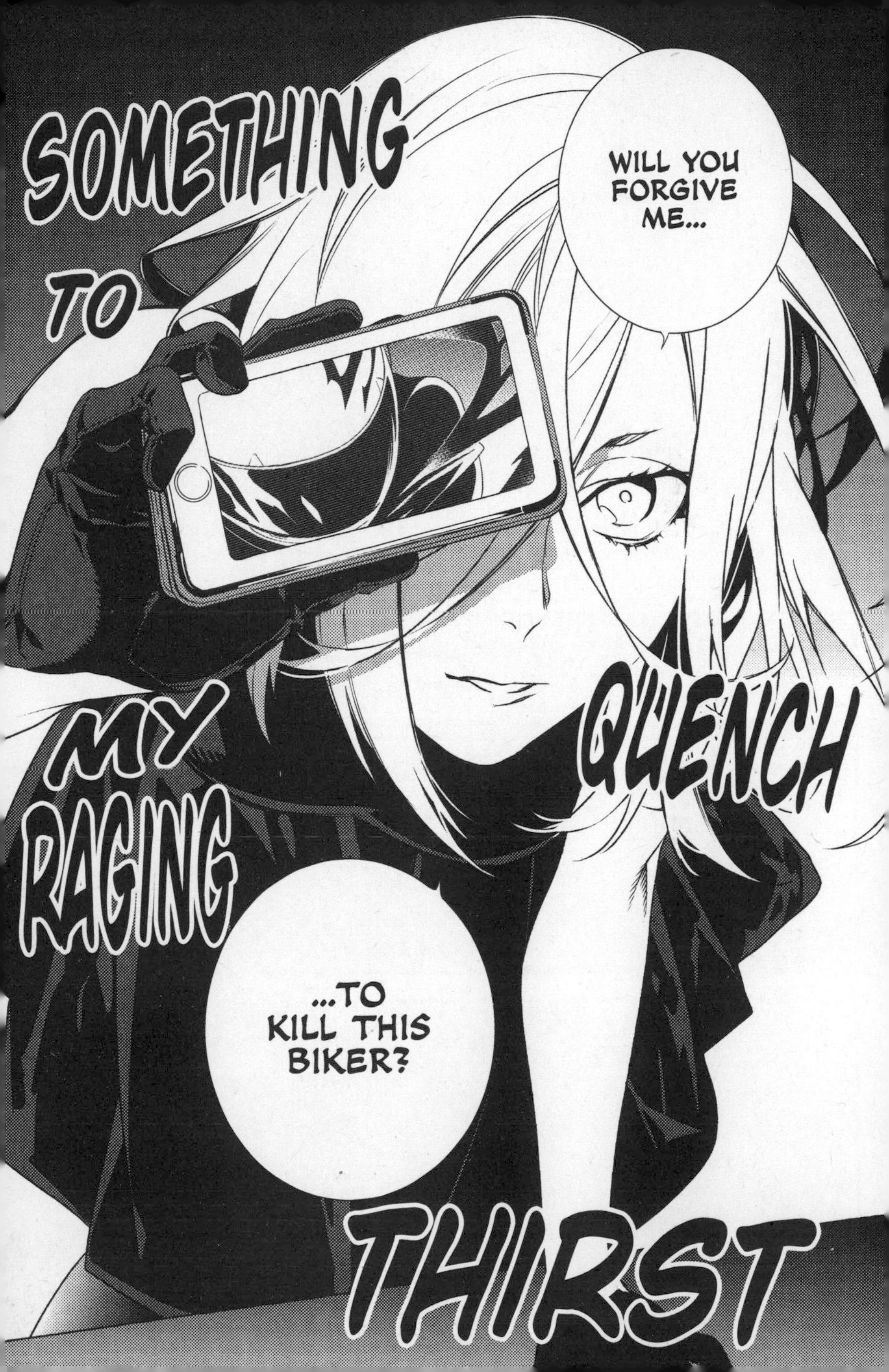
WILL YOU FORGIVE ME...
SOMETHING TO QUENCH MY RAGING THIRST
...TO KILL THIS BIKER?

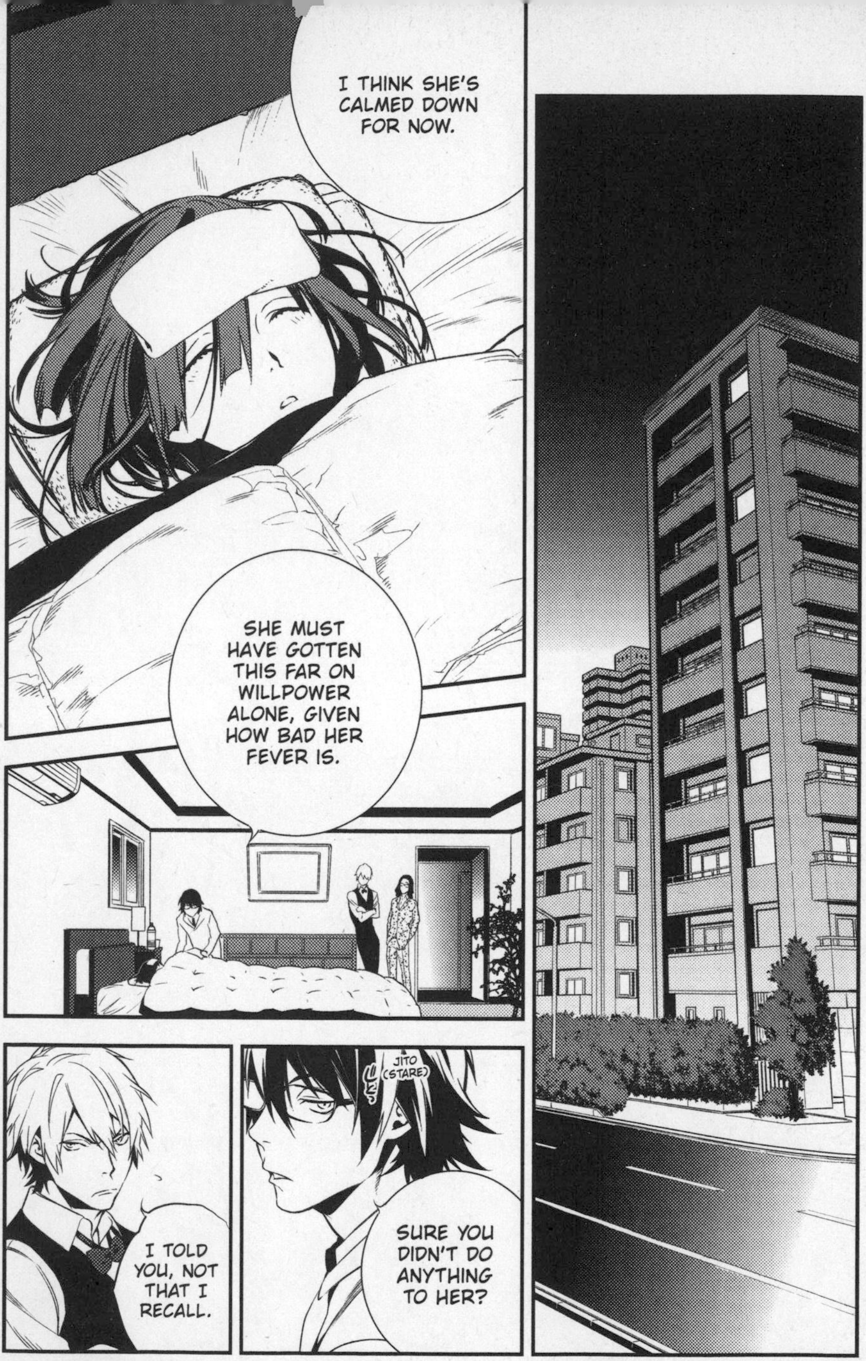
I THINK SHE'S CALMED DOWN FOR NOW.
SHE MUST HAVE GOTTEN THIS FAR ON WILLPOWER ALONE, GIVEN HOW BAD HER FEVER IS.
JITO (STARE)
SURE YOU DIDN'T DO ANYTHING TO HER?
I TOLD YOU, NOT THAT I RECALL.

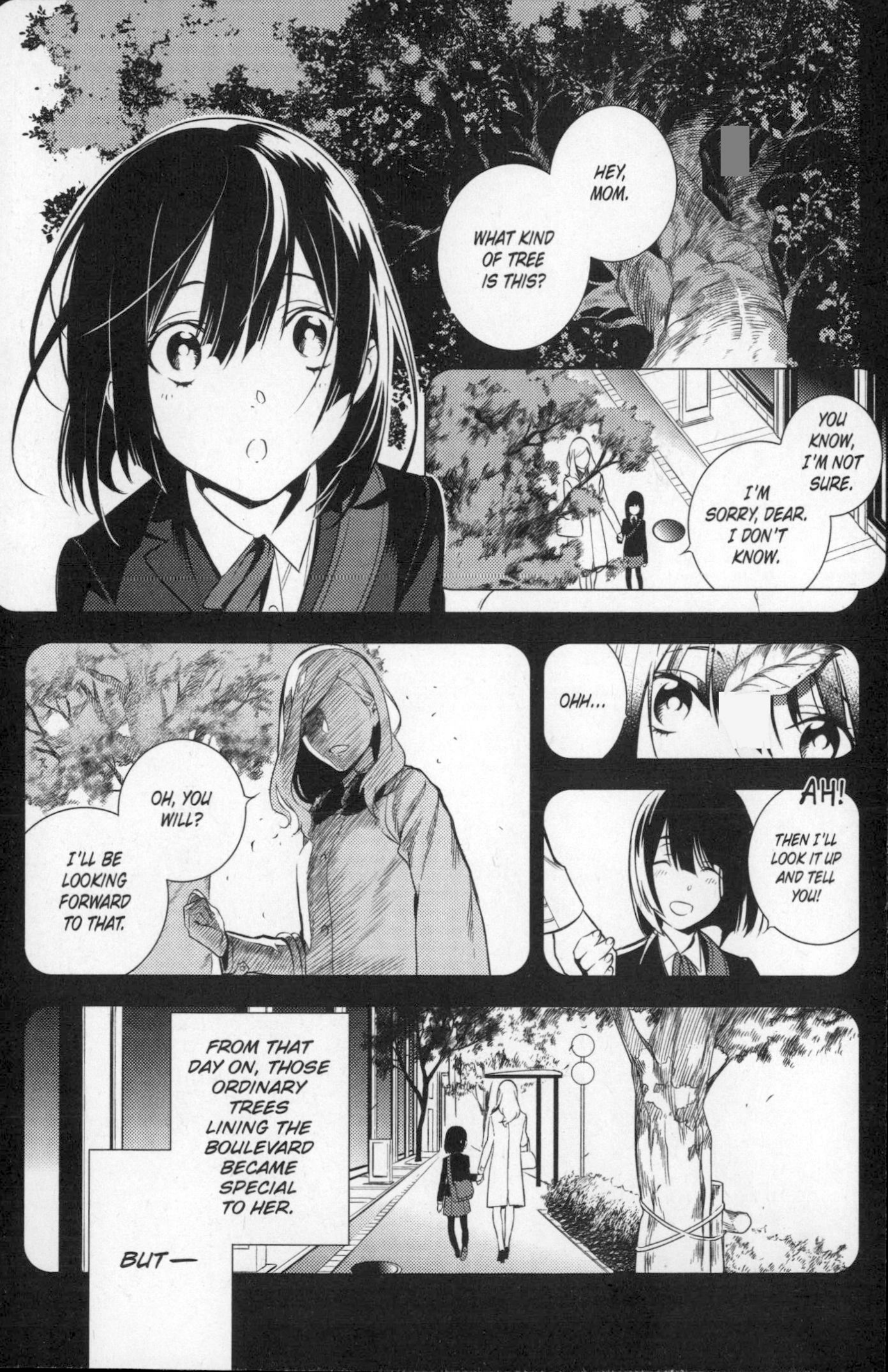
HEY, MOM.
WHAT KIND OF TREE IS THIS?
YOU KNOW, I'M NOT SURE.
I'M SORRY, DEAR. I DON'T KNOW.
OHH...
AH!
THEN I'LL LOOK IT UP AND TELL YOU!
OH, YOU WILL?
I'LL BE LOOKING FORWARD TO THAT.
FROM THAT DAY ON, THOSE ORDINARY TREES LINING THE BOULEVARD BECAME SPECIAL TO HER.
BUT—

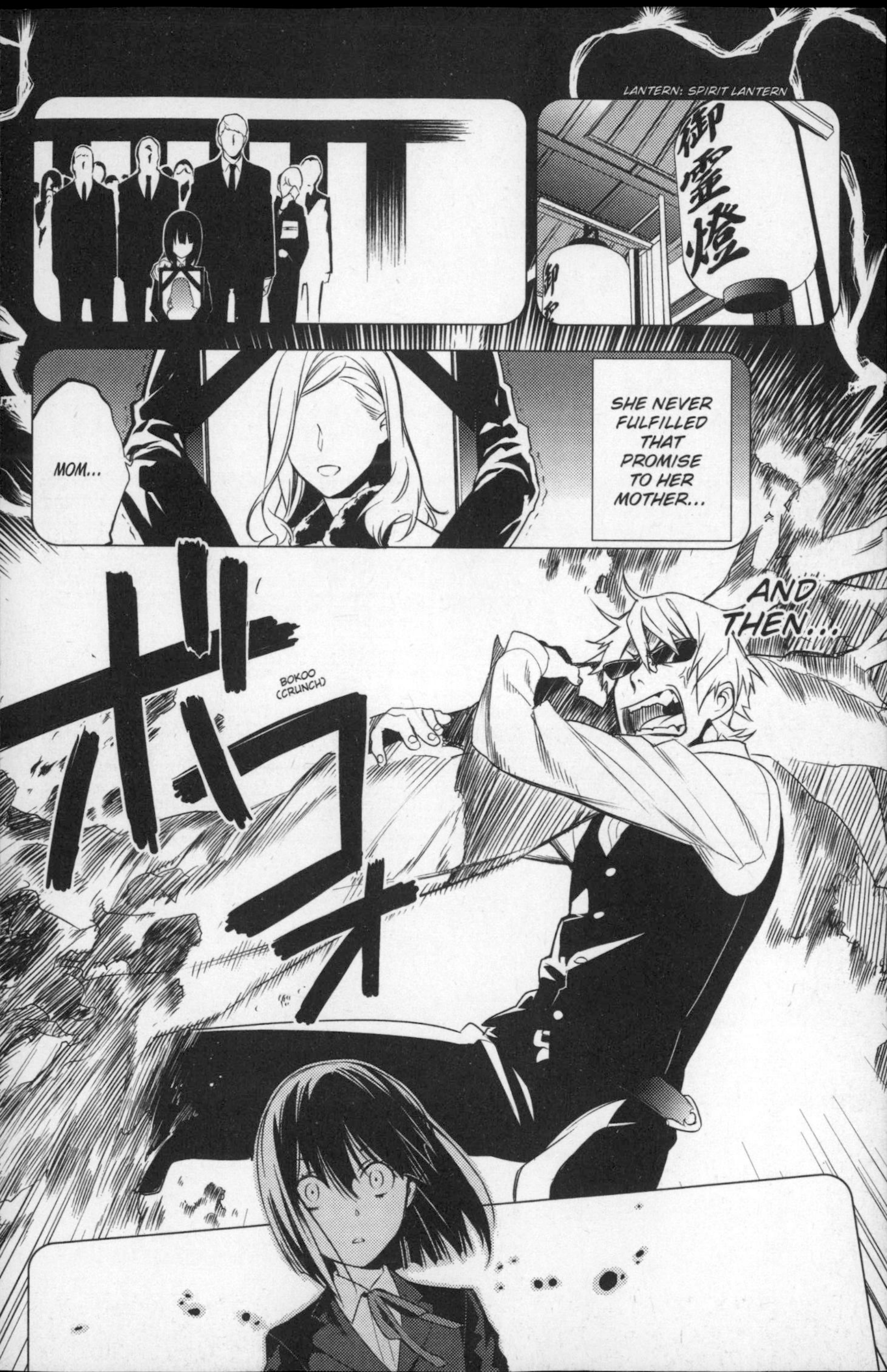
LANTERN: SPIRIT LANTERN
御霊燈
SHE NEVER FULFILLED THAT PROMISE TO HER MOTHER...
MOM...
AND THEN...
BOKOO (CRUNCH)
ボコォ

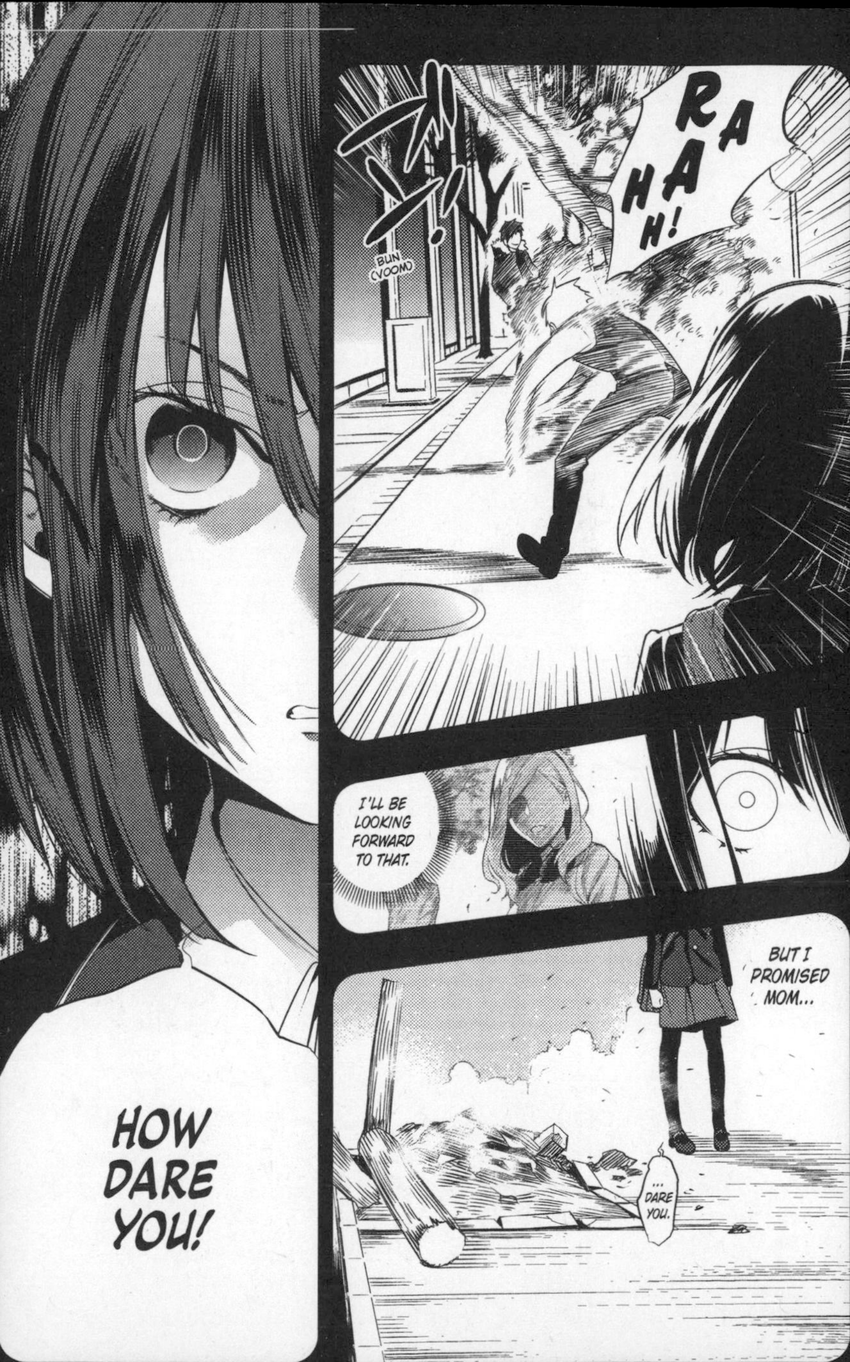
RAHH!
BUN (VOOM)
I'LL BE LOOKING FORWARD TO THAT.
BUT I PROMISED MOM...
...DARE YOU.
HOW DARE YOU!

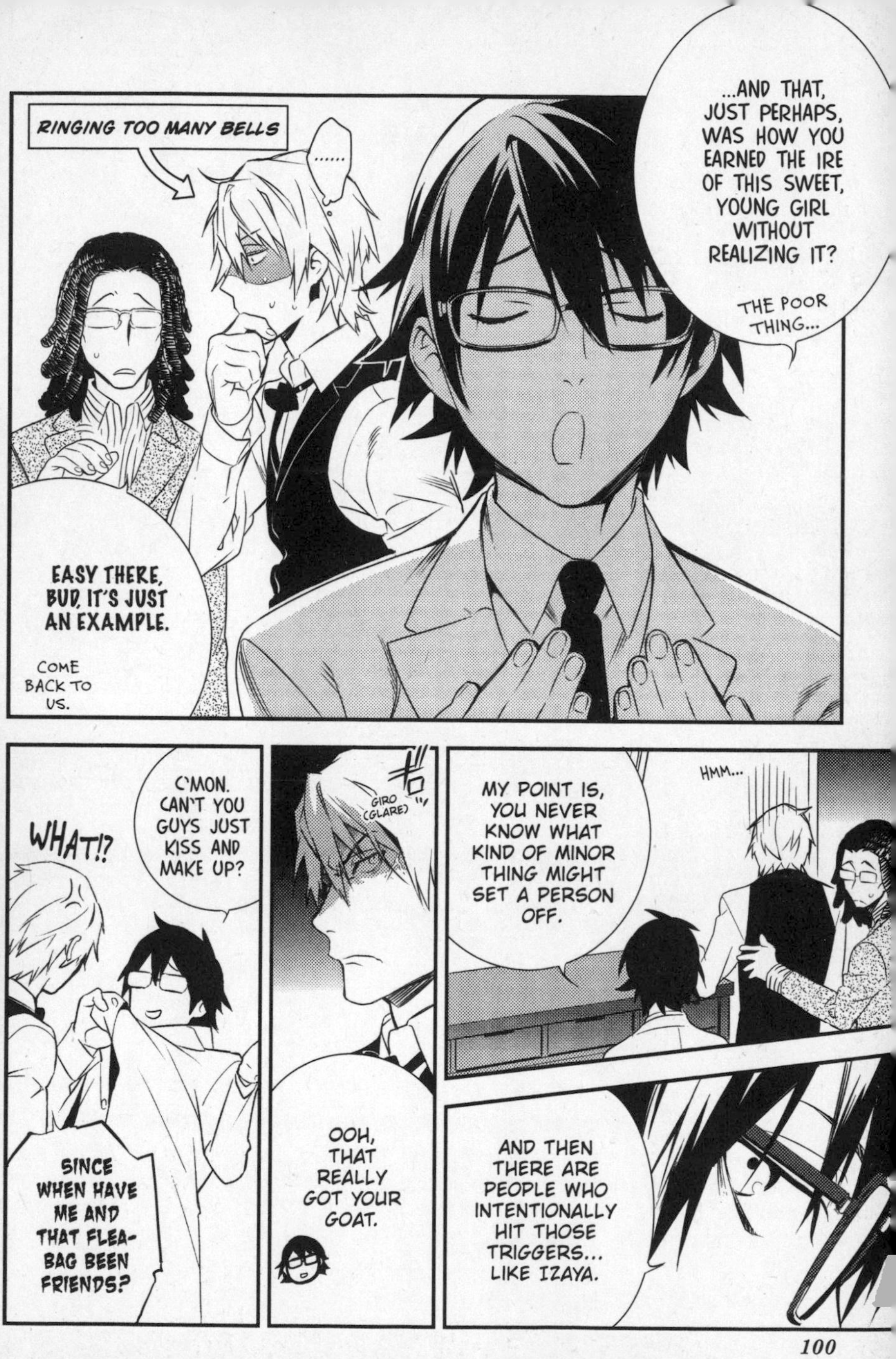
...AND THAT, JUST PERHAPS, WAS HOW YOU EARNED THE IRE OF THIS SWEET, YOUNG GIRL WITHOUT REALIZING IT?
THE POOR THING...
......
RINGING TOO MANY BELLS
EASY THERE, BUD, IT'S JUST AN EXAMPLE.
COME BACK TO US.
HMM...
MY POINT IS, YOU NEVER KNOW WHAT KIND OF MINOR THING MIGHT SET A PERSON OFF.
AND THEN THERE ARE PEOPLE WHO INTENTIONALLY HIT THOSE TRIGGERS... LIKE IZAYA.
GIRO (GLARE)
OOH, THAT REALLY GOT YOUR GOAT.
C'MON. CAN'T YOU GUYS JUST KISS AND MAKE UP?
WHAT!?
SINCE WHEN HAVE ME AND THAT FLEA-BAG BEEN FRIENDS?

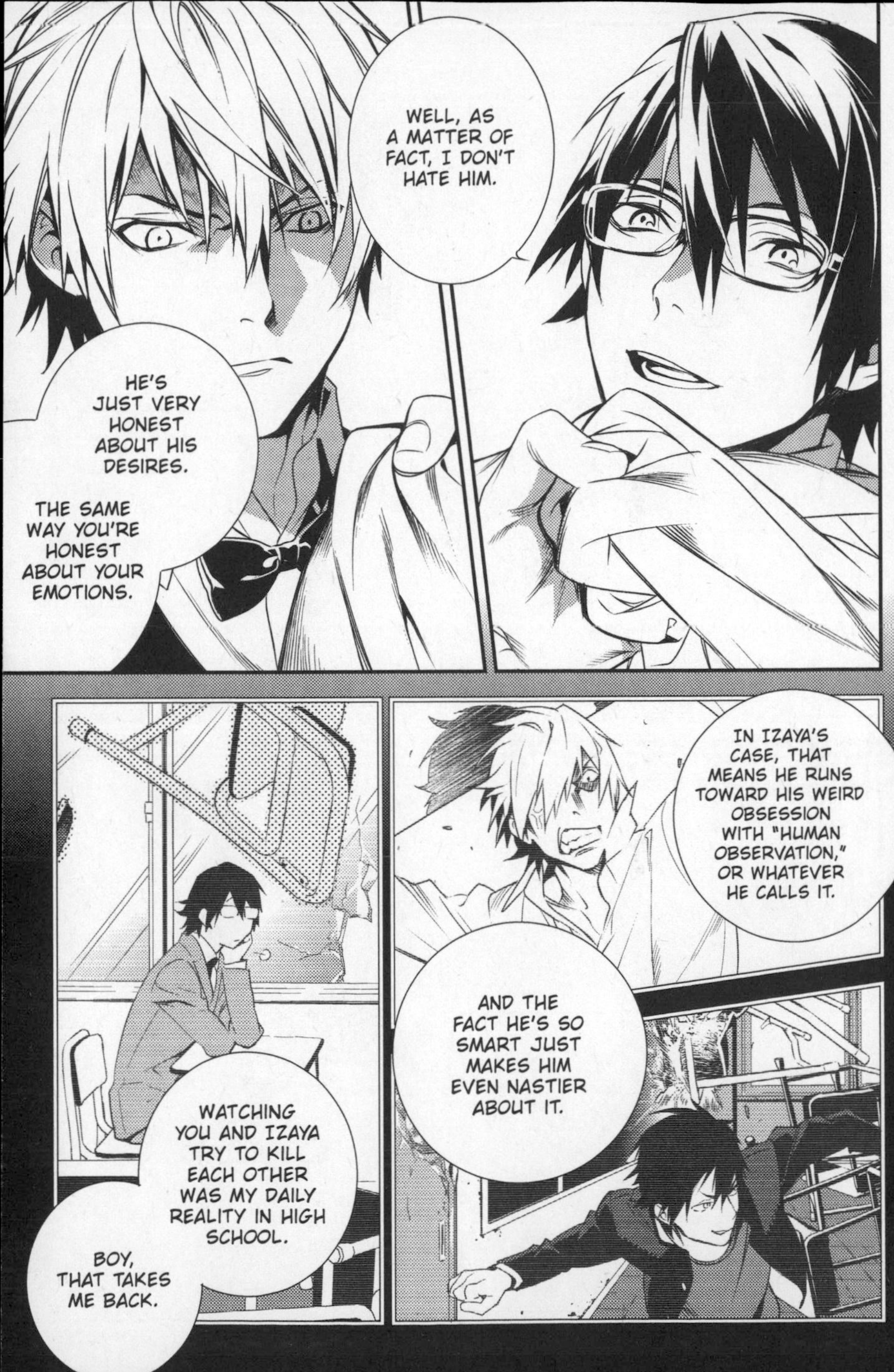
WELL, AS A MATTER OF FACT, I DON'T HATE HIM.
HE'S JUST VERY HONEST ABOUT HIS DESIRES.
THE SAME WAY YOU'RE HONEST ABOUT YOUR EMOTIONS.
IN IZAYA'S CASE, THAT MEANS HE RUNS TOWARD HIS WEIRD OBSESSION WITH "HUMAN OBSERVATION," OR WHATEVER HE CALLS IT.
AND THE FACT HE'S SO SMART JUST MAKES HIM EVEN NASTIER ABOUT IT.
WATCHING YOU AND IZAYA TRY TO KILL EACH OTHER WAS MY DAILY REALITY IN HIGH SCHOOL.
BOY, THAT TAKES ME BACK.

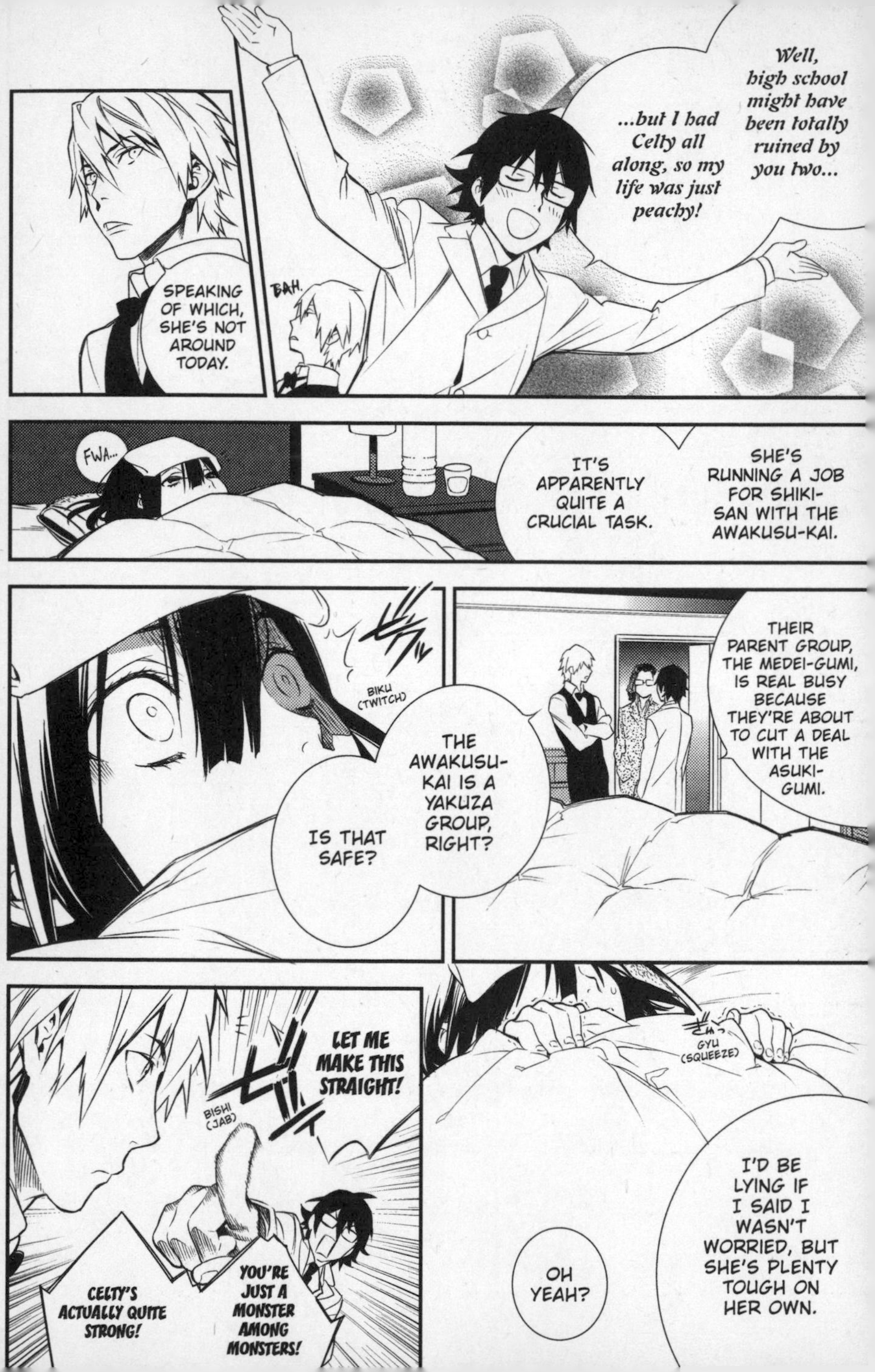
Well, high school might have been totally ruined by you two...
...but I had Celty all along, so my life was just peachy!
BAH.
SPEAKING OF WHICH, SHE'S NOT AROUND TODAY.
SHE'S RUNNING A JOB FOR SHIKI-SAN WITH THE AWAKUSU-KAI.
IT'S APPARENTLY QUITE A CRUCIAL TASK.
FWA...
THEIR PARENT GROUP, THE MEDEI-GUMI, IS REAL BUSY BECAUSE THEY'RE ABOUT TO CUT A DEAL WITH THE ASUKI-GUMI.
BIKU (TWITCH)
THE AWAKUSU-KAI IS A YAKUZA GROUP, RIGHT?
IS THAT SAFE?
GYU (SQUEEZE)
I'D BE LYING IF I SAID I WASN'T WORRIED, BUT SHE'S PLENTY TOUGH ON HER OWN.
OH YEAH?
LET ME MAKE THIS STRAIGHT!
BISHI (JAB)
YOU'RE JUST A MONSTER AMONG MONSTERS!
CELTY'S ACTUALLY QUITE STRONG!

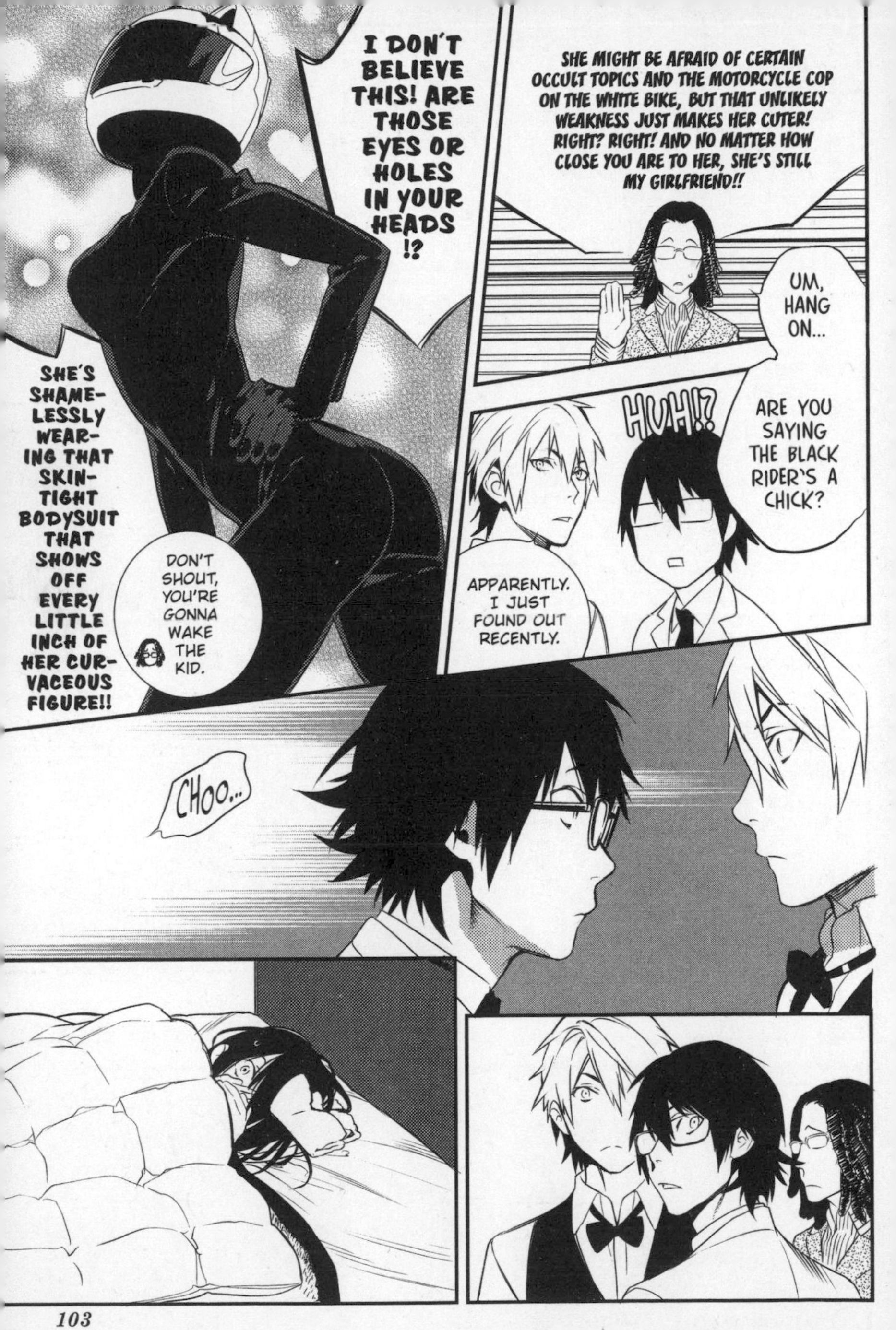
SHE MIGHT BE AFRAID OF CERTAIN OCCULT TOPICS AND THE MOTORCYCLE COP ON THE WHITE BIKE, BUT THAT UNLIKELY WEAKNESS JUST MAKES HER CUTER! RIGHT? RIGHT! AND NO MATTER HOW CLOSE YOU ARE TO HER, SHE'S STILL MY GIRLFRIEND!!
UM, HANG ON...
HUH!?
ARE YOU SAYING THE BLACK RIDER'S A CHICK?
APPARENTLY. I JUST FOUND OUT RECENTLY.
I DON'T BELIEVE THIS! ARE THOSE EYES OR HOLES IN YOUR HEADS!?
SHE'S SHAMELESSLY WEARING THAT SKIN-TIGHT BODYSUIT THAT SHOWS OFF EVERY LITTLE INCH OF HER CURVACEOUS FIGURE!!
DON'T SHOUT, YOU'RE GONNA WAKE THE KID.
CHOO...

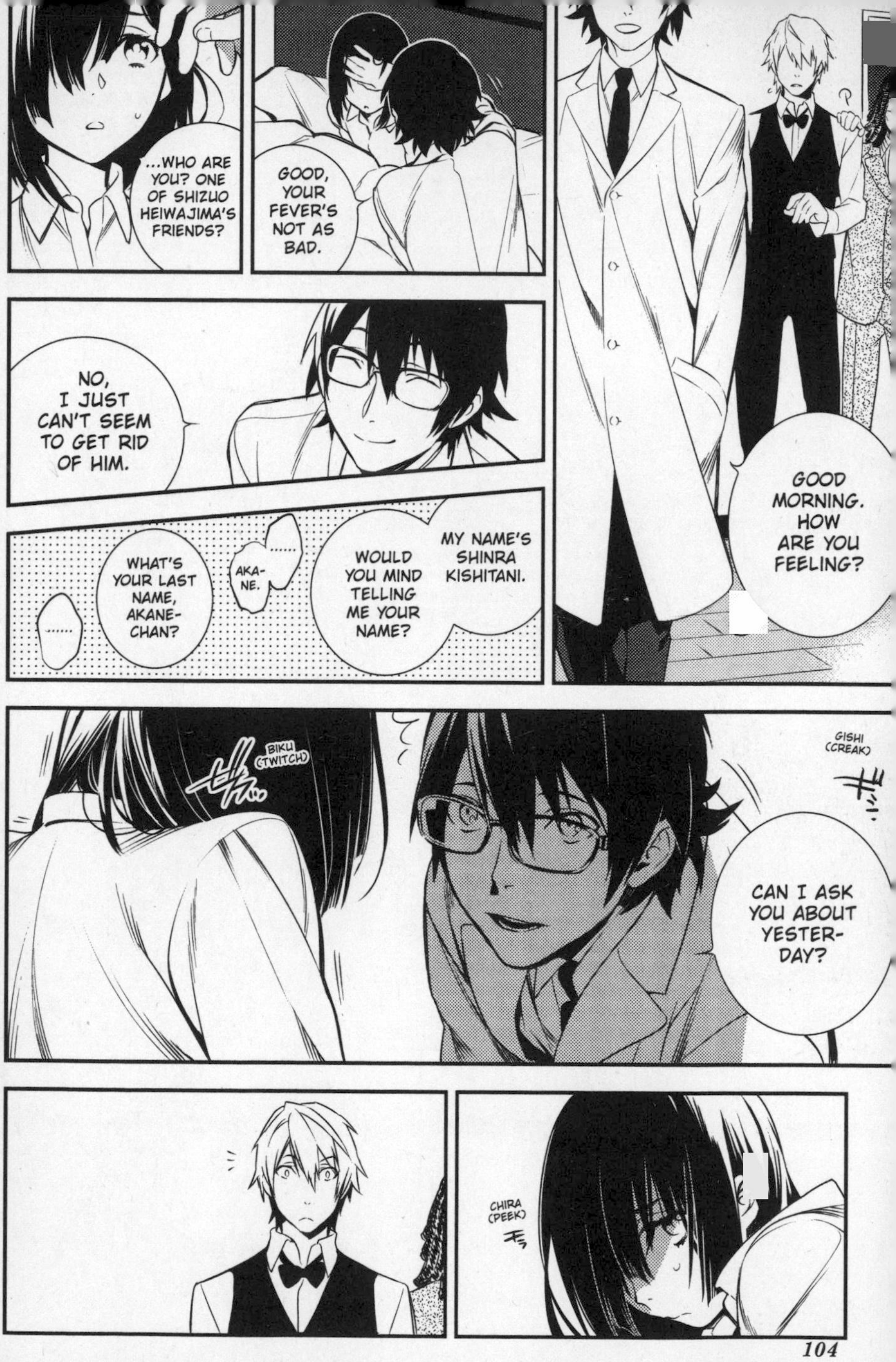
GOOD MORNING. HOW ARE YOU FEELING?
GOOD, YOUR FEVER'S NOT AS BAD.
...WHO ARE YOU? ONE OF SHIZUO HEIWAJIMA'S FRIENDS?
NO, I JUST CAN'T SEEM TO GET RID OF HIM.
MY NAME'S SHINRA KISHITANI.
WOULD YOU MIND TELLING ME YOUR NAME?
......
AKA-NE.
WHAT'S YOUR LAST NAME, AKANE-CHAN?
......
GISHI (CREAK)
CAN I ASK YOU ABOUT YESTER-DAY?
BIKU (TWITCH)
CHIRA (PEEK)

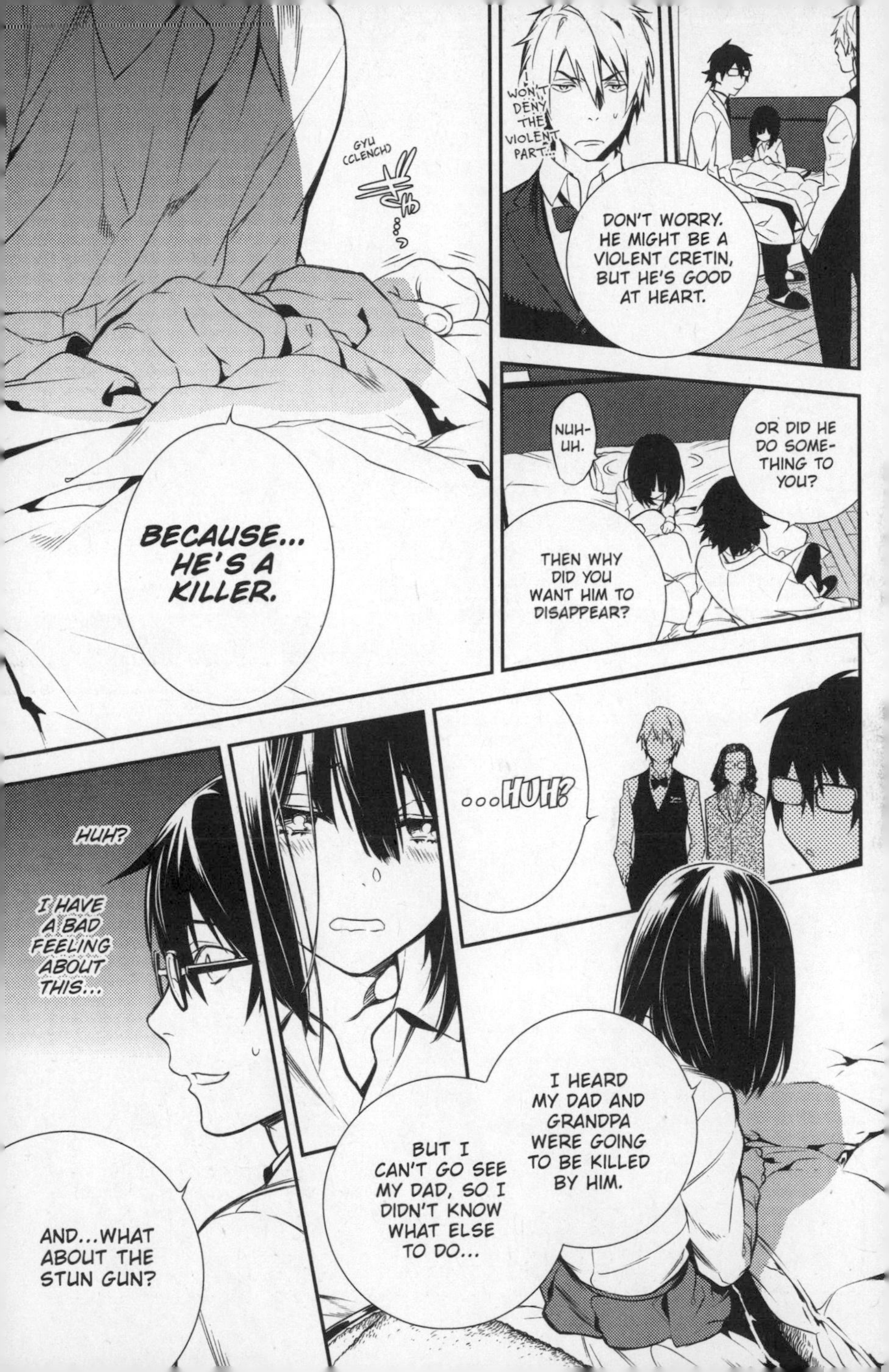
DON'T WORRY. HE MIGHT BE A VIOLENT CRETIN, BUT HE'S GOOD AT HEART.
I WON'T DENY THE VIOLENT PART...
OR DID HE DO SOMETHING TO YOU?
NUH-UH.
THEN WHY DID YOU WANT HIM TO DISAPPEAR?
GYU (CLENCH)
BECAUSE... HE'S A KILLER.
...HUH?
I HEARD MY DAD AND GRANDPA WERE GOING TO BE KILLED BY HIM.
BUT I CAN'T GO SEE MY DAD, SO I DIDN'T KNOW WHAT ELSE TO DO...
HUH?
I HAVE A BAD FEELING ABOUT THIS...
AND...WHAT ABOUT THE STUN GUN?

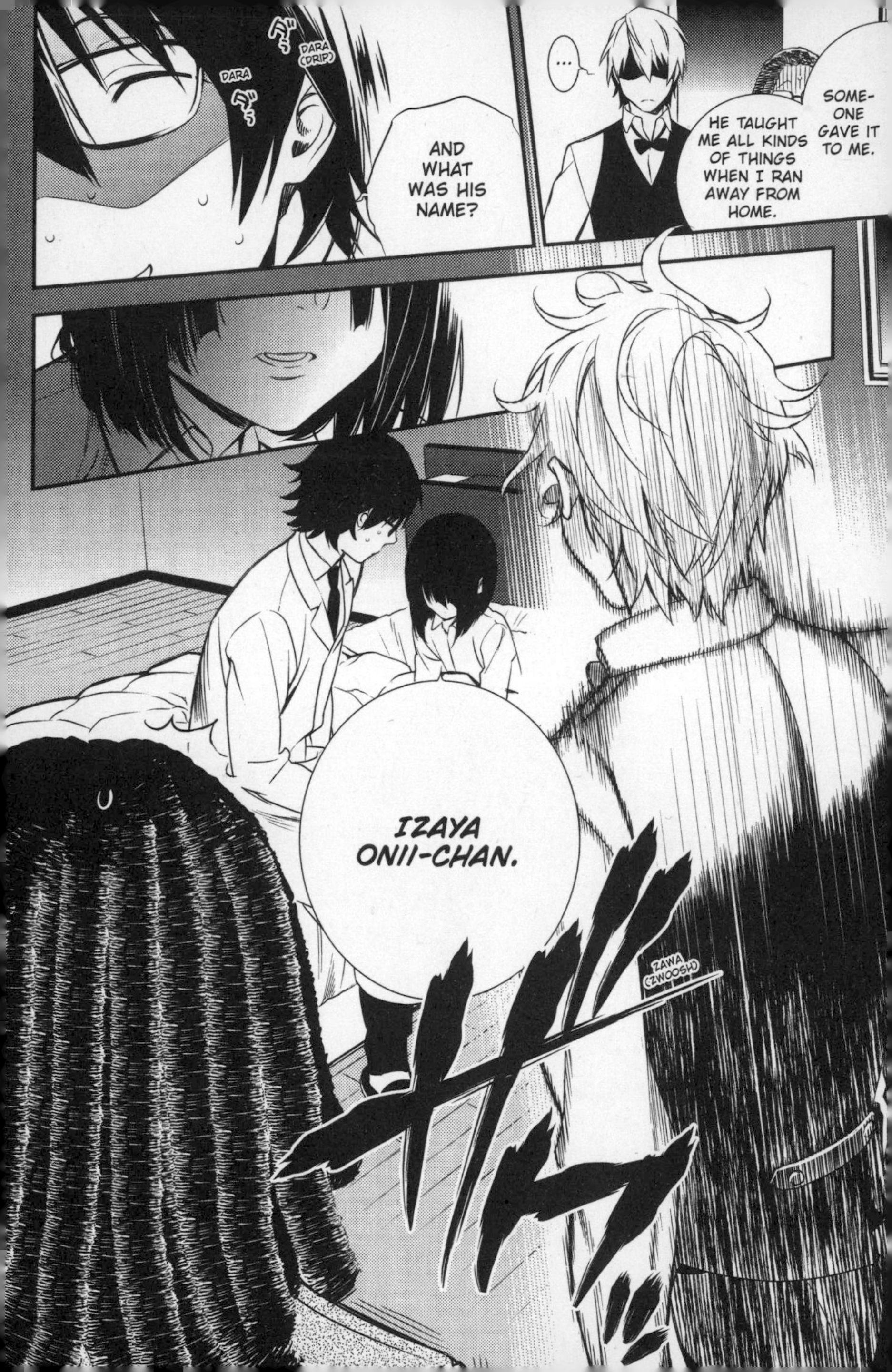
SOME-ONE GAVE IT TO ME.
HE TAUGHT ME ALL KINDS OF THINGS WHEN I RAN AWAY FROM HOME.
...
DARA (DRIP)
DARA
AND WHAT WAS HIS NAME?
IZAYA ONII-CHAN.
ZAWA (ZWOOSH)

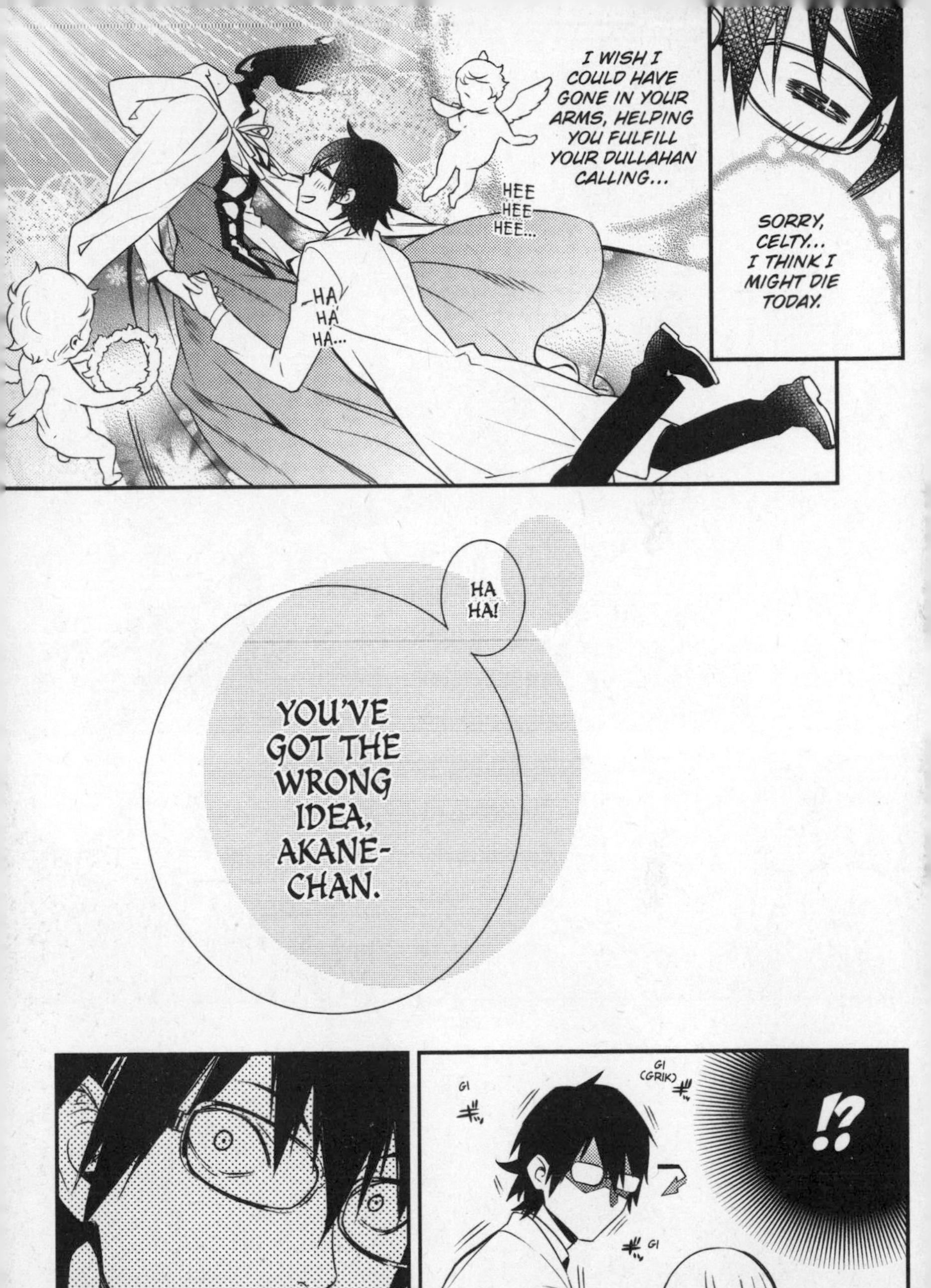
SORRY, CELTY... I THINK I MIGHT DIE TODAY.
I WISH I COULD HAVE GONE IN YOUR ARMS, HELPING YOU FULFILL YOUR DULLAHAN CALLING...
HEE HEE HEE...
HA HA HA...
HA HA!
YOU'VE GOT THE WRONG IDEA, AKANE-CHAN.
GI (GRIK)
GI
GI
!?

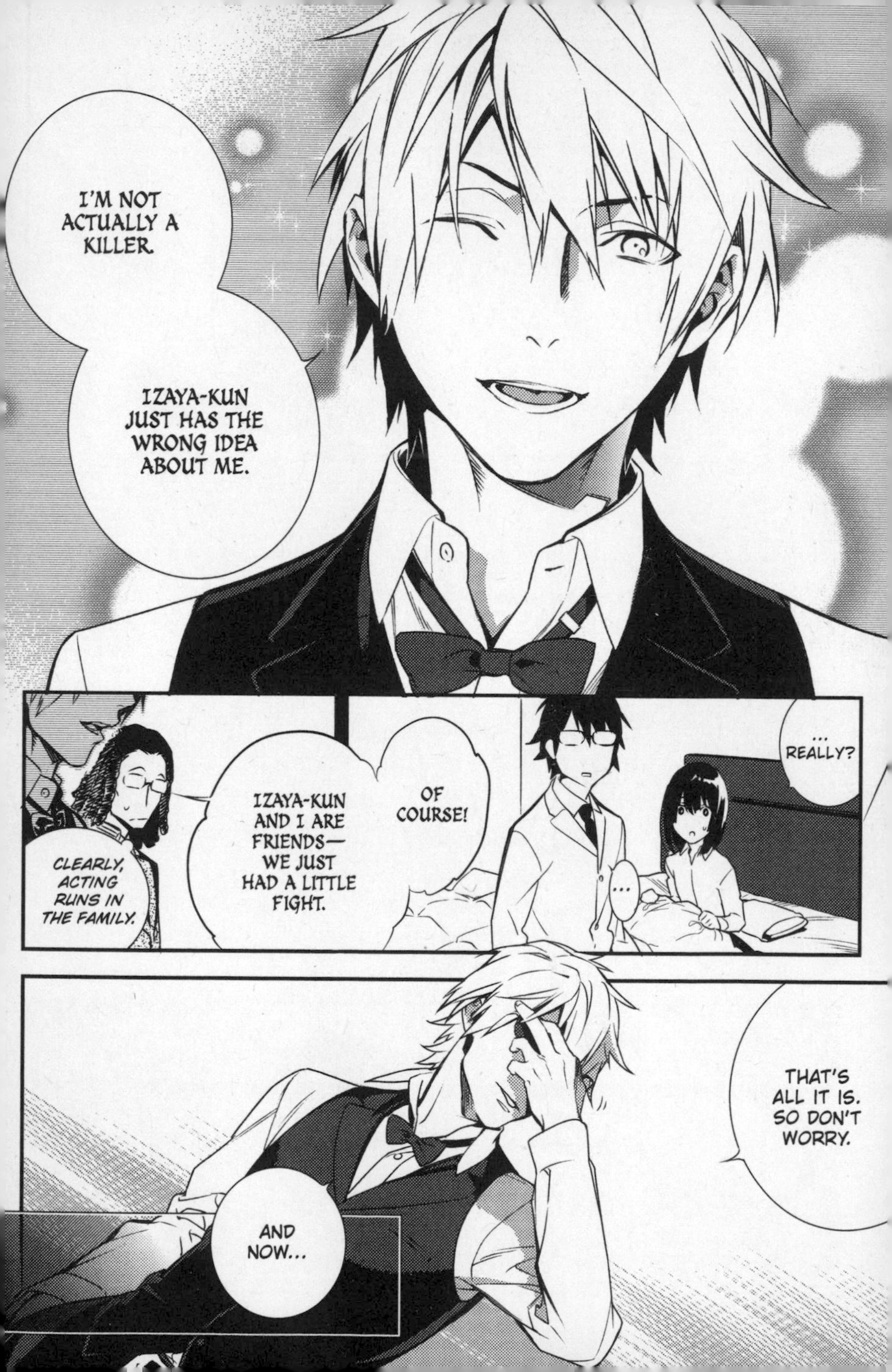
I'M NOT ACTUALLY A KILLER.
IZAYA-KUN JUST HAS THE WRONG IDEA ABOUT ME.
...REALLY?
...
OF COURSE!
IZAYA-KUN AND I ARE FRIENDS— WE JUST HAD A LITTLE FIGHT.
CLEARLY, ACTING RUNS IN THE FAMILY.
THAT'S ALL IT IS. SO DON'T WORRY.
AND NOW...

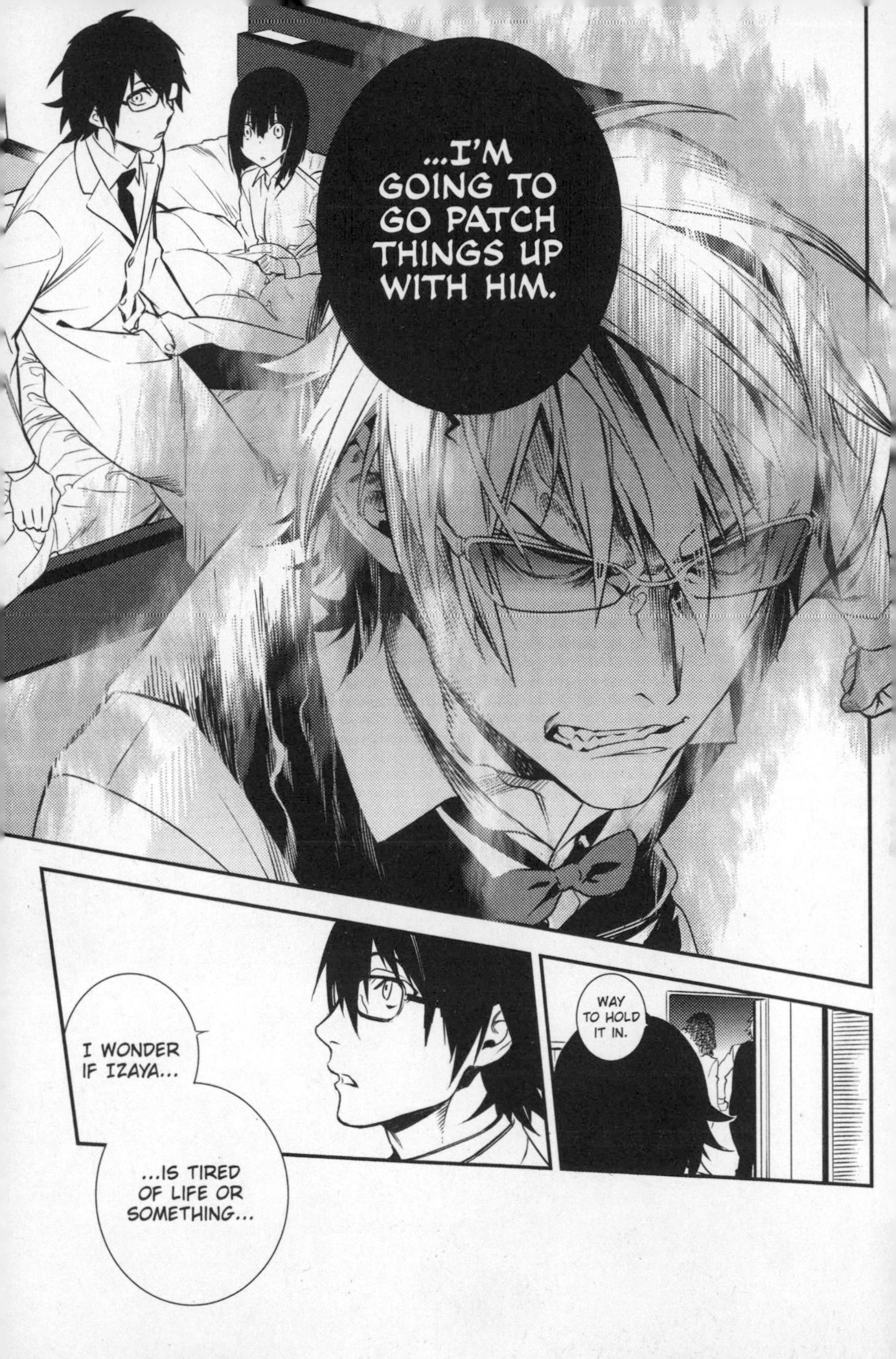
...I'M GOING TO GO PATCH THINGS UP WITH HIM.
WAY TO HOLD IT IN.
I WONDER IF IZAYA...
...IS TIRED OF LIFE OR SOMETHING...

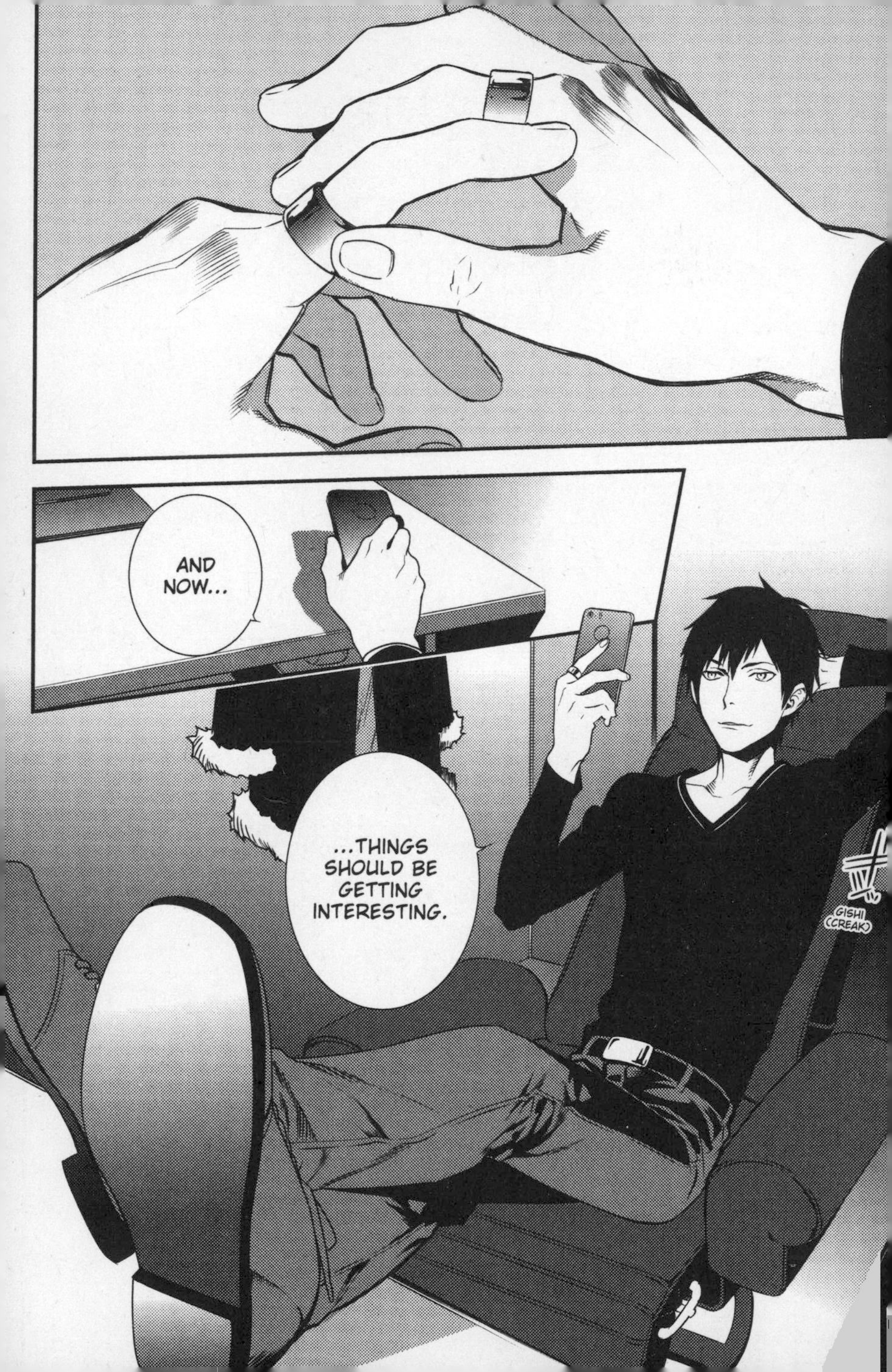
AND NOW...
...THINGS SHOULD BE GETTING INTERESTING.
GISHI (CREAK)

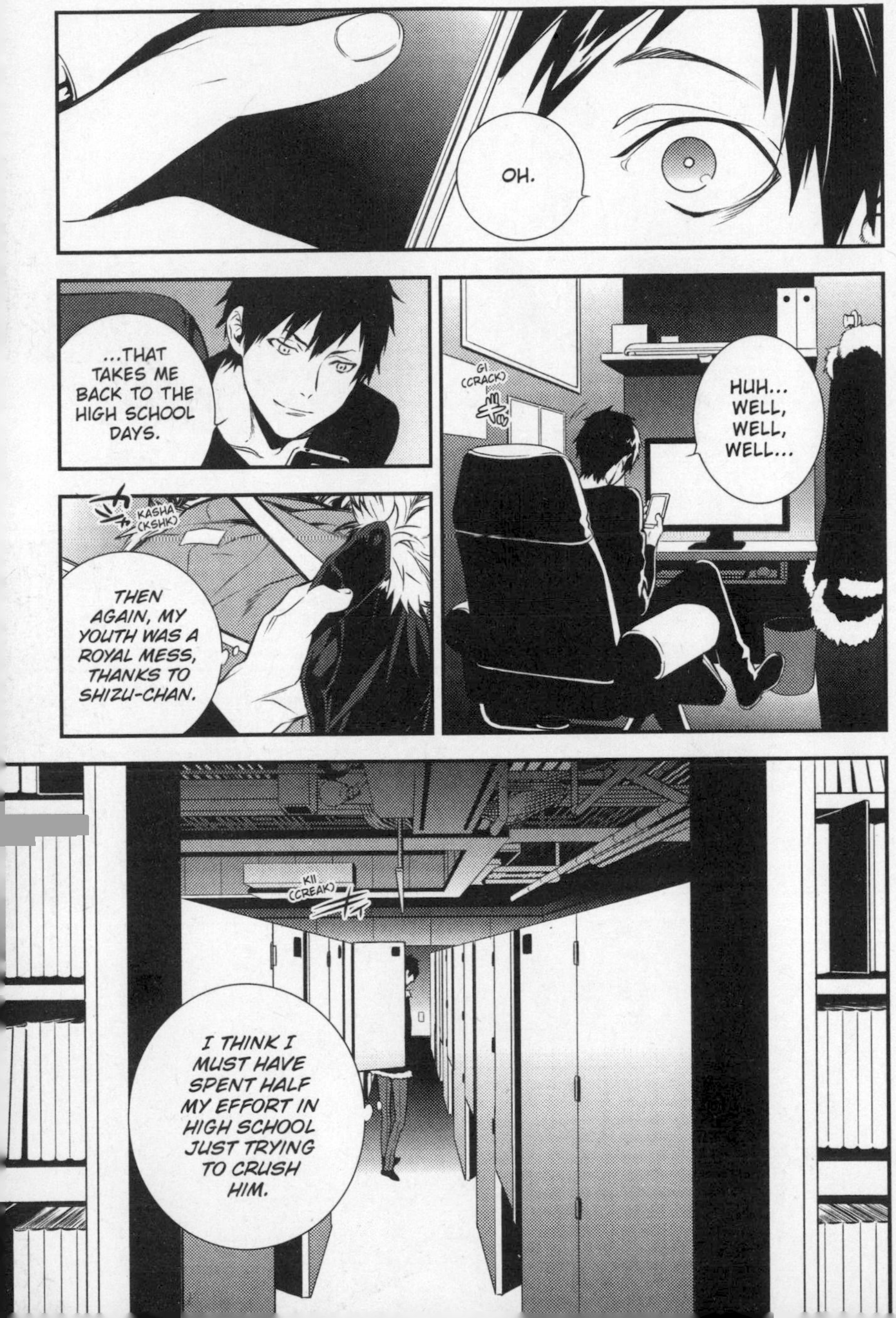
OH.
GI (CRACK)
HUH... WELL, WELL, WELL...
...THAT TAKES ME BACK TO THE HIGH SCHOOL DAYS.
KASHA (KSHK)
THEN AGAIN, MY YOUTH WAS A ROYAL MESS, THANKS TO SHIZU-CHAN.
KII (CREAK)
I THINK I MUST HAVE SPENT HALF MY EFFORT IN HIGH SCHOOL JUST TRYING TO CRUSH HIM.

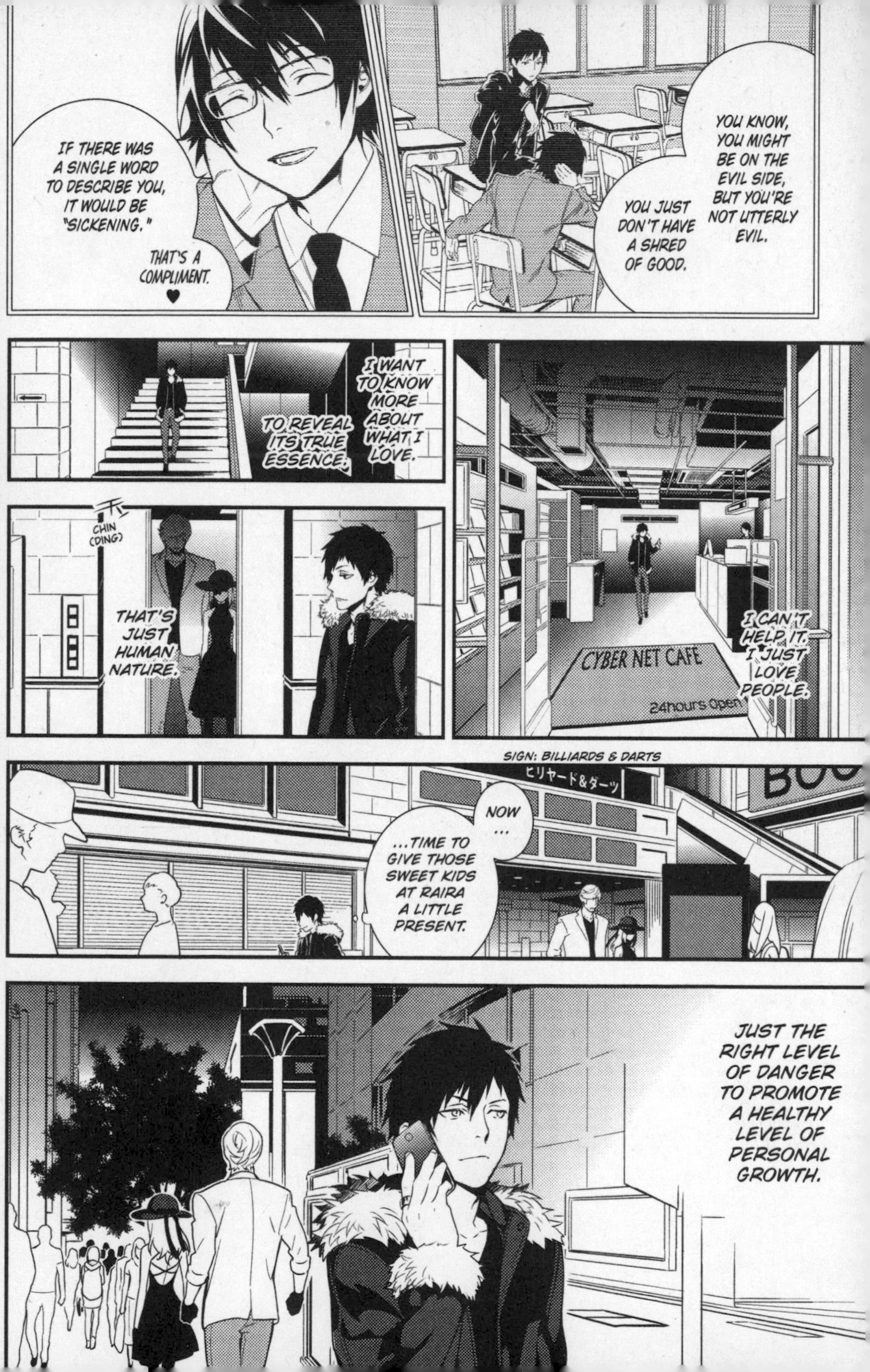
YOU KNOW, YOU MIGHT BE ON THE EVIL SIDE, BUT YOU'RE NOT UTTERLY EVIL.
YOU JUST DON'T HAVE A SHRED OF GOOD.
IF THERE WAS A SINGLE WORD TO DESCRIBE YOU, IT WOULD BE "SICKENING."
THAT'S A COMPLIMENT. ♥
I CAN'T HELP IT. I JUST LOVE PEOPLE.
CYBER NET CAFE
24hours Open
I WANT TO KNOW MORE ABOUT WHAT I LOVE.
TO REVEAL ITS TRUE ESSENCE.
CHIN (DING)
THAT'S JUST HUMAN NATURE.
SIGN: BILLIARDS & DARTS
ビリヤード&ダーツ
NOW ...
...TIME TO GIVE THOSE SWEET KIDS AT RAIRA A LITTLE PRESENT.
JUST THE RIGHT LEVEL OF DANGER TO PROMOTE A HEALTHY LEVEL OF PERSONAL GROWTH.

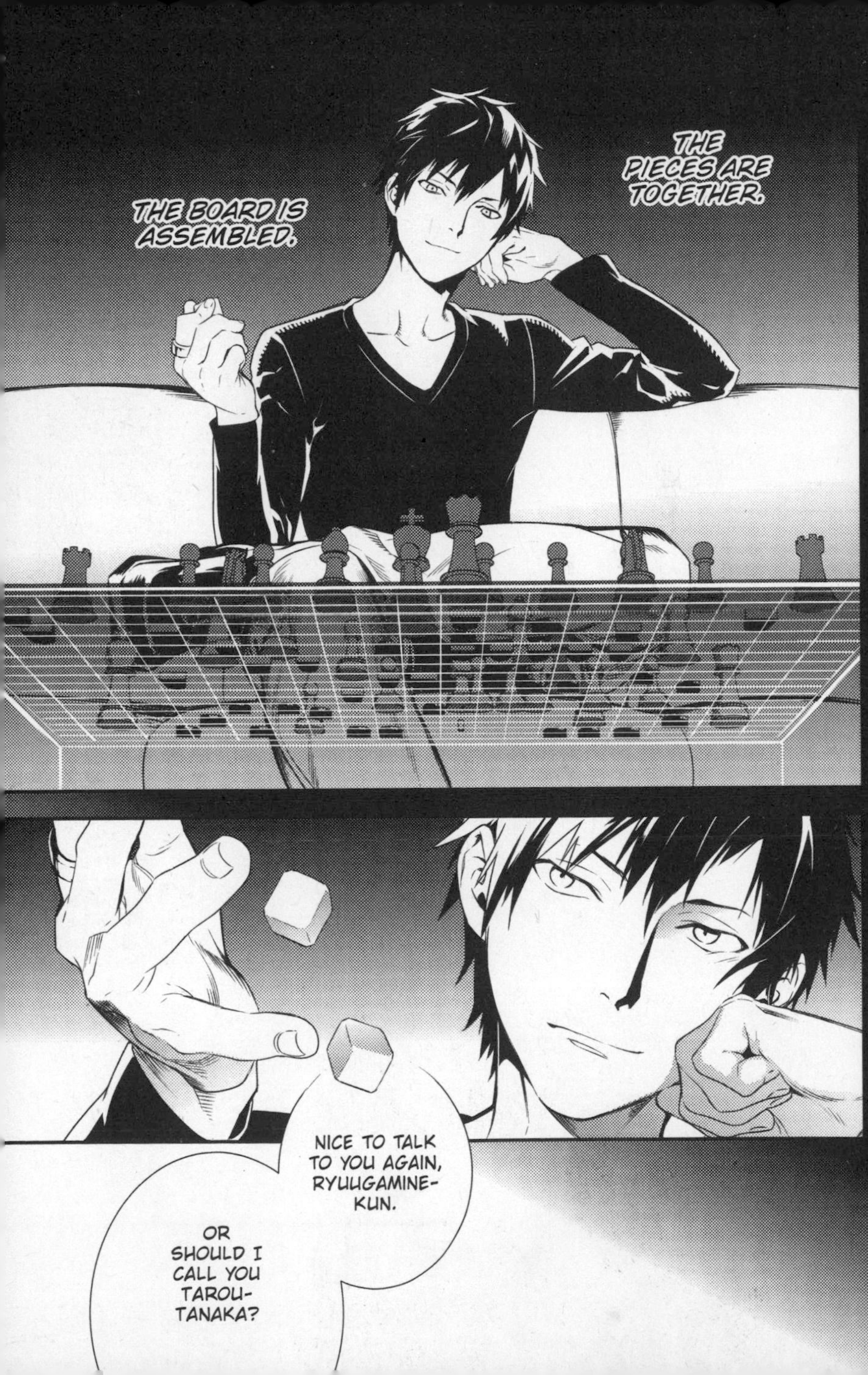
THE PIECES ARE TOGETHER.
THE BOARD IS ASSEMBLED.
NICE TO TALK TO YOU AGAIN, RYUUGAMINE-KUN.
OR SHOULD I CALL YOU TAROU-TANAKA?

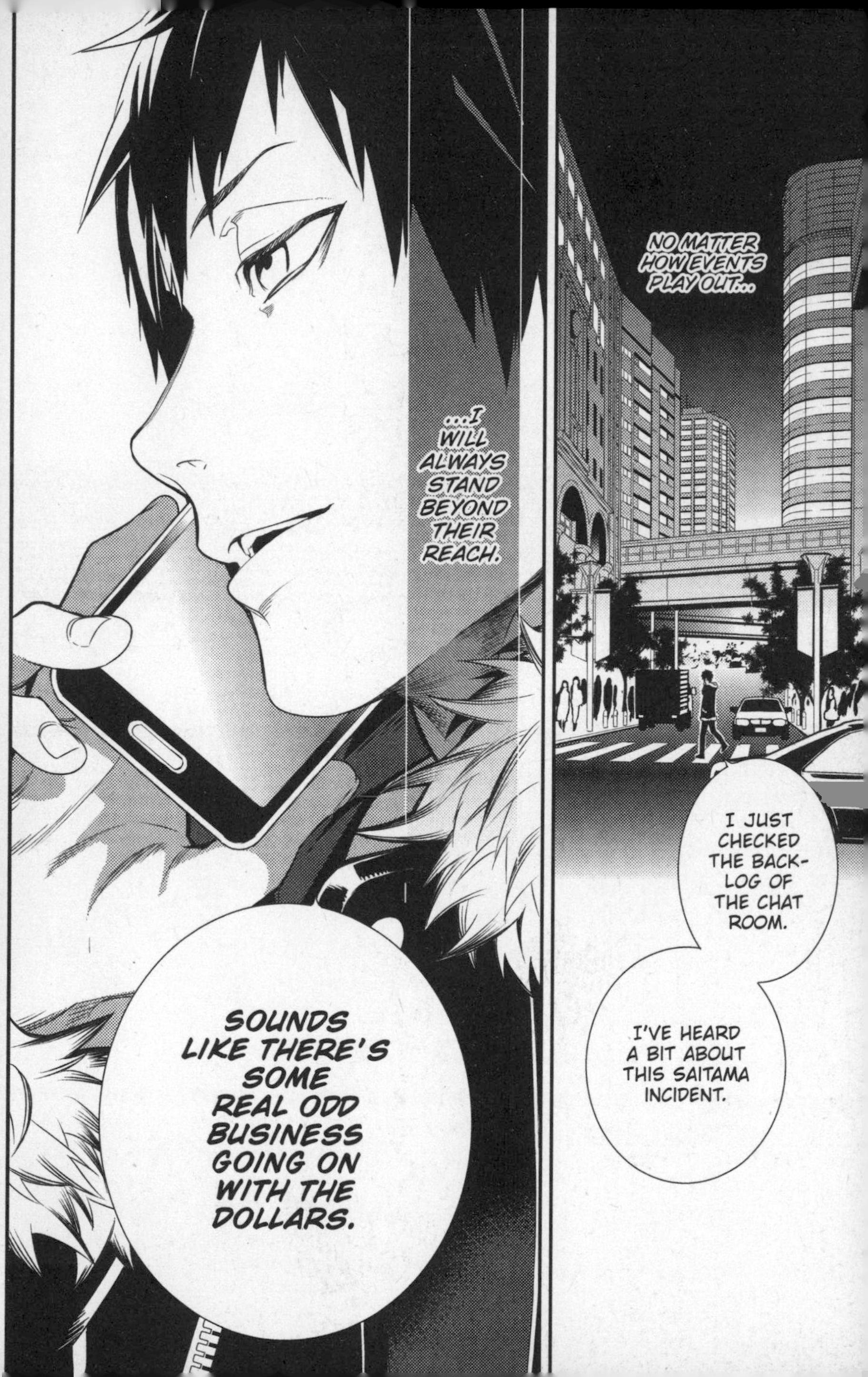
NO MATTER HOW EVENTS PLAY OUT...
I JUST CHECKED THE BACK-LOG OF THE CHAT ROOM.
I'VE HEARD A BIT ABOUT THIS SAITAMA INCIDENT.
...I WILL ALWAYS STAND BEYOND THEIR REACH.
SOUNDS LIKE THERE'S SOME REAL ODD BUSINESS GOING ON WITH THE DOLLARS.

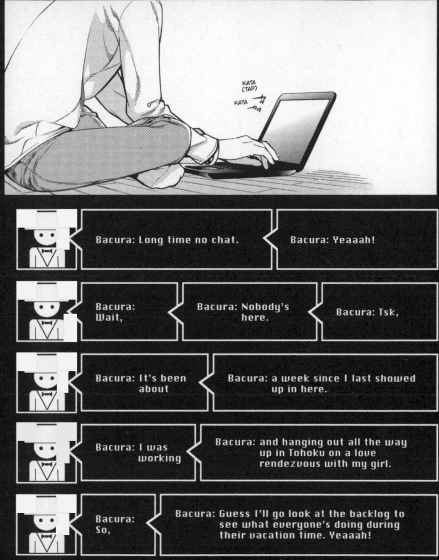

Bacura: Long time no chat.

Bacura: Yeaaah!

Bacura: Wait,

Bacura: Nobody's here.

Bacura: Tsk,

Bacura: It's been about

Bacura: a week since I last showed up in here.

Bacura: I was working

Bacura: and hanging out all the way up in Tohoku on a love rendezvous with my girl.

Bacura: So,

Bacura: Guess I'll go look at the backlog to see what everyone's doing during their vacation time. Yeaaah!

Bacura: Huh?

Bacura: Looks like the log prior to yesterday is just gone.

Bacura: Was there some sort of technical trouble?

Bacura: Anyway,

Bacura: See ya later.

—BACURA HAS LEFT THE CHAT—

—THE CHAT ROOM IS CURRENTLY EMPTY—

—THE CHAT ROOM IS CURRENTLY EMPTY—

⋮

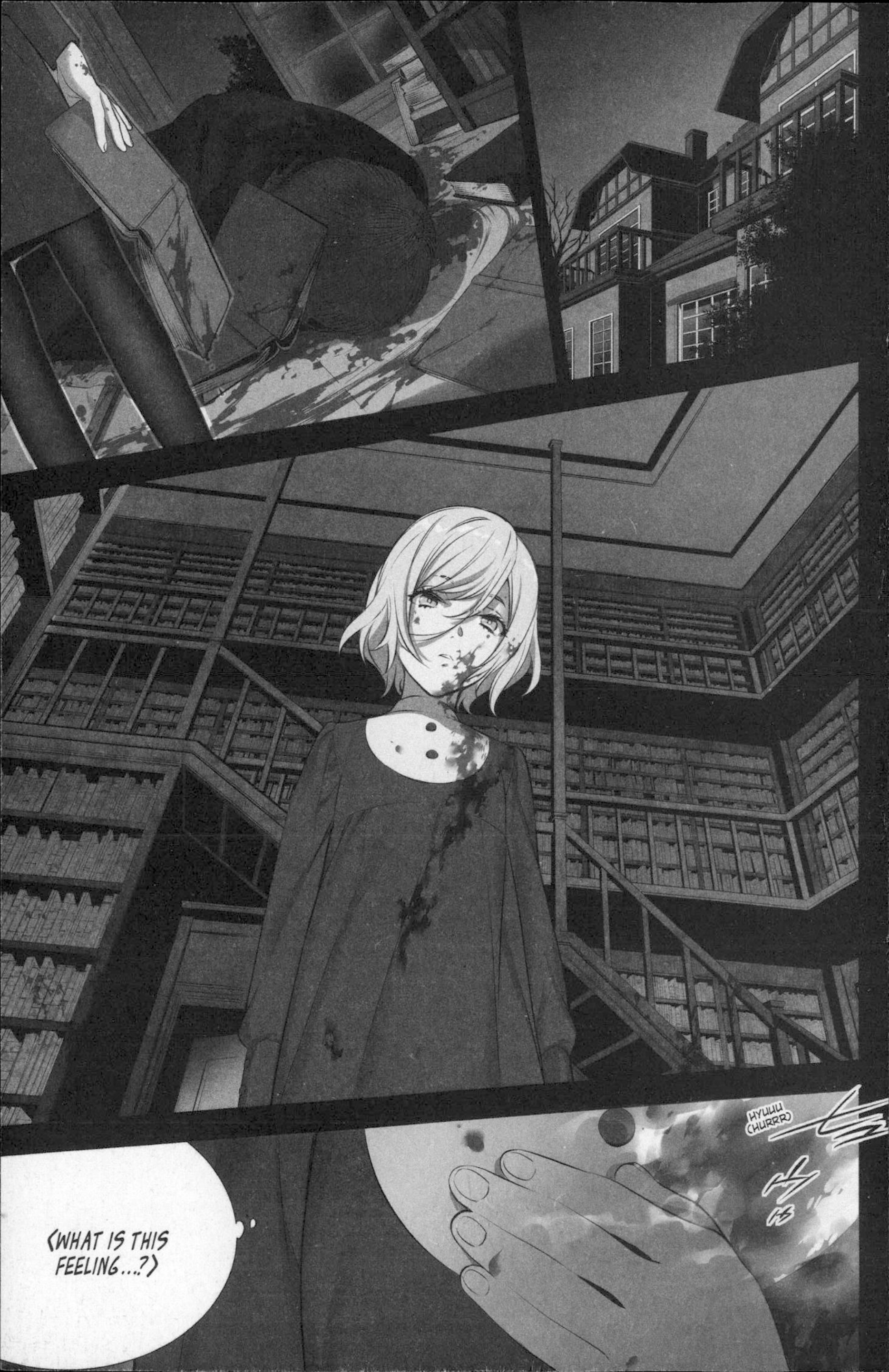
HYUUU (HURRR)
‹WHAT IS THIS FEELING...?›

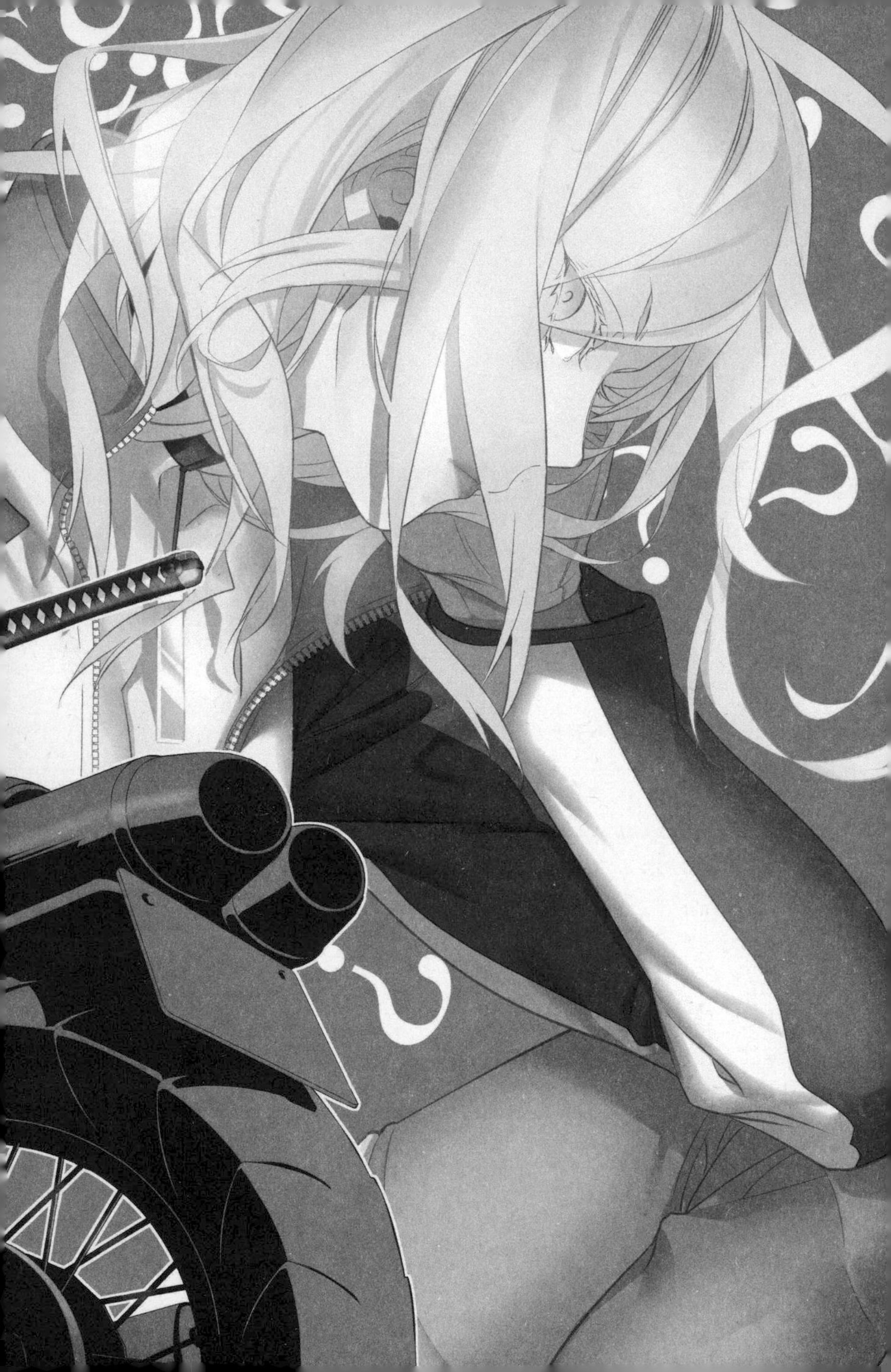

CHAPTER 5 ✕ THE DAYS OF YOUTH SHINE AND CRUMBLE

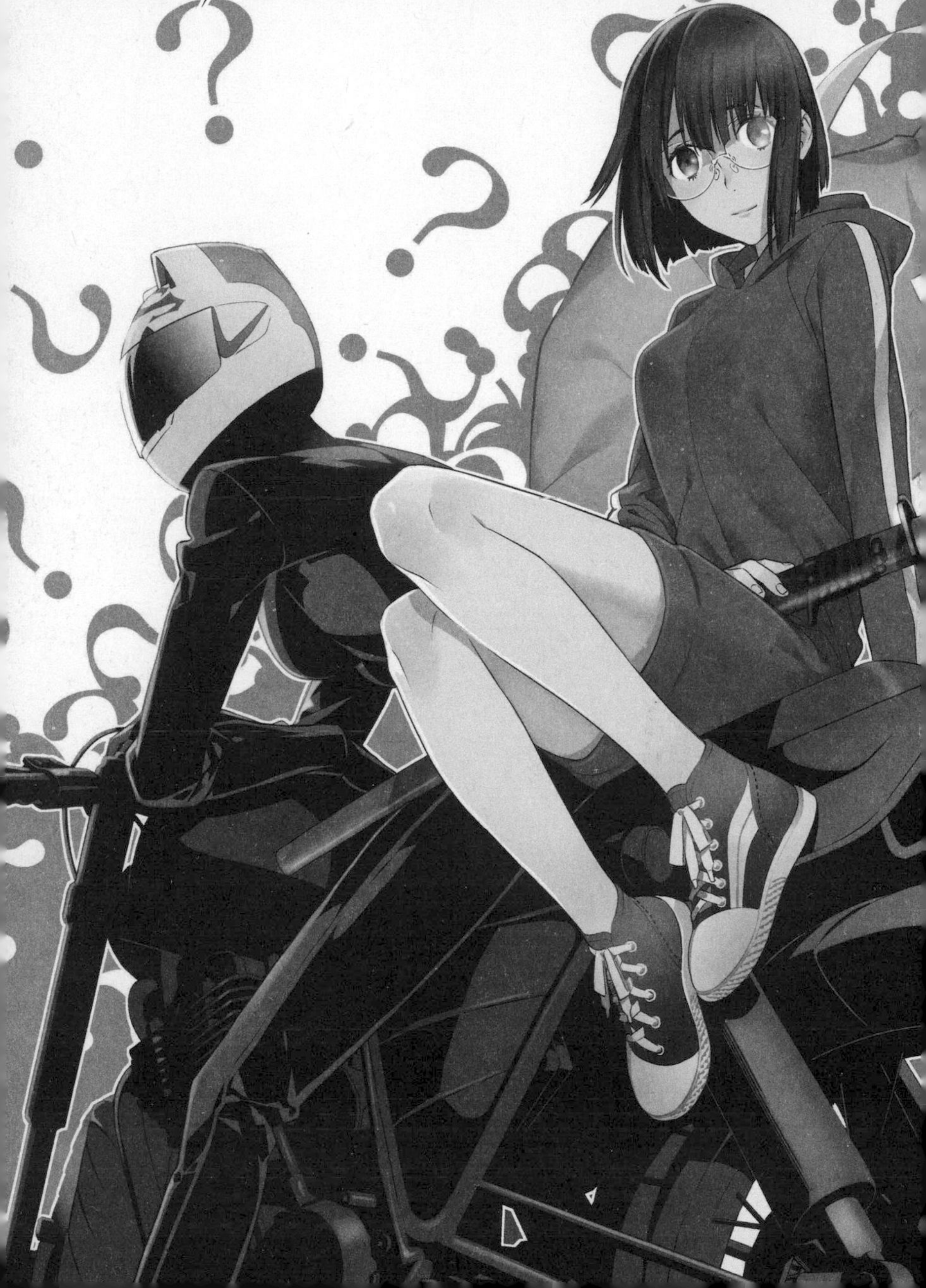

DURARARA!!

DRRR!!

Re;Dollars Arc

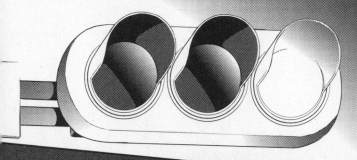

SIGH...

THIS IS A
REAL PAIN
OF A JOB I
TOOK ON.

AS A MATTER
OF FACT, WE NEED
YOU TO FIND AND
PROTECT A CERTAIN
TARGET FOR US.

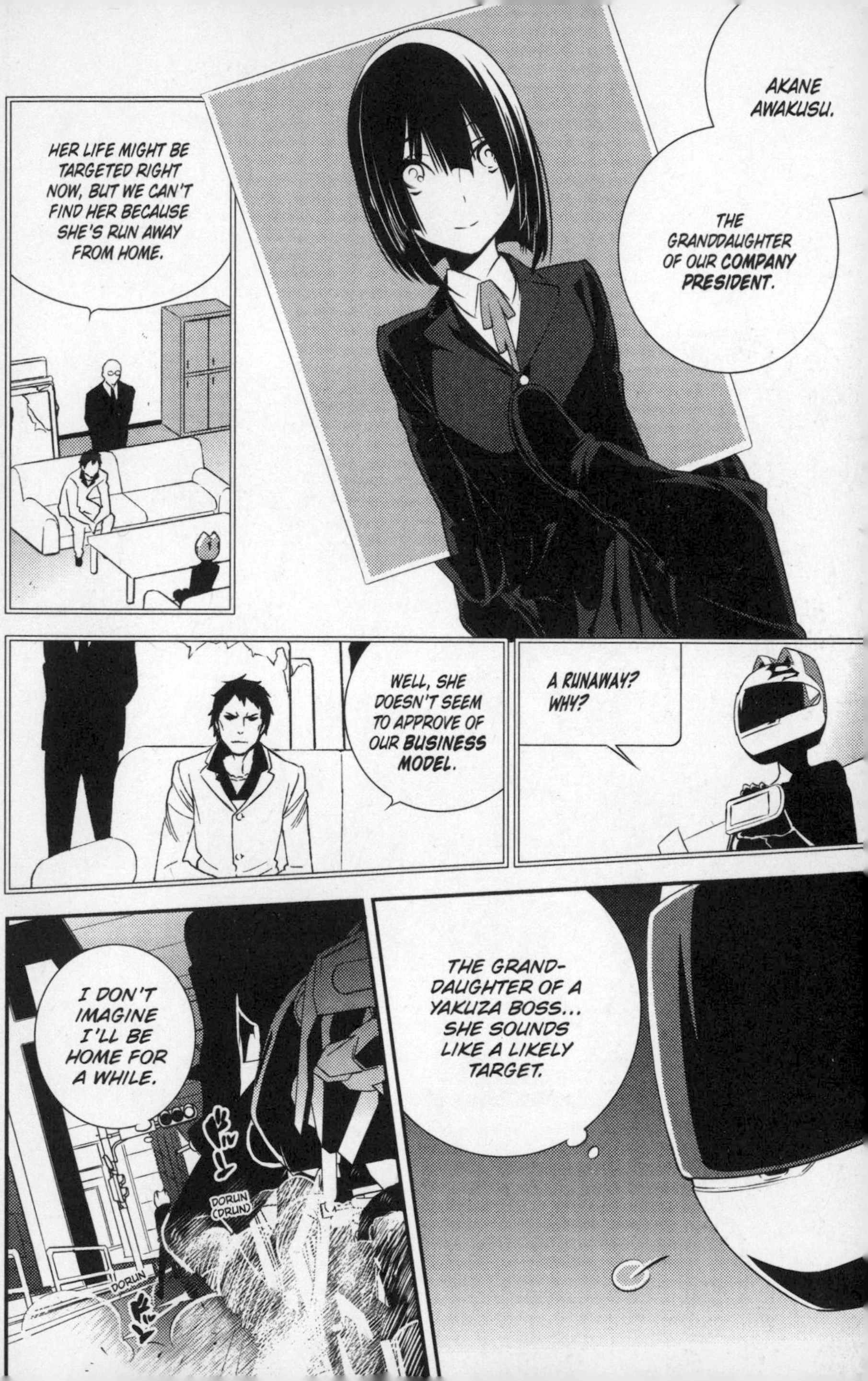
AKANE AWAKUSU.
THE GRANDDAUGHTER OF OUR COMPANY PRESIDENT.
HER LIFE MIGHT BE TARGETED RIGHT NOW, BUT WE CAN'T FIND HER BECAUSE SHE'S RUN AWAY FROM HOME.
A RUNAWAY? WHY?
WELL, SHE DOESN'T SEEM TO APPROVE OF OUR BUSINESS MODEL.
THE GRAND-DAUGHTER OF A YAKUZA BOSS... SHE SOUNDS LIKE A LIKELY TARGET.
I DON'T IMAGINE I'LL BE HOME FOR A WHILE.
DORUN (DRUN)
DORUN

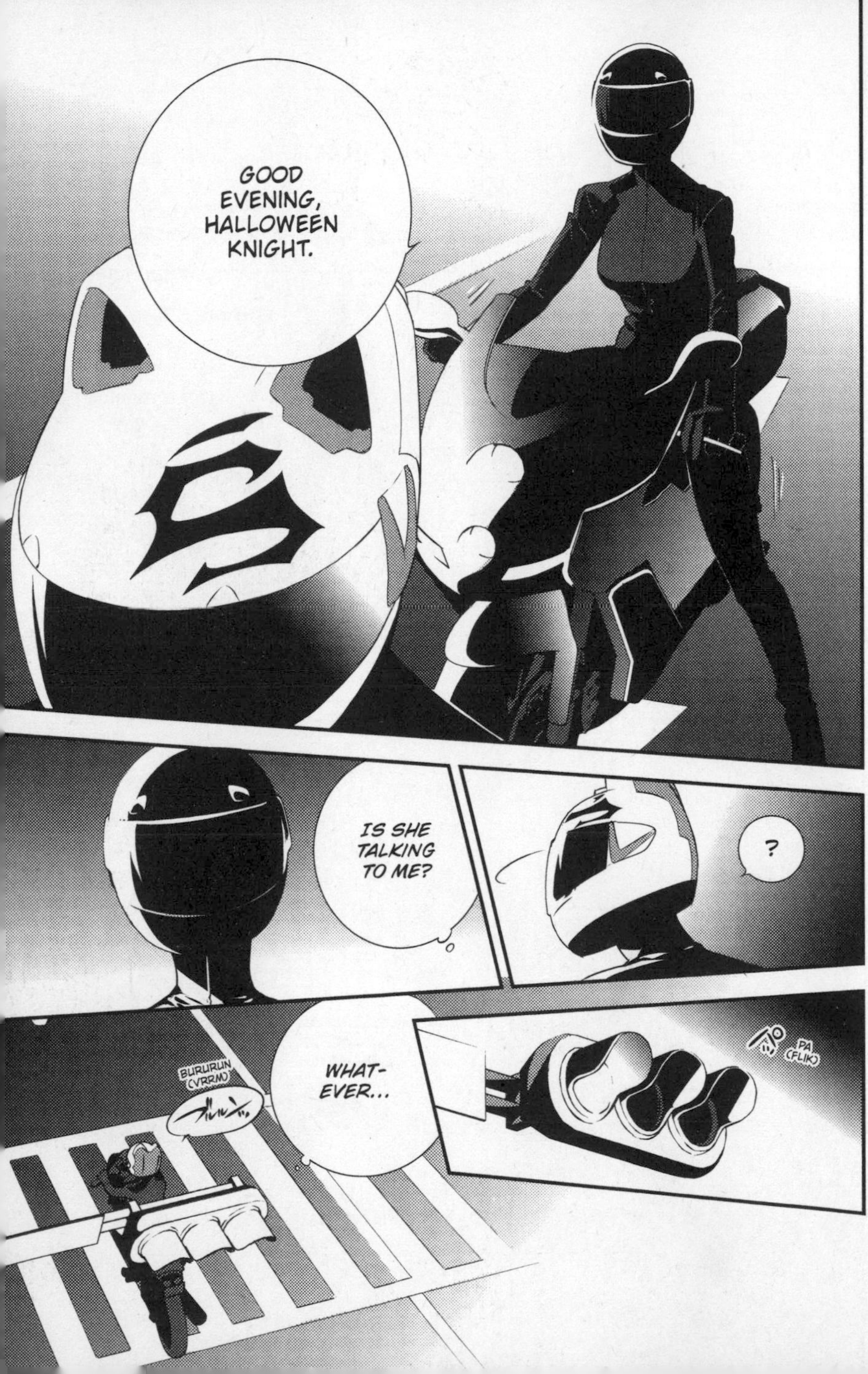

GOOD EVENING, HALLOWEEN KNIGHT.
?
IS SHE TALKING TO ME?
PA (FLIK)
WHAT-EVER...
BURURUN (VRRM)

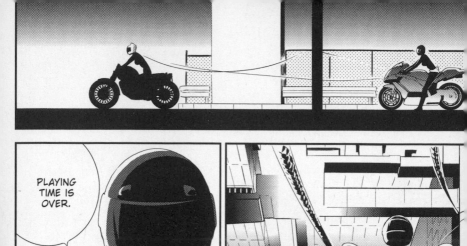

PLAYING TIME IS OVER.

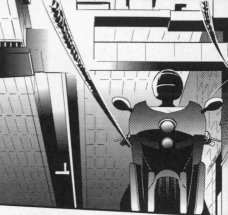

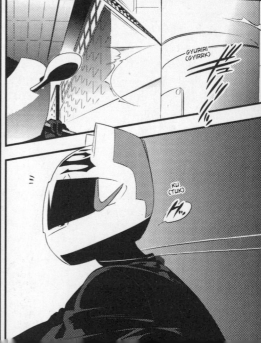

GYURIRI
(GYIRRK)

KU
(TUK)

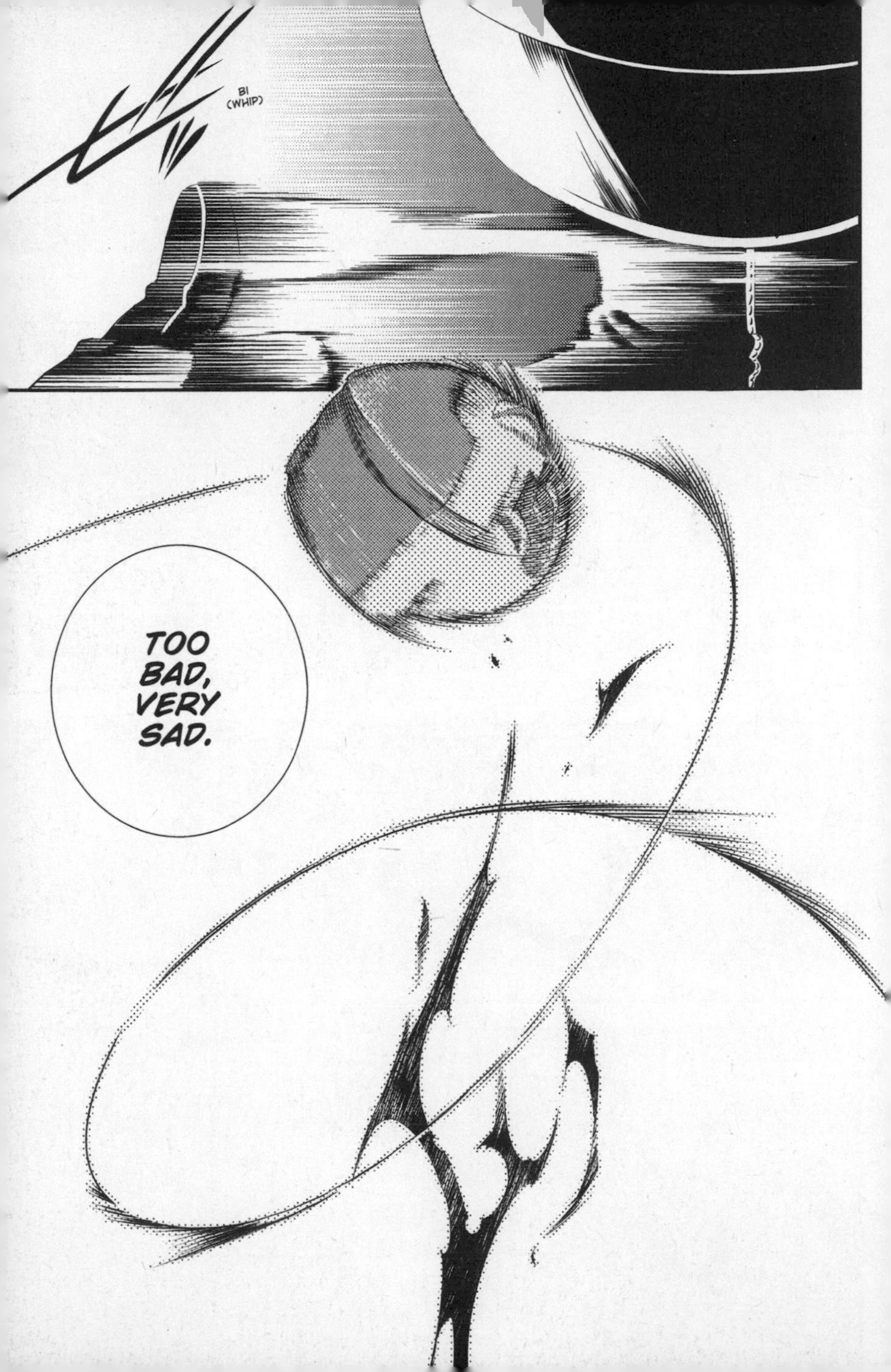
BI (WHIP)
TOO BAD, VERY SAD.

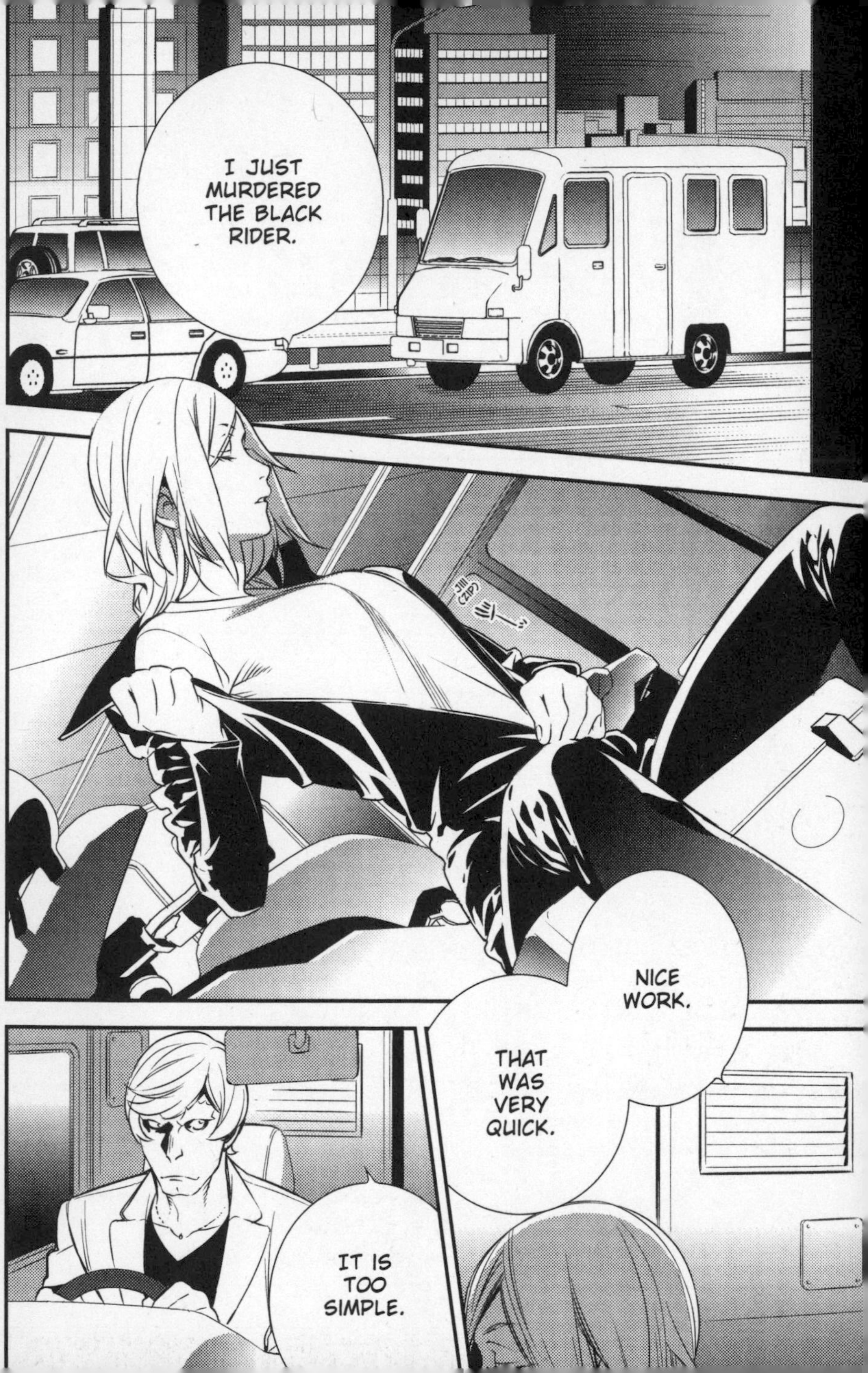
I JUST MURDERED THE BLACK RIDER.
JIII (ZIP)
NICE WORK.
THAT WAS VERY QUICK.
IT IS TOO SIMPLE.

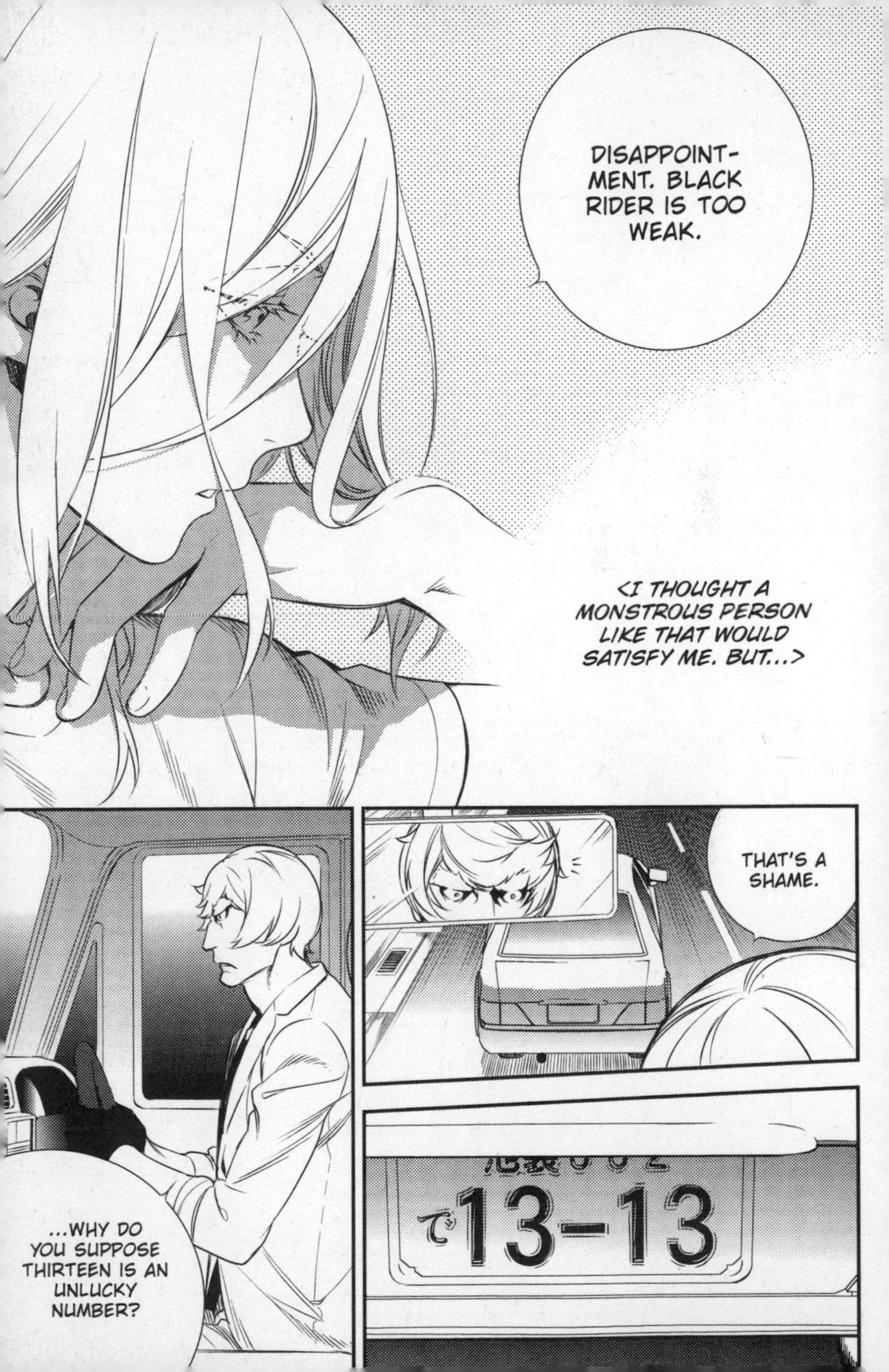
DISAPPOINT-MENT. BLACK RIDER IS TOO WEAK.
<I THOUGHT A MONSTROUS PERSON LIKE THAT WOULD SATISFY ME. BUT...>
THAT'S A SHAME.
て13-13
...WHY DO YOU SUPPOSE THIRTEEN IS AN UNLUCKY NUMBER?

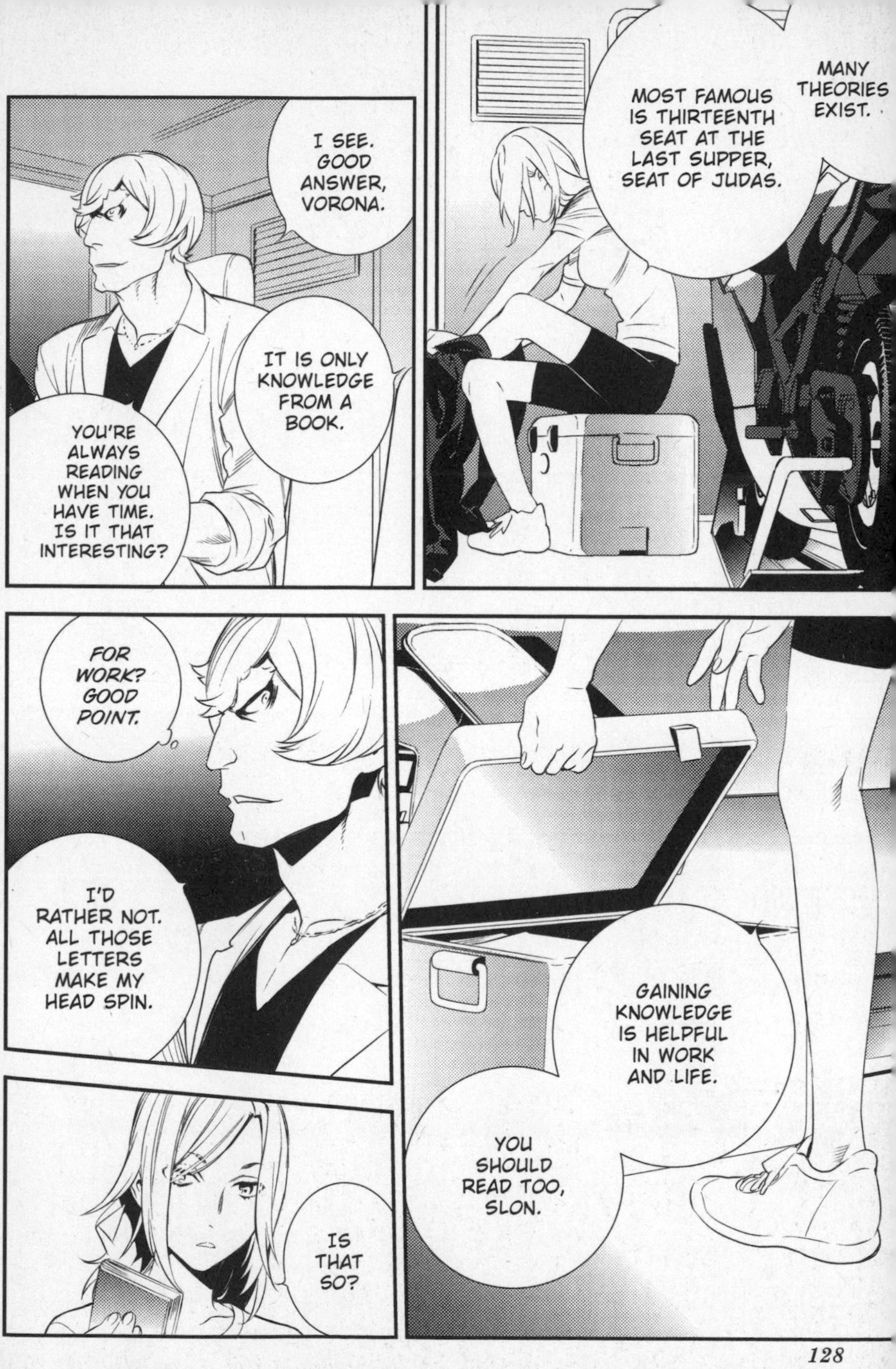
MANY THEORIES EXIST.
MOST FAMOUS IS THIRTEENTH SEAT AT THE LAST SUPPER, SEAT OF JUDAS.
I SEE. GOOD ANSWER, VORONA.
IT IS ONLY KNOWLEDGE FROM A BOOK.
YOU'RE ALWAYS READING WHEN YOU HAVE TIME. IS IT THAT INTERESTING?
GAINING KNOWLEDGE IS HELPFUL IN WORK AND LIFE.
YOU SHOULD READ TOO, SLON.
FOR WORK? GOOD POINT.
I'D RATHER NOT. ALL THOSE LETTERS MAKE MY HEAD SPIN.
IS THAT SO?

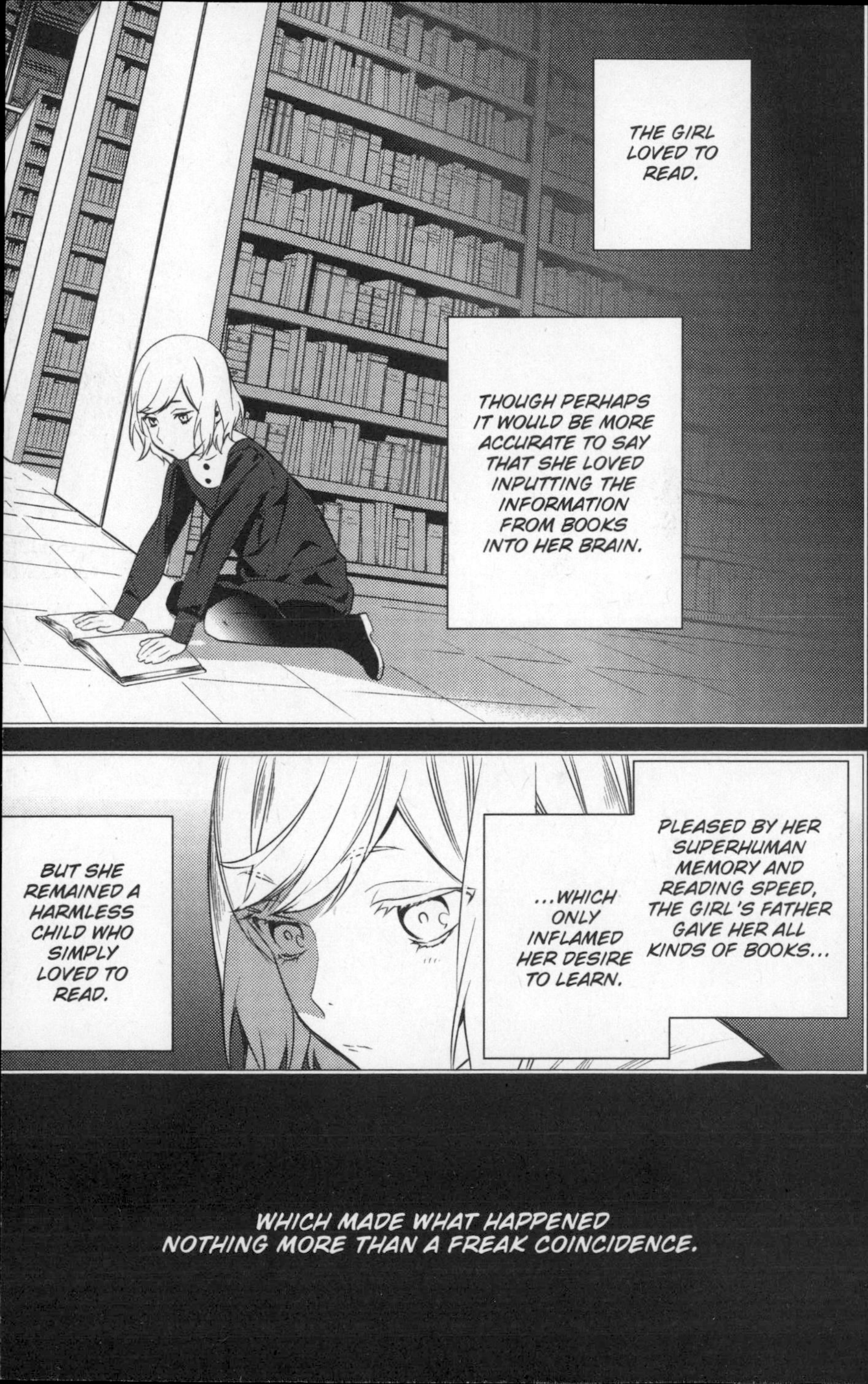
THE GIRL LOVED TO READ.
THOUGH PERHAPS IT WOULD BE MORE ACCURATE TO SAY THAT SHE LOVED INPUTTING THE INFORMATION FROM BOOKS INTO HER BRAIN.
PLEASED BY HER SUPERHUMAN MEMORY AND READING SPEED, THE GIRL'S FATHER GAVE HER ALL KINDS OF BOOKS...
...WHICH ONLY INFLAMED HER DESIRE TO LEARN.
BUT SHE REMAINED A HARMLESS CHILD WHO SIMPLY LOVED TO READ.
WHICH MADE WHAT HAPPENED NOTHING MORE THAN A FREAK COINCIDENCE.

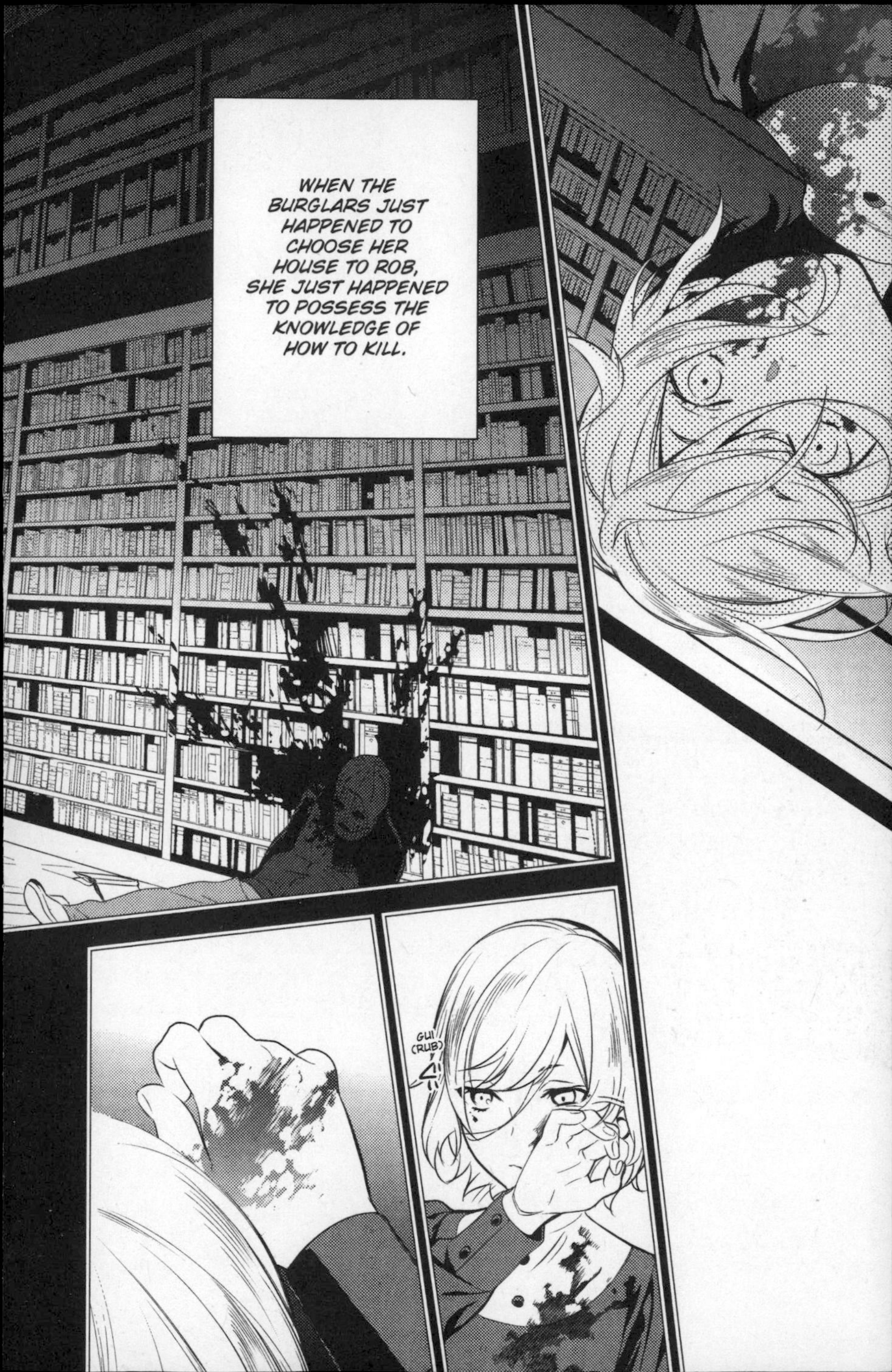
WHEN THE BURGLARS JUST HAPPENED TO CHOOSE HER HOUSE TO ROB, SHE JUST HAPPENED TO POSSESS THE KNOWLEDGE OF HOW TO KILL.
GUI (RUB)

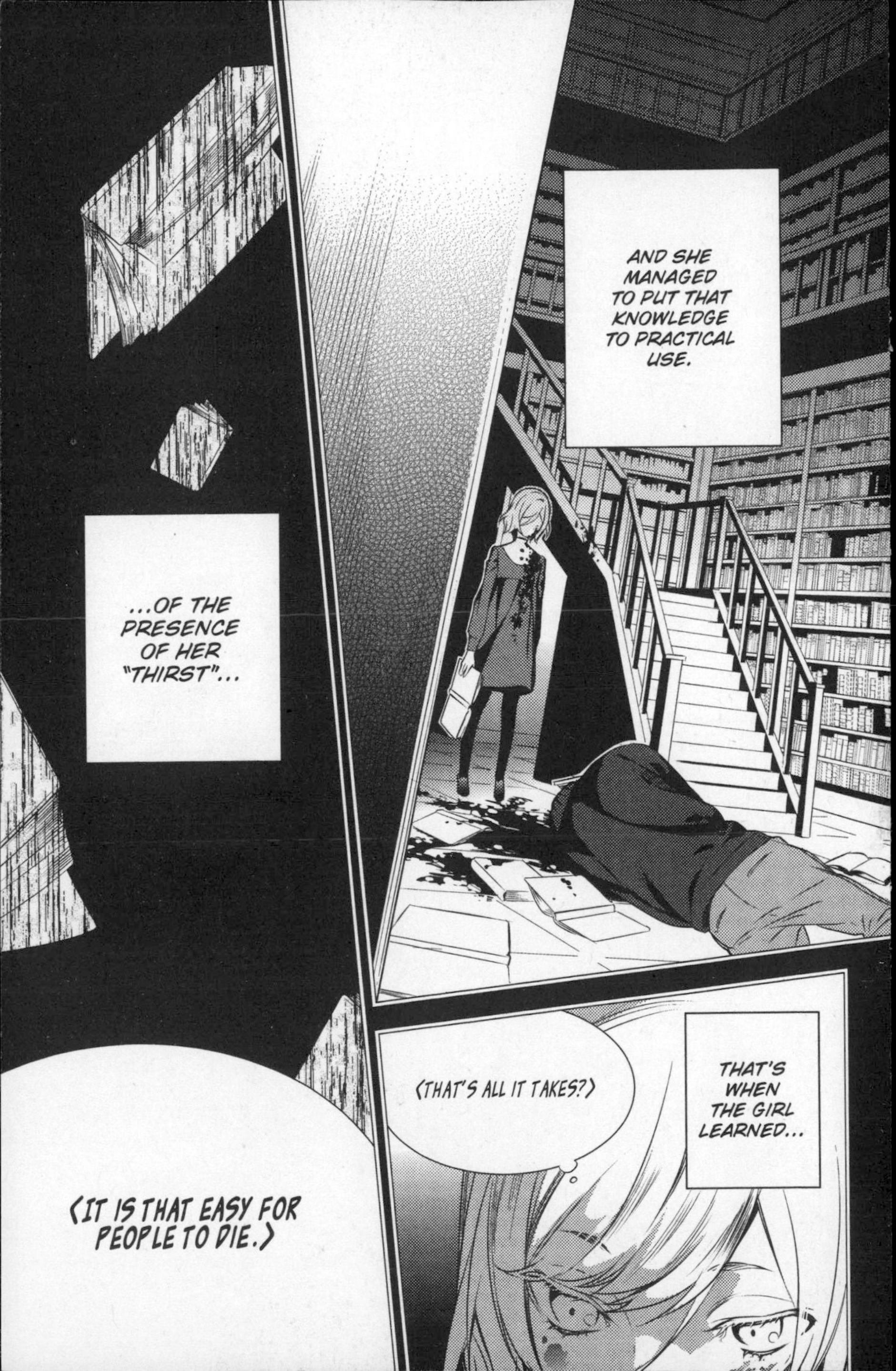
AND SHE MANAGED TO PUT THAT KNOWLEDGE TO PRACTICAL USE.
THAT'S WHEN THE GIRL LEARNED...
〈THAT'S ALL IT TAKES?〉
...OF THE PRESENCE OF HER "THIRST"...
〈IT IS THAT EASY FOR PEOPLE TO DIE.〉

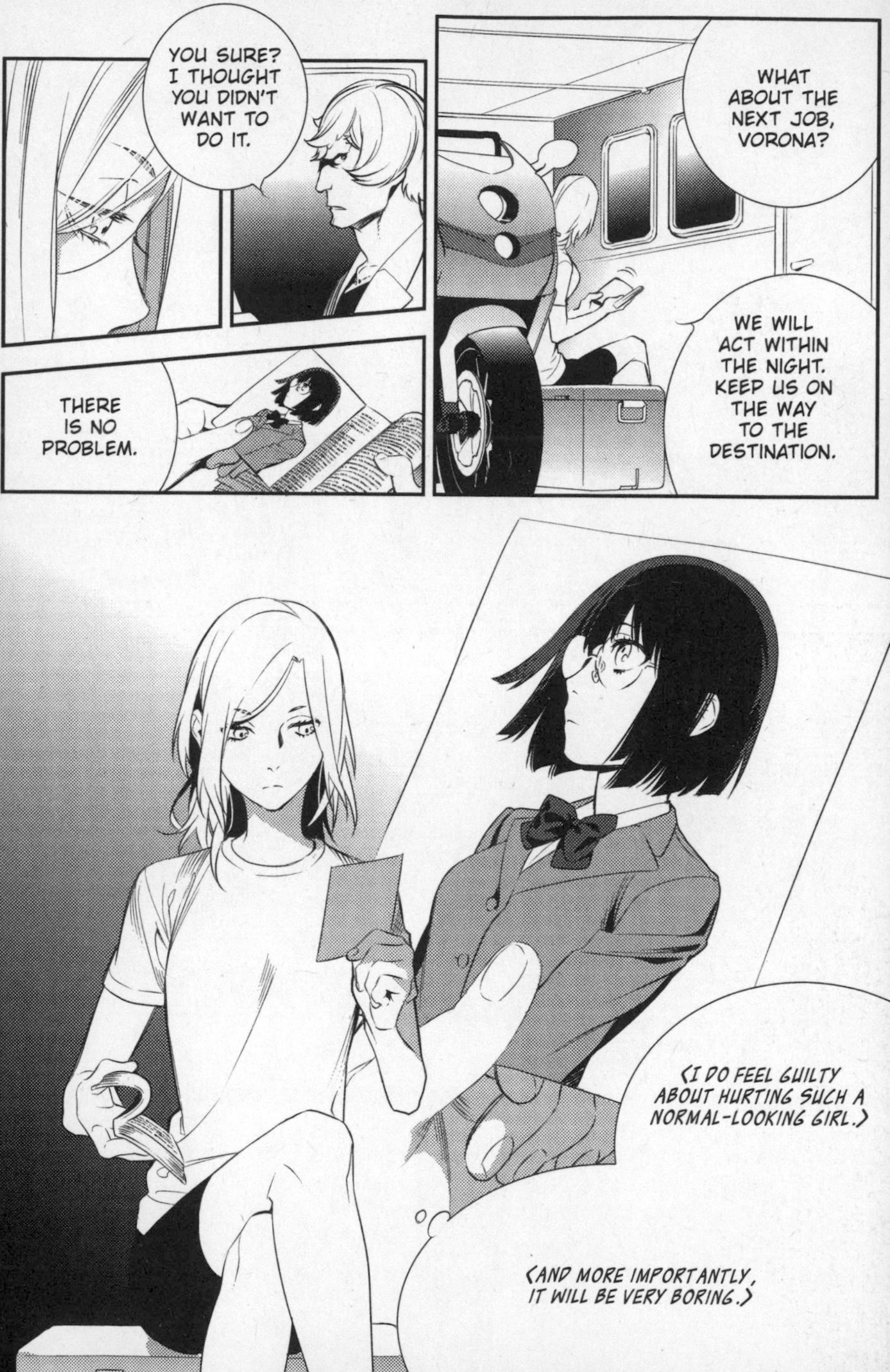
WHAT ABOUT THE NEXT JOB, VORONA?
WE WILL ACT WITHIN THE NIGHT. KEEP US ON THE WAY TO THE DESTINATION.
YOU SURE? I THOUGHT YOU DIDN'T WANT TO DO IT.
THERE IS NO PROBLEM.
<I DO FEEL GUILTY ABOUT HURTING SUCH A NORMAL-LOOKING GIRL.>
<AND MORE IMPORTANTLY, IT WILL BE VERY BORING.>

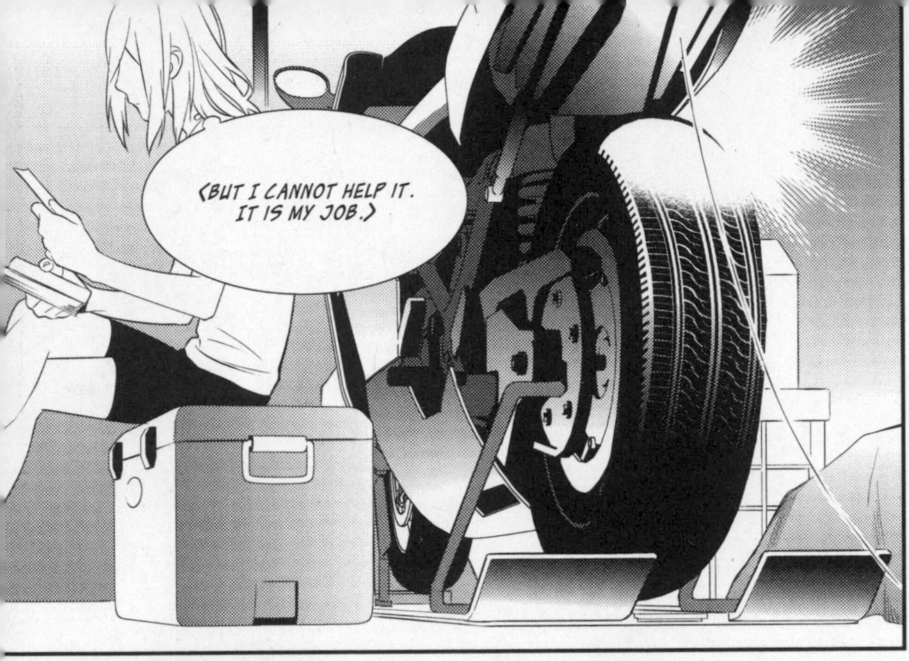
‹BUT I CANNOT HELP IT. IT IS MY JOB.›
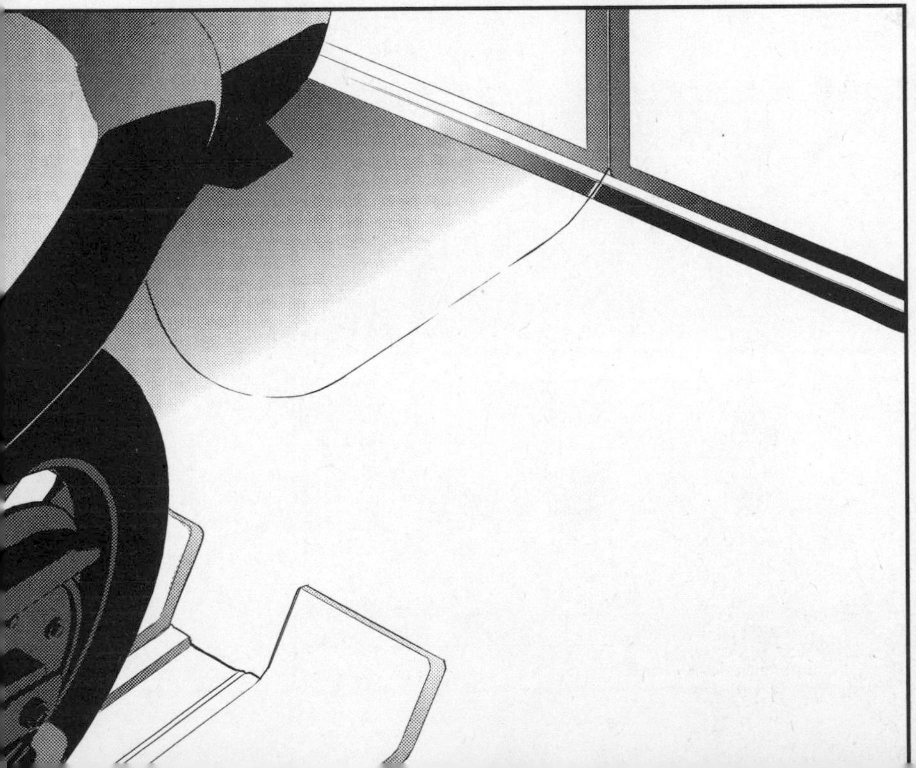

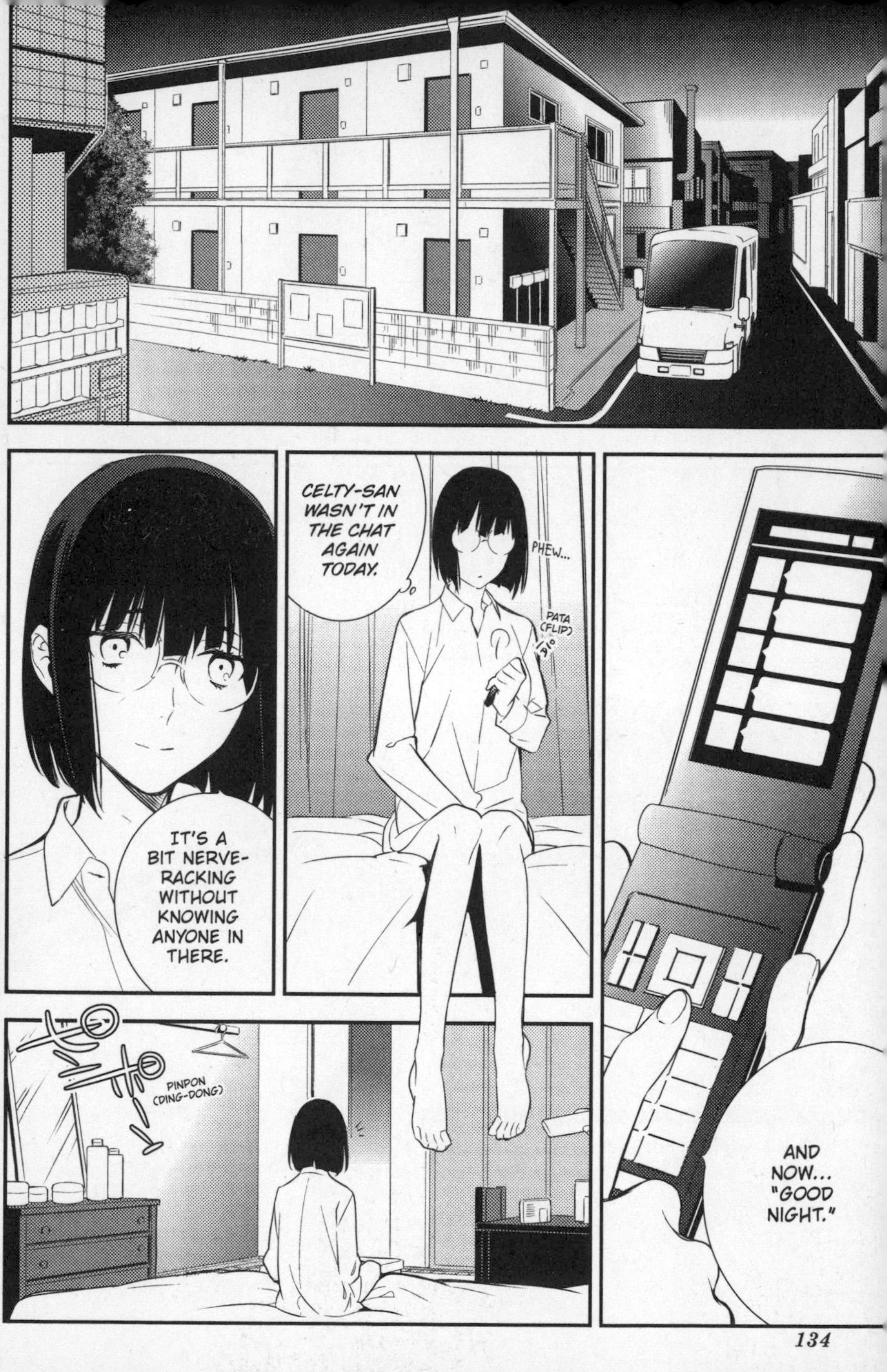
AND NOW... "GOOD NIGHT."
CELTY-SAN WASN'T IN THE CHAT AGAIN TODAY.
PHEW...
PATA (FLIP)
IT'S A BIT NERVE-RACKING WITHOUT KNOWING ANYONE IN THERE.
PINPON (DING-DONG)

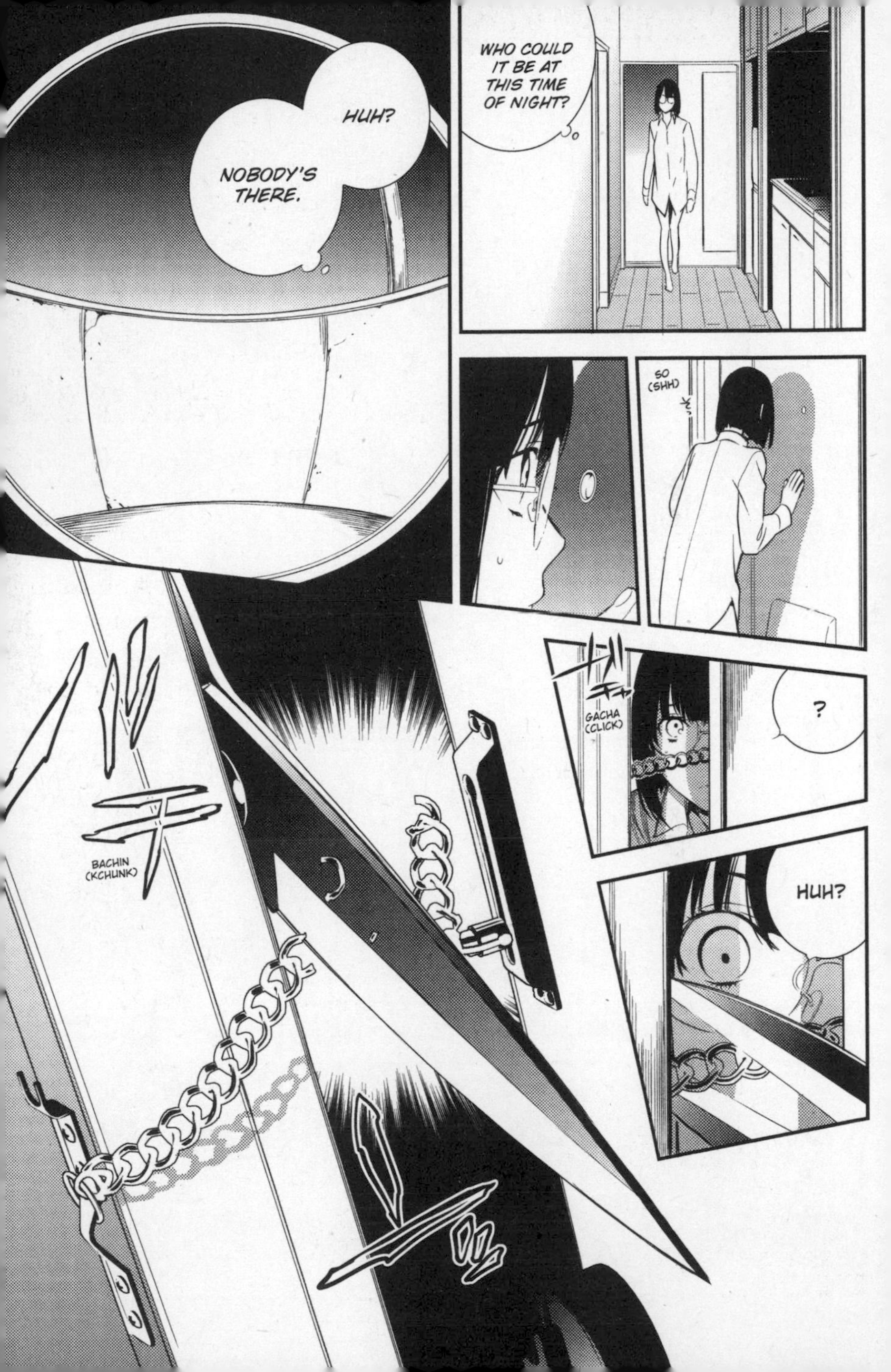
WHO COULD IT BE AT THIS TIME OF NIGHT?
SO (SHH)
HUH?
NOBODY'S THERE.
?
GACHA (CLICK)
HUH?
BACHIN (KCHUNK)

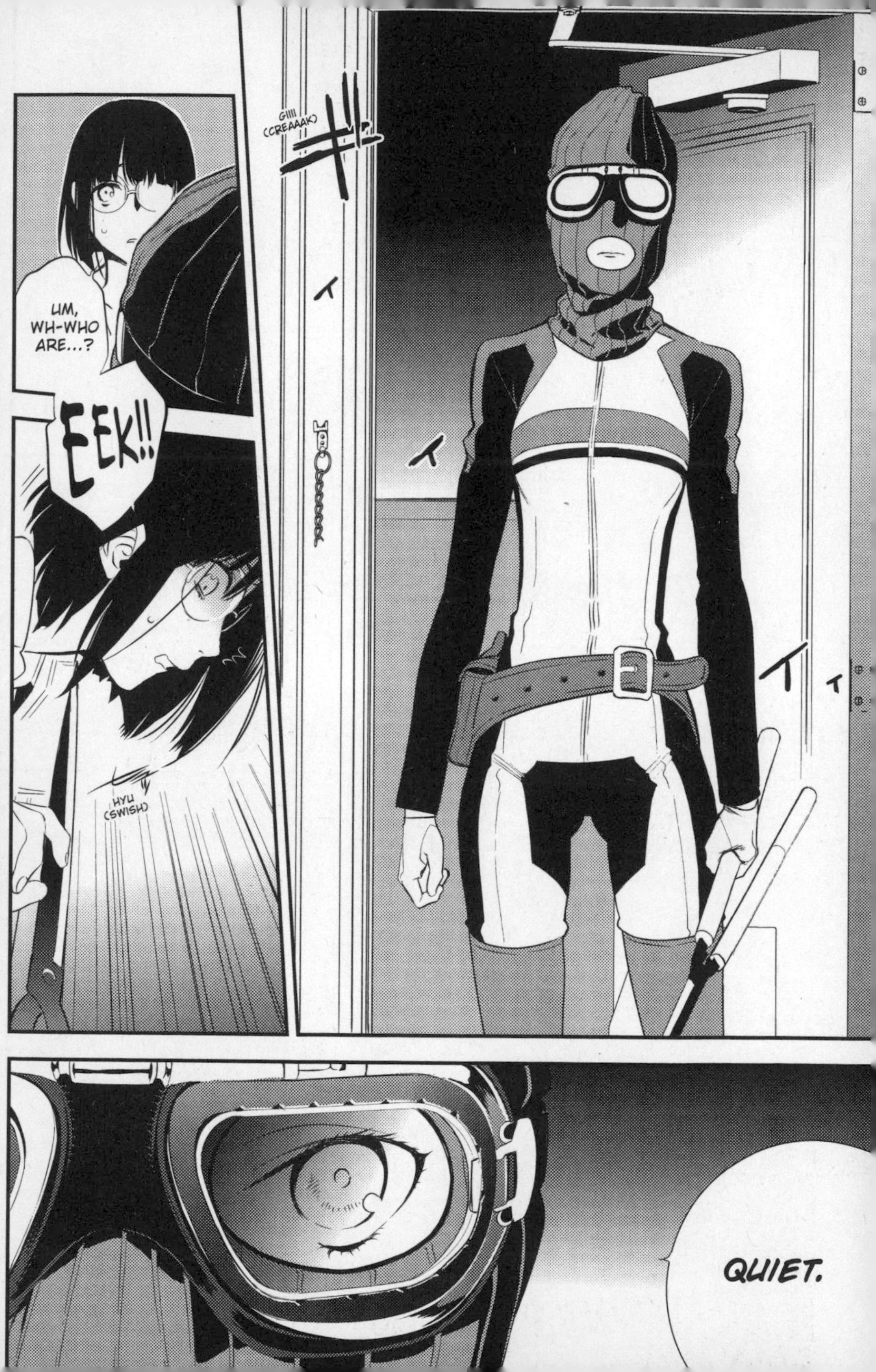
GIIII (CREAAAK)
UM, WH-WHO ARE...?
EEK!!
HYU (SWISH)
QUIET.

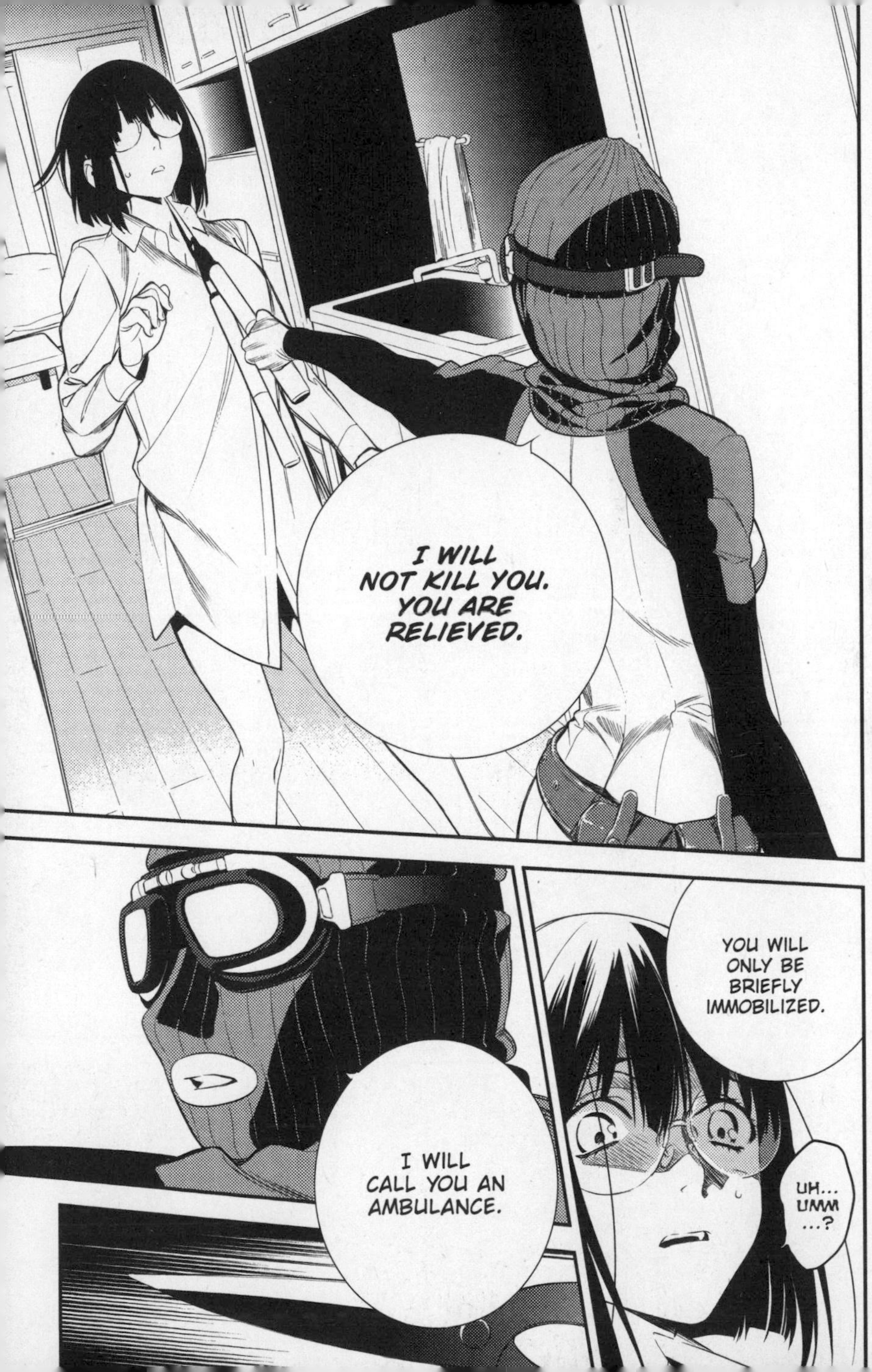
I WILL NOT KILL YOU. YOU ARE RELIEVED.
YOU WILL ONLY BE BRIEFLY IMMOBILIZED.
I WILL CALL YOU AN AMBULANCE.
UH... UMM ...?

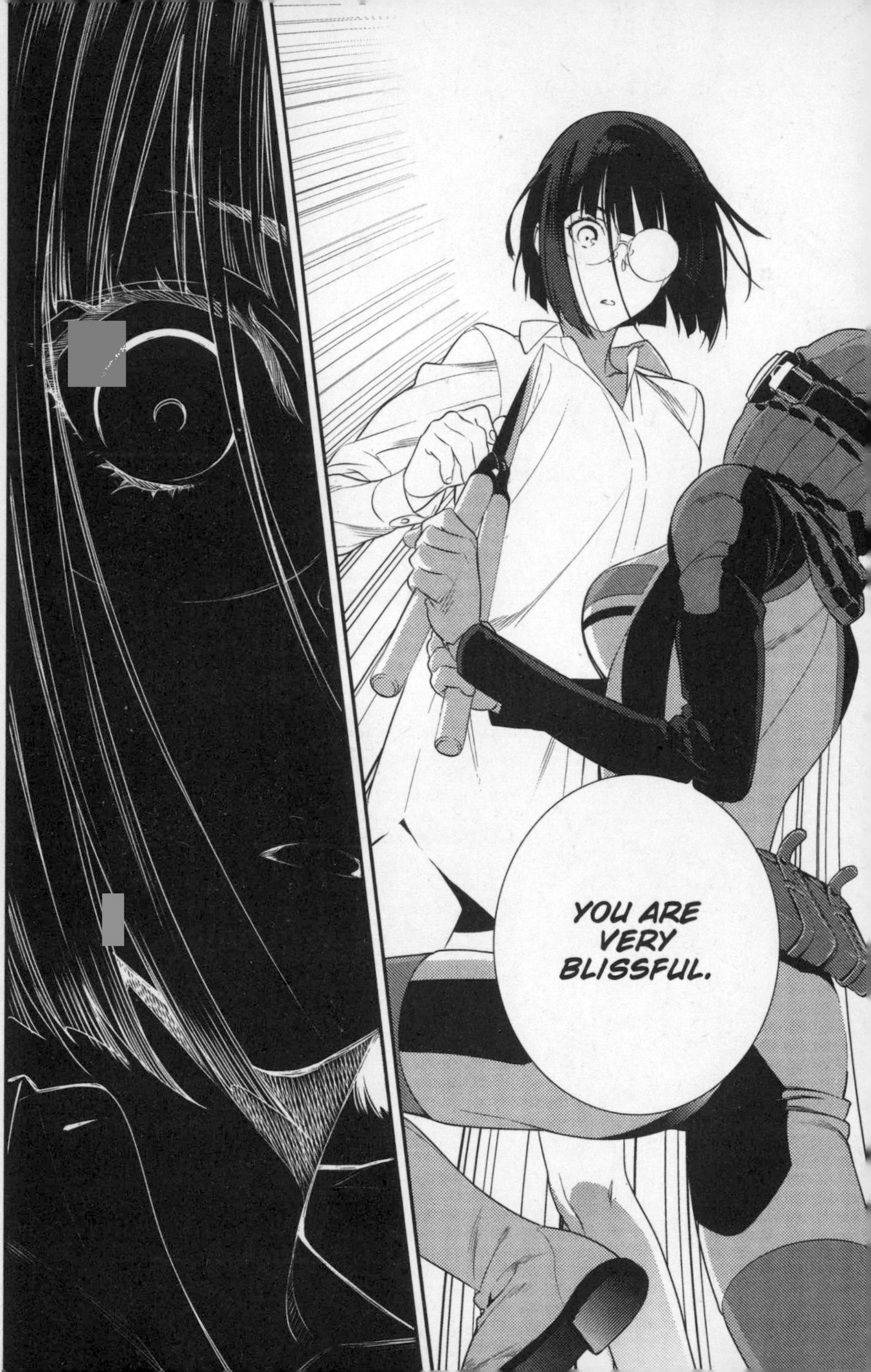
YOU ARE VERY BLISSFUL.

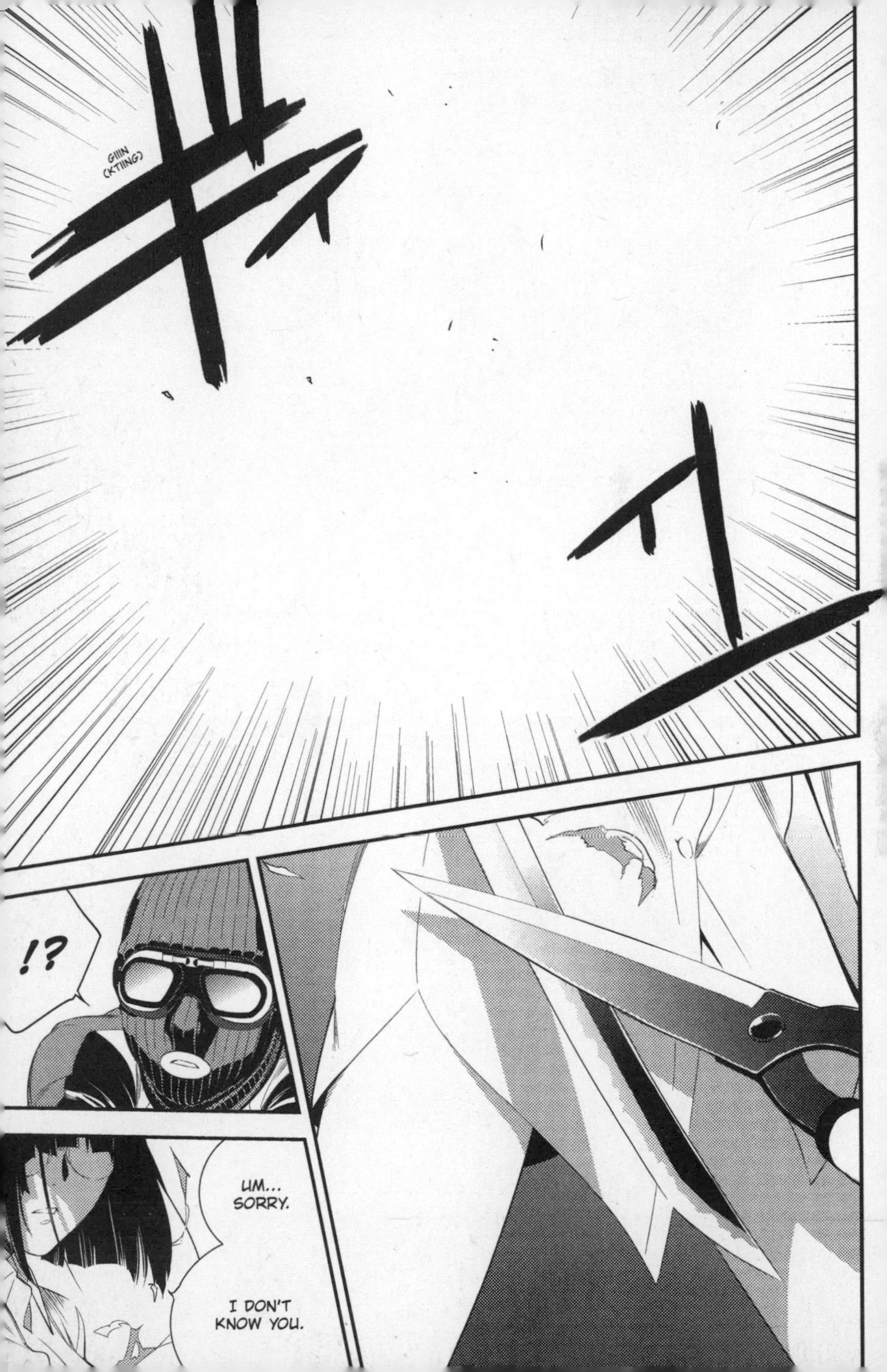
GIIIN (KTIING)
!?
UM... SORRY.
I DON'T KNOW YOU.

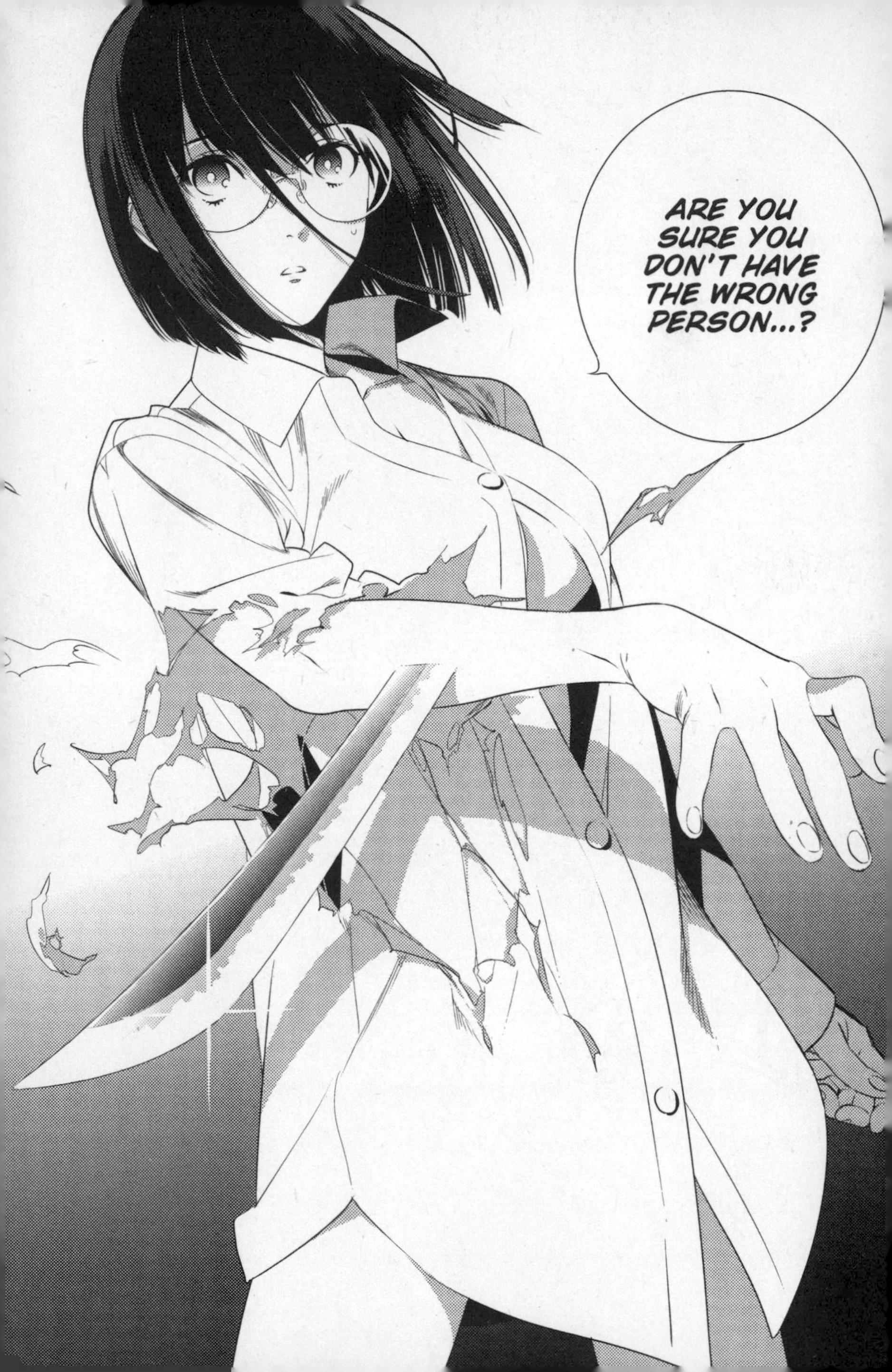
ARE YOU SURE YOU DON'T HAVE THE WRONG PERSON...?

CHAPTER 6 ✗ THE INFO DEALER PLOTS AND DANCES

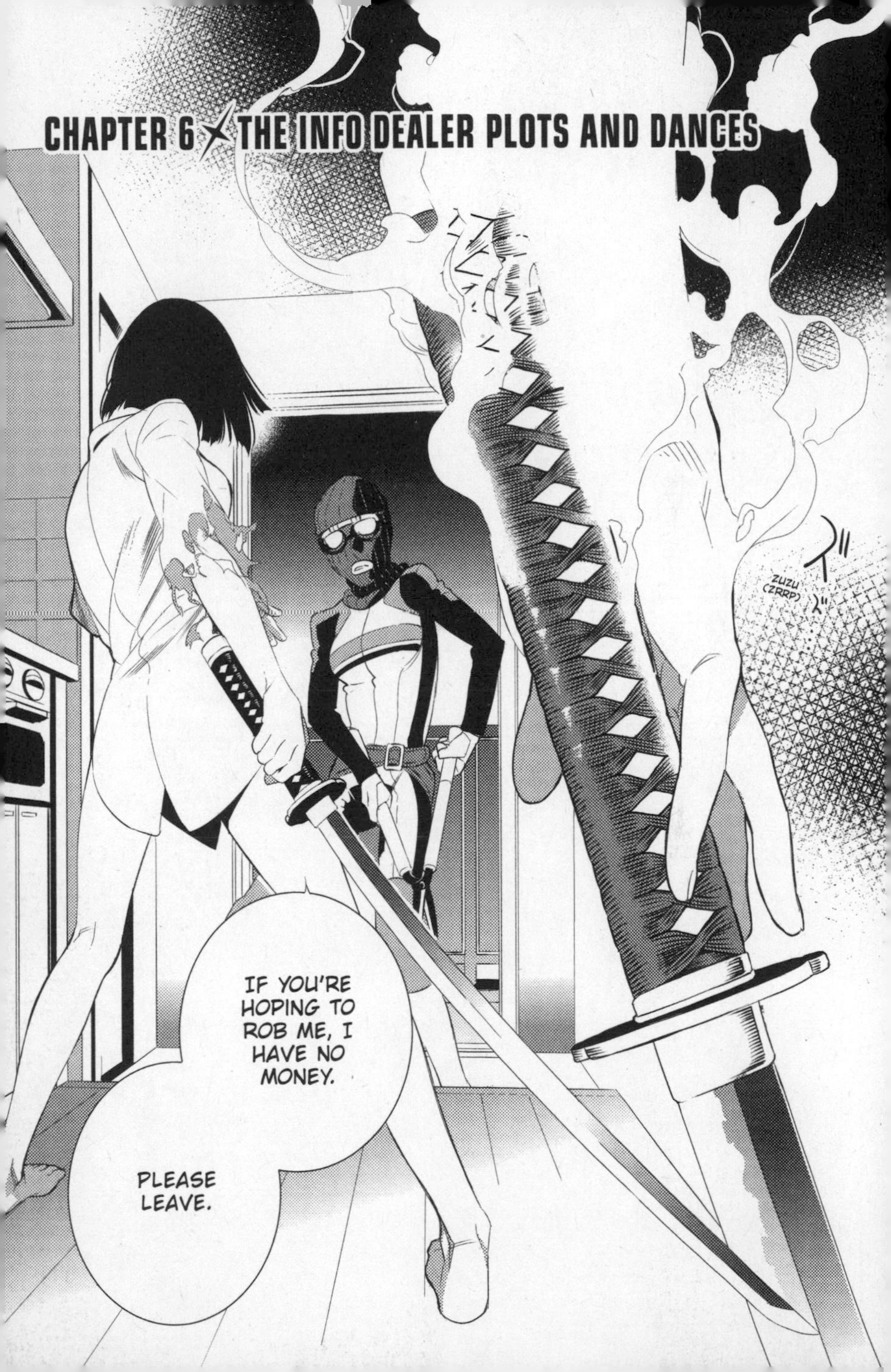
ZUZU (ZRRP)
IF YOU'RE HOPING TO ROB ME, I HAVE NO MONEY.
PLEASE LEAVE.

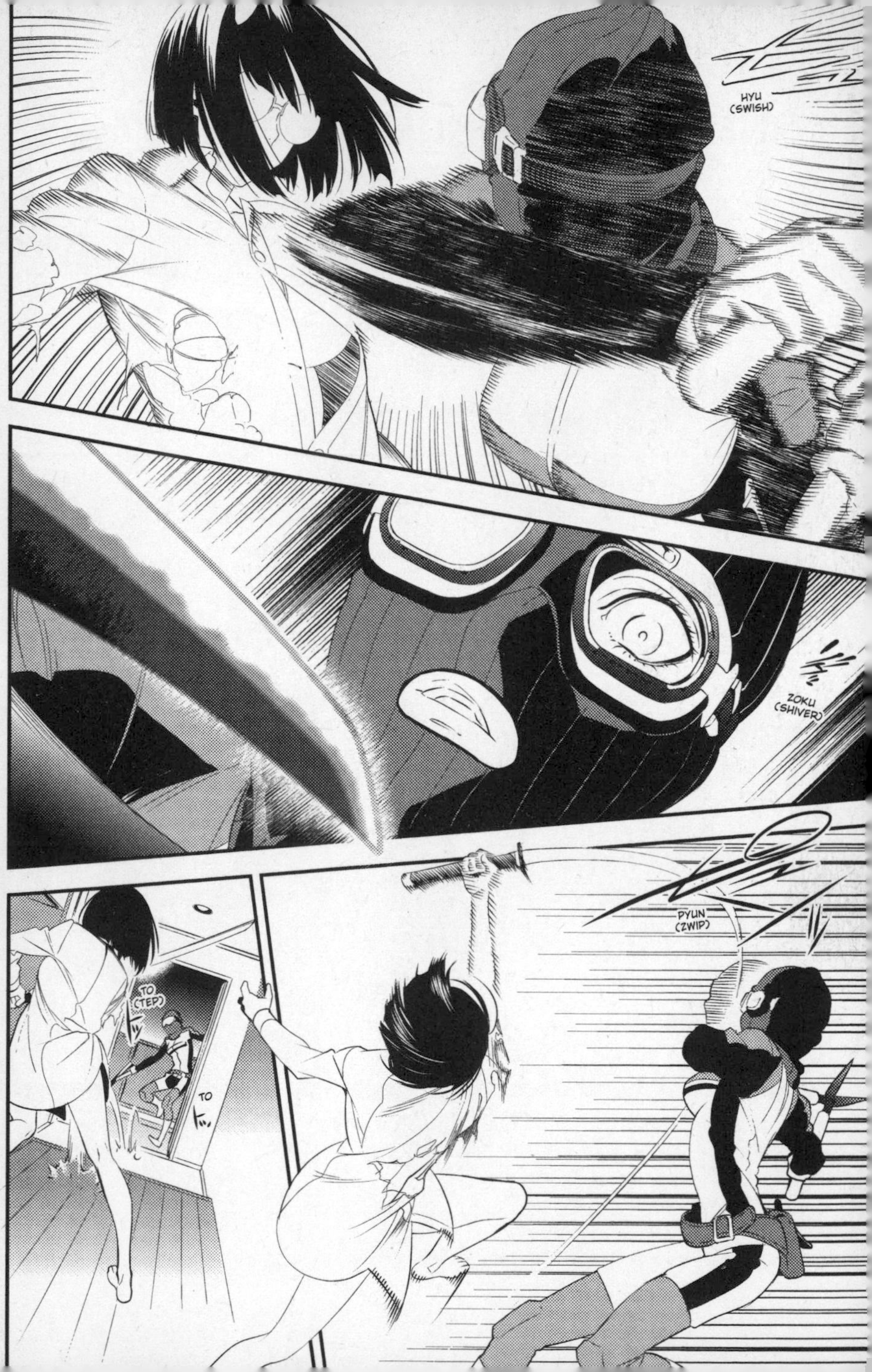
HYU
(SWISH)
ZOKU
(SHIVER)
PYUN
(ZWIP)
TO
(TEP)
TO

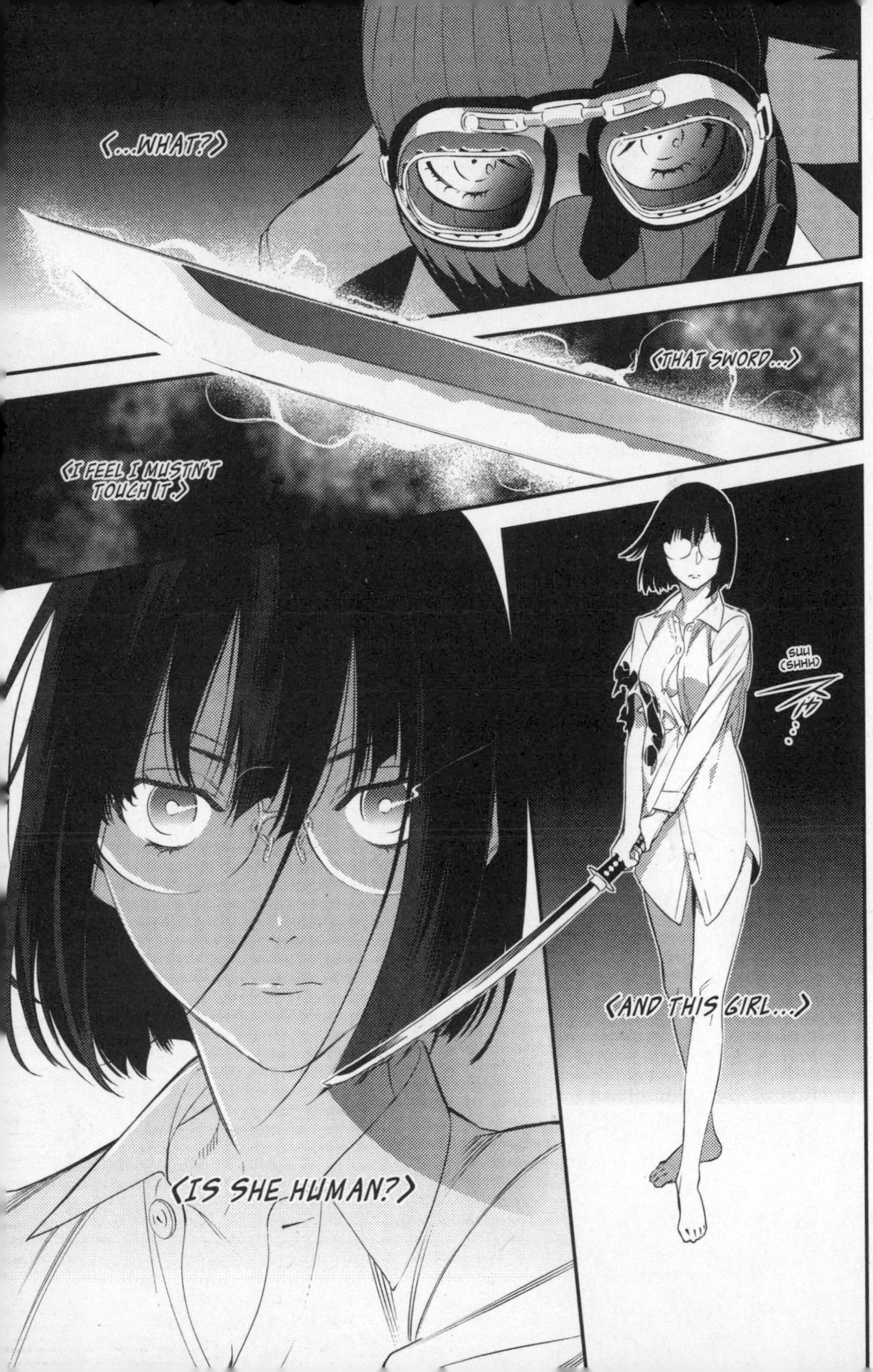
〈...WHAT?〉
〈THAT SWORD...〉
〈I FEEL I MUSTN'T TOUCH IT.〉
SUU (SHHH)
〈AND THIS GIRL...〉
〈IS SHE HUMAN?〉

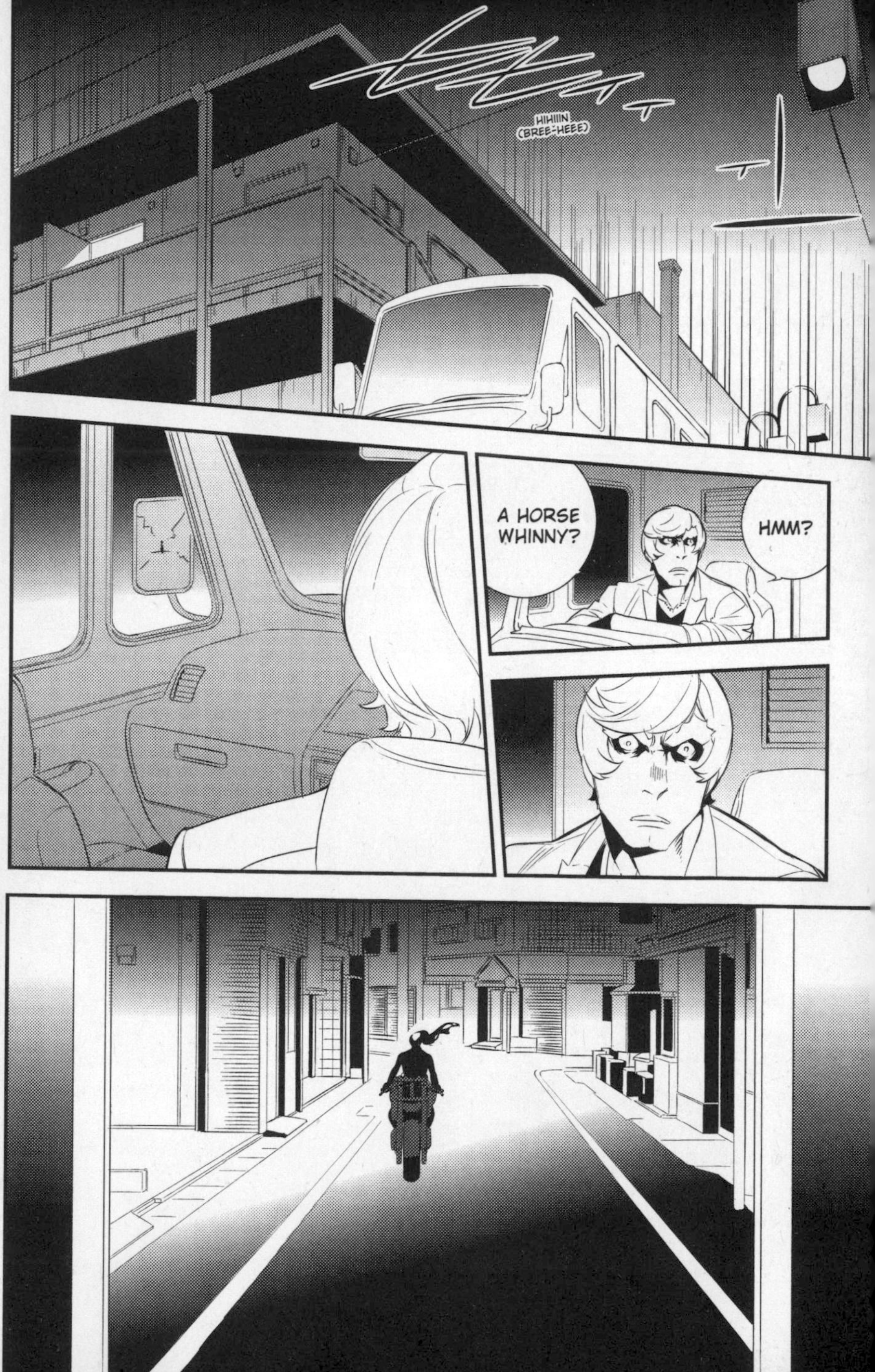
HIHIIIN (BREE-HEEE)
HMM?
A HORSE WHINNY?

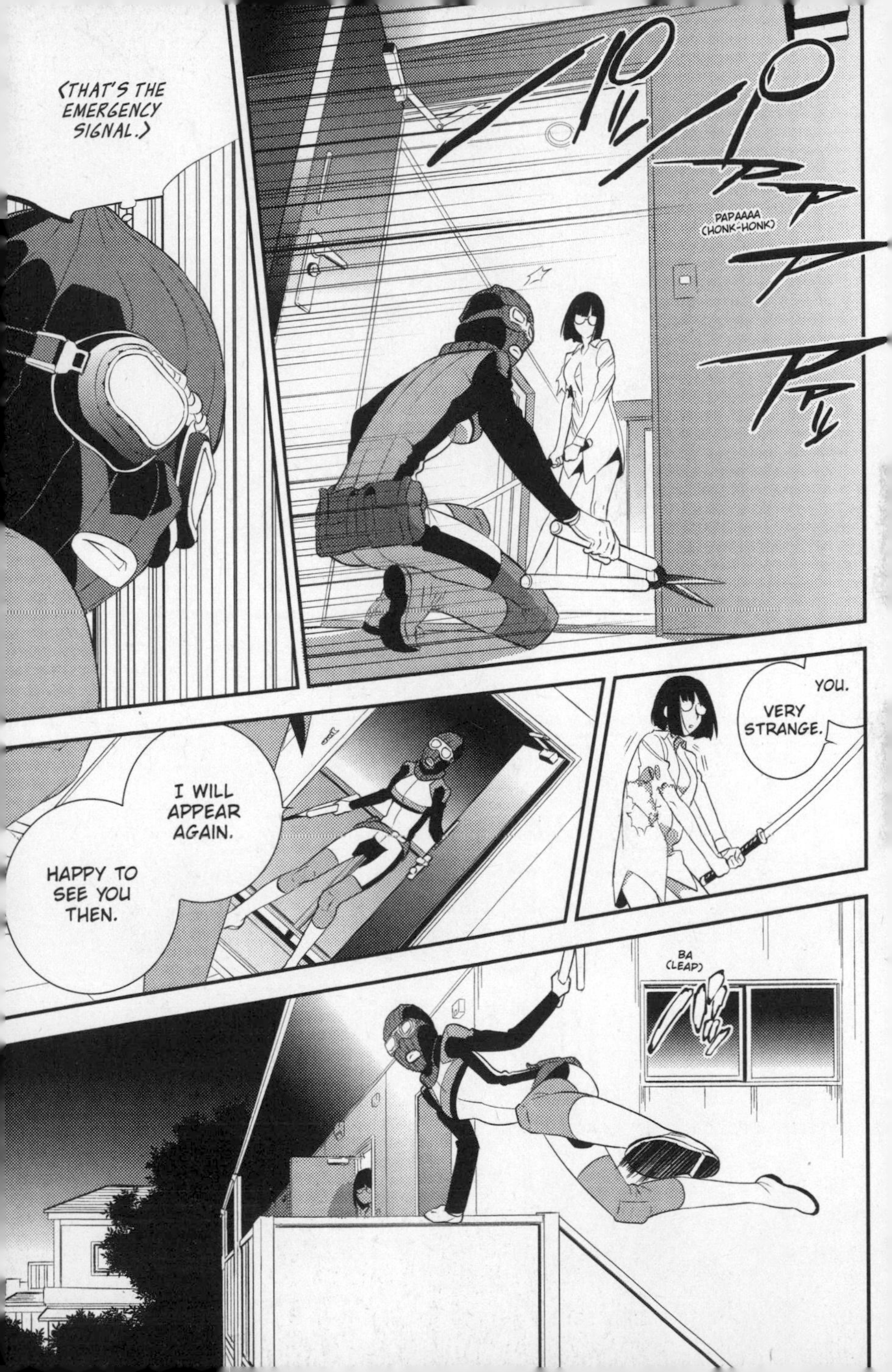
PAPAAAA
(HONK-HONK)
<THAT'S THE EMERGENCY SIGNAL.>
YOU.
VERY STRANGE.
I WILL APPEAR AGAIN.
HAPPY TO SEE YOU THEN.
BA
(LEAP)

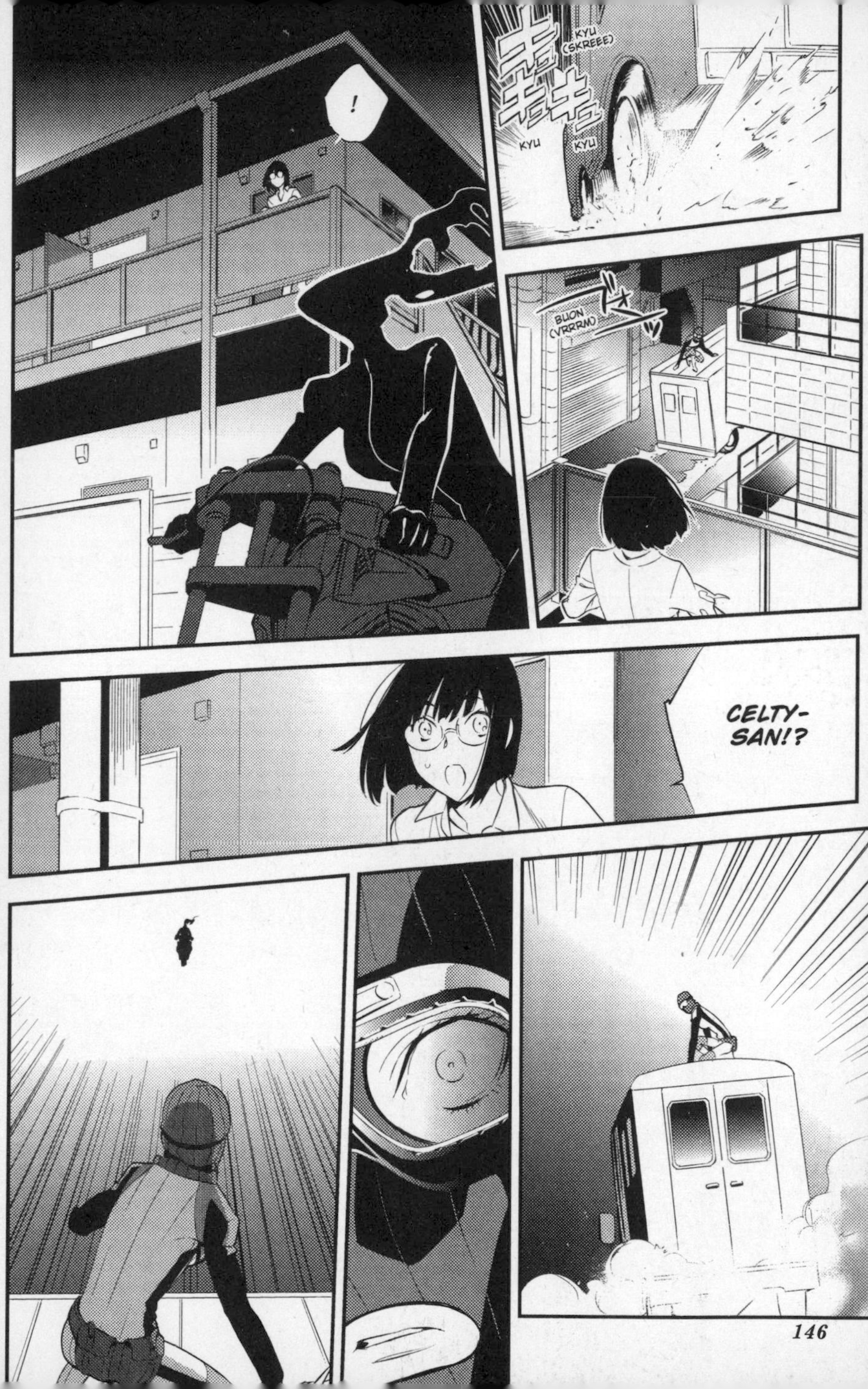
KYU (SKREEE)
KYU
KYU
BUON (VRRRM)
!
CELTY-SAN!?

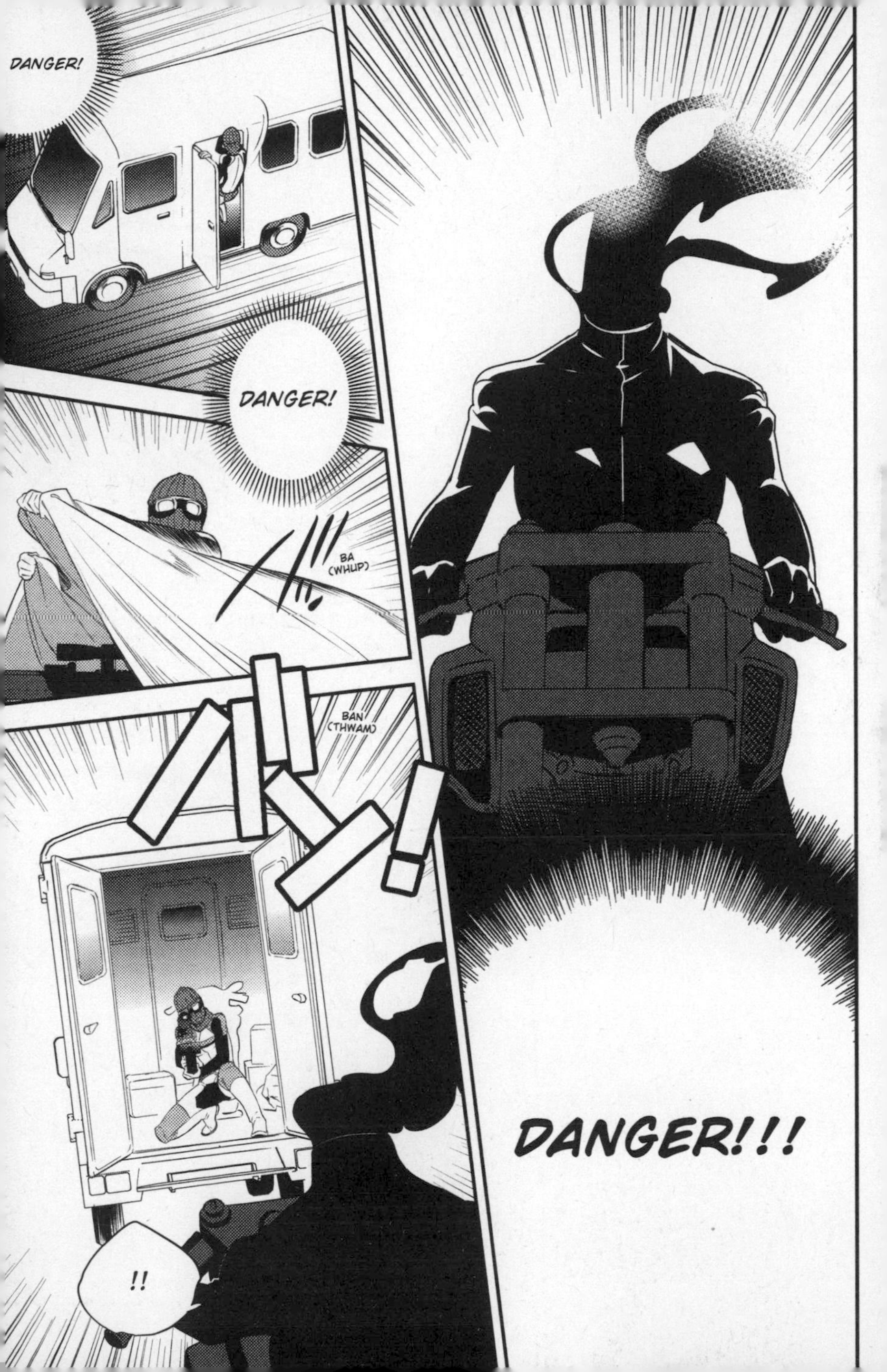
DANGER!!!
DANGER!
DANGER!
BA (WHUP)
BAN (THWAM)
!!

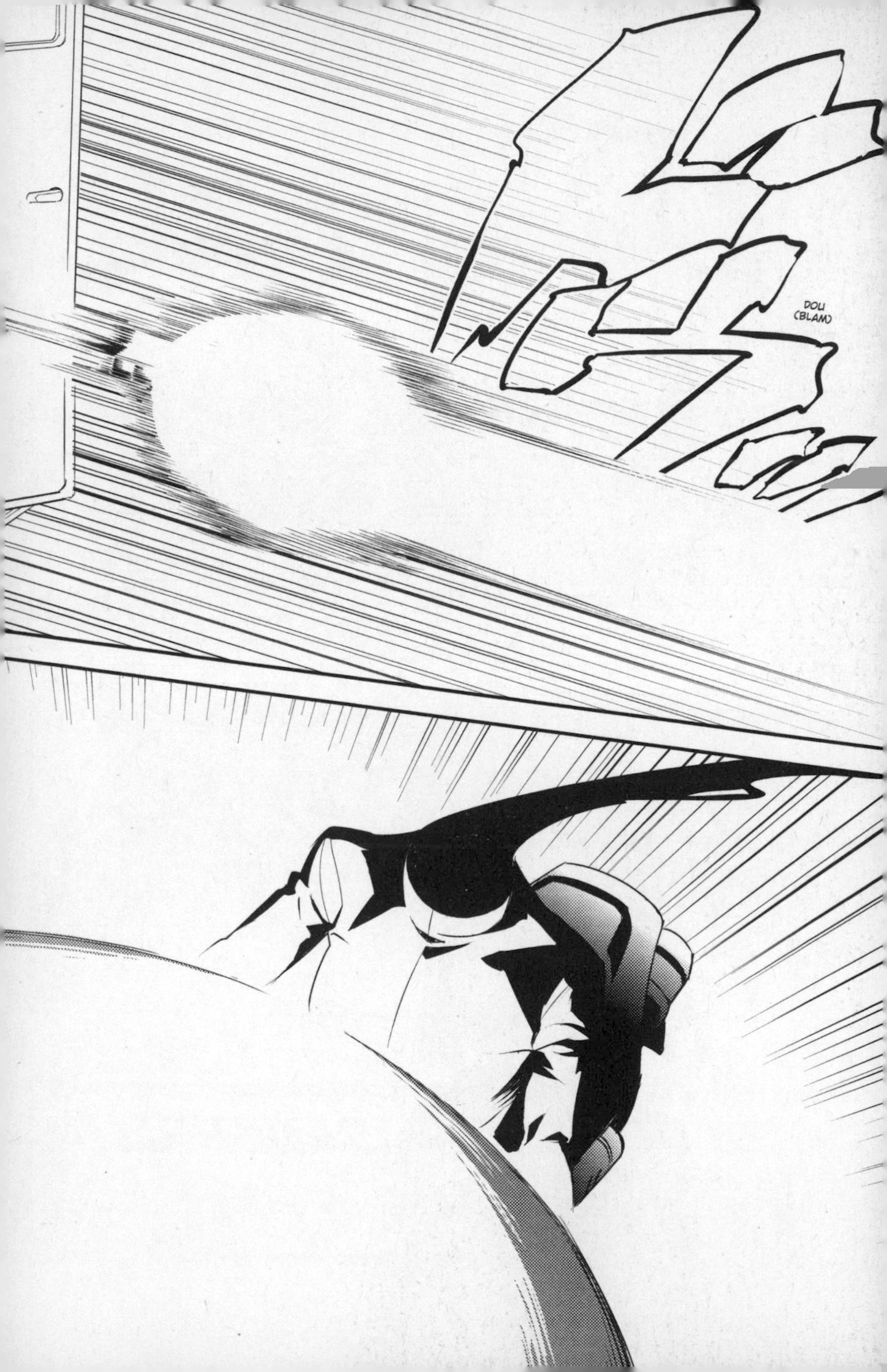
DOU
(BLAM)

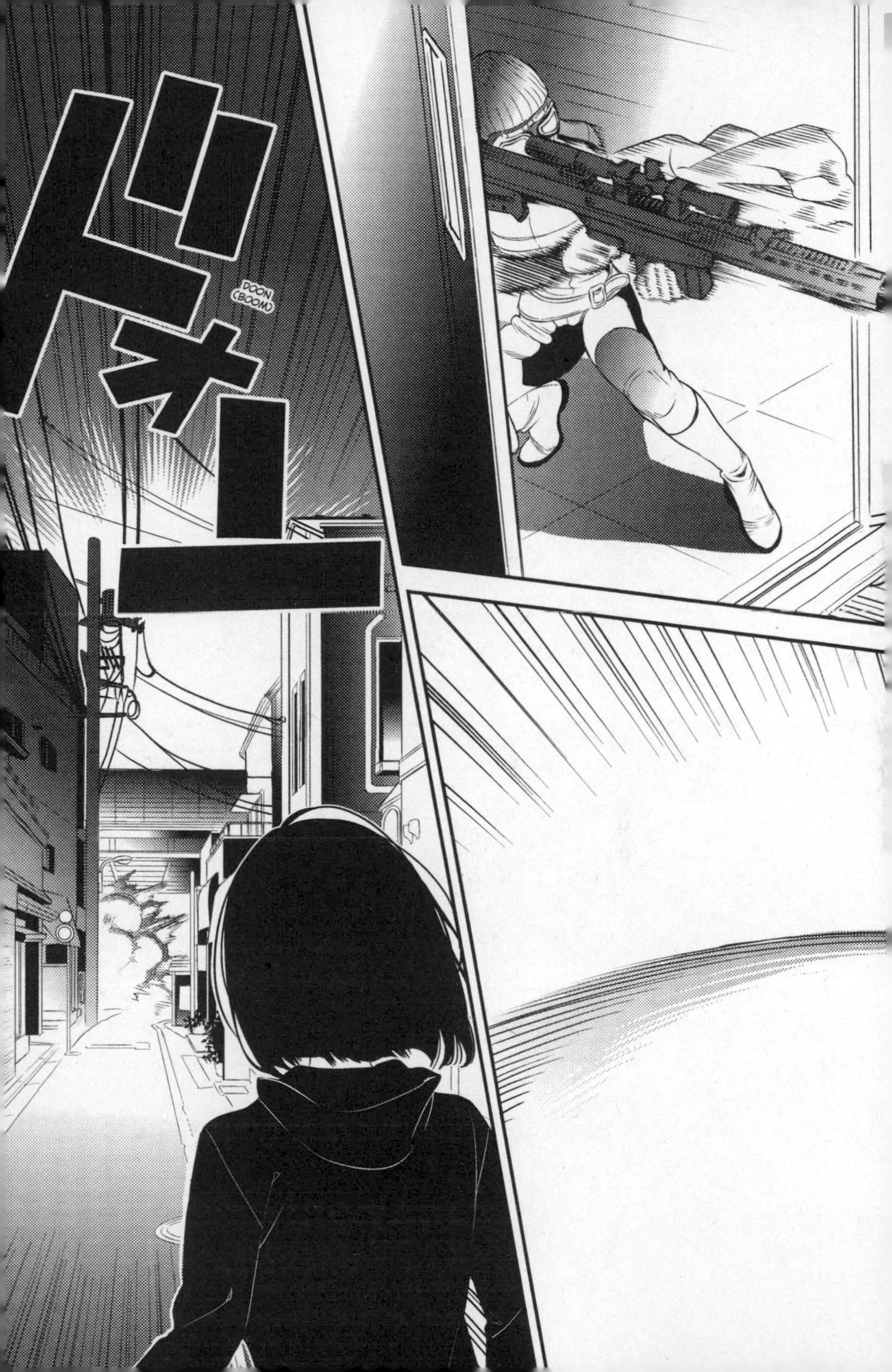
ドォーン
DOON (BOOM)

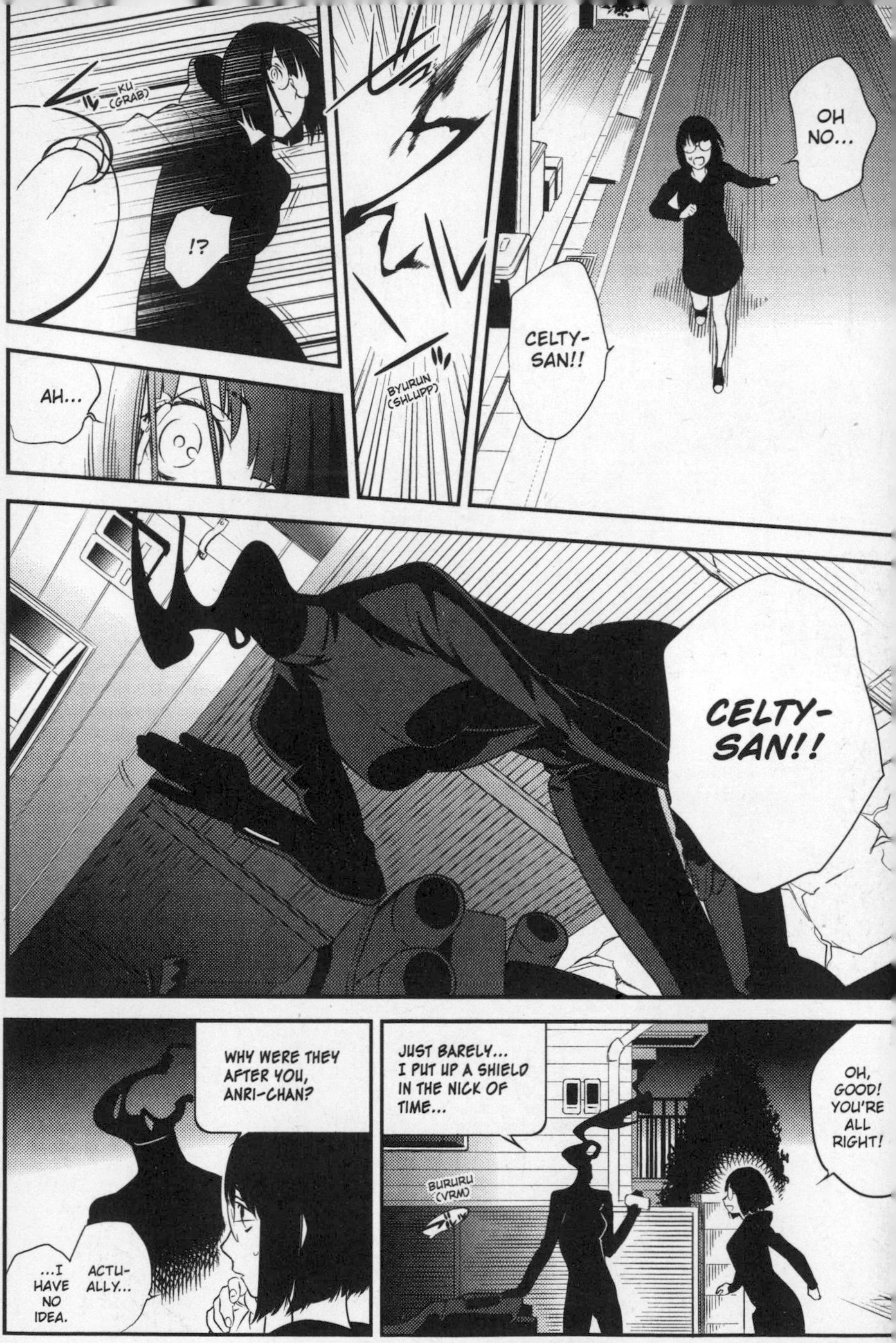
OH NO...
CELTY-SAN!!
BYURUN (SHLUPP)
KU (GRAB)
!?
AH...
CELTY-SAN!!
OH, GOOD! YOU'RE ALL RIGHT!
JUST BARELY... I PUT UP A SHIELD IN THE NICK OF TIME...
BURURU (VRM)
WHY WERE THEY AFTER YOU, ANRI-CHAN?
ACTUALLY...
...I HAVE NO IDEA.

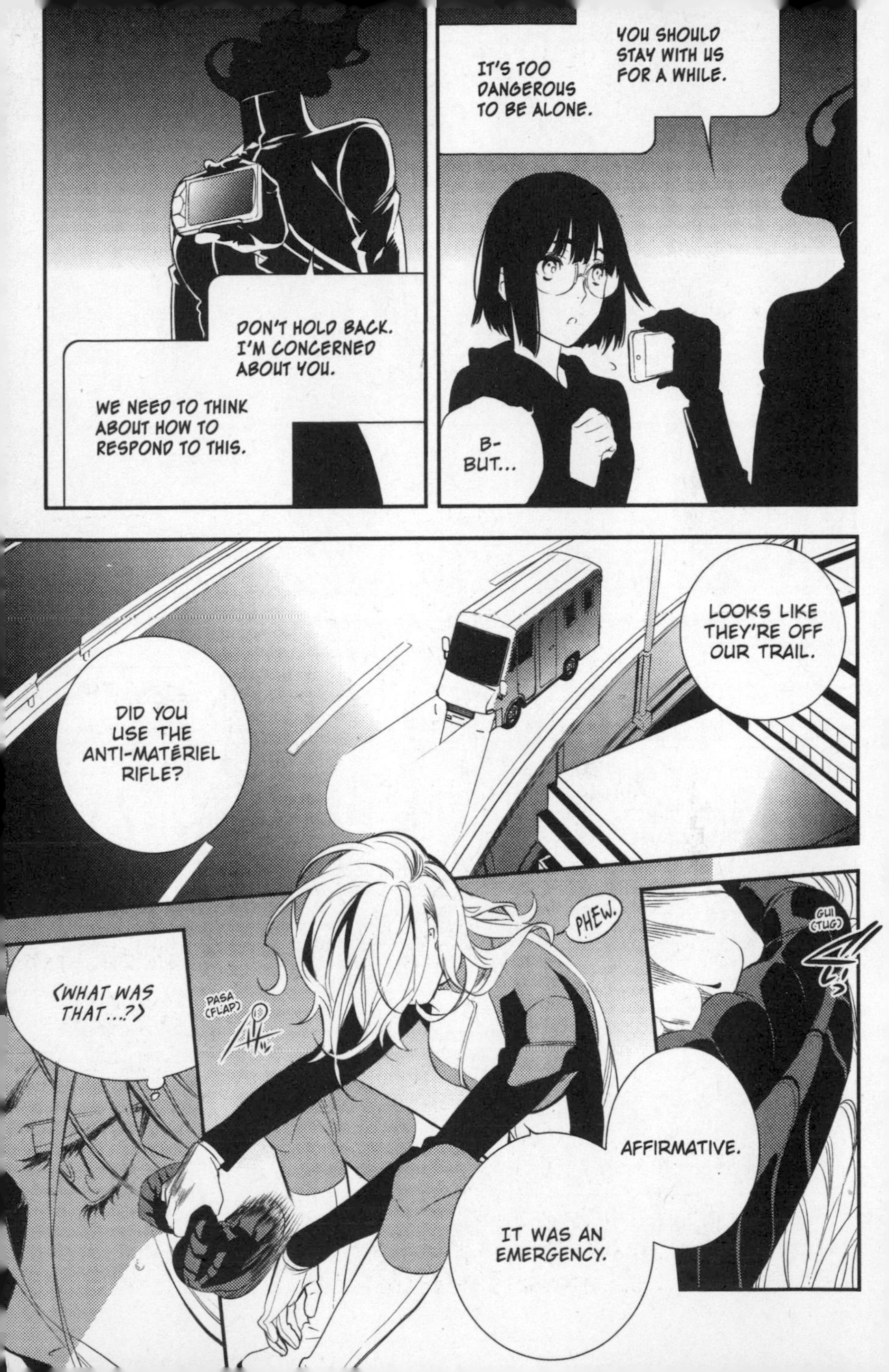

YOU SHOULD STAY WITH US FOR A WHILE.
IT'S TOO DANGEROUS TO BE ALONE.
B-BUT...
DON'T HOLD BACK. I'M CONCERNED ABOUT YOU.
WE NEED TO THINK ABOUT HOW TO RESPOND TO THIS.
LOOKS LIKE THEY'RE OFF OUR TRAIL.
DID YOU USE THE ANTI-MATÉRIEL RIFLE?
GUI (TUG)
AFFIRMATIVE.
IT WAS AN EMERGENCY.
PHEW.
PASA (FLAP)
<WHAT WAS THAT...?>

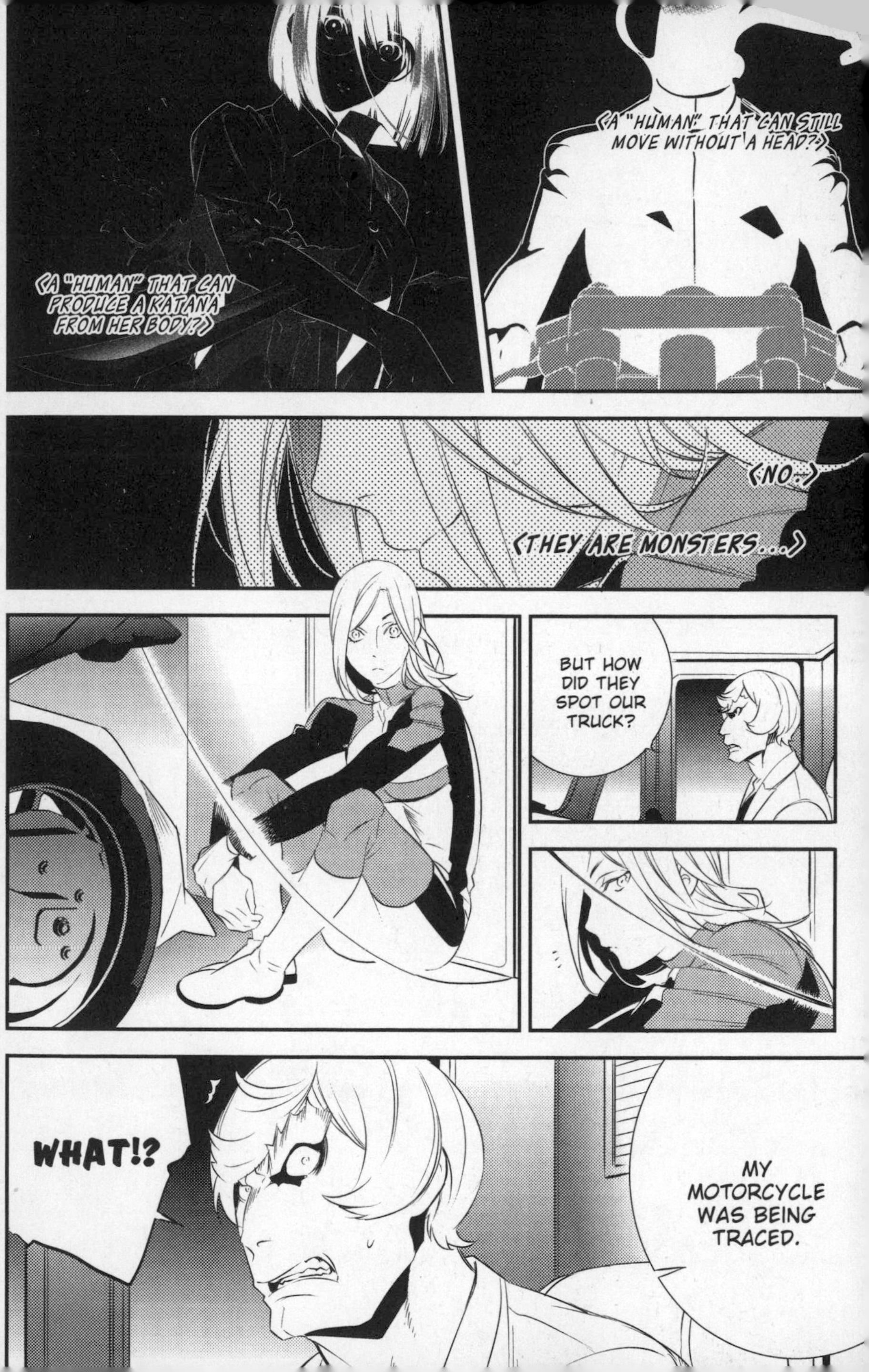

⟨A "HUMAN" THAT CAN STILL MOVE WITHOUT A HEAD?⟩
⟨A "HUMAN" THAT CAN PRODUCE A KATANA FROM HER BODY?⟩
⟨NO...⟩
⟨THEY ARE MONSTERS...⟩
BUT HOW DID THEY SPOT OUR TRUCK?
MY MOTORCYCLE WAS BEING TRACED.
WHAT!?

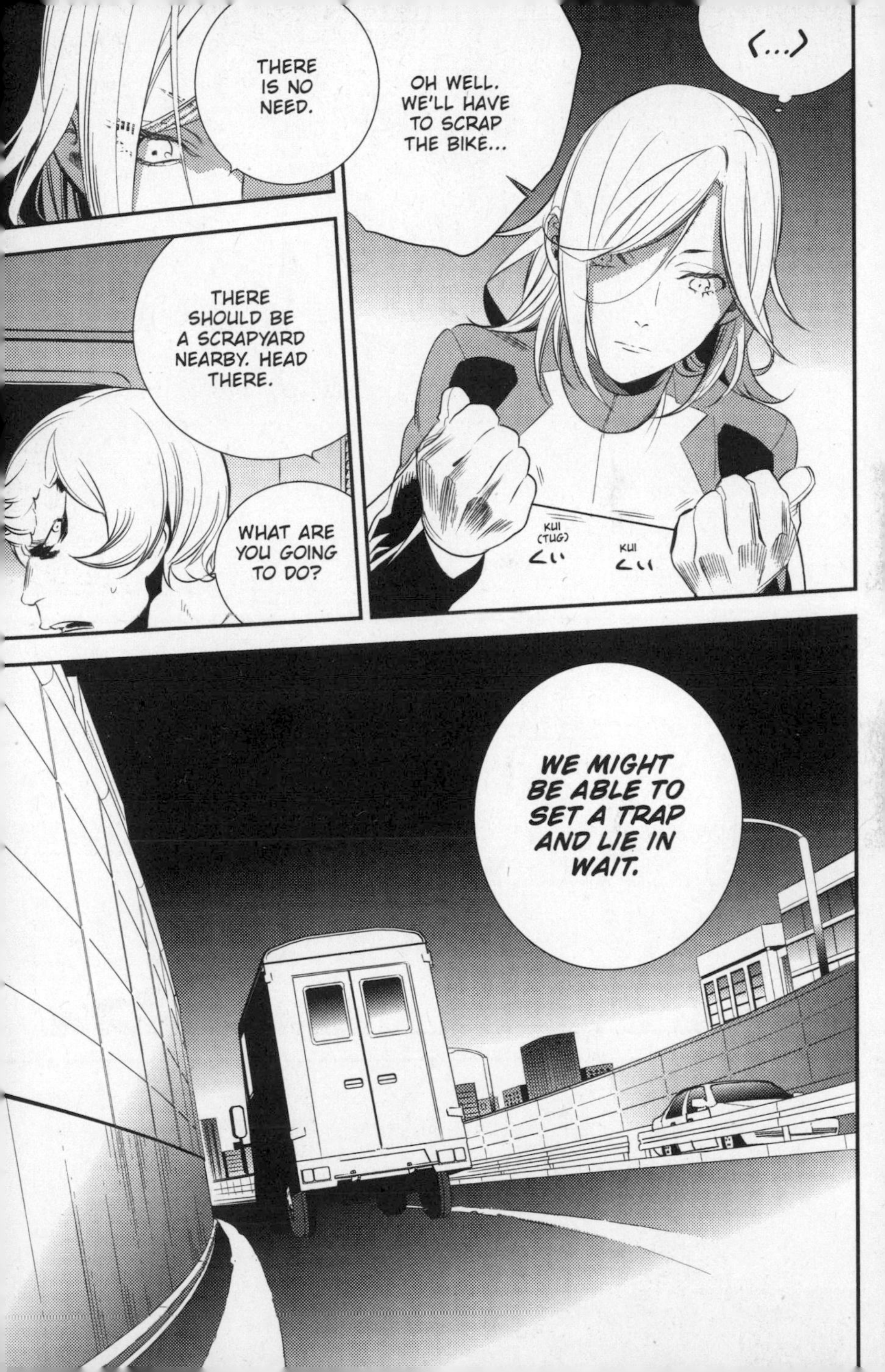
(...)
OH WELL. WE'LL HAVE TO SCRAP THE BIKE...
KUI (TUG) くい
KUI くい
THERE IS NO NEED.
THERE SHOULD BE A SCRAPYARD NEARBY. HEAD THERE.
WHAT ARE YOU GOING TO DO?
WE MIGHT BE ABLE TO SET A TRAP AND LIE IN WAIT.

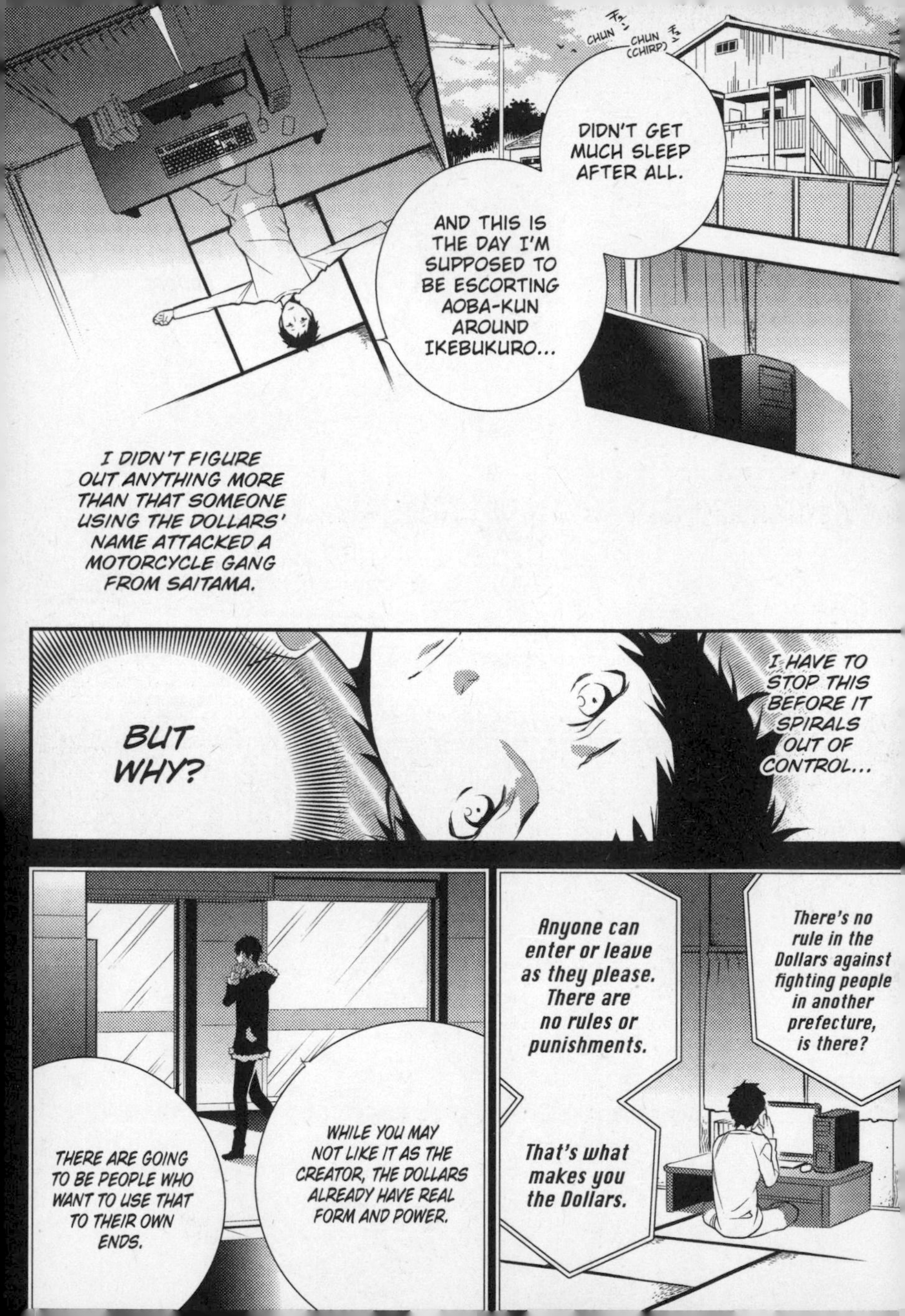
CHUN
CHUN (CHIRP)
DIDN'T GET MUCH SLEEP AFTER ALL.
AND THIS IS THE DAY I'M SUPPOSED TO BE ESCORTING AOBA-KUN AROUND IKEBUKURO...
I DIDN'T FIGURE OUT ANYTHING MORE THAN THAT SOMEONE USING THE DOLLARS' NAME ATTACKED A MOTORCYCLE GANG FROM SAITAMA.
I HAVE TO STOP THIS BEFORE IT SPIRALS OUT OF CONTROL...
BUT WHY?
There's no rule in the Dollars against fighting people in another prefecture, is there?
Anyone can enter or leave as they please. There are no rules or punishments.
That's what makes you the Dollars.
WHILE YOU MAY NOT LIKE IT AS THE CREATOR, THE DOLLARS ALREADY HAVE REAL FORM AND POWER.
THERE ARE GOING TO BE PEOPLE WHO WANT TO USE THAT TO THEIR OWN ENDS.

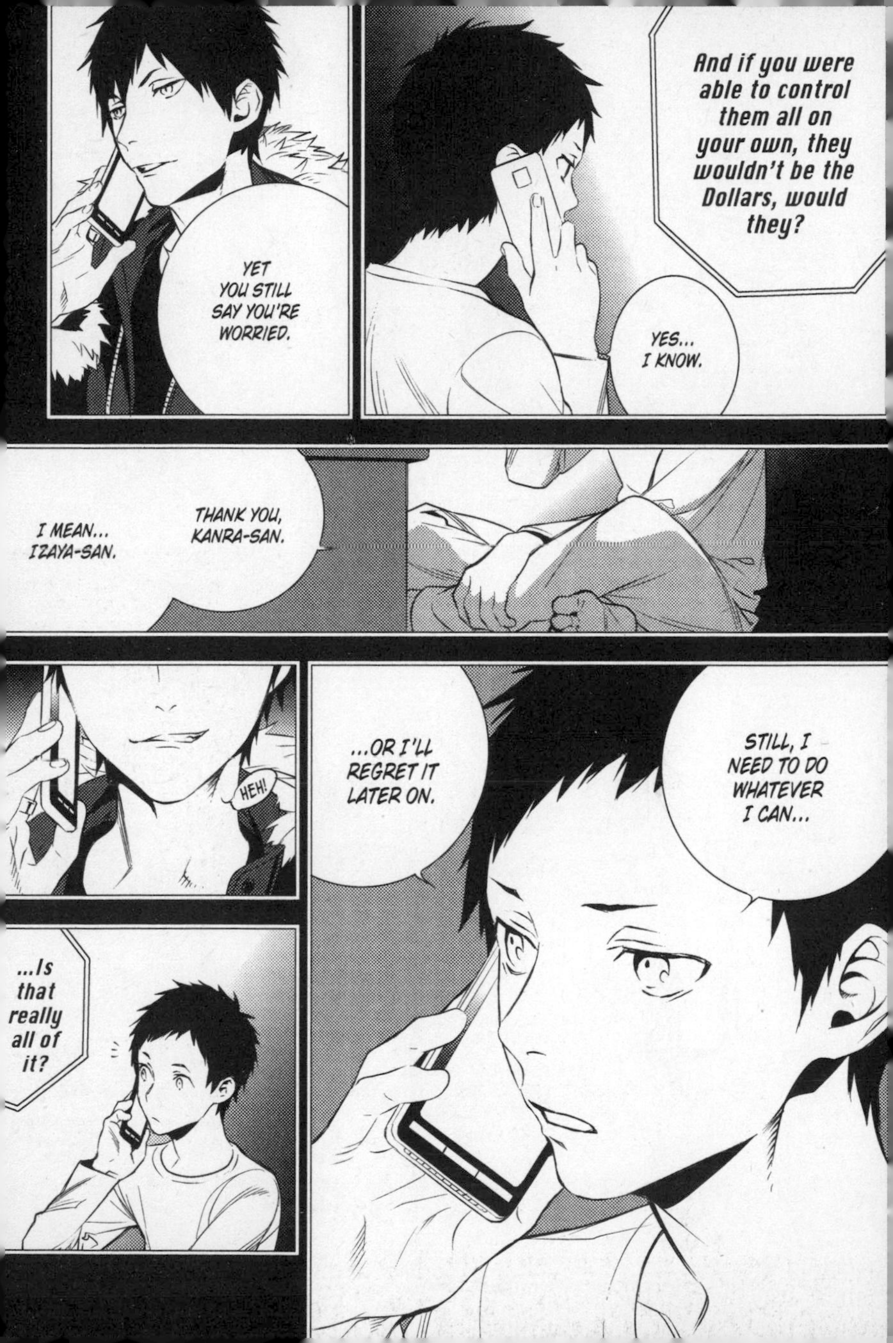
And if you were able to control them all on your own, they wouldn't be the Dollars, would they?
YES... I KNOW.
YET YOU STILL SAY YOU'RE WORRIED.
THANK YOU, KANRA-SAN.
I MEAN... IZAYA-SAN.
STILL, I NEED TO DO WHATEVER I CAN...
...OR I'LL REGRET IT LATER ON.
HEH!
...Is that really all of it?

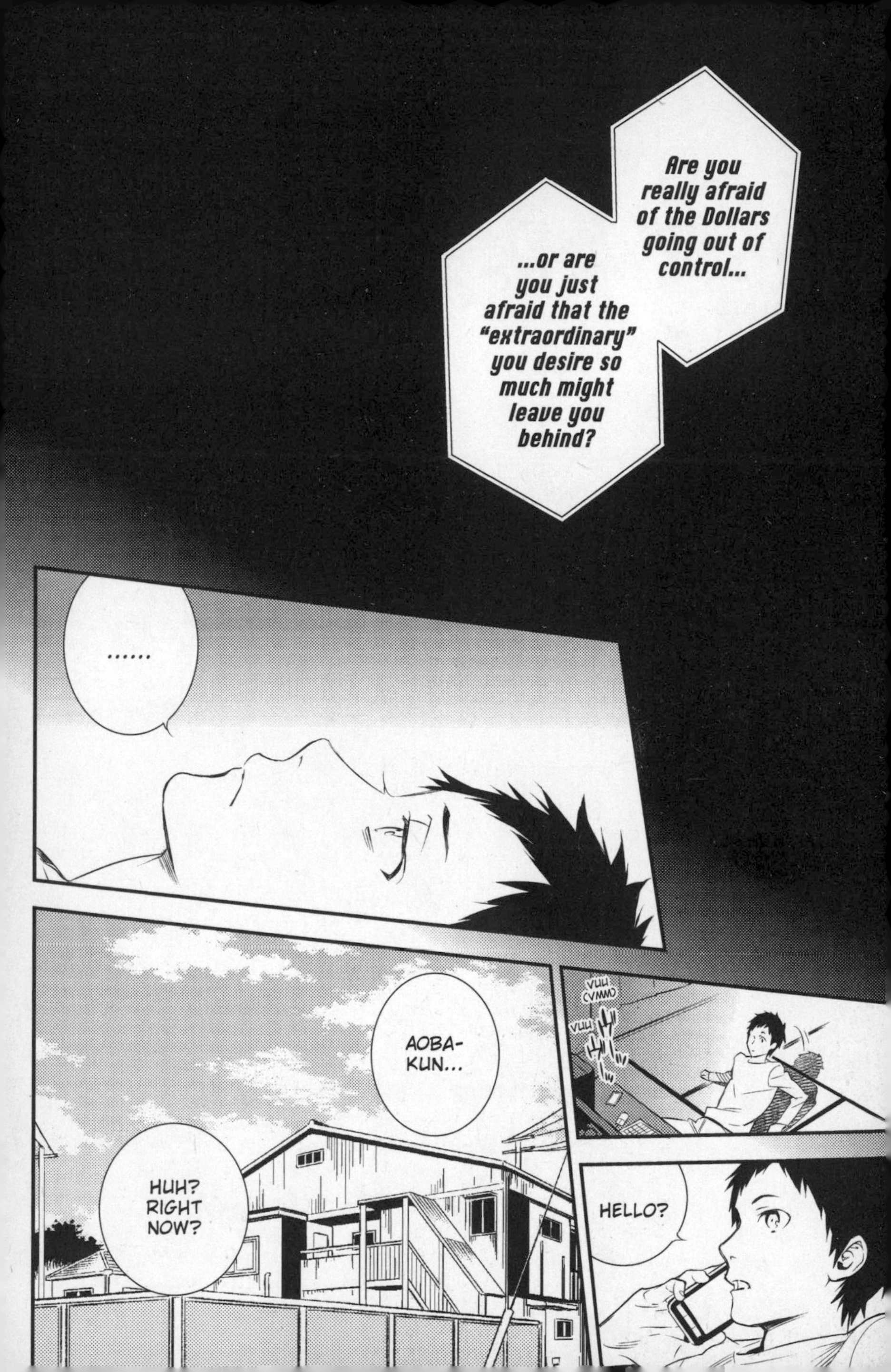
Are you really afraid of the Dollars going out of control...
...or are you just afraid that the "extraordinary" you desire so much might leave you behind?
......
VUU (VMM)
VUU
HELLO?
AOBA-KUN...
HUH? RIGHT NOW?

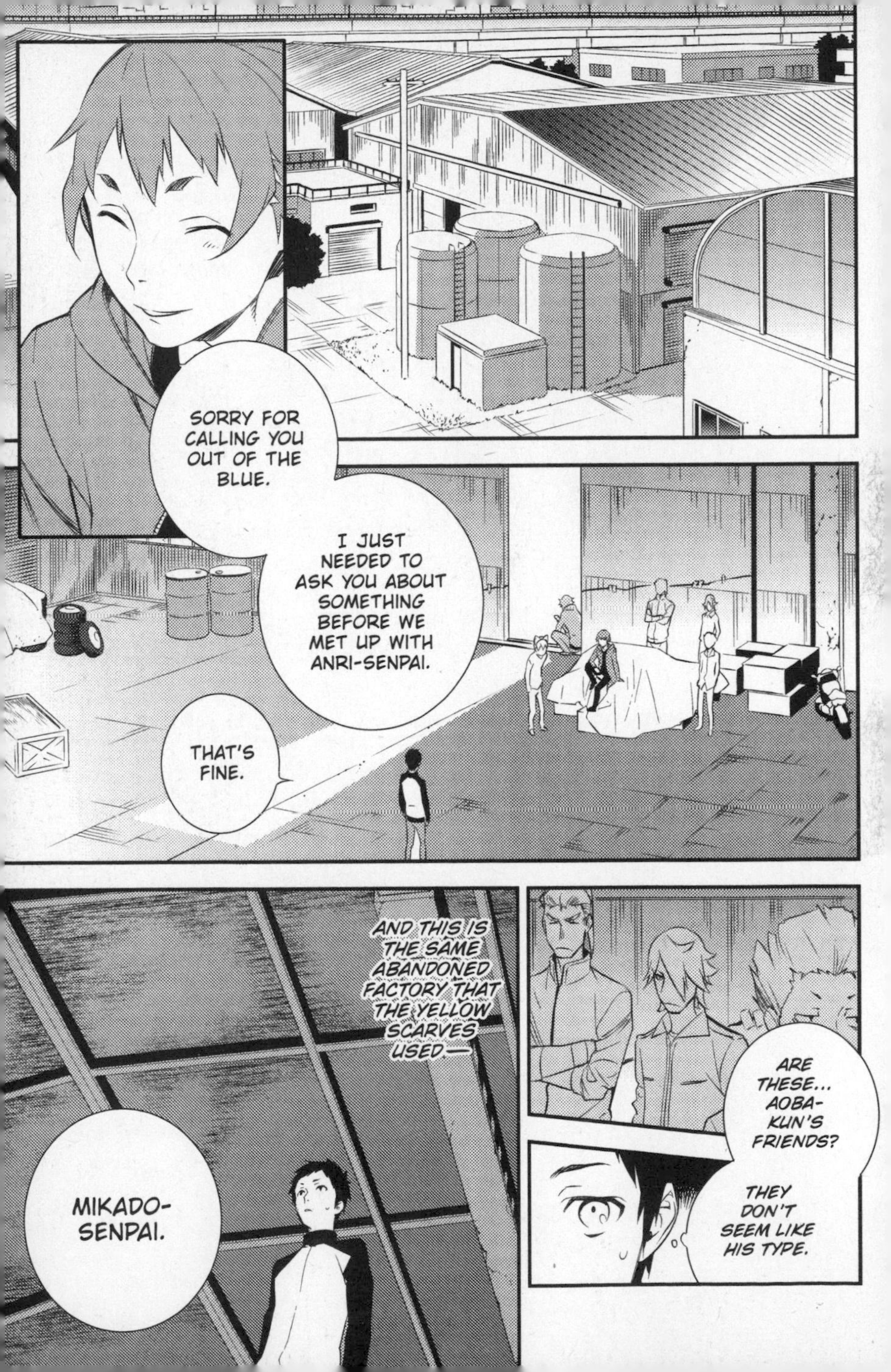
SORRY FOR CALLING YOU OUT OF THE BLUE.
I JUST NEEDED TO ASK YOU ABOUT SOMETHING BEFORE WE MET UP WITH ANRI-SENPAI.
THAT'S FINE.
ARE THESE... AOBA-KUN'S FRIENDS?
THEY DON'T SEEM LIKE HIS TYPE.
AND THIS IS THE SAME ABANDONED FACTORY THAT THE YELLOW SCARVES USED—
MIKADO-SENPAI.

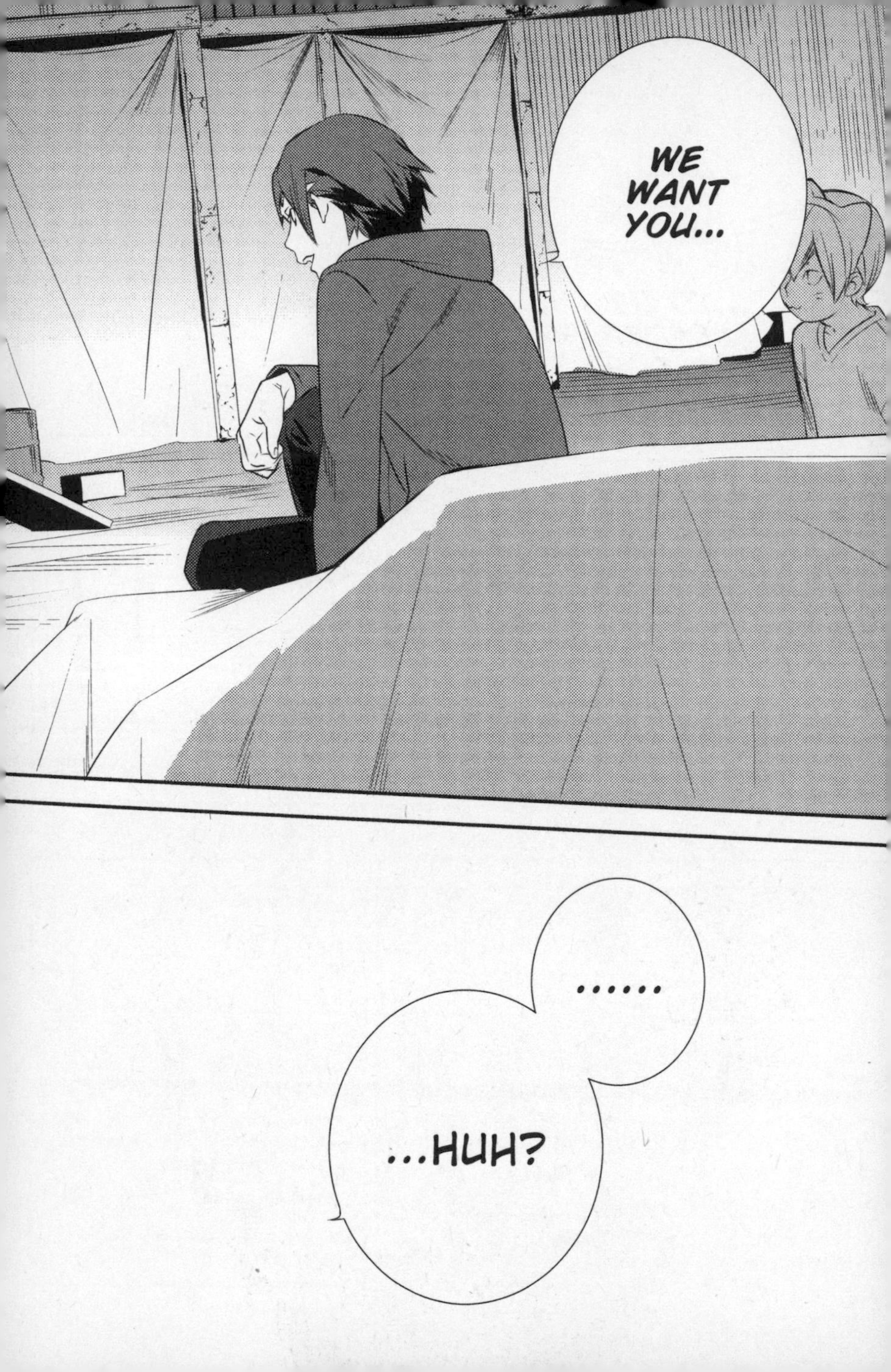
WE WANT YOU...
......
...HUH?

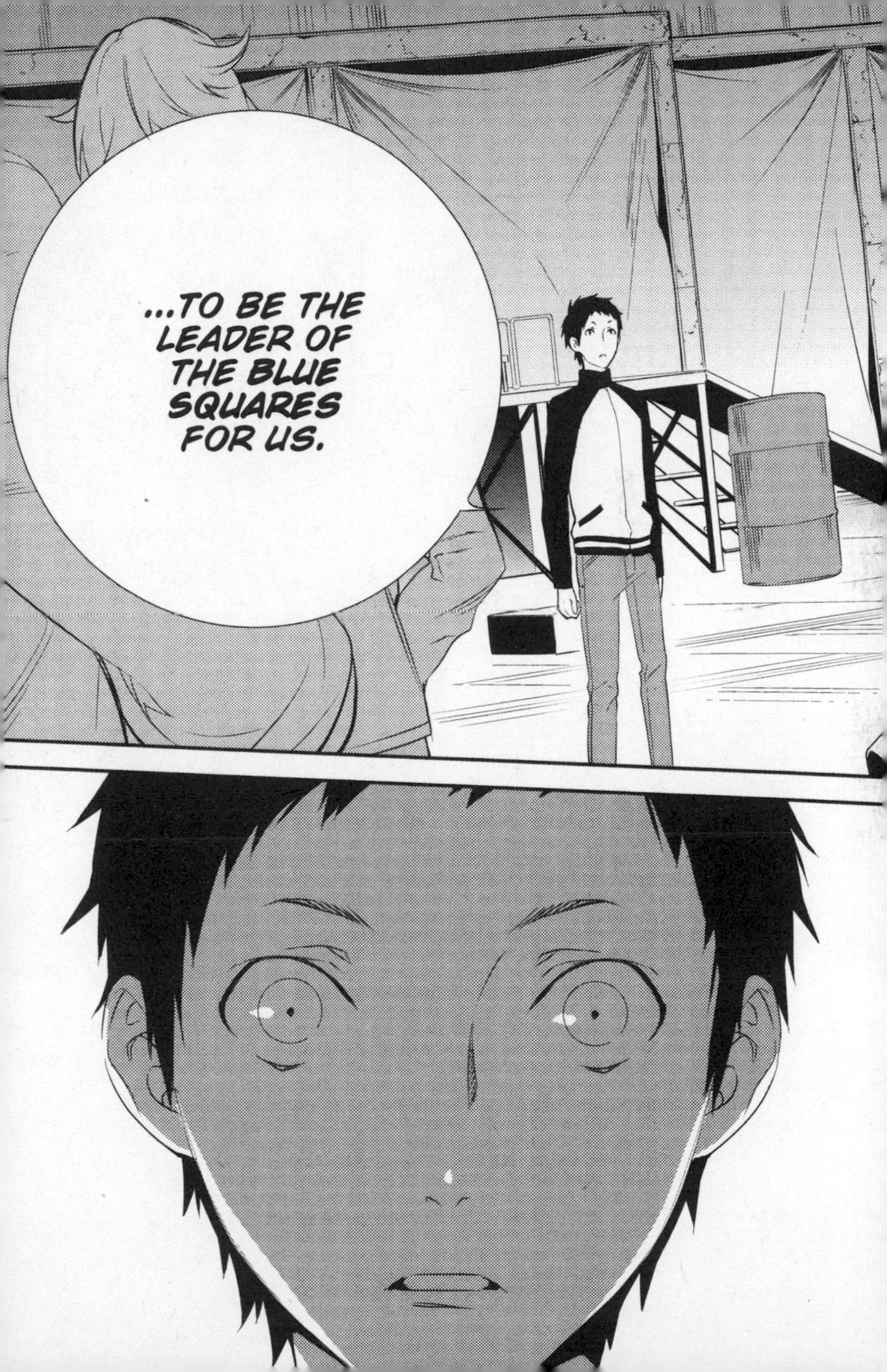
...TO BE THE LEADER OF THE BLUE SQUARES FOR US.

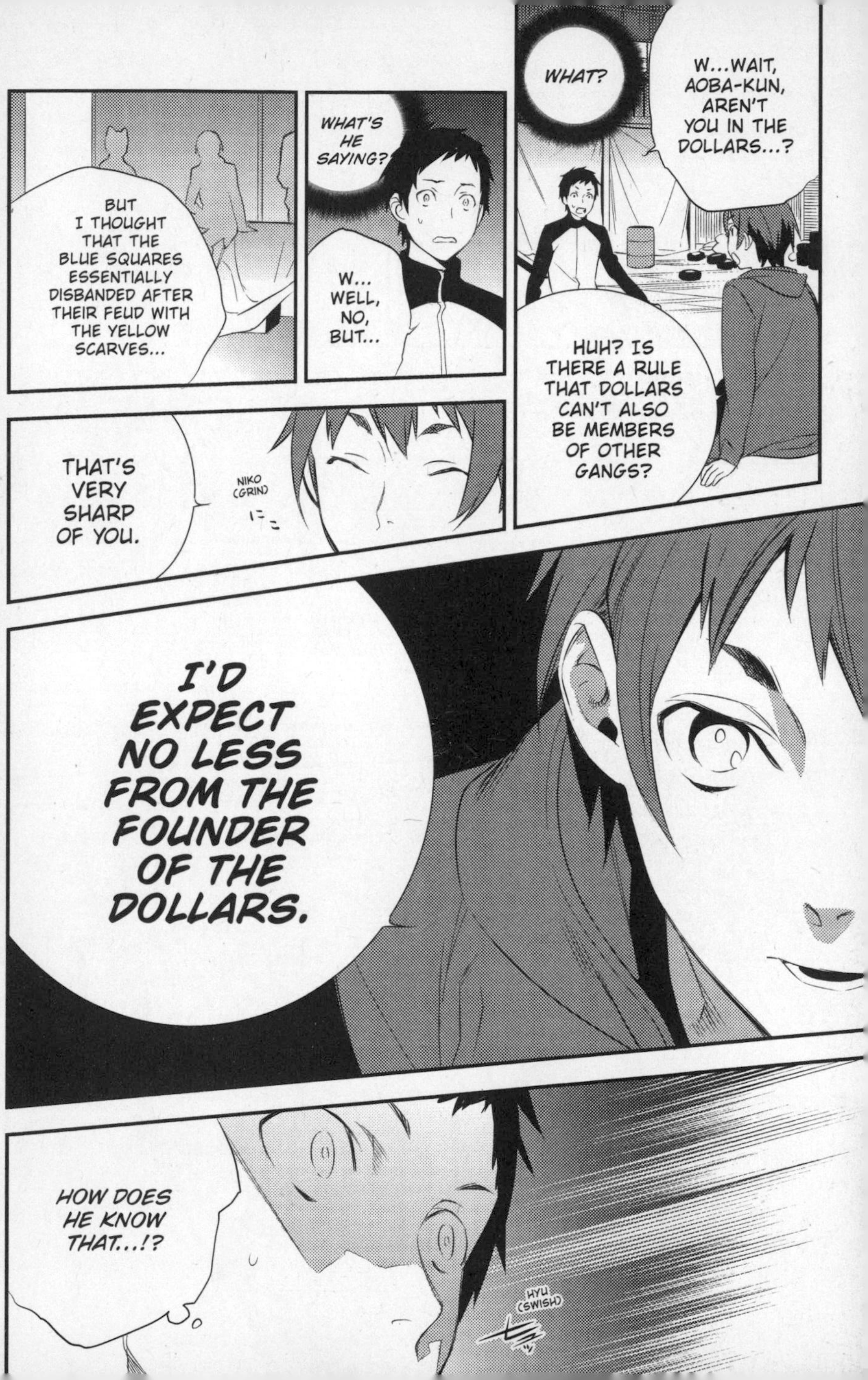
WHAT?
W...WAIT, AOBA-KUN, AREN'T YOU IN THE DOLLARS...?
HUH? IS THERE A RULE THAT DOLLARS CAN'T ALSO BE MEMBERS OF OTHER GANGS?
WHAT'S HE SAYING?
W... WELL, NO, BUT...
BUT I THOUGHT THAT THE BLUE SQUARES ESSENTIALLY DISBANDED AFTER THEIR FEUD WITH THE YELLOW SCARVES...
NIKO (GRIN)
THAT'S VERY SHARP OF YOU.
I'D EXPECT NO LESS FROM THE FOUNDER OF THE DOLLARS.
HYU (SWISH)
HOW DOES HE KNOW THAT...!?

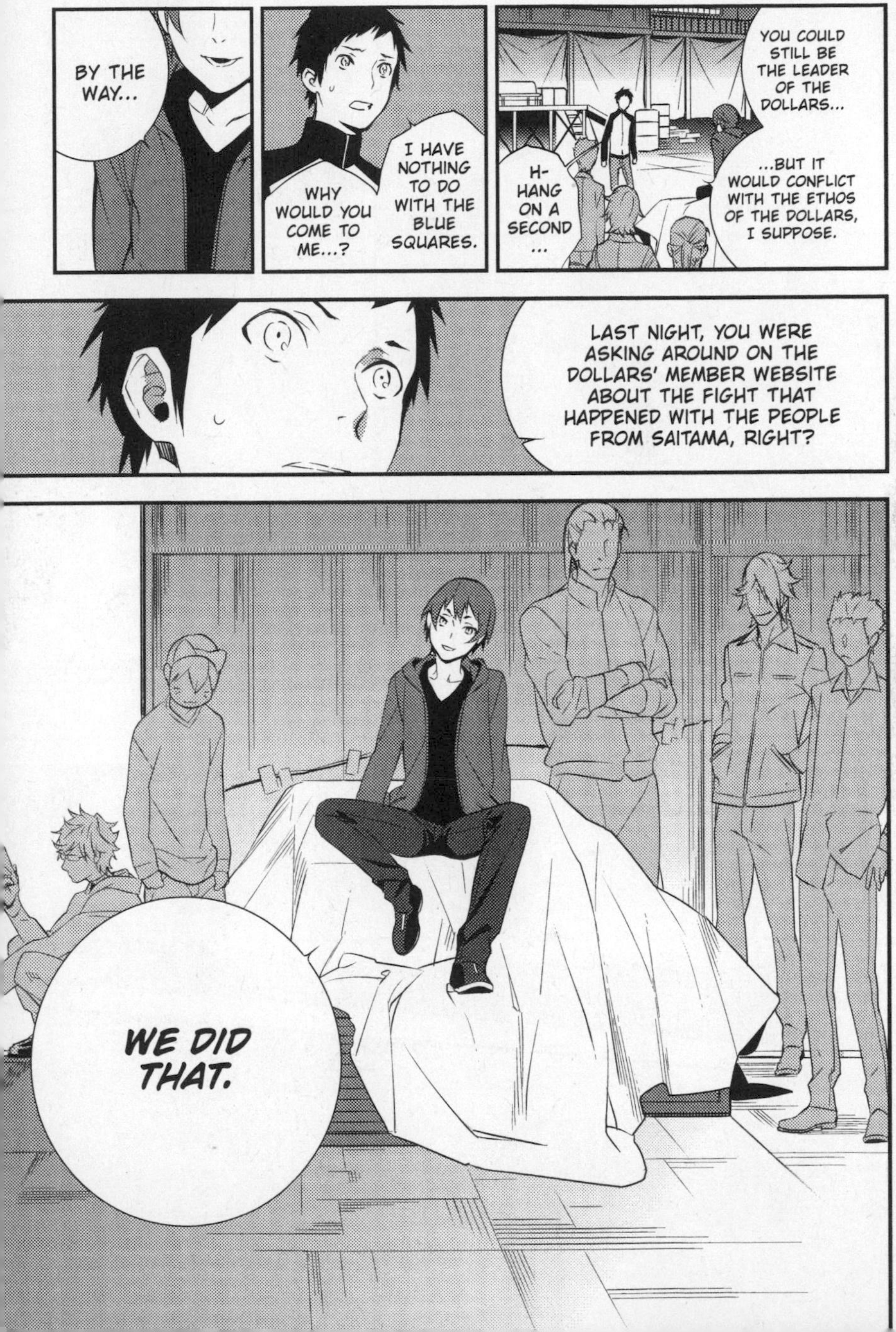
YOU COULD STILL BE THE LEADER OF THE DOLLARS...
...BUT IT WOULD CONFLICT WITH THE ETHOS OF THE DOLLARS, I SUPPOSE.
H-HANG ON A SECOND...
I HAVE NOTHING TO DO WITH THE BLUE SQUARES.
WHY WOULD YOU COME TO ME...?
BY THE WAY...
LAST NIGHT, YOU WERE ASKING AROUND ON THE DOLLARS' MEMBER WEBSITE ABOUT THE FIGHT THAT HAPPENED WITH THE PEOPLE FROM SAITAMA, RIGHT?
WE DID THAT.

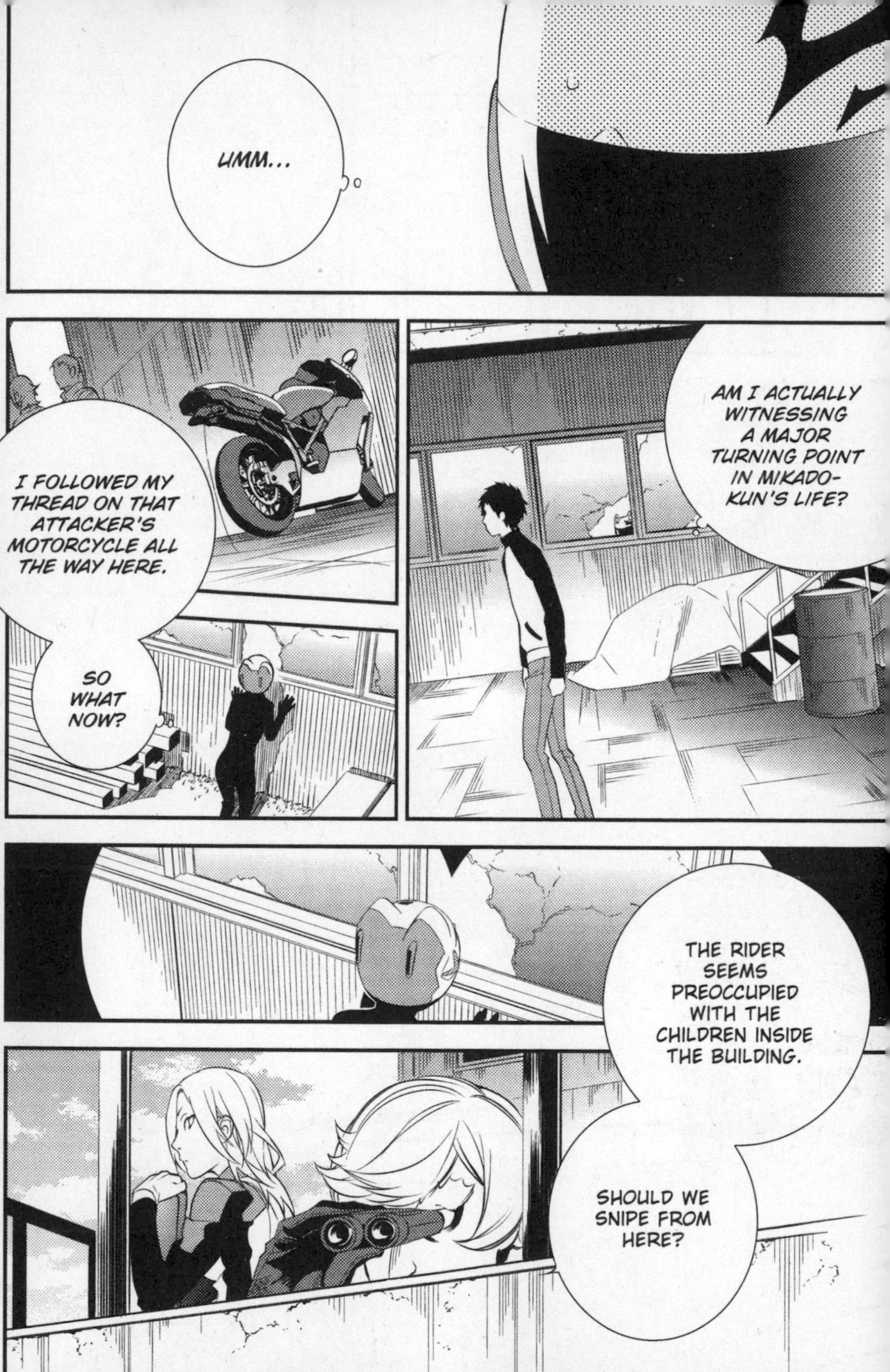
UMM...
AM I ACTUALLY WITNESSING A MAJOR TURNING POINT IN MIKADO-KUN'S LIFE?
I FOLLOWED MY THREAD ON THAT ATTACKER'S MOTORCYCLE ALL THE WAY HERE.
SO WHAT NOW?
THE RIDER SEEMS PREOCCUPIED WITH THE CHILDREN INSIDE THE BUILDING.
SHOULD WE SNIPE FROM HERE?

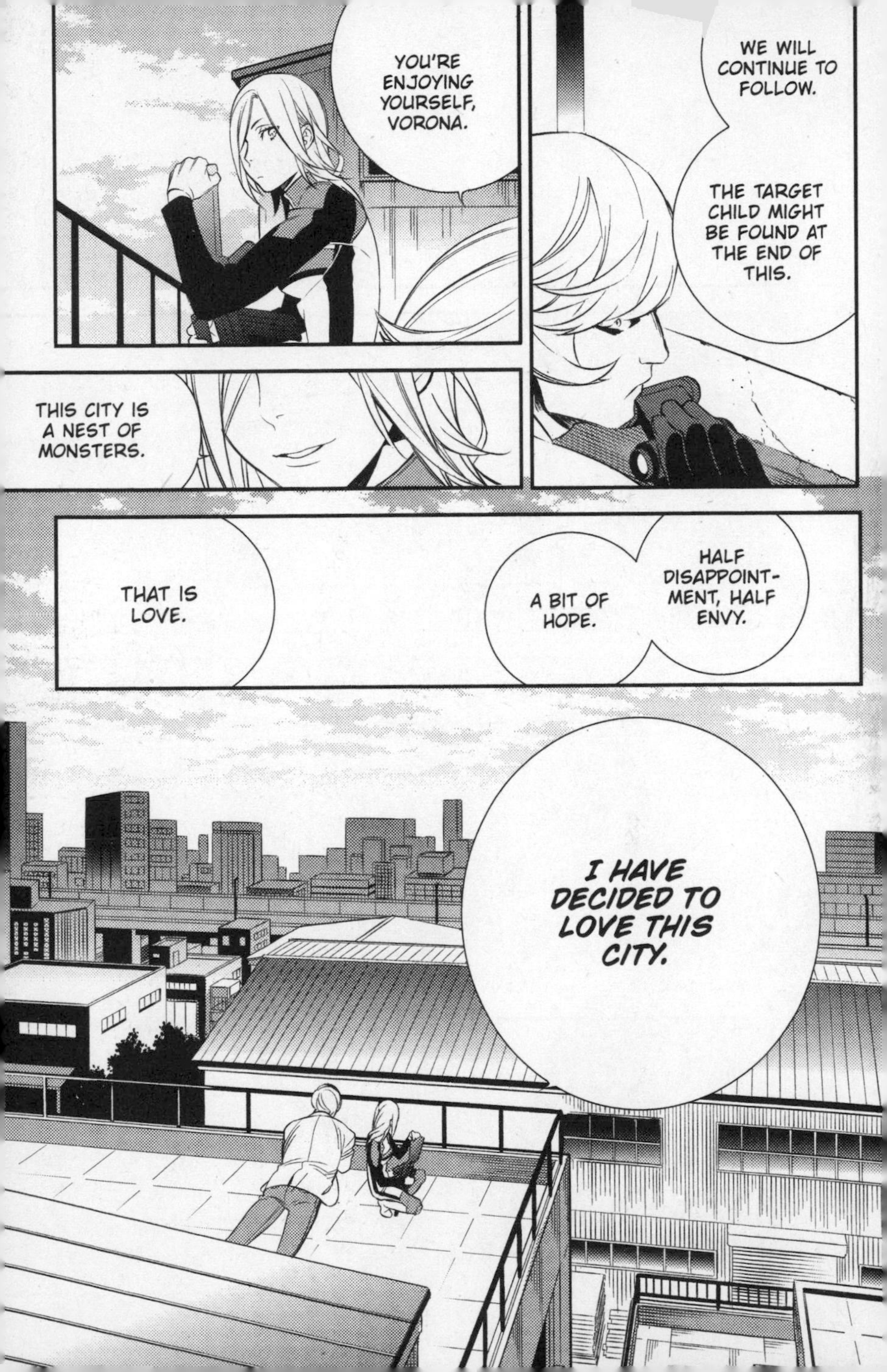
WE WILL CONTINUE TO FOLLOW.
THE TARGET CHILD MIGHT BE FOUND AT THE END OF THIS.
YOU'RE ENJOYING YOURSELF, VORONA.
THIS CITY IS A NEST OF MONSTERS.
HALF DISAPPOINT-MENT, HALF ENVY.
A BIT OF HOPE.
THAT IS LOVE.
I HAVE DECIDED TO LOVE THIS CITY.

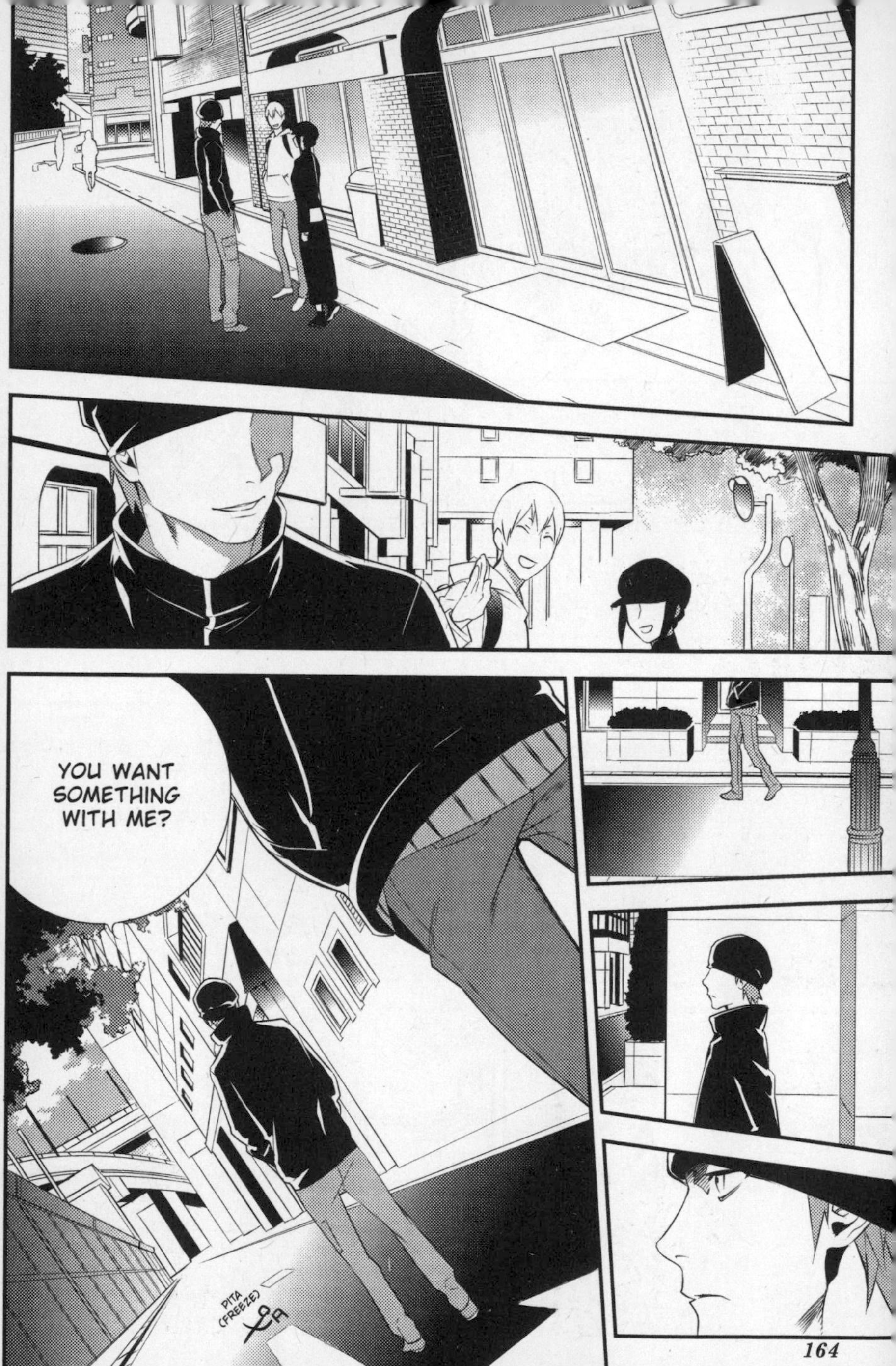
YOU WANT SOMETHING WITH ME?
PITA (FREEZE)

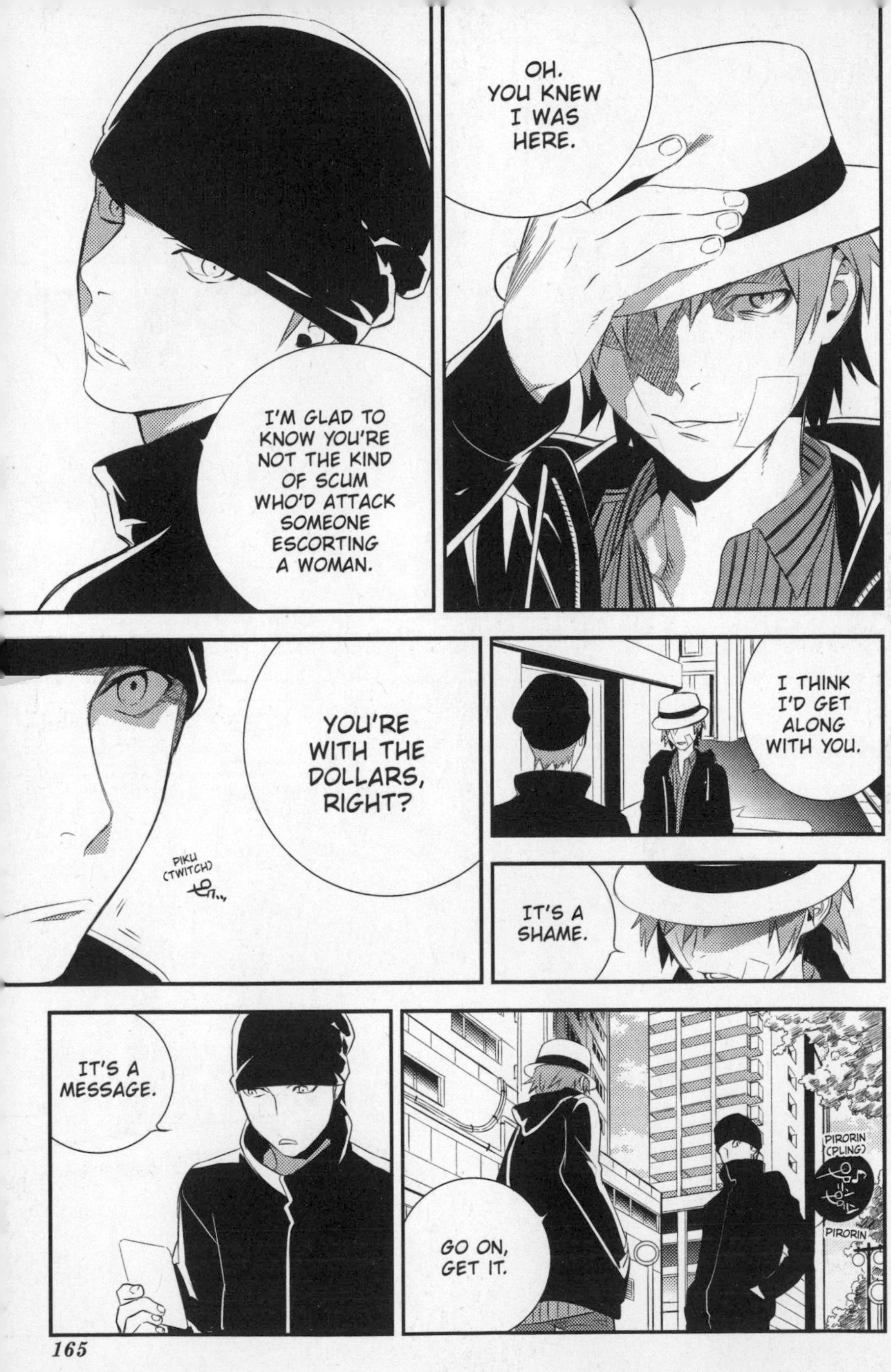
OH. YOU KNEW I WAS HERE.
I'M GLAD TO KNOW YOU'RE NOT THE KIND OF SCUM WHO'D ATTACK SOMEONE ESCORTING A WOMAN.
I THINK I'D GET ALONG WITH YOU.
IT'S A SHAME.
YOU'RE WITH THE DOLLARS, RIGHT?
PIKU (TWITCH)
PIRORIN (PLING)
PIRORIN
GO ON, GET IT.
IT'S A MESSAGE.

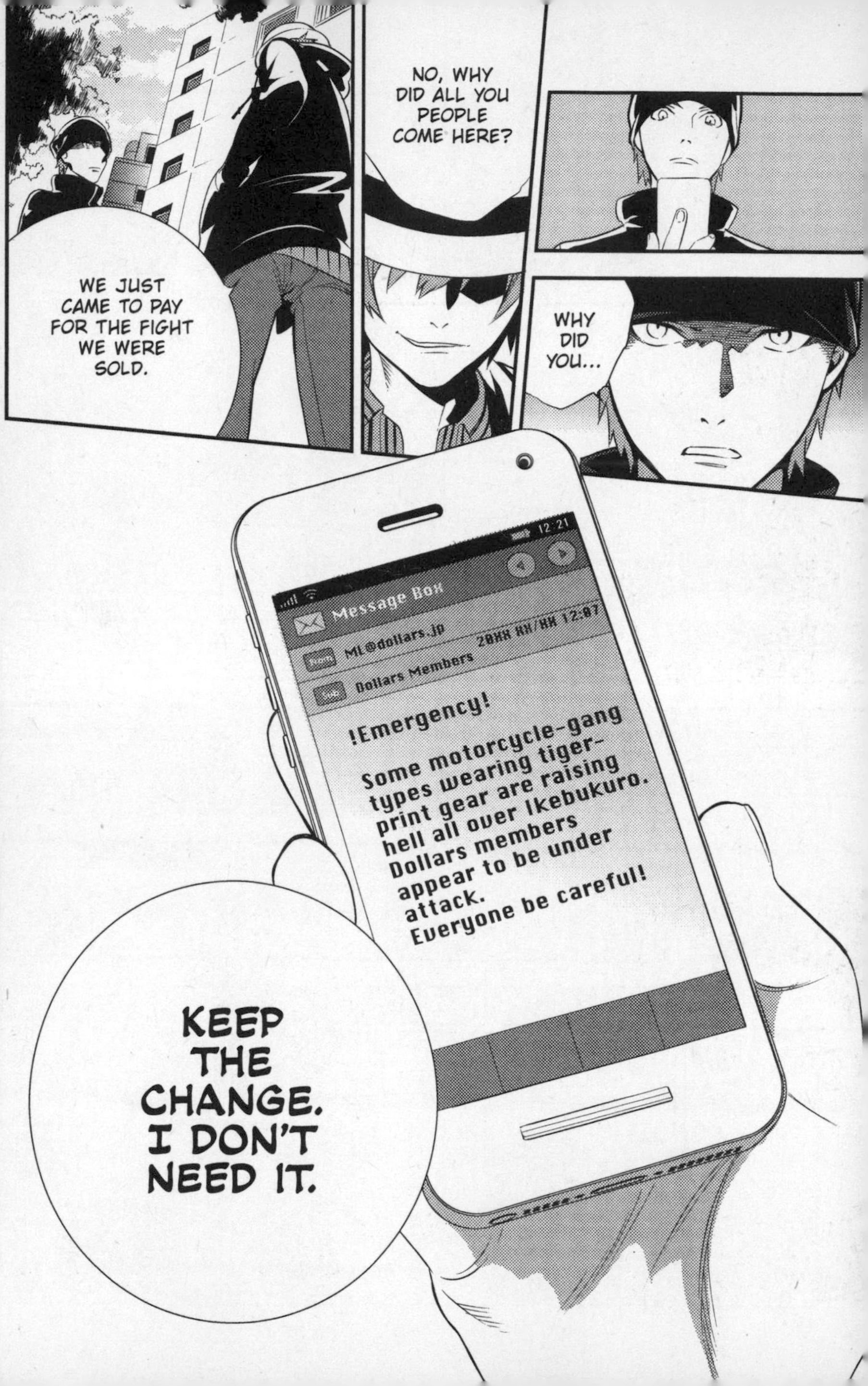
WHY DID YOU...
NO, WHY DID ALL YOU PEOPLE COME HERE?
WE JUST CAME TO PAY FOR THE FIGHT WE WERE SOLD.
12:21
Message Box
From ML@dollars.jp
20XX XX/XX 12:07
Sub Dollars Members
!Emergency!
Some motorcycle-gang types wearing tiger-print gear are raising hell all over Ikebukuro. Dollars members appear to be under attack.
Everyone be careful!
KEEP THE CHANGE. I DON'T NEED IT.

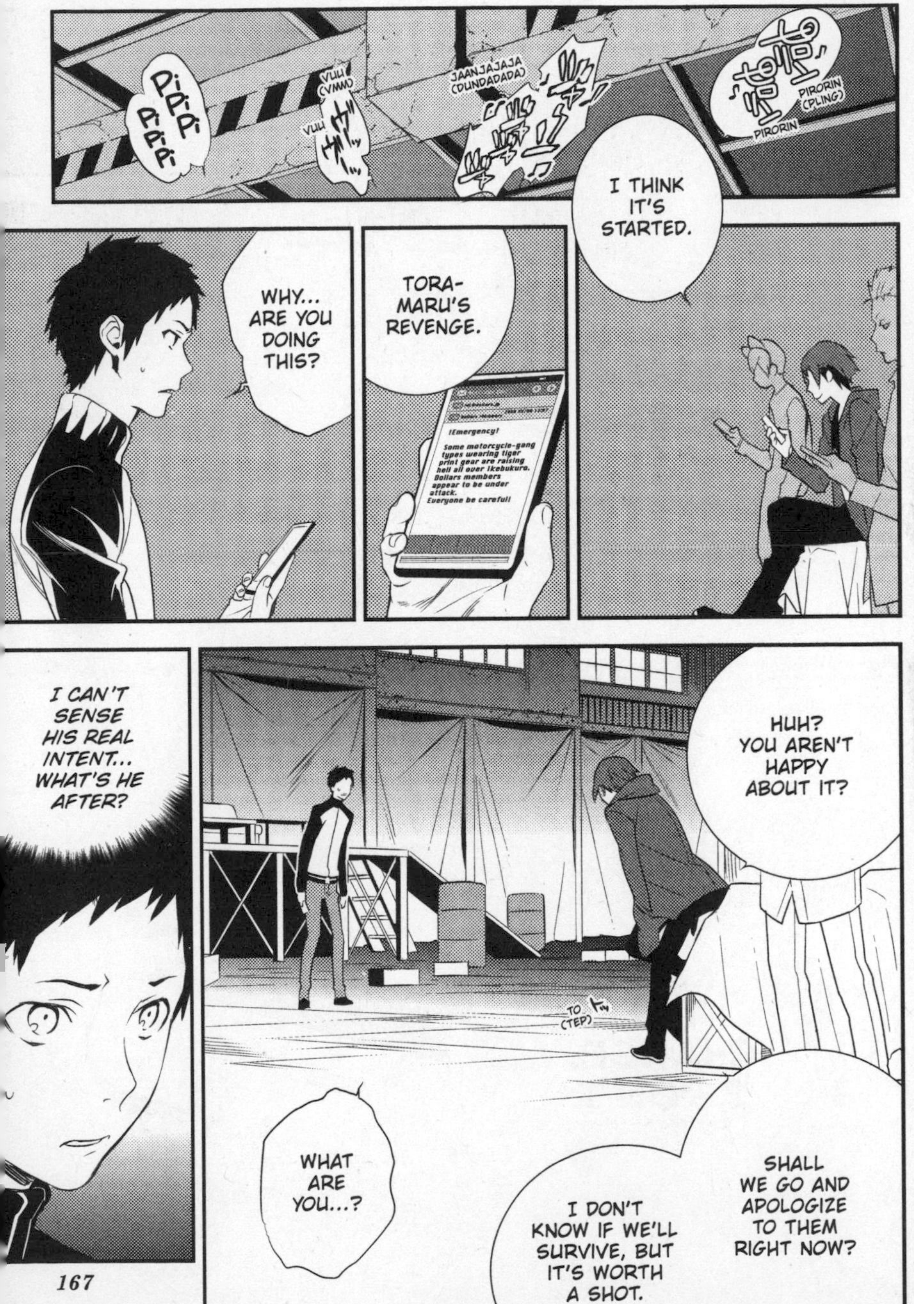
PIRORIN (PLING)
PIRORIN
JAANJAJAJA (DUNDADADA)
VUU (VMMM)
VUU
PiPiPi
PiPiPi
I THINK IT'S STARTED.
TORA-MARU'S REVENGE.
!Emergency!
Some motorcycle-gang types wearing tiger print gear are raising hell all over Ikebukuro. Dollars members appear to be under attack. Everyone be careful!
WHY... ARE YOU DOING THIS?
HUH? YOU AREN'T HAPPY ABOUT IT?
TO (TEP)
SHALL WE GO AND APOLOGIZE TO THEM RIGHT NOW?
I DON'T KNOW IF WE'LL SURVIVE, BUT IT'S WORTH A SHOT.
WHAT ARE YOU...?
I CAN'T SENSE HIS REAL INTENT... WHAT'S HE AFTER?

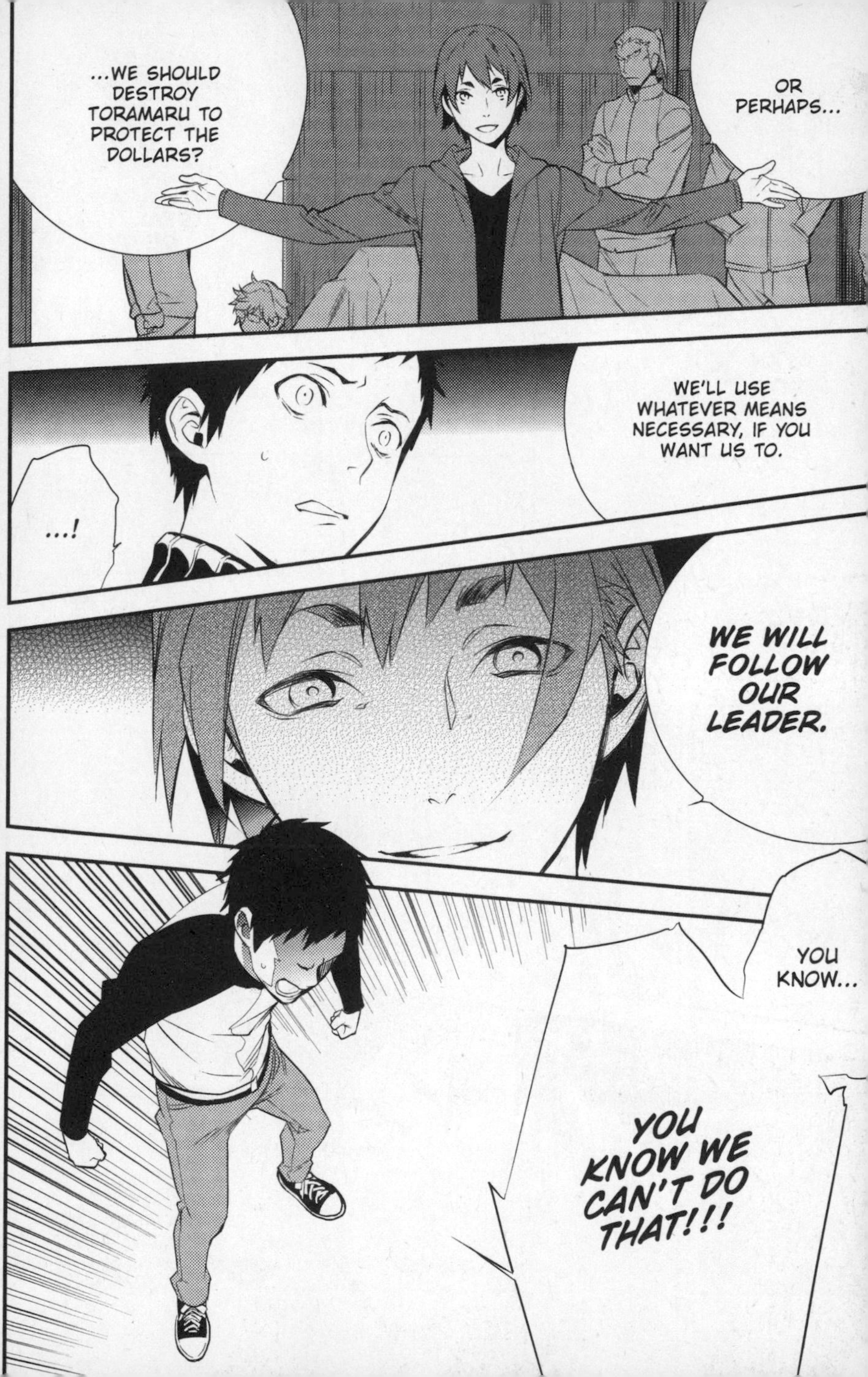
OR PERHAPS...
...WE SHOULD DESTROY TORAMARU TO PROTECT THE DOLLARS?
WE'LL USE WHATEVER MEANS NECESSARY, IF YOU WANT US TO.
...!
WE WILL FOLLOW OUR LEADER.
YOU KNOW...
YOU KNOW WE CAN'T DO THAT!!!

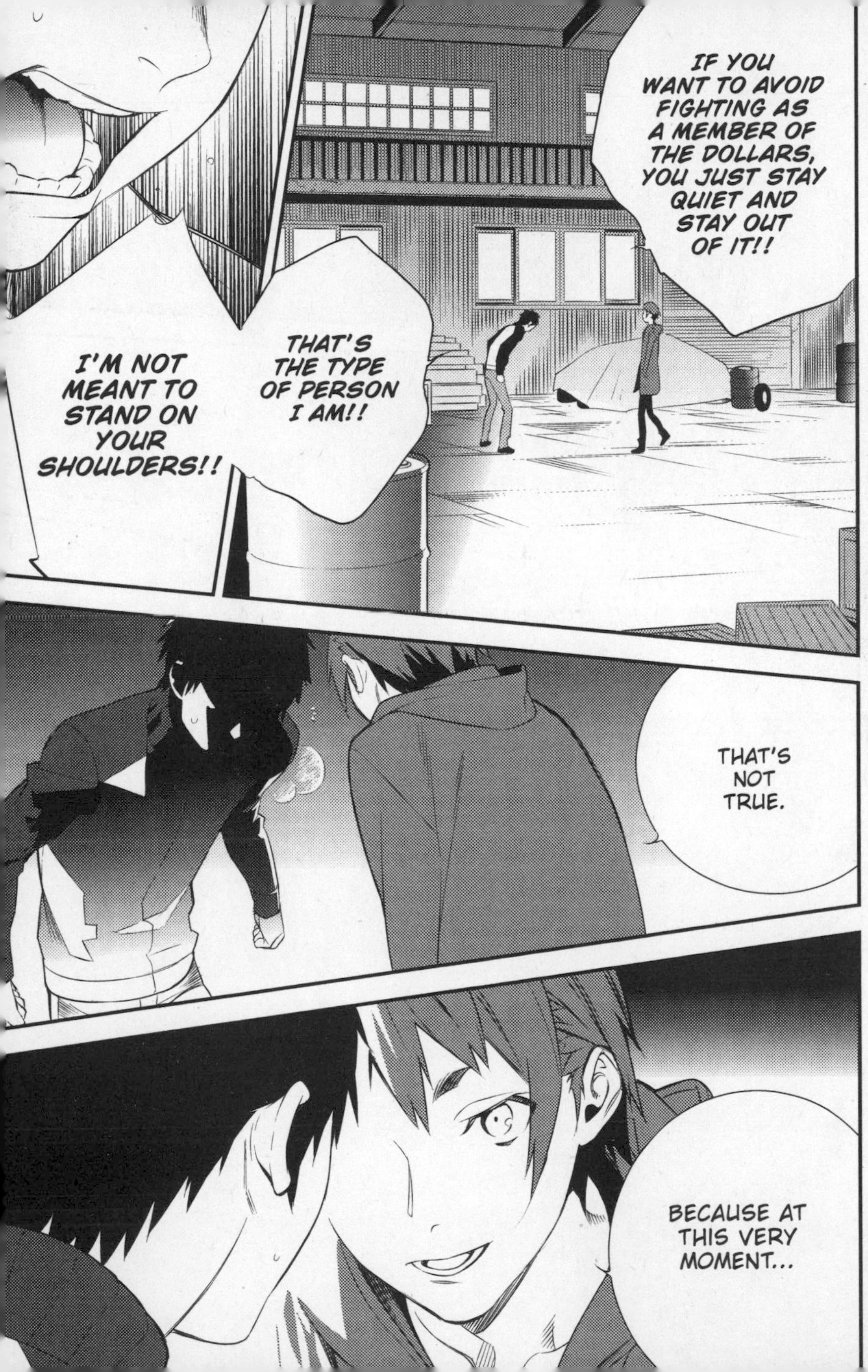
IF YOU WANT TO AVOID FIGHTING AS A MEMBER OF THE DOLLARS, YOU JUST STAY QUIET AND STAY OUT OF IT!!
THAT'S THE TYPE OF PERSON I AM!!
I'M NOT MEANT TO STAND ON YOUR SHOULDERS!!
THAT'S NOT TRUE.
BECAUSE AT THIS VERY MOMENT...

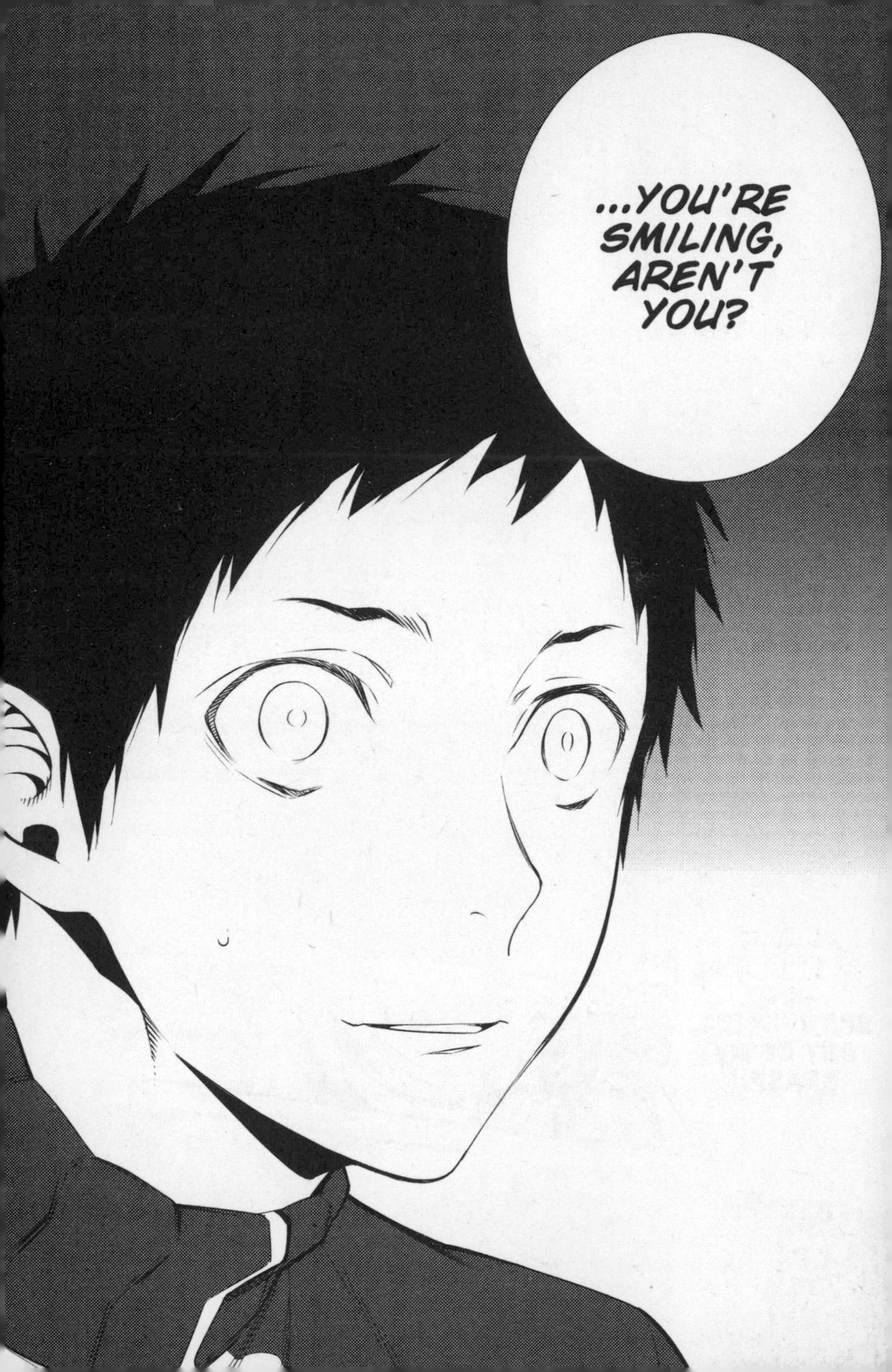
...YOU'RE SMILING, AREN'T YOU?

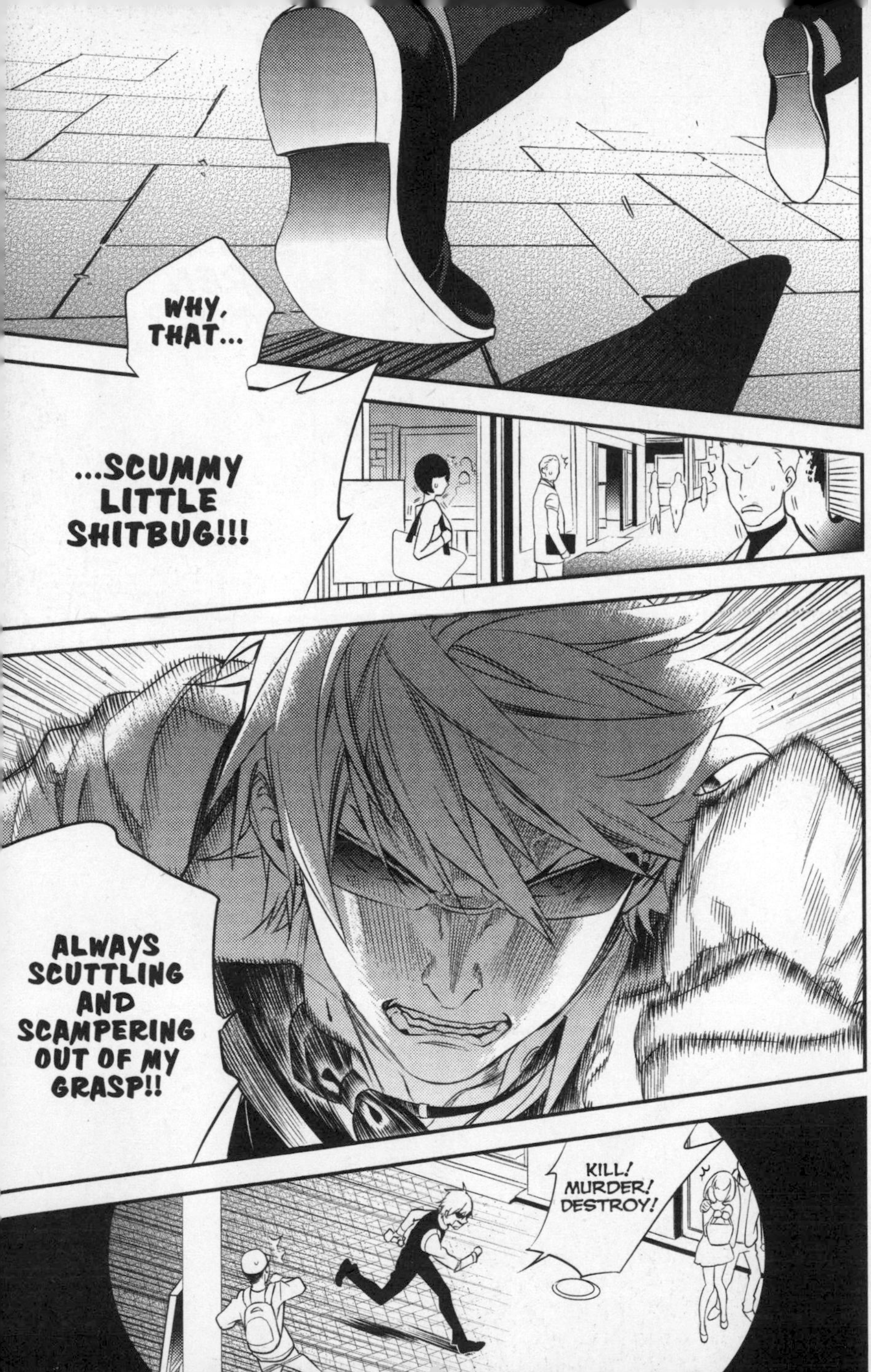
WHY, THAT...
...SCUMMY LITTLE SHITBUG!!!
ALWAYS SCUTTLING AND SCAMPERING OUT OF MY GRASP!!
KILL! MURDER! DESTROY!

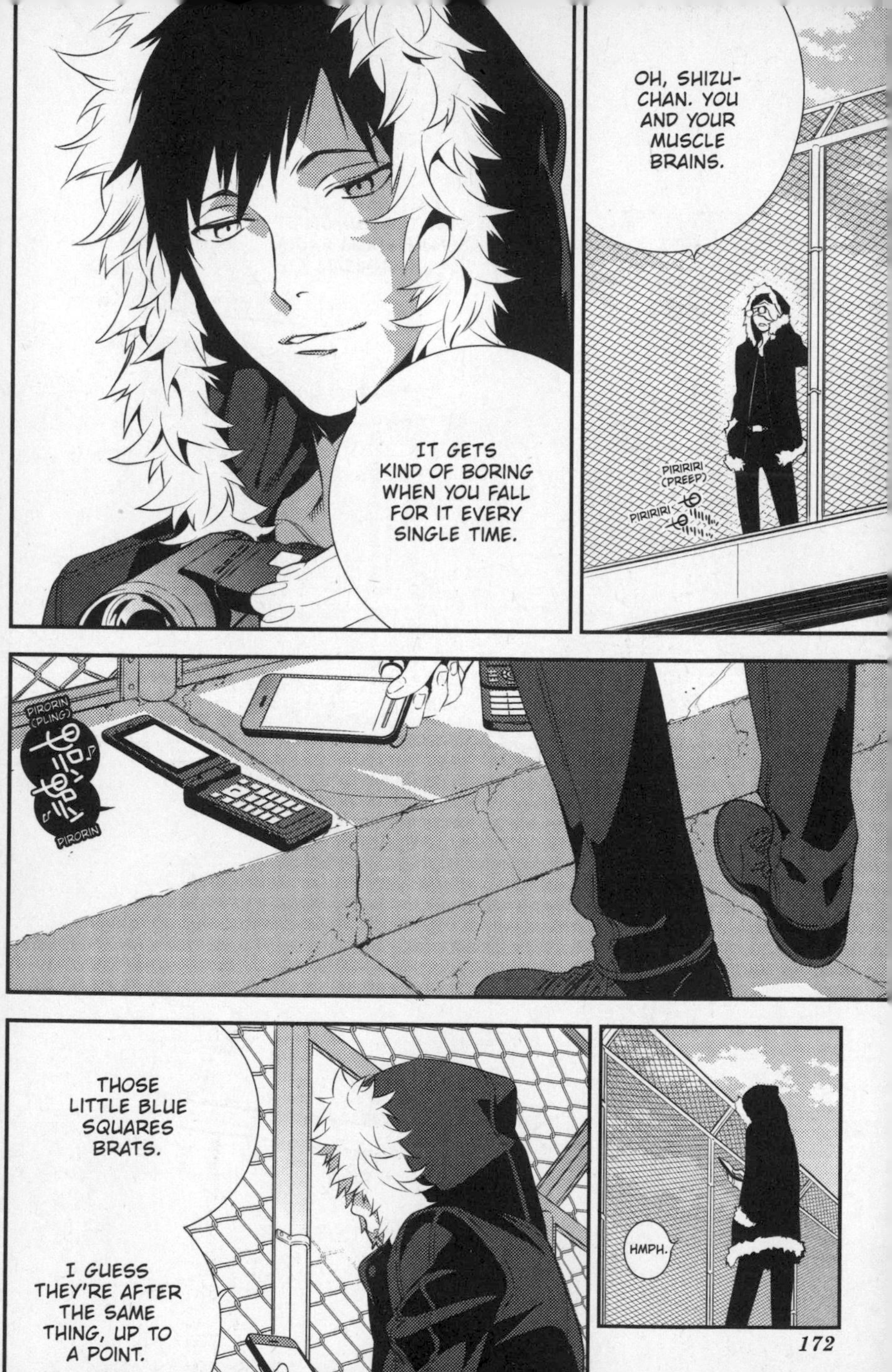
OH, SHIZU-CHAN. YOU AND YOUR MUSCLE BRAINS.
PIRIRIRI (PREEP)
PIRIRIRI
IT GETS KIND OF BORING WHEN YOU FALL FOR IT EVERY SINGLE TIME.
PIRORIN (PLING)
PIRORIN
HMPH.
THOSE LITTLE BLUE SQUARES BRATS.
I GUESS THEY'RE AFTER THE SAME THING, UP TO A POINT.

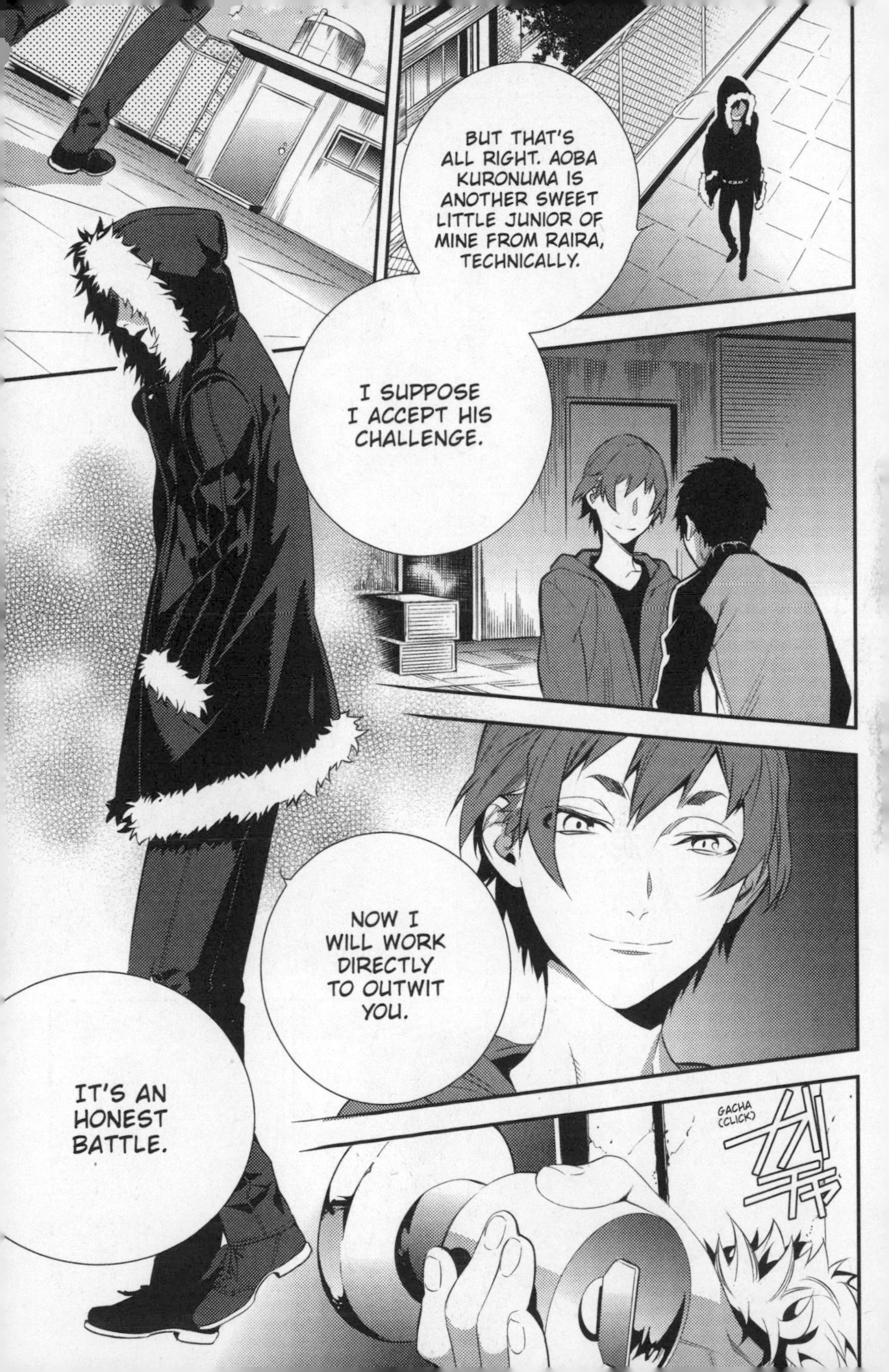
BUT THAT'S ALL RIGHT. AOBA KURONUMA IS ANOTHER SWEET LITTLE JUNIOR OF MINE FROM RAIRA, TECHNICALLY.
I SUPPOSE I ACCEPT HIS CHALLENGE.
NOW I WILL WORK DIRECTLY TO OUTWIT YOU.
GACHA (CLICK)
IT'S AN HONEST BATTLE.

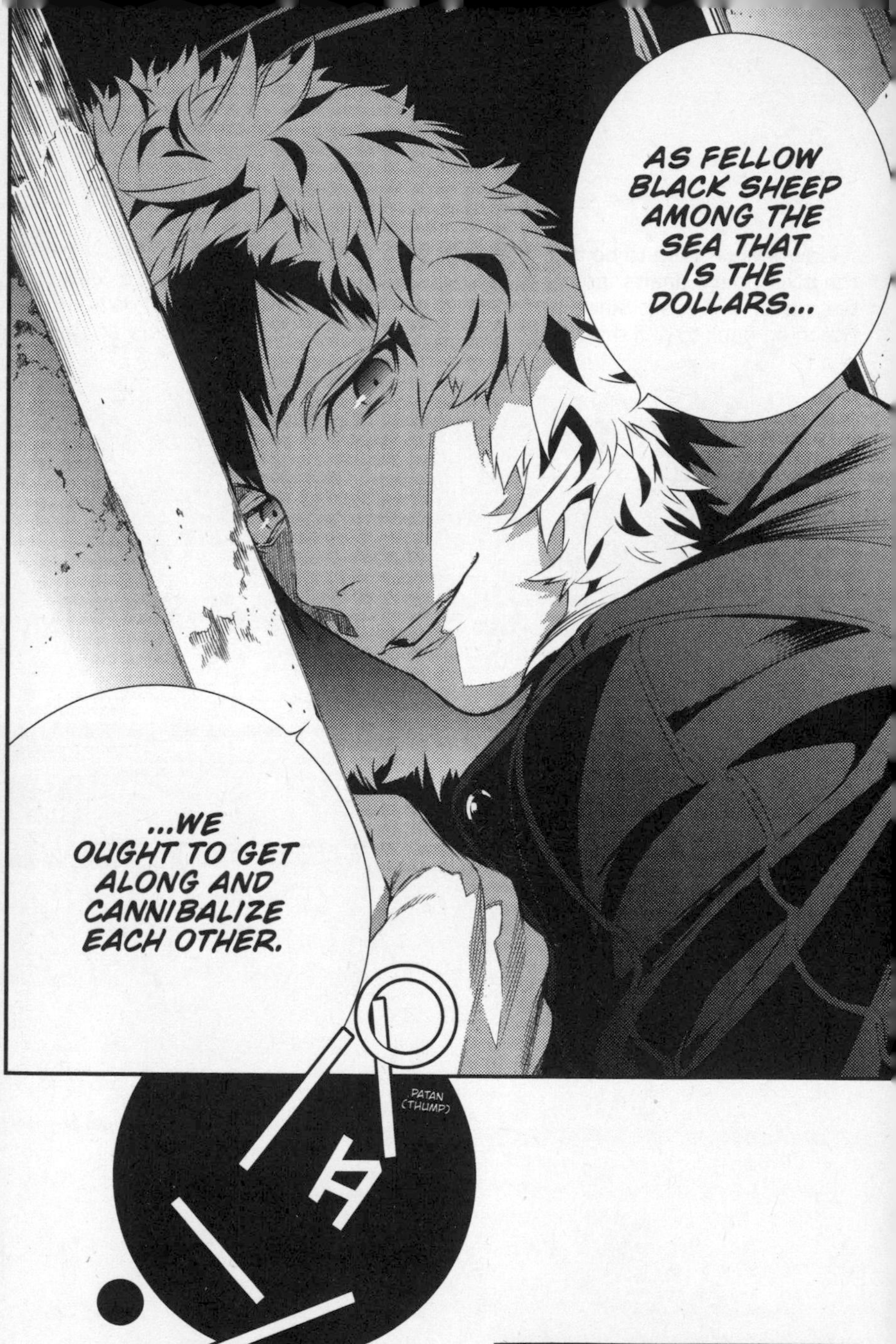
AS FELLOW BLACK SHEEP AMONG THE SEA THAT IS THE DOLLARS...
...WE OUGHT TO GET ALONG AND CANNIBALIZE EACH OTHER.
PATAN (THUMP)

DURARARA!! RE;DOLLARS ARC 1 END

Afterword

Hello, I am Ryohgo Narita, the writer of the original story behind the *Durarara!! Re;Dollars Arc* manga.

Now while I claim to be the "writer," in actuality, all I'm doing is examining the storyboard drafts, so there's hardly any work on my part. It's already been over five years since I wrote this material in my novels, so I've been reaching back to pull the forgotten details from memory as I supervise the drafts.

When I look over the storyboards, I'm always struck, even in the rough draft stage, by how much dynamism Aogiri-san brings to the world of *Durarara!!* through his art. He also elaborates on ideas from the novel in a big way (such as the story of Akane and her mother with the tree, which was only a few lines of text in the novel) so that I often find myself saying, "Oooh, wow, an original scene...wait, is this actually based on the book?"

As a reader, I find *Re;Dollars* to be quite thrilling, and as the author, it's simply delightful. I hope to do my own part to keep the *Durarara!!* series evolving, as I look forward to how this manga will grow!

To Aogiri-san, the editors Kuma-san and Haseyama-san, the editorial staff of *G Fantasy*, and of course, to all the readers of this manga, I send my greatest appreciation!

Thank you so much! Hope you keep tuning in!

Ryohgo Narita

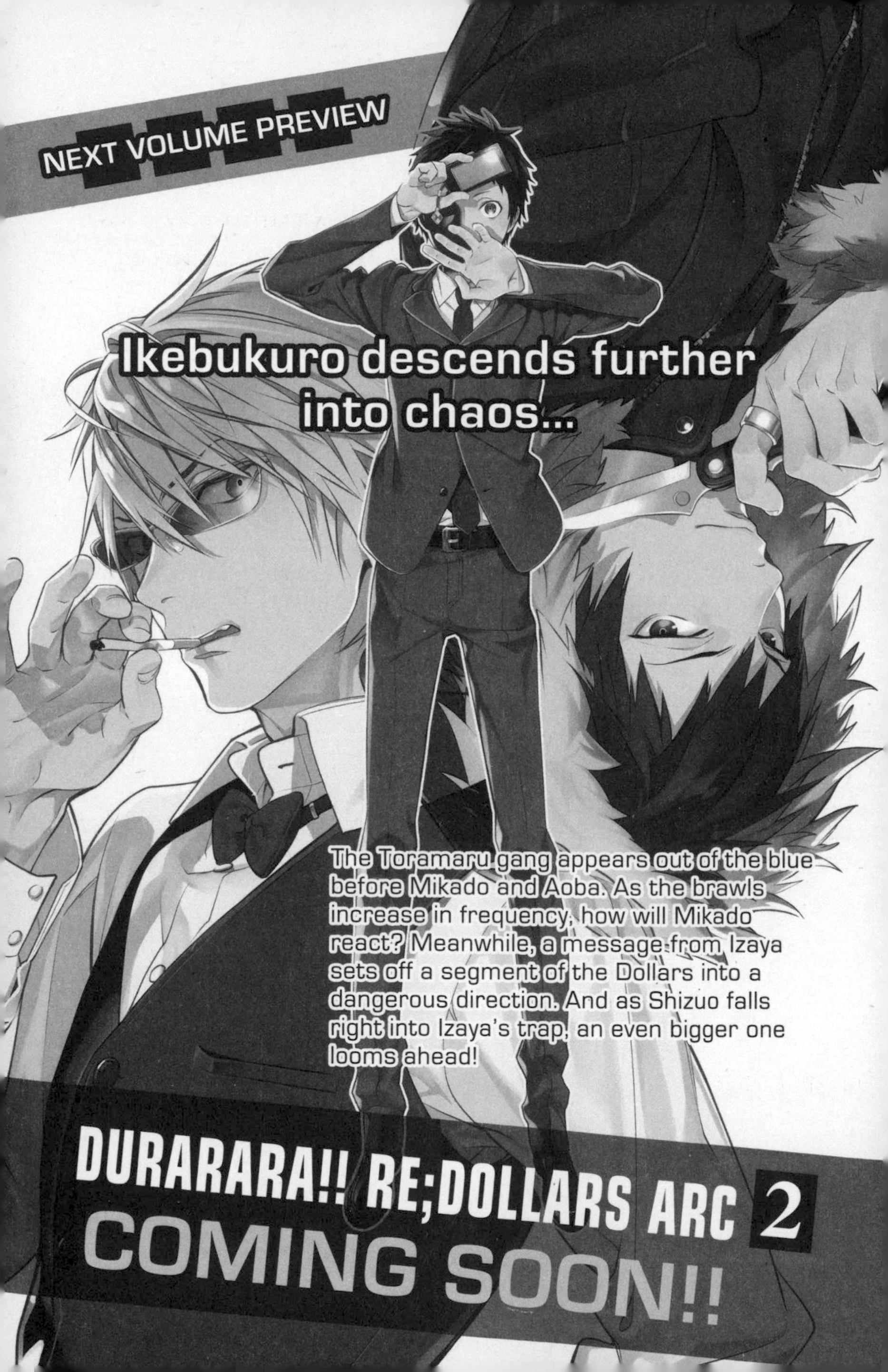
NEXT VOLUME PREVIEW
Ikebukuro descends further into chaos...
The Toramaru gang appears out of the blue before Mikado and Aoba. As the brawls increase in frequency, how will Mikado react? Meanwhile, a message from Izaya sets off a segment of the Dollars into a dangerous direction. And as Shizuo falls right into Izaya's trap, an even bigger one looms ahead!
DURARARA!! RE;DOLLARS ARC 2
COMING SOON!!

TRANSLATION NOTES

Common Honorifics

no honorific: Indicates familiarity or closeness; if used without permission or reason, addressing someone in this manner would constitute an insult.

-san: The Japanese equivalent of Mr./Mrs./Miss. If a situation calls for politeness, this is the fail-safe honorific.

-sama: Conveys great respect; may also indicate that the social status of the speaker is lower than that of the addressee.

-kun: Used most often when referring to boys, this indicates affection or familiarity. Occasionally used by older men among their peers, but it may also be used by anyone referring to a person of lower standing.

-chan: An affectionate honorific indicating familiarity used mostly in reference to girls; also used in reference to cute persons or animals of either gender.

PAGE 14
Toramaru: While the initial *tora* means "tiger," explaining the tiger-print designs of the gang, in the original Japanese, the *To* is represented in English letters, followed by kanji characters. This is actually a play on *To Love-Ru,* a romantic comedy manga from *Shonen Jump* that utilized a similar styling, creating a pun on the verb "to love" and the word "trouble" (*toraburu*).

PAGE 25
Silence of the Manservants: A pun between *hitsuji* (sheep/lamb) and *shitsuji* (butler/manservant), creating a play on the film *Silence of the Lambs.*

PAGE 61
Mark Wakaba: The given name *Aoba* means "fresh leaves." A related term, *wakaba,* meaning "young leaves," is also utilized for what is called the Wakaba Mark, an insignia of a green-and-yellow leaf that newly-registered drivers must place on their cars for one year after receiving their license to alert fellow drivers to the potential for inexperienced driving.

PAGE 85
Vorona: This name is derived from the Russian word for "crow."

Slon: Similar to Vorona, this name is Russian for "elephant."

PAGE 115
Tohoku: Meaning "northeast," this is the northern region at the tip of Honshu, the main island of Japan. Compared to the rest of Honshu, it is quite rural and sparsely populated.

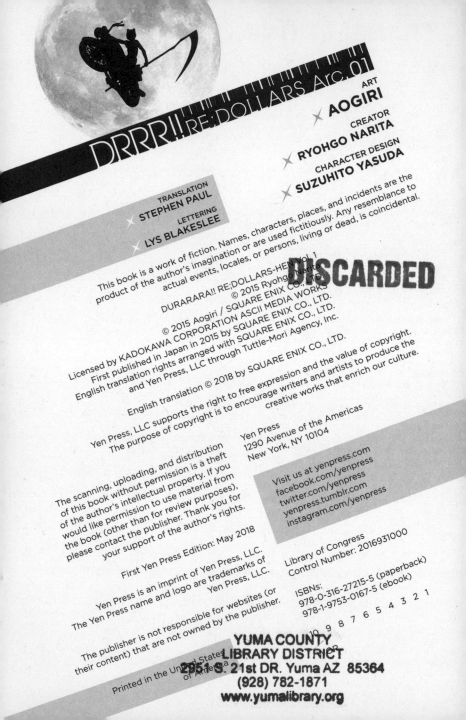

DRRR!! RE;DOLLARS Arc. 01

ART
✕ AOGIRI

CREATOR
✕ RYOHGO NARITA

CHARACTER DESIGN
✕ SUZUHITO YASUDA

TRANSLATION
✕ STEPHEN PAUL

LETTERING
✕ LYS BLAKESLEE

DISCARDED

DURARARA!! RE;DOLLARS-HEN Vol. 1
© 2015 Ryohgo Narita
© 2015 Aogiri / SQUARE ENIX CO., LTD.
Licensed by KADOKAWA CORPORATION ASCII MEDIA WORKS
First published in Japan in 2015 by SQUARE ENIX CO., LTD.
English translation rights arranged with SQUARE ENIX CO., LTD.
and Yen Press, LLC through Tuttle-Mori Agency, Inc.

English translation © 2018 by SQUARE ENIX CO., LTD.

Yen Press
1290 Avenue of the Americas
New York, NY 10104

Visit us at yenpress.com
facebook.com/yenpress
twitter.com/yenpress
yenpress.tumblr.com
instagram.com/yenpress

First Yen Press Edition: May 2018

Yen Press is an imprint of Yen Press, LLC.
The Yen Press name and logo are trademarks of
Yen Press, LLC.

The publisher is not responsible for websites (or
their content) that are not owned by the publisher.

Printed in the United States of America

Library of Congress
Control Number: 2016931000

ISBNs:
978-0-316-27215-5 (paperback)
978-1-9753-0167-5 (ebook)

10 9 8 7 6 5 4 3 2 1